THE AUSTRALIAN
KETTLE
BARBECUE
COOKBOOK

THE AUSTRALIAN
KETTLE
BARBECUE
COOKBOOK

BRIDGET JONES

NEW
BURLINGTON
BOOKS

A QUINTET BOOK

Published by New Burlington Books
6 Blundell Street
London N7 9BH

ISBN 1-85348-289-7

This book was designed and produced by
Quintet Publishing Limited
6 Blundell Street
London N7 9BH

Creative Director: Peter Bridgewater
Art Director: Ian Hunt
Designers: James Lawrence, Peter Radcliffe
Artwork: Danny McBride
Project Editor: David Barraclough
Photographers: Steve Alley and Amber
Wisdom

Typeset in Great Britain by
Central Southern Typesetters, Eastbourne
Manufactured in Hong Kong by
Regent Publishing Services Limited
Printed in Hong Kong by
Leefung-Asco Printers Limited

Contents

CHAPTER ONE

Barbecuing

Barbecue cooking is unique, both in the flavours it produces and in the cooking techniques that are used. These can often reflect the character of the cook: large chunks of meat, raw on the inside, charred on the outside, and washed down with strong drink for those with hearty appetites, or a delicate chicken wing for the socialite. The devotee of junk food can load up on prepared meat and poultry full of sulphites and preservatives, seasoned with a little synthetic 'liquid smoke', while the lover of good food, at whom this book is aimed, can prepare an extraordinary range of dishes, cooked with a variety of barbecue techniques or with a mixture of conventional and barbecue cooking methods, whether boiling, microwaving or steaming.

If you want to explore the full potential of a barbecue, it is a good idea not to have too many fixed ideas. Many people refuse to use aluminium foil when they are cooking on a barbecue, with the result that the wings and legs of chicken, and the small bones of some chops, are hopelessly charred long before the rest of the meat is cooked. Others believe that a barbecue isn't ready to use unless the temperature is sufficiently intense to blister unprotected skin (and indeed paintwork) an arm's length away. Their penalty too is food that is burned on the outside, and raw on the inside. It is *much* easier to cook large pieces of meat in a covered kettle barbecue, with reduced risk of flare-ups, less charring, and increased chances of success.

At its most basic, a barbecue is simply a method of cooking out of doors, using burning charcoal or wood to create a smoky flavour, perhaps over a pit in the ground lined with *maguey* leaves or over a vast fire for roasting an ox. However, this book concentrates on a particular type of barbecue – the kettle barbecue – and using it for cooking a wide variety of informal meals. From food with the family to a fun day with a host of friends, the kettle barbecue is particularly versatile.

Why do it? The food tastes good; it's a great opportunity for entertaining; it's surprisingly easy, and informal; it's a welcome change from the kitchen, especially in hot weather; and best of all, it's just plain *fun*.

RIGHT **One of the advantages of the kettle barbecue is that it can be used both open and closed.**

The Kettle Barbecue

The kettle barbecue is distinguished by two features: its shape and the fact that it has a close-fitting lid. Shape-wise, the kettle barbecue has a domed fire bowl and a domed lid so that the cooking process may be carried out on the open grill or in the covered barbecue. The shape and heavy-duty finish on the bowl and lid provide maximum heat reflection for efficient cooking.

Buying a Kettle Barbecue – Options Available

The first point to remember is to look for a good-quality product, one that is made from heavy-duty materials with a finish that will withstand both weather and the burning charcoal without deteriorating. Look for a manufacturer's guarantee – better kettle barbecues come with a five year guarantee.

Next, think about the size of barbecue – they range from small, portable kettles with carrying handles to large ones for coping with cooking for crowds. Compare the surface area of the cooking grill and the height of the lid. The overall height is important if you want to take full advantage of the kettle barbecuing method for cooking large cuts of meat, whole turkeys or the like. The small to middle size kettles usually have sufficient height between the cooking rack and the top of the lid to accommodate a

good-sized chicken, but they are not always large enough to take a turkey or a large joint of beef or ham.

There should be vents in the bowl of the kettle to allow air to enter and for easy ash removal. Look for removable ash catchers too. The lid should also be vented to allow smoke to escape and air to enter. The vents in the lid should be adjustable so that the cooking process may be slowed down.

Some barbecues have a dual-purpose thermometer which fits in the lid to record the temperature in the barbecue as well as for use as a meat thermometer. On some models the lid clips on the outside of the fire bowl to act as a low wind shield – useful for open cooking and for keeping the lid out of the way.

Fire Racks and Cooking Grill

The fire rack fits in the base of the barbecue – the fuel is lit on top of this rack. Fire separators are available to keep the burning fuel towards the sides of the rack so that a drip tray may be placed in the middle for indirect cooking. The cooking rack slots into place at a fixed height above the fire rack. Look for cooking racks that have gaps where extra fuel may be fed through the rungs to the barbecue if necessary – important if you intend cooking for a long period of time; particularly large birds or cuts of meat.

Accessories

Tool holders which hook on the side of the fire bowl are really useful and they come as standard with the larger barbecues. Similar accessories include a condiment holder or small wooden work table – rather like a chopping board – helpful for holding small pots of oil or seasoning but otherwise of questionable value (particularly on smaller models).

Special cooking racks for containing food which fit on top of the grill come in many shapes and sizes, from vegetable holders that slot around the side of the barbecue to roast holders that take a large joint. Rib racks of different types and kebab holders are also available. Heavy-duty foil drip trays are for once-only use, alternatively use an old baking tin (pan).

Lastly, weather-proof covers are available to protect the outside of the kettle when not in use.

Cooking in a Kettle Barbecue

So, what is different about using a kettle barbecue instead of an open grill? If you use the kettle barbecue open, then all the instructions that apply to ordinary barbecue cooking should be adopted – the food should be turned frequently and the same cooking times should be followed.

With the lid on the kettle barbecue the top of the food begins to cook even though it is not facing down towards the hot coals. When the kettle is covered it creates an 'oven' space. This is a real plus for cooking larger cuts of meat or whole poultry as the cooking time is reduced.

There are two methods of cooking: direct cooking or indirect cooking. For direct cooking, the coals are spread evenly under the cooking rack and the food is placed over the heat. For indirect cooking the hot fuel is piled to both sides of the fire rack and a drip tray is placed in the middle. The food is cooked over the drip tray. The indirect method may be used on an open barbecue but it is considerably slower as a good deal of heat is lost. With the lid on the kettle barbecue the indirect method is quick and it usually means that flare-ups are avoided.

In a larger kettle barbecue, food may be cooked by the indirect method towards the middle of the cooking rack and, at the same time, small items may be placed over the hot coals for direct cooking at both sides of the rack.

Controlling the Cooking Rate

The height of the cooking rack is usually fixed on kettle barbecues. However, by using the vents under the fire bowl and in the lid, the heat inside the barbecue is fairly easily controlled. If the fire is too fierce, then simply close the vents underneath and half or three-quarters close the vents in the lid. As the fire subsides, regulate the heat by opening the vents in the lid. The amount of fuel placed in the barbecue in the first place also determines the extent of the heat when the lid is in place.

If the fire needs a boost, open the vents in the fire bowl as well as those in the lid. Alternatively, keep the lid off the barbecue for a few minutes.

When the lid is firmly in place on the kettle there is far less risk of fat flaring because of the reduced air supply and lack of draught. This applies to direct cooking as well as when a drip tray is used. When you take the lid off to turn food, if cooking by the direct method fat tends to flare. If the lid is left open for some time when a drip tray containing fat is positioned between the hot coals, then the fat in the tray may well flare up quite fiercely. Solve this problem by pouring some cold water directly into the drip tray occasionally. Take care to ensure that a foil drip tray does not disintegrate or burn through after long cooking, spilling burning fat into the ashes below. It is a good idea to use tongs to lift and empty the drip tray occasionally if there is a lot of fat in it. Remove the drip tray when you have finished cooking.

Smoking in a Kettle Barbecue

Food which is cooked with the lid on has a better flavour than open-cooked food. Herbs and spices or barbecue smoking mixtures may be placed on the coals. (Follow the manufacturer's instructions for pre-soaking some of the herb mixtures). Soaked wood chips may also be added to flavour food.

Since the food is cooked over coals this is not a form of smoking in the same way as the use of a slow-smoker, where the food is left for many hours until it is thoroughly penetrated with the flavour of the smoke. However, more flavour and a deeper colour is imparted in a kettle barbecue than over an open grill.

Barbecue Cooking with a Difference

As well as all the usual (and unusual) foods that may be barbecued, the covered kettle may be used as a primitive oven for baking cakes, breads, pastries and similar items. However, this is not really utilizing the barbecue to its best advantage as the flavour imparted from the fire does not contribute to the end results. This is, of course, a personal opinion and there are plenty of recipes available for barbecued cakes or puddings.

Griddles and cooking plates are available for use on the cooking rack and woks are made to fit into certain models of kettle barbecues. The wok may be used for stir-frying and some sources even suggest that you start deep-frying in the wok over the hot coals. Common sense suggests that you are better off restricting this cooking method to the safety of the kitchen, using appliances that are equipped with accurate controls. As an aside, the smaller portable kettles make good alternatives to camping stoves, in which situation a suitably sized wok would be a useful piece of equipment for cooking meals.

This book concentrates on using the kettle for barbecuing in the traditional sense, for fun and for flavour.

Food to Barbecue

There are many things you can cook on a barbecue that are quite unexpected – and indeed, some of the methods are unexpected too. How about onions or baby pumpkins roasted in the coals? Or baked apples cooked in foil ?

For most people, barbecue means chicken or simply-cooked meat, often in the form of hamburgers or sausages. There are, however, many other ways to enjoy barbecued meat, especially if you utilize the kettle barbecue to the full and explore international cuisines. Both Greece and India make versions of meatball kebabs; from East Asia comes satay, tiny kebabs on bamboo skewers, served with a peanut sauce; Tex-Mex cooking, from the southern borders of the United States, gives us *fajitas;* in Portugal, fresh sardines are grilled whole.

Even if you confine yourself to a single type of food, the sausage, there is an extraordinary variety available, including: the North American frankfurter (or regional variants such as the 'red hot' and 'white hot'); the Portuguese *linguica;* the Spanish or Mexican *chorizo;* the British 'banger'; the Cornish 'hog's pudding'; the German *weisswurst, blutwurst* or *knackwurst* (among many others); the French *andouilles* and *saucissons secs;* Italian *mortadella . . .* The list is tremendous.

Barbecue food has its own terminology. 'Spare ribs' are actually *spar* ribs, cooked on a stick or spar; and the unlikely-sounding 'buffalo wings' are actually chicken wings cooked in a style that originated in Buffalo, New York – which does not improve them much, as they remain bony, gristly, and messy, like all chicken wings.

Chicken wings, or the tiny bits of meat on satay, are a little out of the mainstream of real barbecues, however. Barbecue cooking has often been associated with hard-working if unconventional men and not surprisingly, it is generally hearty fare. It can also be quite cheap: sausages rarely cost much and chicken is no longer reserved for the rich. In the United States, the price of skirt steak (for *fajitas)* is ridiculously high but in many other countries, this American delicacy can be bought for next to nothing.

Tools and Accessories

Although you won't need many complicated tools for your barbecue, a pair of long-handled metal tongs at the very least will make it easier to manipulate the food, and will not cause loss of juices in the same way as a large, stout knife or even a meat-fork. As you learn more about barbecues, and decide on what and how you want to cook, you will evolve your own preferences; but the following 'star-rated' guide to accessories should be useful if you are just starting to take barbecues seriously. Three stars means 'must have'; two stars, either that something is essential only for some kinds of cookery, or that it is useful but not essential in other kinds; and one star means that you shouldn't throw it away if you receive it as a present, but that it's not worth rushing out and buying.

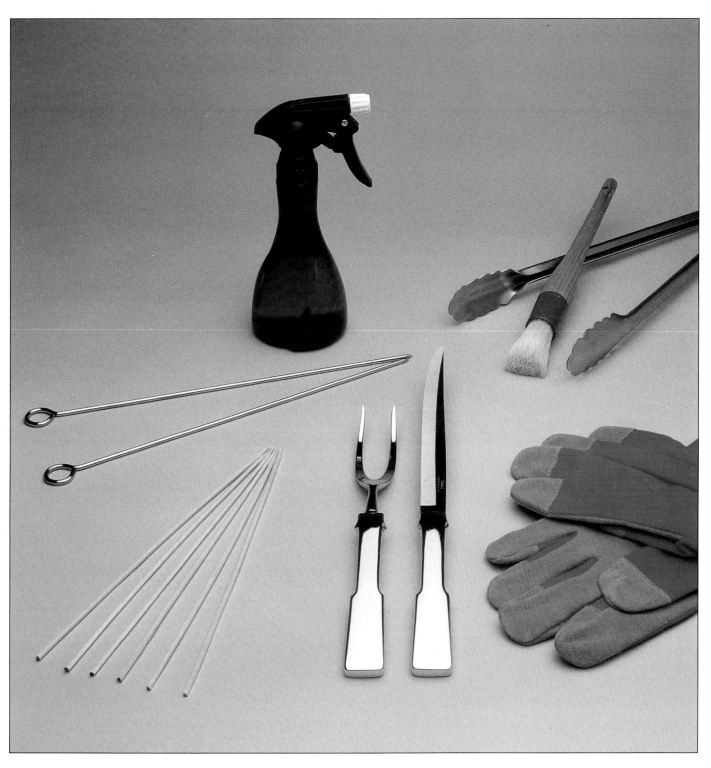

ABOVE A selection of necessary equipment for barbecuing – gloves, skewers (both metal and bamboo), water-sprayer, tongs, basting brush, and a carving fork and knife.

Aluminium foil***   This offends some purists, but it's useful stuff. Wrap around chicken wings and other small parts of larger cuts to avoid charring. Also use as a parcel-wrap for some kinds of fish and vegetable cooking, on the grill or in the coals.

You can also use aluminium foil to make drip pans (see below) and saucepans, and you can use it to keep cooked food warm.

Basting brush***   You can survive without this, provided you never want to do any basting (moistening your meat, chicken or fish with the cooking juices), and you can do a surprising amount of cooking without it. Buy one with a long, stainless steel wire handle – or better still, buy a couple.

Drip trays**   If you want to cook large cuts, as already mentioned, put a drip tray under the meat or poultry and bank the coals around the edge. Disposable aluminium trays are ideal, although you can use cheap non-disposable cookware, or make the drip tray yourself from foil.

Fork**   A useful companion to tongs, but not essential. A heavy meat-carving fork is more useful than small cocktail forks with wooden handles and long metal rods terminating in a little fork: they are hardly big enough to pick up a large prawn.

Gloves***   These are essential, and although purpose-made barbecue gloves are all very well, gardening gloves are safer, more comfortable, and last infinitely longer. Welders' gloves are another alternative.

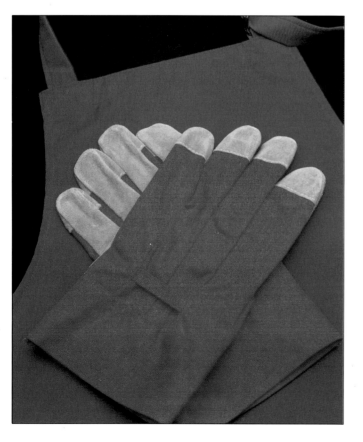

Grill basket*   A wire mesh basket which opens like a book can be useful if you want to cook whole, delicate fish or anything else that is likely to fall apart when cooked.

Meat thermometer*   These are no substitute for experience, and are never very accurate anyway. The only real use for them is to help you gain experience in cooking times.

Poker**   You can rearrange the coals with almost anything, but a metal poker or rake is useful. Alternatively, keep a separate pair of tongs (see below) for adding and moving coals.

Rack*   Like a grill basket, this sits on the grill and holds things in place. It is moderately useful for roasts, which otherwise tend to be difficult to rotate evenly.

Skewers**   Long metal skewers are essential for most kinds of kebabs. Stainless steel is far and away the best choice for most purposes, although short bamboo skewers are used in some kinds of cooking, notably satay (page 53). Soak these in water before use so they will slip through the food easier, and won't burn as fast. They won't burn at all if you are careful.

Spatula**   A metal spatula or fish slice is once again an adjunct to the tongs (below), and not essential. It does make it easier to cook hamburgers, though.

Tongs***   Like the gloves, these are absolutely essential. Go for the spring-loaded, stainless steel variety, as these give a much stronger and more secure grip than the scissor-type, and are much easier to use. As already mentioned, a second set of tongs is useful for adding fuel and rearranging the fire.

Vegetable racks*   These are available to hold vegetables at an angle to the cooking rack near the side of the kettle barbecue. They are useful for long cooking of potatoes or cobs of corn, but it is just as easy to cook many types of vegetable briefly on the cooking rack.

Water-sprayer**   Used to suppress flare-ups, a water-sprayer is essential if you want to cook large cuts or fatty meat. The choice of sprayer varies widely, and while some cooks like an ordinary water-pistol (squirt-gun), others use a well-cleaned squeeze-type detergent bottle, and yet others prefer a gardener's misting spray.

LEFT Apron and gloves are both essential items as protection against heat, spillage and sparks.

RIGHT The usual wood for fuel is oak, although almost any kind can be used.

Fuel

· · · · · · · · · · · · · · · · · · ·

There are various types of barbecue fuel, each of which has its own advantages and disadvantages – and each of which affects the flavour of the food in a different way. They are wood, charcoal and charcoal briquettes.

Wood is still preferred by many people for both the flavour it produces in the food and the aroma of the wood smoke. Well dried hardwoods are the most usual choice, as many softwoods add unwanted resinous flavours to the food – although if you like retsina (Greek wine flavoured with pine-resin), you might like to try cooking with pine chips. It is, apparently, very good for some kinds of fish.

The most usual wood employed is oak, closely followed by hickory, but you can use almost any type. Apple and pear wood are well regarded, and the roots of old grapevines are said to make a good fuel, although it is hard to find anyone who has actually used them, so this may be just a piece of barbecue folklore. Mesquite, which is often used after it has been turned into charcoal, is not good for a fire: it crackles and spits alarmingly, and was described by one enthusiastic barbecuer as being like something out of a science fiction movie.

Charcoal has almost as long a history as wood. It produces a much fiercer heat, and the coals are longer lasting, so it requires less attention and is more versatile. It is possible to find charcoal with different flavours: the distinctive smell and taste of mesquite is almost compulsory in the American South-West, for example.

If you buy 'real' charcoal (as distinct from the briquettes described below), it usually comes in lumps of widely varying size. Building a fire from these is quite an art, and it is generally easiest to smash the largest and least manageable lumps with a hammer and chisel before you use them.

Charcoal briquettes, according to one legend, were invented by the Ford Motor Company to use up the sawdust that was left over from making the floorboards of the Model T. Whether this is true or not, they are probably the most popular and convenient of barbecue fuels. One problem with briquettes, however, is that some brands impart a faint chemical taste to the food; this comes from the 'mastic' that is used to bind the powdered charcoal. You can't really taste it if you drown the food in sugary commercial barbecue sauce (which tastes like a distillery by-product anyway), but if you have spent hours preparing delicately marinated food, it is worth remembering. For this reason, those who care passionately about barbecues rarely use them. If they do, they test several different brands until they find one which cooks like real charcoal, as some brands use much more petrochemical mastic binder than others. In addition to 'plain vanilla' briquettes, you can also get briquettes with a touch of mesquite, and even some made from old Jack Daniels whiskey barrels!

Ingredients and Techniques

Some kinds of barbecue cooking are surprisingly simple – steaks, for example, or even quite large cuts of meat – whereas others are unexpectedly difficult. Acceptable hamburgers are easy, but *good* hamburgers are another matter. Practice is essential to develop the mixture of experience and knowledge that you need in order to become a really good barbecue cook.

Pay attention when you are cooking. Barbecue temperatures are not easily controllable, and unlike roasting meat in an oven, barbecuing is not a 'set it and forget it' process. Take both interest and pride in what you are doing.

Most importantly, choose your ingredients carefully. Good meat can be cooked simply, but cheap meat requires help. There is plenty of information about both in here.

If you want to take short-cuts – for example ground ginger instead of freshly chopped ginger root – by all means do, but the more care you put into the preparation, the finer the results.

Beer Beer and barbecues are inseparable to many people, but instead of drinking generic 'maltade', readers might care to try some of the products of smaller breweries, which have vastly more flavour, or to drink imported beer.

BELOW Garlic, mushrooms, ginger, mustard and tomatoes are just some of the basic ingredients for barbecuing.

RIGHT A delicious, yet simple, barbecue meal.

Exotic ingredients From time to time, recipes in this book call for unusual ingredients such as sesame oil or *mirin* (cooking sake). Substitutes are suggested, but the real thing will taste better. Unless you live in the back of beyond, most ingredients will be available from a speciality or ethnic shop near you.

Garlic A head of fresh garlic costs very little, and will keep for a long time (completely odourlessly).

Ginger Ginger root is readily available in many supermarkets and in most oriental, Indian and other ethnic speciality shops. Skinned and grated or finely chopped, it is infinitely superior to – and in fact quite different from – dried, powdered ginger. It also keeps well in the refrigerator.

Herbs Fresh herbs are best, but dried herbs can also be excellent, provided they have not been on your shelf too long. Dried herbs should be strongly aromatic when you rub them in your fingers, not dusty and musty.

Mustard Mustard powder tastes completely different from prepared mustard, and which one you choose will depend on what you are preparing. Sweet, mild American mustard is great for burgers, but is not much use for mixing sauces; coarse-milled Dijon mustard is excellent with sausages.

Oil Olive oil tastes good, and is good for you. The strongest flavour comes from Greek 'extra virgin' olive oil, (taken from the first pressing of the olives) and the best Italian, Spanish and even French oils are equally good. Second-pressing oil is weaker in flavour and lighter in colour, and 'pomace oil', extracted from the third pressing with the help of steam, is all but tasteless. Other good oils include walnut and grapeseed, and safflower and peanut oils are more appropriate for South-East Asian food, where olive oil is not authentic, or for blander food. Sesame oil has a unique hot, spicy flavour, whereas corn oil is barely adequate for frying: its only virtue is that it is cheap.

Pepper Generally use fresh-ground black pepper, from a pepper-mill, and for marinades in which the meat will rest for many hours, whole black peppercorns. Ready-ground black pepper is a poor substitute, and ready-ground white pepper is no substitute at all.

Wine You don't need fine vintages for barbecues, but hearty, drinkable wines (reds in particular) can greatly improve a meal. Sparkling wines are ideal.

Temperatures

Throughout this book, the following descriptions of temperature are used. Holding your hand above the coals at grill height (remove the grill first!), count how many seconds you can stand it. Unless you are unusually slow on the uptake, heat ratings are (approximately):

5 seconds	Low
4 seconds	Low-medium
3 seconds	Medium
2 seconds	Hot
Can't do it	Fierce

Increase the heat by opening the air vents or pushing the coals closer together.

Quantities

Throughout this book, quantities are given in metric US and imperial (English) measures. The more eagle-eyed readers will note that the equivalents are not always absolutely precise, and it is worth noting that measuring dry ingredients by the cup can be inaccurate: a lot depends on how tightly you pack the ingredients, how finely they are chopped, and so forth. Although the 'standard cup' is 8 fluid ounces, the Australian standard tablespoon is 20 ml or ½ fl oz, while the American standard tablespoon is 15 ml.

None of this is very important. Cooking is not a precise science, and you should always reckon that a recipe may need 'fine tuning'. This is particularly true when using garlic: quantities suggested in this book are on the low side, but they may often be doubled (or more) by garlic lovers. Similarly, ginger, sugar, pepper and salt can also be varied within very wide limits.

Getting ready for a Barbecue

Until you are reasonably experienced at the barbecue grill, don't invite friends over unless you know them well. If they are the sort you can fill up with liquor, so they don't worry about half-raw or half-charred mistakes, fine; but if you want to serve them good food, you'll have to learn what you are doing first.

First, plan your shopping. Go for something easy to begin with – preferably steaks – and don't forget the aluminium foil and (very important) the fuel.

Second, plan when you are going to eat. You will need to start the fire about half an hour before you want to begin cooking – maybe less for a small wood fire, maybe more for a large charcoal fire. Starting the fire late will mean tiresome delays, but starting it too early may mean adding another half-sack of fuel before you start cooking, because the first lot has burned away.

Third, get organized. Have everything set up so that you know where it is. Ten minutes wasted while you look for the tongs can be disastrous. If it's a social occasion, make sure there is room for other people to cluster around the barbecue and talk to you.

Fourth, do any advance cooking that you can. Make the garlic bread; set the potatoes baking in the oven, if you are going to do it that way; cut up vegetables, whether for *crudités* or for cooking, and make the dips.

Finally, start the fire. Check the manufacturer's instructions supplied with your kettle barbecue to calculate the amount of fuel you will need. Alternatively, here is a rough guide. Spread a layer at least 4 cm (1½ in) deep across the floor of the barbecue. If you are cooking a small amount of food on a large barbecue, the area of coals should be at least 5 cm (2 in) bigger than the area that will be covered by the food. If you are using wood, you will need more fuel – at least 5 cm (2in) – and if you are cooking larger cuts of meat, you should have extra fuel heaped at the sides of the barbecue to add later.

Make a mound of the fuel for lighting and if you are using wood or real charcoal, put the smaller bits at the bottom and the larger ones on top. The fuel is now ready to light. Keep the lid off the barbecue until the charcoal is ready for cooking.

If you think that charcoal briquettes impart a chemical taste, the oily aroma of 'starter fluids' (or, worse still, waxes) will really offend your nose and your taste buds. Electric fire-starters are a much better idea as are the 'chimney' starters that you prime with wadded newspaper. A gas-powered blowtorch is also clean and fairly easy to use. These are available cheaply at all good hardware stores. Start the coals in a mound, then spread them out when they are burning well. Do not cover the barbecue until you reach this stage.

The coals are not ready for cooking until they are just what their name suggests – coals – with no visible flame. Charcoal and wood should be covered with a fine layer of grey-white ash: if there is still any black showing on charcoal (including briquettes), the fire is not ready. At night, there should be an even red glow with just the suspicion of a blue haze around the coals.

While you are cooking, you can throw any or all of the following onto the coals for flavour:

Soaked wood chips
Cloves of garlic
Bay leaves
Onion skins
Salt
Peppercorns
Dried or fresh herbs (such as sage, oregano, rosemary).

RIGHT **Just a few of the many ingredients that can be used to barbecue, including plenty of items to be served before and during a meal.**

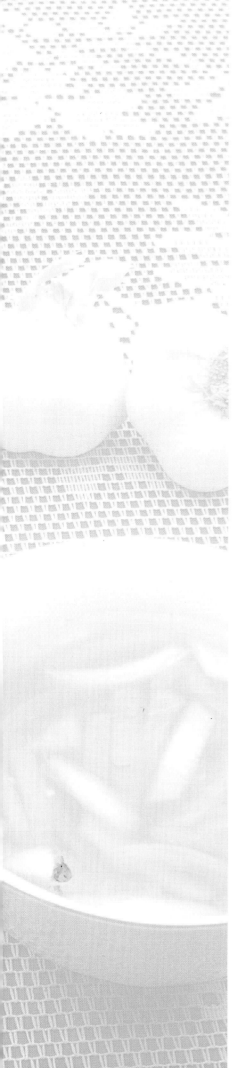

Marinades, basting, and sauces

A marinade is intended to flavour and (usually) to tenderize meat before it is cooked, while a basting sauce is intended to keep it moist while it is cooking. Sometimes, marinating and basting may be done with the same sauce, whereas other dishes have one sauce that is made for a marinade and another for basting. Usually (though not invariably), both sauces are fairly thin: the marinade quite liquid, and the basting sauce rarely thicker than cream.

Barbecue sauces are something else again, and are mainly a North American phenomenon. At their worst, these thick, sugary sauces disguise the taste of almost anything, and are often used indiscriminately as a marinade (when they are too thick to soak into the meat); as a basting sauce (when they usually burn and caramelize); and as a garnish.

Soaking in almost any liquid – even water – will tenderize meat, especially if you leave it overnight; but some liquids add more flavour than others, and some actually have a chemical action which helps to tenderize tough cuts. Pawpaw (papain) juice is probably the most powerful of these tenderizers, and indeed the enzyme extracted from pawpaw was the first commercially popular meat tenderizer. Fresh pineapple juice is almost as effective.

The trouble with commercial tenderizers, as well as with soaking in pawpaw or pineapple marinades for too long, is that they can be altogether too effective: the meat is reduced to pulp. In general, a commercial tenderizer (which is *only* a tenderizer, and does nothing for flavour) should not be used for more than an hour or two, and a pawpaw or pineapple tenderizer should only be used for two to four hours. Tenderizers which use citrus juice (usually lime or lemon) can be left overnight, although much more than 12 hours in a strong citrus marinade can be too much. Marinades based on beers, wines and spirits are fine for as long as you want to leave the meat: overnight is the minimum you should consider, 24 hours is better, and two or even three days is not too long, provided everything is in the refrigerator.

When you leave meat in a marinade, use a glass or ceramic bowl or (easiest of all) a self-sealing plastic bag. Some stainless steel bowls will be all right, and enamel is fine if there are absolutely no chips in the finish, but iron will react with many marinades to give an unattractive metallic taste, and it is unadvisable to use aluminium as it may dissolve entirely, especially if the marinade is acidic. Depending on the shape of the container, the size of the meat, and the shape of the cut, you should turn the meat in the marinade a few times in order to make sure that it is uniformly soaked. Usually, four to six turns and rearrangements should be enough, or in other words, every 20–30 minutes in a two-hour marinade, and two or three times before you go to bed and three or four times after you

get up if you are marinating overnight.

To baste, use a basting brush. Keep it clean when you are not using it, and make sure that you have somewhere clean to rest it on (a plate, or a piece of aluminium foil) while you are cooking.

Marinades

All of the marinades in this book can also be used as basting sauces. In the list of recipes that follow, marinades are graded from 'savoury' to 'sweet'. By varying the ingredients, you can make up your own favourites, but beware: if it is too sweet, you run the risk of caramelizing the sugar.

All recipes are for approximately 2 cups/450 ml/16 fl oz. You may wish to make double or half recipes, according to the amount of meat you are marinating.

RIGHT **Ingredients for a cider marinade.**

CIDER MARINADE

	US	Metric	Imperial
Dry cider ('Scrumpy')	2 cups	450 ml	16 fl oz
Small onion, thinly sliced	1	1	1
Garlic cloves, crushed	4	4	4
Pepper and salt			

● Superb with pork, 12–36 hours.

● 'Scrumpy' can be hard to find, but you can make a good approximation by allowing fresh, unpasteurized apple juice to ferment to completion. For an extra kick, add a slug of calvados or apple brandy.

WHITE WINE MARINADE

	US	Metric	Imperial
Dry white wine	1½ cup	330 ml	12 fl oz
Lemon or lime juice	½ cup	110 ml	4 fl oz
Dry mustard	1 tsp	1 tsp	1 tsp
Salt and fresh-ground pepper			

- Use for fish, 12–48 hours.
- Add olive oil to taste for dry fish.

BEER MARINADE

	US	Metric	Imperial
Beer (1 can)	1½ cups	330 ml	12 fl oz
Cider or wine vinegar	2 tbs	2 tbs	2 tbs
Olive oil	½ cup	110 ml	4 fl oz
Small onion, thinly sliced	1	1	1
Garlic cloves, finely chopped	2	2	2
Salt and fresh-ground black pepper			

- Use for beef, 8-48 hours.
- Ideally, use beer you can actually taste, such as Guinness or any other strong flavoured beer.

RED WINE MARINADE

	US	Metric	Imperial
Red wine	1¼ cup	280 ml	10 fl oz
Olive oil	⅔ cup	150 ml	5½ fl oz
Small onion, finely chopped	1	1	1
Garlic cloves, finely chopped	2	2	2
Salt and fresh-ground black pepper			

● Use for beef, 12–48 hours.

TERIYAKI

	US	Metric	Imperial
Soy sauce	1 cup	225 ml	8 fl oz
Cooking sake *(mirin)*	⅔ cup	150 ml	5½ fl oz
Vinegar	⅓ cup	75 ml	3 fl oz
Sesame oil	2 tbsp	2 tbsp	2 tbsp
Garlic cloves, finely chopped	2	2	2
Ginger root, finely chopped	1 tsp	1 tsp	1 tsp
Salt and fresh-ground black pepper			

● Use with any meat, poultry or seafood, 2 hours to overnight.

● If you can't get cooking sake, use regular sake or sherry plus one-third of its own volume of sugar. Sesame oil, which is hot and spicy, is available in oriental shops. Ground ginger may be subsituted for fresh chopped ginger, but is very inferior.

RIGHT **Teriyaki marinade ingredients.**

APPLE TARRAGON

	US	Metric	Imperial
Fresh apple juice or cider	1 cup	225 ml	8 fl oz
Cider vinegar	⅓ cup	75 ml	3 fl oz
Olive oil	¼ cup	55 ml	2 fl oz
Bunch of shallots (whole with tops), chopped			
Honey	3 tbsp	3 tbsp	3 tbsp
Tarragon leaves	1½ tbsp	1½ tbsp	1½ tbsp
Salt and fresh-ground black pepper			

- Use with chicken and lamb, 4 to 24 hours.

- This sauce is cooked. Mix all the ingredients, bring to the boil, and simmer for 20 minutes. Cool before using.

PINEAPPLE MARINADE

	US	Metric	Imperial
Mashed fresh pineapple	1½ cups	330 ml	12 fl oz
Dry sherry	½ cup	110 ml	4 fl oz
Garlic cloves, crushed	2	2	2
Rosemary leaves	½ tsp	½ tsp	½ tsp

- For pork, 2–6 hours.

- If you have a very sweet tooth, add 2 tbsp honey or brown sugar.

TANDOORI

	US	Metric	Imperial
Small dried red chillies	4	4	4
Coriander seeds	2 tbsp	2 tbsp	2 tbsp
Turmeric	1½ tbsp	1½ tbsp	1½ tbsp
Garam masala	2 tsp	2 tsp	2 tsp
Garlic cloves, crushed	6	6	6
Medium onion, chopped	1	1	1
Root ginger, grated	½ oz	15 gm	½ oz
Lemon juice	2 tbsp	2 tbsp	2 tbsp
Salt	2 tsp	2 tsp	2 tsp

- Grind together all the ingredients, except the salt and lemon juice, to make a smooth paste. Add the salt and lemon juice. Use either as a brushing sauce for chicken grilled conventionally, or as a marinade (rubbed onto the skin of the chicken) and then cook the chicken in foil.

ABOVE Generic barbecue
sauce ingredients.

Barbecue Sauces

You can vastly improve the flavour of barbecued spare ribs
and such like by making up your own barbecue sauces
instead of using commercial bottled sauce. Remember two
things. First, thin sauces make better marinades. Second,
both tomato and sugar will burn if they are applied too
early. Sweet, thick barbecue sauces should only be applied
just before the meat is almost cooked, about 10–15 minutes
before it is ready.

   Once again, the sauces are graded from savoury to sweet.
This time, quantities are for 1 cup/225 ml/8 fl oz, as these
sauces are brushed on during cooking. The only exception
is the recipe listed as 'generic' barbecue sauce: this is a
home-made alternative to the syrupy bottled varieties, and
is likely to be used in larger quantities, so the quantity
is doubled.

GENERIC BARBECUE SAUCE
(2 cups/450 ml/16 oz)

	US	Metric	Imperial
Fresh tomato purée (sauce)	1¼ cups	225 g	8 oz
Vinegar	⅓ cup	75 ml	3 fl oz
Brown sugar	⅓ cup	85 gm	3 oz
Medium onion, chopped	1	1	1
Garlic cloves, finely chopped	1–4	1–4	1–4
Chilli powder	1 tbsp	1 tbsp	1 tbsp
American (mild) mustard	2 tbsp	2 tbsp	2 tbsp

- Mix all the ingredients, bring to the boil and simmer for 5 minutes.

- This recipe is authentically American, but others may care to reduce the sugar and use 1 tbsp of dry mustard.

BEER-CHILLI-HORSERADISH

	US	Metric	Imperial
Beer	⅓ cup	75 ml	3 fl oz
Chilli sauce	½ cup	110 ml	4 fl oz
Grated horseradish	2 tbsp	2 tbsp	2 tbsp
Very finely chopped onion	1 tbsp	1 tbsp	1 tbsp
Sugar	½ tsp	½ tsp	½ tsp
Salt	½ tsp	½ tsp	½ tsp
Fresh-ground black pepper	¼ tsp	¼ tsp	¼ tsp
Dry mustard	¼ tsp	¼ tsp	¼ tsp

- This requires no cooking; just mix, and use on beef. Bottled chilli sauce can be used for this mixture as once it's been grilled, no-one will know that it wasn't home made!

RIGHT **Apricot and ginger sauce.**

PINEAPPLE

	US	Metric	Imperial
Canned crushed pineapple	1 cup	225 ml	8 fl oz
Cornflower (cornstarch)	2 tsp	2 tsp	2 tsp
Honey	3 tbsp	3 tbsp	3 tbsp
Soy sauce	2 tbsp	2 tbsp	2 tbsp
Cider vinegar	2 tbsp	2 tbsp	2 tbsp

FAR RIGHT **Pineapple barbecue sauce.**

● Combine the pineapple and the cornflour in a saucepan and add the other ingredients. Heat for 5 minutes, stirring constantly. Use for chicken and pork.

APRICOT-GINGER

	US	Metric	Imperial
Apricot jam	¾ cup	225 gm	8 oz
Cider vinegar	2 tbsp	2 tbsp	2 tbsp
Melted butter	2 tbsp	2 tbsp	2 tbsp
Root ginger, finely chopped	1 tsp	1 tsp	1 tsp

● This may be a little sweet for some tastes and substituting fresh apricots, which are then puréed in a food processor, results in a remarkable sauce! It requires no cooking: just mix and use.

MUSHROOM AND TOMATO SAUCE
(Serves 6)

ABOVE Mushroom and tomato sauce.

	US	Metric	Imperial
Large onion, chopped	1	1	1
Garlic clove, crushed	1	1	1
Olive oil	1 tbsp	1 tbsp	1 tbsp
Bay leaf	1	1	1
Parsley sprig	1	1	1
Tomatoes, peeled and chopped	2 lb	1 kg	2 lb
Red wine	½ cup	110 ml	4 fl oz
Sugar	1 tsp	1 tsp	1 tsp
Chicken stock	½ cup	110 ml	4 fl oz
Salt and fresh-ground black pepper			
Button mushrooms, sliced	½ lb	225 g	½ lb
Butter	1 tbsp	1 tbsp	1 tbsp

• Cook the onion and garlic in the oil over a fairly low heat until the onion is soft but not browned – this will take about 15 minutes. Add the bay leaf, parsley and tomatoes, then cook, stirring until the tomatoes are beginning to soften – about 5 minutes. Pour in the wine, stir in the sugar and add the stock. Sprinkle a little seasoning in to the sauce, bring to the boil and then reduce the heat so the mixture is only just bubbling. Cover and simmer very gently for 40 minutes.

• Sieve the sauce. Cook the mushrooms briefly in the butter over a fairly high heat, then stir them into the sauce and heat through. Taste and adjust the seasoning before serving. The sauce is good with meat, poultry, fish or vegetables. The stock may be varied accordingly. If you prefer, the sauce may be thickened by stirring in 1– 2 tbsp flour before adding the tomatoes.

CUCUMBER AND TARRAGON SAUCE
(Serves 4)

	US	Metric	Imperial
Walnut oil	2 tbsp	2 tbsp	2 tbsp
Cucumber, peeled and diced	½ lb	225 gm	½ lb
Flour	2 tbsp	2 tbsp	2 tbsp
Salt and fresh-ground black pepper			
White wine	1 cup	225 ml	8 fl oz
Tarragon sprig	1	1	1
Soured cream	½ cup	110 ml	4 fl oz

● Heat the walnut oil very gently in a saucepan. Add the cucumber and cook, stirring occasionally, for 10 minutes. Do not increase the temperature above a medium setting as the oil will become bitter if it is overheated.

● Stir in the flour, salt and pepper, and then cook for a minute. Pour in the wine, stirring all the time, and bring the sauce to the boil. Reduce the heat, add the tarragon and cover the pan. Simmer the sauce for 10 minutes. Stir in the cream and heat for a minute or so but do not allow the sauce to bubble or else the cream will curdle. Taste and adjust the seasoning, then discard the tarragon sprig before serving. The sauce is good with chicken, fish and seafood.

RIGHT **Cucumber and tarragon sauce.**

HORSERADISH-MUSTARD CREAM
(Serves 4)

	US	Metric	Imperial
Wholegrain mustard	3 tbsp	3 tbsp	3 tbsp
Grated fresh horseradish or horseradish sauce	2 tbsp	2 tbsp	2 tbsp
Honey	1 tsp	1 tsp	1 tsp
Soured cream	1 cup	225 ml	8 fl oz
Chives, snipped	2 tbsp	2 tbsp	2 tbsp

• Mix the mustard and horseradish or horseradish sauce with the honey. Stir in the soured cream and chives. Chill the sauce for an hour or so, then leave it at room temperature for 30 minutes before serving. The mustard and horseradish provide enough flavour not to have to add extra seasoning.

• As a healthier alternative, use yoghurt instead of the soured cream. The sauce is good with all meats and some poultry, particularly beef steaks and duck.

Butters
If you are not too worried either about cholesterol or about keeping kosher, flavoured butters are a traditional accompaniment to many barbecued dishes. Soften the butter (to room temperature) before trying to mix any of the following, which are based on 110 gm/4 oz of butter.

Anchovy butter: Chop or shred two or three anchovy fillets (or to taste – it could be a whole can!) and pound well with the butter.
Garlic butter: Add 1 tsp each of finely chopped parsley and garlic ground in a pestle and mortar. Use with steak, bread and shrimp.
Herb butter: Add 2 tbsp each of finely chopped spring (green) onions and parsley, and ½ tsp tarragon leaves. Use with chicken, fish and vegetables.
Herb and cheese butter: Add 3 tbsp grated Parmesan cheese, 1 tbsp finely chopped parsley, ½ tsp basil leaves and 1 clove garlic crushed and chopped. Use with vegetables.
Blue cheese butter: Add 60 g crumbled blue cheese, 1 tbsp sliced shallots with tops and 1 clove garlic, crushed and chopped. Use with beef.
Mustard butter: Add 2 heaped tbsp Dijon mustard, 1 tbsp sliced shallots with tops and 1 clove garlic, crushed and chopped. Use with beef or poultry.

RIGHT **Horseradish-mustard cream.**

Seasoned butters may be served at room temperature, or melted for brushing.

LEFT **Herb butter and ingredients.**

CHAPTER THREE

Basic grilling

Basic grilling is very much like cooking over a camp fire, normally using the open barbecue and small pieces of meat. The thicker the piece of meat, the longer it will take to cook all the way through; hence if it is more than about 5 cm (2in) thick, put the lid on the barbecue for effective cooking.

When you are grilling smaller pieces of meat (including hamburgers and chicken) it is important to avoid two things: charring and flare-ups. You can reduce both to a minimum by intelligent trimming, taking off any protruding, meatless bones or small flaps of carelessly cut meat. Bones will char, and small bits of meat will burn. Small, exposed areas that cannot be trimmed, such as chicken wings and the bones which protrude from lamb chops, should be wrapped in aluminium foil to prevent charring.

Next, cut off all fat that is more than about 6 mm (¼ in) wide; as the meat is cooking, the fat will melt and this is what causes flare-ups. Do not try to remove *all* fat, as this will result in meat that is dry and tough: there has to be some fat for flavour and tenderness.

For fat remaining around the edge of the meat, you should cut through the fat to the meat – although not actually *into* the meat – to prevent the meat from curling. Both meat and fat contract slightly as they are cooked, but meat contracts faster, hence the curling.

Steaks

Steaks and barbecues go extremely well together – and luckily, steaks are about the easiest thing in the world to barbecue to perfection. Crisp on the outside, tender in the middle, aromatic with the smoke of the barbecue – delicious!

Many people tend to serve massive steaks – weighing at least 450 g (1 lb) and often 650 g (1¼ lb). In part, this is because a steak *must* be big if it is to be cooked in the traditional barbecue manner. Thinner steaks can be barbecued, but the effect is very different. A steak for traditional barbecuing must be at least 2.5 cm (1 in) thick, and 5 cm (2 in) is by no means unusual. While some cuts can be conveniently shared between two people, it is difficult to divide most steaks so that both people get an equal amount of the good meat and the bone, fat, etc.

The best steaks for frying or grilling (broiling) are not

BELOW A T-bone steak.

necessarily the best for barbecuing. Fillet steak, for example, is almost wasted on a barbecue. The delicate flavour of the meat is overwhelmed by the smoke, and the contrast in texture between the crisp outside and the tender inside is a little too great: the inside can seem mushy and flavourless. What is more, a fillet steak that is big enough to barbecue properly will be extremely expensive, and will better serve two or three people than one, as with *chateaubriand,* cut from the centre of the fillet. Small fillet steaks require enormous concentration if they are not to be overcooked.

The classic steaks for barbecuing are, therefore, T-bones and their close relatives, porterhouse and club (or Delmonico) steaks; rib steaks *(entrecotes);* strip steaks (made from the non-fillet side of the T-bone or porterhouse, and also called New York Strip, or *contrefilet);* sirloin; and the rather tougher rump steak. A 'London Broil' (unknown in London, but popular in the United States) is, or should be, a thick piece of high-quality top rump. But these are not the only possibilities: the Far Western Tavern in Guadalupe (California), one of the world's great steak houses, has registered the name 'Bull's Eye' for a big steak taken from the eye or interior of the rib.

All of these steaks are best served plain-barbecued, with no marinating and no sauce, although some people like to dress them with butter (including flavoured butter, see page 26) for serving. The smallest steaks that are normally served are 180 gm (6 oz) although a more usual small steak is about 225 gm (½ lb); 350 gm (¾ lb) is a typical large

ABOVE **A small steak, served with salad.**

steak in Britain, whereas 450 gm (1 lb) is an Australian-style portion. All weights are uncooked; a steak typically loses 10–20 per cent of its weight during cooking, depending on how it is cooked and for how long.

For the best results, sear one side over a high heat, and then finish cooking the other over a medium-to-low heat. Searing times are fairly consistant whether the steak is to be rare, medium, or well done.

The first table below is for high quality, tender steaks such as T-bone, porterhouse, and sirloin. For thicker 5 cm (2 in) steaks, use a slightly lower heat on the second side. Both sets of timings are for the open barbecue.

THICKNESS	FIRST SIDE (High)	SECOND SIDE (Medium-low)
2.5 cm (1 in)	2–3 minutes	Rare: 2–3 minutes
		Medium: 5–8 minutes
		Well done: 10 minutes or more
5 cm (2 in)	4–6 minutes	Rare: 8–10 minutes
		Medium: 12–15 minutes
		Well done: 20 minutes or more

To cook tougher cuts, first marinate the meat – a red wine marinade (see page 19). Puncture the steak both with and across the grain using a sharp knife; this will help the marinade to penetrate. No cooking information is given for 'well-done' steaks here – they would be too tough. Slice the thicker steaks diagonally to serve.

THICKNESS	FIRST SIDE (High)	SECOND SIDE (Medium-low)
2.5 cm (1 in)	5–6 minutes	Rare: 15 minutes
		Medium: 20 minutes
5 cm (2 in)	8 minutes	Rare: 20 minutes
		Medium: 23 minutes

MINTED APPLE LAMB STEAKS
(Serves 4)

	US	Metric	Imperial
Juniper berries, crushed	6	6	6
Mint sprigs	2	2	2
Salt and fresh-ground black pepper			
Apple juice	6 tbsp	6 tbsp	6 tbsp
Lamb steaks, off the leg, about 225–350 gm (½–¾ lb) each	4	4	4
Dessert apples	2	2	2
A little lemon juice			
Brown sugar	3 tbsp	3 tbsp	3 tbsp

- It is best to crush the juniper berries in a heavy pestle and mortar. Add the mint leaves (discard the stalks) and crush them lightly, then mix in plenty of seasoning and pour in the apple juice.

- Place the lamb steaks in a dish and spoon the apple juice mixture over them. Cover and chill overnight or for up to 24 hours.

- Peel and core the apples just before cooking the steaks. Cut each apple into four slices and sprinkle with a little lemon juice. Cook the steaks over a medium heat for 5–10 minutes on each side. Brush with any remaining marinade during cooking.

- When the steaks have been turned, sprinkle the sugar over the apples. Turn the slices in the sugar and lemon juice, then grill them briefly until they are just beginning to brown: 1–2 minutes on each side is usually long enough. Top each lamb steak with a slice of apple before serving.

LEFT **Lamb steak.**

RIGHT **Carpetbag steak on the grill.**

CARPETBAG STEAK
(Serves 4)

. . . .

	US	Metric	Imperial
Slice of rump steak, 5 cm (2 in) thick	3 lb	1.5 kg	3 lb
Fresh oysters, shelled	10	10	10
Salt and fresh-ground black pepper			
Butter, melted	2–3 tbsp	2–3 tbsp	2–3 tbsp

. . . .

● Cut a horizontal slit into the middle of the steak to make a neat pocket. Take care not to cut right through the steak.

● Mix the oysters with plenty of seasoning, then put them into the pocket in the steak. Secure the opening with two short metal meat skewers and string to keep the steak in a neat shape. Brush the steak all over with melted butter.

● Cook the steak over low to medium heat with the cover on the barbecue. Allow 40–50 minutes, turning the steak twice during cooking and brushing occasionally with the remaining butter. To serve the steak, remove the skewers and trussing string, then cut the steak across into slices.

● If fresh oysters are not available, canned shellfish may be substituted. Good-quality smoked oysters give a different flavour which is also good.

Korean Barbecue and Beef Teriyaki

In the Far East, beef is often barbecued in much thinner strips than in the West. For success, you will need a *very* sharp chopping knife to slice the meat; partially freezing it will make cutting very much easier.

RIGHT **Korean-style beef and salad.**

KOREAN BEEF
(Serves 4–6)

	US	Metric	Imperial
Sesame seeds	1 tbsp	1 tbsp	1 tbsp
Shallots, finely chopped	1 cup	2 large	2 large
Garlic cloves, very finely chopped	2–4	2–4	2–4
Soy sauce	¼ cup	55 ml	2 fl oz
Sugar	2 tbsp	2 tbsp	2 tbsp
Dry sherry or *sake*	2 tbsp	2 tbsp	2 tbsp
Peanut or sesame oil	2 tbsp	2 tbsp	2 tbsp
Beef (chuck, round or sirloin) in a slice about 2.5 cm (1 in) thick	1½ lb	750 gm	1½ lb

● Toast the sesame seeds in a heavy iron skillet, shaking frequently to avoid burning and popping, until golden. Grind the toasted seeds in a pestle and mortar or spice grinder. Mix thoroughly with the shallots, garlic, soy sauce, sugar, wine and oil.

● Slice the meat into strips about 6 mm thick. Add to the marinade, stirring to coat thoroughly. Marinate for an hour or two.

● Over a high or even fierce heat, grill the strips until the meat is browned, but still rare – about 30 seconds to 1 minute per side.

● In Korea, this would be served with *kimchi* (pickled, salty cabbage, available at Korean stores), stir-fried bean sprouts and plain boiled rice. If you can't get *kimchi,* try a coleslaw or cucumber salad with vinegar dressing.

BEEF TERIYAKI

● Use the teriyaki sauce recipe from page 19 for this dish. Teriyaki sauce straight from the bottle can be quite good, and you can add a little freshly chopped garlic to taste if you like.

● For 4–6 people, you need 1–1.5 kg (2–3 lb) of beef. It need not be of outstanding quality: top round or chuck is fine, but it should be in a single slice, at least 2.5 cm (1 in) thick. With the meat semi-frozen, cut strips as thin as you can, across the grain: 3 mm (⅛ in) is about right.

● Soak bamboo skewers in water to avoid charring, and then thread the meat onto them. Pour the marinade over the skewered meat and turn the sticks frequently to assure even coverage and penetration. 30 minutes of soaking is enough.

● Grill over a hot or fierce fire for 3–4 minutes until the meat is browned but not dried out. Serve as an *hors d'oeuvres* (for up to 12 people) or with rice and vegetables cooked in the Japanese style.

Chops and Cutlets

The techniques used for cooking chops and cutlets are much the same as those for cooking steaks, although you have to make adjustments according to the type of meat used.

A chop or cutlet consists of a rib bone and the meat attached to it. For pork, it is normally called a chop; for lamb and veal, 'chop' and 'cutlet' and for venison, 'cutlet' or 'noisette' are the usual terms.

Pork Chops

Hind loin chops are dryer than fore loin ones, and so are less suitable for barbecuing. Shoulder chops are the fattiest, but have an excellent flavour. True chop-lovers would grill them unadorned but you can both marinate them and use some kind of basting or barbecue sauce. With hind loin chops, this is probably a good idea. A cider marinade (page 17) is ideal, or use one of the sweet marinades such as pineapple.

Unlike steaks, pork chops are not seared as it toughens them. Trim the fat as described on page 28, and cook a 2.5 cm (1 in) chop over a medium to low heat for 25 – 30 minutes, turning once. Thinner chops may be cooked in as little as 12–15 minutes: be careful to avoid over-cooking, or the meat will be tough. The chop is cooked when the juices run clear if you pierce the meat with a skewer or knife – but don't test it too often, or the meat will dry out.

Smoked chops cook faster than unsmoked chops: a 2.5 cm (1 in) chop should be cooked in 15 – 20 minutes.

Lamb Chops

Rib cutlets are distinguished by a long bone and a small 'nut' of lean meat surrounded by fat. You need to watch these carefully if they are not to be overcooked, but they taste excellent. Loin chops are the easiest of all to cook, because they are usually biggest and thickest, and they have the most meat. The most impressive chops to look at are butterfly chops (two chops joined at the bone, cut across both sides of the carcass) and are cooked in exactly the same way.

Cook over a medium heat: a chop 2.5 cm (1 in) thick should take 15 minutes or a little less, while thin chops can be cooked in 5 –10 minutes. Turn once.

Lamb chops can be eaten with the meat a little pink, although well-done lamb is less tough than well-done pork or beef.

BUTTERFLY LAMB CHOPS WITH BASIL
(Serves 4)

RIGHT **Coriander pork chops.**

	US	Metric	Imperial
Butterfly lamb chops (double loin chops)	4	4	4
Garlic clove, chopped	1	1	1
Olive oil	1 tbsp	1 tbsp	1 tbsp
Handful of fresh basil leaves, shredded			
Pine nuts, toasted	3 tbsp	3 tbsp	3 tbsp
Salt and fresh-ground black pepper			
Lemon wedges	4	4	4

• Place the chops in a dish. Sprinkle the garlic, oil and about a quarter of the basil over the chops, then cover and chill for a couple of hours.

• Meanwhile, mix the remaining basil with the pine nuts and seasoning. Cook the chops over a medium heat for 5 – 8 minutes on each side, according to whether you like your chops rare or well done.

• Sprinkle the basil and pine nut mixture over the cooked chops. Serve the lemon wedges with the chops so that the juice may be squeezed over before eating the meat.

RIGHT **Pork chops on the grill.**

CORIANDER PORK CHOPS
(Serves 4)

	US	Metric	Imperial
Pork loin chops, about 2.5 cm (1 in) thick	4	4	4
Coriander seeds, coarsely crushed	3 tbsp	3 tbsp	3 tbsp
Garlic clove, chopped	1	1	1
Grated lemon rind	1 tsp	1 tsp	1 tsp
Salt and fresh-ground black pepper			
Sunflower oil	2 tbsp	2 tbsp	2 tbsp
Greek-style yogurt	4 tbsp	4 tbsp	4 tbsp
Shallot, chopped	4 tbsp	4 tbsp	4 tbsp

● Trim the rind off the chops and cut into the fat in a few places. Mix the coriander, garlic, lemon rind and plenty of seasoning.

● Brush the chops all over with oil, then rub the coriander mixture over both sides of them. Place in a dish, cover and leave to marinate in the refrigerator for several hours or overnight.

● Cook the chops over a medium heat, turning once or twice, for about 30 minutes, or until they are cooked through. Top each chop with some yogurt and sprinkle with chopped shallot before serving.

Sausages

Although it is possible to cook almost any sausage on the barbecue, it is a good idea to pre-cook fresh sausages and then to cook them by indirect heat over a drip-pan.
All sausages are fatty, and flare-ups are a virtual certainty if you do not take these precautions. With some cooked sausages, such as frankfurters, fat is not a problem, while other seem to contain almost as much fat as fresh sausages.

The best way to pre-cook fresh sausages is on the barbecue, very slowly, a long way above or to one side of the coals, and let the fat drip out and burn. The easiest way, however, is in the microwave. Prick the skins, and cook at one of the lower settings until the fat begins to run out (use a sloping 'bacon tray' for convenience). Alternatively, use the grill (broiler) in the oven, turning frequently. If you want to pre-cook them on the barbecue, you can also wrap them in aluminium foil with a couple of tablespoons of water, and allow to render for 10–15 minutes. But be careful when you unwrap them.

Black pudding, blutwurst, blood sausage – A cooked sausage which may be barbecued in slices 2.5–5 cm (1–2 in) long without very great risk of flare-up, although a drip-tray is a better idea. Great for a hearty brunch. Takes 5–10 minutes over low heat.

Bologna – Cook as for black pudding, above.

Bratwurst – Pre-cook, or buy ready-cooked bratwurst. Prick the skin, and cook over a drip-tray.

'Bangers' – Prick skins and cook over a low heat until the fat has rendered out – this will take longer for the less 'meaty' varieties. These taste surprisingly good if they are left to go cold after they are fully cooked.

Chorizo – Pre-cook these. Thin chorizo can be cooked in the same way as 'Bangers' (above), but thick chorizo should be split lengthways with a knife (though not all the way through) and grilled over a low heat for 10–20 minutes.

Frankfurters – Ideally, these should be smoked in a water-smoker until they are hot, then finished on the grill. In practice, they can be grilled straight from the can, without drip-trays or any other precautions, in well under 10 minutes. Turn frequently. The same goes for 'red hots' and 'white hots', which are regional variants with a skin.

LEFT **Linguisa, also known as Italian pork sausages.**

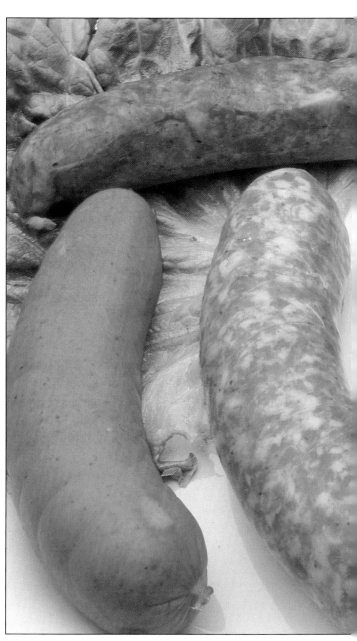

Linguisa (Italian pork sausage) – Cook as for thick chorizo, above.

Polish smoked sausage – Cook as for thick chorizo.

Salami – Dry sausages of all kinds can be cooked. They will render out a lot of fat, and become very crumbly, but the flavour is excellent. Cook as for black pudding, above.

Weisswurst – This is normally boiled, but a whole boiled weisswurst can be finished on the barbecue and will taste all the better for it. Cook briefly from hot, turning often.

To accompany sausages, consider sauerkraut, German potato salad (page 100), and potato pancakes.

ABOVE **Knockwurst and bratwurst sausages.**

LEFT **A selection of sausages from the wide variety available.**

Burgers

Nothing is easier to make than a hamburger, but cooking them successfully is another matter.

If you want to save calories, use lean (22 per cent fat) mince (ground beef) rather than extra lean (15 per cent). Much of the fat will render out anyway, and the extra lean meat can be rather dry. The smallest hamburgers that can conveniently be barbecued are 110 gm (¼ lb), but 175 gm (6 oz) or 225 gm (½ lb) are better. Anything much larger can be awkward to keep in one piece, and will certainly be harder to cook evenly. Once again, all weights are before cooking: a hamburger can lose up to 25 per cent of its weight in cooking, through loss of moisture and fat.

For a first-class basic hamburger, you need add absolutely nothing to the meat: it's the meat, the whole meat, and nothing but the meat. You do *not* need egg, which will spoil the flavour. Shape the meat (at room temperature) into patties that are about 2.5 cm (1 in thick). Handle the hamburger as little as possible – this will help to keep it tender – before cooking as follows on the open barbecue:

FIRST SIDE (High)	SECOND SIDE (Medium/low)
2–4 minutes	Rare: 4–5 minutes
	Medium: 6–8 minutes
	Well done: 10–15 minutes

If you want to add barbecue sauce, the 'generic' recipe on page 21 is probably the most suitable.

Drop the burger on the (oiled) grill and brush the upper surface with sauce. When you flip the burger, brush the cooked side. For a patty melt, add the sliced cheese 2–5 minutes before cooking is complete: some cheeses melt faster than others.

Stuffed Hamburgers

You may also care to try stuffed hamburgers. Make the patties 1.3 cm (½ in) thick and between the two layers try any or all of the following. Seal the edges as best as you can (don't use too much stuffing!) and cook as for a regular hamburger:

Cheese (Cheddar, Mozarella, or Blue)
Cooked bacon
Chopped onion
Pickles
Capsicum
Olives

Presentation

Whether plain, flavoured or stuffed hamburgers, the classic presentation is in a large, soft, tasteless hamburger bun which has to be toasted over the barbecue in order to impart any flavour or texture to it at all. But all kinds of other breads – French bread, sourdough rolls, muffins, bagels and even pumpernickel or croissants – can also be used.

Classic salad accompaniments are iceberg lettuce and tomato, and cucumber and sliced dill pickles are also usual. For onion, use thinly sliced red onion or chopped shallots for a milder flavour than raw white onion. Whereas in Australia and Britain, fried onions are sometimes served with hamburgers, in the United States, they are more likely to be raw.

Other garnishes include sour cream; bottled or home-made chili con carne or pizza sauce; sliced olives; sliced avocado; crispy-friend bacon; mustard; tomato sauce and many kinds of proprietary salad dressings.

TOP RIGHT **Chicken cooked in foil.**

BOTTOM RIGHT **Chicken pieces served with rice and salad.**

LEFT **A hamburger served with salad.**

Chicken

Barbecuing is one of the very best (and easiest) ways of adding flavour to cheaper chickens. You can cook chicken pieces (legs, wings, quarters and halves) over the open barbecue; but they cook more evenly and with more flavour with the lid on. Whole chickens cook very quickly and evenly in the covered barbecue. If you are using a meat thermometer, look for an interior temperature of 85°C (185°F).

Chicken Pieces
Cook over a medium, direct heat with no drip tray. Turn every 10 minutes, basting from time to time with melted butter: herbs, such as oregano or sage, or garlic butter (page 26) can be added for extra flavour. Sprinkle the chicken with pepper and salt before cooking; both to add flavour and to crisp the skin.

	Open Barbecue	Covered Barbecue
Breasts, boned	12–15 minutes	10–12 minutes
Wings, legs	35–40 minutes	30–35 minutes
Quarters	40–50 minutes	30–40 minutes
Halves	1 hour or more	45 minutes or more

Whole Chicken
Wipe the bird inside and out; do not stuff. Season with pepper and salt.

Truss carefully, and cover wingtips and leg ends with aluminium foil. Cook over medium, indirect heat (use a drip tray) in a covered barbecue. A middling-size chicken of 1.25–1.75 kg (2½–3½ lb) should cook in about 1¼–1½ hrs. Turn three or four times during that time.

For faster cooking, prepare a Spatchcock bird: take a heavy knife and split the bird along the backbone. Pull hard, cracking the breastbone, and flatten the chicken.

Undercut the wing and leg joints slightly, if necessary, to help the bird lie flat. Lean on the whole with the heel of your hand to flatten thoroughly and slit the thigh to help it cook more evenly. Marinate in red wine marinade (page 19) for at least a couple of hours. Grill over a medium, direct heat, with the cover on the barbecue, skin side first until it is golden and crispy, then place bone side downwards. Baste with olive oil, turning occasionally. Total cooking time will be 35–45 minutes for an average-size chicken.

LEFT Barbecue chicken.

CHICKEN WITH AVOCADO
(Serves 4)

	US	Metric	Imperial
Chicken quarters	4	4	4
Chilli powder	½ tsp	½ tsp	½ tsp
Thyme leaves	1 tsp	1 tsp	1 tsp
Salt and fresh-ground black pepper			
Groundnut oil	1 tbsp	1 tbsp	1 tbsp
Avocados	2	2	2
Tomatoes, diced	4	4	4
Shallots, chopped	2	2	2
Soured cream	4 tbsp	4 tbsp	4 tbsp

● Trim the leg and wing ends off the chicken if necessary and cut away any flaps of skin or lumps of fat. Mix the chilli powder, thyme and plenty of seasoning. Brush the chicken quarters with the groundnut oil, then rub the seasoning mixture all over them.

● Cook the chicken by the indirect method, over a drip tray, with the lid on the barbecue. Allow about 45–50 minutes, turning once or twice, until the chicken is golden and crisp all over. Check that the meat is cooked through by piercing it at the thickest part with the point of a knife. If there is any sign of blood in the juices cook the chicken a little longer.

● Halve, peel and dice the avocados, then mix them with the tomatoes and shallots. Pile this mixture next to the chicken on plates and top each portion with some soured cream. The fresh, creamy avocado mixture complements the slightly spicy, full-flavoured barbecued chicken.

RIGHT **A whole chicken on the grill with pineapple rings.**

Pre-cooking

To save time, part-cook half and whole chickens in a microwave oven before barbecuing. Cook in the microwave for half of the oven manufacturer's recommended time and finish on the grill with half of the recommended times in this book.

Checking the chicken is cooked

Always take great care to ensure that chicken meat is cooked right through to the bone. Pierce the meat at the thickest point: if there are any signs of blood in the juices, or pink meat, then continue cooking: if the outside of the bird is in danger of overcooking, then wrap it loosely in foil or shield small areas.

Other poultry

· · · · · · · · · · · · · · · · · · · ·

The kettle barbecue cooks whole fowl, large and small, to perfection. It may not have occurred to you that it is

perfectly possible to cook everything from a pigeon weighing under 450 gm (1 lb) to a turkey that weighs 7 kg plus (15–16 lb).

Turkey

Wipe and season the bird, inside and out. An 3½ kg (8 lb) turkey will serve 6–8 people, with leftovers; a 6.8 kg (115 lb) turkey will serve 12–15.

Cook over a medium heat with a drip tray, turning every 15 minutes or so and basting with melted butter. As with chicken pieces, use herb or garlic butter for extra flavour. An 3.6 kg (8 lb) bird should take 2–2½ hours, while a 6.8 kg (15 lb) bird will take at least 4 hours.

With birds of this size, though, the meat will continue to cook for 20–30 minutes after it is removed from the heat. On the meat thermometer look for a temperature of 85°C (185°F): then the bird is cooked. Allow it to rest for about 5 minutes, or slightly longer.

Duck

Wild duck is covered on page 90, but domestic fresh or (defrosted) frozen ducks can be cooked in the same way as chicken. A 2.5 kg (4–5 lb) duck should be cooked in about 2 hours, but start checking after about 1¾ hours. A duck this size will serve four.

Because duck is so very fatty, indirect, covered cooking is absolutely essential to avoid flare-ups.

RIGHT A Cornish game hen, served with pasta and salad.

DUCK BREASTS WITH PINEAPPLE AND BAY

(Serves 4)

	US	Metric	Imperial
Vegetable oil	2 tbsp	2 tbsp	2 tbsp
Fresh green chilli, seeded and sliced	1	1	1
Bay leaves	4	4	4
Shallots, chopped	4	4	4
Can pineapple rings in syrup	½ lb	225 gm	½ lb
Duck breasts	4	4	4

● Heat the oil gently in a small saucepan. Add the chilli rings and bay leaves and cook gently, stirring occasionally, for 5 minutes. Stir in the shallots and cook for a further 5 minutes before pouring in the syrup from the can of pineapple. Bring it slowly to the boil and simmer for 2 minutes, then leave the mixture to cool completely.

● Place the duck breasts in a dish and pour the cooled marinade over them. Cover and chill overnight. Drain the duck breasts before cooking them. Pour the marinade into a small pan and bring it to the boil, reduce the heat and simmer the liquid for about 10 minutes, or until it is reduced to a small amount of glaze.

● Cook the duck breasts over a medium heat for about 10 minutes on each side, or until the skin is crisp and well browned and the meat is cooked to your liking. Discard the bay leaves from the marinade and pour it over the duck before serving.

Pigeon

Allow one whole pigeon per person. Wrap a slice of bacon around the breast and back – pigeons are not particularly fatty – and roast over a medium-high direct heat for 15–25 minutes, turning once. Unlike other whole fowl, you can cook pigeons with an open grill, but the covered barbecue is quicker and gives a better flavour.

Cornish Game Hen

A small chicken, completely unknown in Cornwall, this is a popular dish in the United States. The nearest equivalent is a small spring chicken: whole hens typically weigh 750 gm (1½ lb). One hen can serve two people easily.

Cook for 25–30 minutes over medium heat, with a drip tray.

LEFT Duck with bay leaves.

CHAPTER FOUR

Kebabs

Kabab, an Arab word also found in Persian and Urdu, has been spelled in a wide variety of ways including 'cabob' and 'keebaub'. It is only quite recently that most of the English-speaking world has standardized on 'kebab', while Americans have settled for 'kabob'.

Although kebabs are found throughout the Near East, and indeed throughout the world, the Greeks (and for that matter, the Yugoslavs and Albanians) make some of the simplest: cubes of lamb or pork, cooked on a skewer, and served either with rice or in a pocket of pita bread (or pitta bread – again, the spelling isn't standardized) with a squeeze of lemon juice, a salad, and a couple of ferocious capsicums.

Greek Pork Kebabs

A couple of pounds (just under one kilo) of boned pork meat will make enough kebabs for 4–6 people if served with rice, or 6–8 if served with plenty of salad in pita bread. The meat is usually marinated for at least 1 hour in a mixture of lemon juice and oil: two or three parts of oil to one part of lemon juice is ideal. The marinade is also used for basting.

Shoulder of pork is traditional and economical, and tastes very good, but it may be a little fatty for some tastes; and although the loin is delicious and tender, it will require constant basting with a mixture of olive oil if it is not to become tough. So leg of pork is probably the best compromize: it tastes good, and it has enough fat to keep it juicy while still being high-quality meat.

Whichever cut you choose, dice it into cubes approximately 3 cm (1¼ in) square, and thread these onto a skewer so that they are touching: you do not want any space between the pieces of meat. Marinade for at least 1 hour – overnight will do no harm, although a marinade with more oil and less lemon juice may be advisable (three-to-one instead of two-to-one).

Cook over a medium-low fire which extends somewhat beyond the meat on the kebab: cooking on a too-small grill tends to mean the meat in the middle will be cooked while the ends are not. Four 10 cm (4 in) of tight-packed meat is (just) sufficient for one pita filling, with salad. Cook for at least 15 minutes, turning frequently.

Greek Lamb Kebabs

The basic procedure is the same as for pork kebabs: again,
shoulder is traditional, but leg is better. Cooking times are
slighly shorter than for a similar-sized skewer of pork.

● Barbecue over medium-low heat for 10–15 minutes, turning and basting frequently.
Sprinkle with parsley and serve with the remaining lemon butter, salad and garlic bread
as a main course or as an appetizer before steak.

SKEWERED VENISON WITH PRUNES
(Serves 4)

	US	Metric	Imperial
Boneless venison, for example, haunch or steak	2 lb	900 g	2 lb
Red Wine Marinade (page 19)			
Bacon rashers	16	16	16
Ready-to-eat prunes	32	32	32
Bay leaves	16	16	16

● Trim any small areas of fat off the venison, then cut it into chunks. Place them in a dish
and pour the marinade over. Cover and chill overnight.

● Cut the rinds off the bacon and cut each rasher in half. Wrap a piece of bacon around
each prune. Remove the meat from the marinade. Thread the meat, wrapped prunes and
bay leaves on eight metal skewers. Brush the kebabs all over with marinade, then cook
them over medium heat for 15–20 minutes, turning two or three times and brushing often
with the marinade. The venison may be served cooked through or pink in the middle
according to personal preference.

LEFT **Skewered venison
with prunes.**

TURKEY KEBABS
(Serves 4)

	US	Metric	Imperial
Boneless turkey breast	2 lb	900 g	2 lb
Fresh rosemary, chopped	1 tbsp	1 tbsp	1 tbsp
Grated rind and juice of 1 orange			
Garlic clove, crushed	1	1	1
Olive oil	2 tbsp	2 tbsp	2 tbsp
Salt and fresh-ground black pepper			

- The turkey meat should be skinned and trimmed of any small pieces of fat. Cut the meat into large chunks of about 5 cm (2 in) in size. Place them in a bowl. Add the rosemary, orange rind and juice, garlic and plenty of seasoning. Mix well to coat all the pieces of turkey in marinade. Cover and chill for 2–6 hours.

- Remove the turkey from the marinade and thread the chunks on to eight metal skewers. Cook over medium heat, brushing often with the marinade, for about 30 minutes. Turn the kebabs three or four times so that the turkey is evenly well browned and crisped in parts. The kebabs are good with a salad of endive and Chinese cabbage.

PORK 'N' PEPPER KEBABS
(Serves 4)

	US	Metric	Imperial
Lean boneless pork	2 lb	900 g	2 lb
Red capsicums	2	2	2
Green capsicums	2	2	2
Dried sage	1 tbsp	1 tbsp	1 tbsp
Vegetable oil	2 tbsp	2 tbsp	2 tbsp
Medium sherry	2 tbsp	2 tbsp	2 tbsp
Salt and fresh-ground black pepper			

- Cut the pork into 2.5 cm (1 in) cubes. Halve the red and green capsicums, remove their seeds and stalk, and then cut them into 2.5 cm (1 in) squares.

- Thread the meat and capsicums on four metal skewers. Mix the oil, sage, sherry and plenty of seasoning, then brush this all over the kebabs. Cook the kebabs over medium heat, with the lid on, for 30–35 minutes. Turn the kebabs twice and brush with any remaining oil and sherry mixture. The meat should be evenly browned and cooked through.

TOP RIGHT **Turkey kebabs on the grill.**

BOTTOM RIGHT **Pork 'n' pepper kebabs.**

CHICKEN TIKKA
(Serves 4)

	US	Metric	Imperial
Fresh root ginger, grated	2 tbsp	2 tbsp	2 tbsp
Garlic cloves	3	3	3
Onion, grated	1	1	1
Turmeric	½ tsp	½ tsp	½ tsp
Ground coriander	1 tbsp	1 tbsp	1 tbsp
Ground cumin	1 tbsp	1 tbsp	1 tbsp
Natural yogurt	4 tbsp	4 tbsp	4 tbsp
Lemon juice	2 tbsp	2 tbsp	2 tbsp
Salt and fresh-ground black pepper			
Large boneless chicken breasts	4	4	4

• Mix the ginger, garlic, onion, turmeric, coriander and cumin. Stir in the yogurt and lemon to make a paste, then add seasoning.

• Remove the skin from the chicken and cut each breast into six pieces. Place the chicken in a bowl and pour the spice mixture over them. Mix thoroughly, cover and chill overnight or for up to two days (the chicken must be absolutely fresh if it is to be marinated for this long).

• Thread the chicken on four metal skewers and cook over high heat, turning often, for 20–25 minutes. The chicken should be very well browned and cooked through.

RIGHT **Steak kebabs.**

Serving with Pita
Heat the pita bread for 15–30 seconds on each side: it should puff up and make it easy to slit for filling. The traditional Greek salad filling consists of shredded white cabbage with a dressing of olive oil and lemon juice, about three parts oil to one part of lemon juice. Add a couple of slices of tomato; 1 tbsp or so of diced cucumber; and a couple of thin slices of raw, or 1 tsp of chopped onion. Give your guests the option of extra Green capsicums: Italian *pepperoncini* are an acceptable substitute although not quite as good.

Put the salad in first; strip the meat off the skewer, into the pita; then lay a capsicum over the top. Serve with wedges of lemon to squeeze over the meat.

Half a head of cabbage, two or three tomatoes, one cucumber and one medium onion should provide plenty of salad for four people.

RIGHT **Chicken tikka.**

Steak Kebabs

A basic steak (or beef) kebab – Basque-style, for example – is very much like a Greek-style kebab: the same 3 cm (1¼ in) cubes, with no other ingredients. Some people like to push the meat close together, like pork and lamb, while others prefer to leave a small space between the pieces, as this gives a larger area to crisp on the outside.

There is a major difference, however, in cooking times and temperatures. Steak kebabs are normally cooked over a medium-hot or even hot fire, and if the pieces of meat are separated instead of being pushed together, a rare kebab might be cooked for as little as 3–4 minutes over hot coals, being turned once a minute or more frequently. Even if the meat is pushed together, 10 minutes is as long as most people would want to cook a beef kebab even over medium-hot coals.

What is more, steak kebabs are more often served with baked potatoes and beans or other vegetables, rather than with bulky breads and salads, so the quantities of meat required per person tend to be higher: 225 gm (½ lb) of boneless beef (uncooked weight) per person is a reasonable minimum.

Garnished Kebabs

In general, it is a good idea to avoid excessive cleverness or creativity when dealing with steak kebabs: those wonderful cookery-book pictures which show meat alternated with wedges of onion, cherry tomatoes, capsicums and mushrooms are virtually impossible to cook, because all the ingredients cook at different rates. If you are determined to make this sort of kebab, note the following points:

● Use only beef. The risk of undercooking pork is too great, though if you like underdone lamb, by all means consider that.

● Cut the meat smaller than you would for an all-meat kebab. Instead of a 3 cm (1¼ in) cube, try cutting squares that are 3 cm (1¼ in) on each side but only about 1.5 cm (½–¾ in) thick.

● Unless the meat is *very* thin – 6 mm (¼ in) or so – do not press moist vegetables close against it: the steam from the vegetables will keep the temperature too low to allow the meat to cook properly.

• The best way to make a garnished kebab is probably to cut long, thin strips of meat. Begin with a piece of medium-quality steak about 3 cm (1¼ in) thick. Chill it to make cutting easier, and with a *very* sharp knife, slice off pieces 6 mm (¼ in) thick. Marinate to tenderize, using one of the marinades on page 17.

Weave the strips of meat accordion-style onto the skewer. Between the folds of the accordion, insert vegetables or even fruit: wedges of orange, pineapple, banana, cherry tomatoes, mushrooms (previously steamed for a minute or two), small stewing onions, or whatever you like.

Cook over medium coals for about 15 minutes.

Meatball Kebabs

The humble meatball takes amazingly well to being barbecued. The important thing is to ensure that the meatball mixture is really well mixed and pounded on the skewers. The meatballs should be lightly oiled and turned with great care to prevent them sticking, or else the meatball is likely to disintegrate as you try to pull it away. Here are two recipes, one relatively simple and Greek, the other a much subtler Indian dish.

LEFT **Meatball kebab.**

ABOVE **Steak kebab, with pasta and salad.**

KEFETHES (Greek)

(Serves 8)

	US	Metric	Imperial
Dry white wine	½ cup	110 ml	4 fl oz
Water	1 cup	225 ml	8 fl oz
Stale bread	½ lb	225 gm	½ lb
Medium onions, finely chopped	2 or 3	2 or 3	2 or 3
Minced (ground) beef or veal	2 lb	900 gm	2 lb
Minced (ground) pork	½ lb	225 gm	½ lb
Freshly chopped mint or spearmint	2 tbsp	2 tbsp	2 tbsp

● Mix the wine and water; soak the bread in this. Parboil the onions for three minutes. Drain, and chop finely when cool. Mix all the ingredients together, and leave for at least 20 minutes for the flavours to blend.

● Form into about three dozen sausage-shaped patties, and thread on to skewers pressing them on well. Brush with olive oil. Cook over a medium to low heat for at least 20 minutes, turning frequently and basting occasionally with olive oil or a mixture of olive oil and lemon juice, as for Greek-style kebabs (page 44).

● Serve with salad, garnished with fried potatoes. This is hearty food: a bottle of *retsina* (resinated Greek wine) is a good accompaniment.

SEEKH KEBAB (India)

(Serves 6: ingredients marked with an asterisk* can be found in Indian or Oriental shops)

	US	Metric	Imperial
Minced (ground) mutton or lamb	1½ lb	750 gm	1½ lb
Grated root ginger	1 tsp	1 tsp	1 tsp
Large onion, finely chopped	1	1	1
Gram flour*	4 tbsp	4 tbsp	4 tbsp
Fresh hot green chillies, chopped	2	2	2
Green mango powder*	1 tsp	1 tsp	1 tsp
Salt	1 tbsp	1 tbsp	1 tbsp
Juice of half a lemon			
Large egg	1	1	1
Chopped coriander leaves	2 tbsp	2 tbsp	2 tbsp
Ghee (clarified butter)	4 tbsp	60 gm	2 oz
Tomato, onion and lemon to garnish			
SPICES:			
Poppy seeds, roasted and ground	½ tsp	½ tsp	½ tsp
Garam masala*	1 tsp	1 tsp	1 tsp
Red chilli powder	1 tbsp	1 tbsp	1 tbsp
Fresh-ground black pepper	½ tsp	½ tsp	½ tsp
Black cumin seeds*, roasted, ground	1 tsp	1 tsp	1 tsp
Ground coriander seeds	1 tbsp	1 tbsp	1 tbsp

• Mix all the ingredients together except the egg, coriander and ghee. Leave for 30 minutes, then add the egg and coriander.

• Knead the mixture until it is sticky, then divide into 18 portions and form into sausage shapes. Thread these onto skewers, pressing them on well.

• Melt the ghee in a bowl on the side of the grill and brush the meat with this. Cook over a medium-hot fire for about 20 minutes, brushing with ghee occasionally. Seekh kebabs are normally served garnished with tomato and chopped onion, with lemon wedges for squeezing, as appetizers.

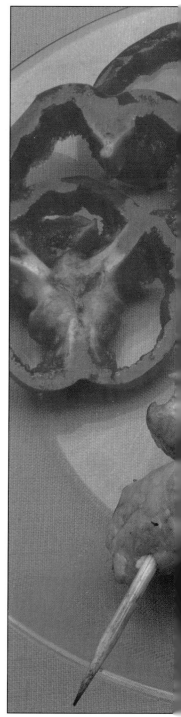

ABOVE **Satay pork.**

preference), pork (any lean cut), firm-fleshed fish and prawns.

For meat or fish satay, cut the meat into 12mm (½ in) cubes and thread on bamboo skewers that have been soaked for at least 1 hour in water – for prawns, use fair-size tails (frozen will do). Marinate the skewers for at least 1 hour, turning occasionally.

Pork marinade: 4 tbsp oil, 4 tbsp soy sauce, 33 tbsp honey, 2 tbsp vinegar, 1 tsp aniseed, 2 cloves of garlic (crushed), salt and fresh-ground black pepper to taste. Squeeze a piece of very fresh root ginger in a garlic press to get a little ginger juice for an additional, tangy ginger flavour.

Lamb marinade: In an electric blender, purée an onion with 4 tbsp each of peanut oil and soy sauce, plus salt and pepper to taste.

Beef marinade: Dilute ½ tsp pure tamarind extract (try oriental stores) in 2 tbsp water. Add the juice of half a lemon, 4 tbsp soy sauce, 1 tsp sugar, 3 cloves of garlic (crushed) and one grated or puréed onion. Again, add salt and pepper to taste.

Chicken marinade (1): 4 tbsp soy sauce, 1 tbsp honey, 2 tbsp ginger juice (see pork marinade, above), 2 tbsp dry sherry, salt, and either fresh ground black pepper or chilli powder.

Chicken marinade (2): Dissolve 85 g (⅓ cup/3 oz) of cream of coconut in 150 ml (⅔ cup/5½ fl oz) of hot water; softening the cream of coconut in a microwave will make this easier. Beat to a thick cream. Add 1 tsp pure tamarind extract, 1 tbsp ground coriander, 1 tbsp dried fennel, 2 tsp cumin, 2 tsp ground cinnamon, ¾ tsp turmeric, the seeds of 3 white or green cardamoms, nutmeg and chilli to taste. Beat well, then add 1 onion (grated or chopped in a food processor or liquidizer), 1 tbsp ginger juice, and 2 crushed garlic cloves.

Seafood marinade (1): 5 tbsp soy suace, 1 tbsp ginger juice, 3 tbsp dry sherry; pepper and salt to taste.

Seafood marinade (2): for a hotter, spicier version of the above, crush two cloves of garlic and chop two (or more) hot green chillies. Add these to the mixture.

Seafood marinade (3): Add 2 tbsp each of vinegar and honey to either of the above recipes for a sweet-and-sour taste.

Seafood marinade (4): Dissolve 60 g (¼ cup/2 oz) cream of coconut in 75 ml (⅓ cup/3 fl oz) of hot water. Liquidize with 1 small onion, 1 clove of garlic, 2 small fresh hot chillies, and the grated zest of about half a lemon. Add salt and freshly ground black pepper to taste.

Seafood marinade (5): Dissolve 1 tsp pure tamarind extract in 5 tbsp water. Add an equal quantity of peanut oil or sesame oil, plus salt and pepper to taste.

Satay

. . . .

Satay is one of the glorious of barbecued appetizers. Satay is quite time consuming to prepare, and each skewer contains very little meat, but it is so delicious that it is well worth the effort. It is impossible to give quantities – people will eat satay as long as it is available, and still look for more – but to allow less than three or four skewers per person is sheer cruelty. The secret of the taste lies in the marinades and the peanut sauce.

The meat is usually of high quality, and very carefully trimmed: possibilities include steak (especially sirloin, and even fillet), lamb (especially leg), chicken (breast for

PEANUT SAUCE

	US	Metric	Imperial
PART 1			
Medium onions	2	2	2
Garlic cloves	4–6	4–6	4–6
Fresh hot chillies	4	4	4
Prawn paste (from oriental shops)	1 tbsp	1 tbsp	1 tbsp
Ground coriander	2 tsp	2 tsp	2 tsp
Ground cumin	2 tsp	2 tsp	2 tsp
Dried fennel	1 tsp	1 tsp	1 tsp
Peanut oil for frying	4 tbsp	4 tbsp	4 tbsp
PART 2			
Creamed coconut	¾ cup	180 g	6 oz
Water	1 cup	225 ml	8 fl oz
Tamarind extract	2 tsp	2 tsp	2 tsp
Ginger juice	2 tbsp	2 tbsp	2 tbsp
Soy sauce	2 tbsp	2 tbsp	2 tbsp
Sugar	1 tbsp	1 tbsp	1 tbsp
Crunchy peanut butter	1½ cups	350 g	12 oz
Juice of 1 lime			
Grated rind of 1 lemon			
Salt and fresh-ground black pepper			

● Proportions may be varied widely to suit individual tastes: in particular, the number of chillies may be halved, doubled or even tripled; and the quantities of garlic, prawn paste, soy sauce and sugar may be increased by 50–100 per cent.

● Dissolve the cream of coconut in the water, in a saucepan or using a microwave oven. Dissolve the tamarind extract in 3–4 tbsp of water.

● In a blender, liquidizer or food processor, purée together all of the ingredients for Part 1 except the oil. Fry the paste in the oil until it is strongly aromatic. Then add all the ingredients from Part 2 with enough water to make it thin enough to stir easily. Heat, and simmer gently for up to 10 minutes, by which time the sauce should be thick and creamy (with grains) like a Dijon mustard. Reheat in the microwave, or in a pot on the barbecue to serve.

ABOVE **Satay beef.**

Seafood Kebabs

Because most kinds of seafood cook faster than meat, it is often possible to make garnished kebabs with olives, tomatoes and onions, on the skewer along with the fish or shellfish. Here are some examples:

PRAWN KEBABS

	US	Metric	Imperial
Fresh prawns	1 lb	450 g	1 lb
Melted butter	¼ cup	55 ml	2 fl oz
Lemon juice	¼ cup	55 ml	2 fl oz
6–8 rashers bacon			

- Combine the melted butter and lemon juice, to use as a basting sauce.

- Shell the prawns, and remove the veins. Remove the rind from the bacon and cut each rasher into halves or thirds – a piece big enough to wrap each prawn, which is then threaded onto a skewer.

- Cook over medium to hot coals until the prawns are cooked and the bacon is crisp, about 10–15 minutes. Turn and baste frequently; baste again just before serving, and serve any remaining butter-lemon mixture as a sauce.

LOBSTER-PRAWN-SCALLOP KEBABS

	US	Metric	Imperial
Melted butter	¼ cup	55 ml	2 fl oz
Lemon juice	2 tbsp	2 tbsp	2 tbsp
Small lobster, about 900 g/2 lb	1	1	1
Fresh prawns	½ lb	225 g	½ lb
Shelled fresh scallops	½ lb	225 g	½ lb
Cherry tomatoes	24	24	24
Large stuffed green olives	24	24	24
Fresh parsley, chopped finely	2 tbsp	2 tbsp	2 tbsp
Salt and fresh-ground pepper			

- Combine the melted butter and the lemon juice as a brushing sauce.

- Remove the meat from the tail of the lobster, and cut into chunks. Shell the prawns, and remove the veins. Alternate the ingredients on the skewers and sprinkle with salt and pepper.

FOLLOWING PAGE **Prawn kebabs and clams on the grill.**

CHAPTER FIVE

Shellfish and fish

Most people think automatically of prawns when they think of barbecuing shellfish. But in practice, you can barbecue a far wider range of shellfish than that: clams, lobsters, oysters and crab legs are all possibilities.

Clams: Sort the clams, discarding any that are open or suspiciously light: a fresh clam is heavy, and sealed up tight – 'clammed up', in fact.

Scrub the clams, and place them on the grill over a medium-high direct heat. Cook until the shells just begin to open, then turn and cook for another 5–15 minutes or until they pop fully open. The size of the clams, the thickness of their shells, how long they have been out of water, and how well done (or otherwise) you like your clams will all affect cooking times, but overcooking will make them tough. Once they're open, they're ready to eat, but be careful not to burn yourself on the hot shell.

Crab: King crab is the only crab that is easy to barbecue, but with other crabs the big middle section of the leg barbecues very well. You can use frozen crab legs if you defrost them first.

Split the leg with a big, heavy knife and flex it slightly to open the slit. This is a three-handed job, as you need two hands to flex the leg and the other to pour in a 50/50 mixture of lemon juice and melted butter. Barbecue for a total of about 10 minutes over medium coals, basting occasionally with the lemon-butter mixture. Serve with more of the basting sauce, or with lemon juice and melted butter separately.

Crayfish/Rock lobster: Only the tails are usually cooked, and as with crab, frozen will do.

Cut off the thin shell on the lobster's or crayfish's underside with kitchen shears. Bend the thick upper shell backwards to expose the meat and to help flatten out the tails. Brush with lemon-butter mixture (see *Crab*, above).

Barbecue over a medium heat, shell-side down, for about 10 minutes, basting frequently. Turn over, flesh-side down, to complete the cooking for about another 5 minutes. The

meat is cooked when it is opaque (rather than translucent) and flakes easily with a fork, although some people prefer their crayfish less cooked than this.

Lobsters: There are two (or possibly even three) schools of thought on barbecuing lobsters. One advocates parboiling; a second splits the fish, but cooks it from raw in much the same way as crayfish; and the third school reckons that you can't improve on boiling anyway. Parboiling is the method recommended here.

To parboil, plunge the live lobster head-first into a large saucepan or kettle of rapidly boiling water. Hold it under with a wooden spoon: it should be dead within 15 seconds. Remove as soon as the water comes to the boil again. Preparation thereafter is as for raw lobster.

To kill a live lobster other than by boiling, the most humane method is apparently to put it inside a strong plastic bag in a freezer (at −10°C/15°F or below): it will gradually lose consciousness and die. This is less cruel than it sounds: after all, a lobster is cold-blooded and lives in cold water, so death by cold is allegedly not painful. You can also parboil the lobster after this treatment.

Split the lobster in half lengthways – a job for a large, stout knife, or for a *very* stout cook's knife, possibly in association with a mallet – and remove the stomach and gut. The green liver and the pink coral (roe) of the female are both regarded as delicacies.

Brush with a mixture of melted butter and lemon juice, or olive oil and lemon juice, with two or three or even four parts butter or oil to one part lemon juice. Add salt and

pepper to taste. Grill over a medium-low heat, shell-side down, for 10–20 minutes, then turn over and finish for 3–5 minutes. Remove the claws and drop them in the embers for a further two or three minutes.

Serve with melted butter and wedges of lemon.

Oysters: Cook as for clams.

Prawns: As long as a prawn is big enough not to fall through the grill, it can be barbecued. Shell before cooking smaller prawn tails can be cooked whole, while larger prawns can be 'butterflied' (split almost in two lengthwise, and opened out) before cooking. Cooking time varies according to the size of the prawn and the taste of the diner, but 5 minutes over a low heat is a good average. Brush with a 50/50 mixture of melted butter and lemon juice.

Grilled Fish

The simplest way to cook whole fish on the barbecue is to choose very fresh, small-to-medium size fish. Clean them and grill over a relatively low heat, having greased or oiled the grill thoroughly before you start, to avoid sticking. Turn the fish with tongs occasionally. The outside will be crispy and a little burned in places, but the interior will be delightfully moist and smoky.

With any small fish, cooking recommendations are next to impossible: too much depends on the size and thickness of the fish and on personal preference. However, 2–5 minutes a side over medium or low coals is a good starting

LEFT **Grilled lobster.**

RIGHT **Prawns with salad.**

point. As with meat, allow the fish to reach room temperature before you cook it as refrigerated fish is harder to cook evenly, and frozen fish is virtually impossible to cook satisfactorily.

In Portugal, *sardinhas assadas* (fresh grilled sardines) are a favourite dish, served as a plate of 12 or twenty, with no more garnish or ornament than a few lemon wedges.

Medium-size fish such as trout, red snapper (pargo) or bass are much easier to handle with a couple of aluminium-foil loops, especially when they are almost fully cooked. To make the loops, tear off a 30-cm (12-in) length of heavy foil about 15 cm (6 in) wide and fold it four times so that you end up with a strip 30 cm (12 in) wide and about 2 cm (¾ in) wide. Oil the side that will be against the fish, and loop around to make 'handles'.

Cook the fish under a covered grill over medium heat, turning occasionally and basting frequently with melted

butter. A 1.5 kg (3 lb) fish should take 30–40 minutes. It is ready when the flesh flakes easily with a fork, the juices run clear when pricked with a fork, or the pectoral (side) fin detaches easily.

To cook large fish, over 1.8–2.25 kg (4–5 lb), wrap it with three foil loops. Cook as for medium-sized fish, but allow as much as 1 hour for cooking. You may find that two spatulas are the easiest way to lift the cooked fish.

You can also cook whole fish such as mackerel or snapper in a grill basket.

Fish steaks

While whole fish may appeal to the traditionalist and to the true fish lover, fish fillets and fish steaks are easier to cook, contain few or no bones, and are generally more convenient.

The best fillets and steaks to barbecue are from firm-fleshed fish: tuna, flake and swordfish are particularly delicious, especially if they are not overcooked. Bass and salmon are good, and cod tastes better this way although it tends to fall apart. Fillets and steaks should be at least 2.5 cm (1 in) and preferably 4 cm (1½ in) thick or they will dry out, as well as being more likely to fall apart.

Marinate the fish for half an hour or so in lemon juice and olive oil (one part lemon juice to two parts oil), with chopped parsley or tarragon, and pepper and salt to taste. Coat with flour if you want a crispy crust, although this is optional. Cook over a low heat for 1–4 minutes per side, depending on your tastes, the thickness of the steak, and the kind of fish used.

Fish in foil

While cooking fish in foil may offend purists, there is no doubt that it offers many advantages – not least, that the fish won't fall apart on the barbecue or stick to it.

ABOVE **Whole small fish served with rice and salad.**

RIGHT **Grilled shark with salad.**

ABOVE **Poached bass fillets with salad.**

FISH FILLETS

(Serves 4)

	US	Metric	Imperial
Fish fillets, about 180 g (6 oz) each	4	4	4
Melted butter	2 tbsp	2 tbsp	2 tbsp
Lemon juice or dry white wine (or a mixture of both)	2 tbsp	2 tbsp	2 tbsp
Fresh parsley, chopped	1 tbsp	1 tbsp	1 tbsp
Salt and fresh-ground black pepper			

• Measure the thickness of the fillets at their thickest point. This determines the cooking time: allow 12–15 minutes per in, 5–6 minutes per cm.

• To make a parcel, put a sheet of foil about 50 cm (18 in) square on a plate and make a depression in the centre so the liquid does not run out. Lay the fillets side by side making more than one parcel if you have too many fillets to fit in without overlapping. (If they overlap, it will spoil your estimate of cooking time.)

• Add the butter and lemon juice/wine and season with salt, pepper and parsley. Fold the foil over the top to create a baggy enclosure. Cook over medium-hot coals.

GRILLED SALMON IN FOIL
(Serves 6)

	US	Metric	Imperial
Whole salmon, cleaned weight	2½–3 lb	1.25–1.5 kg	2½–3 lb
Juice of 1 lemon	–	–	–
Olive oil	1 tbsp	1 tbsp	1 tbsp
Salt and fresh-ground black pepper			
Fresh dill, chopped	¼ cup	30–40 g	1–1½ oz
Butter	¼ cup	60 g	2 oz
Dijon mustard	1 tsp	1 tsp	1 tsp
Oil or butter to grease foil			
Lemon wedges			

• The foil is used as a cradle, rather than as a wrap. It should be long enough to cradle the whole fish, with a bit at either end for ease in handling. Grease the foil thickly with butter (or brush it all over with olive oil) to prevent sticking, and poke holes in it with a knitting needle or something similar so that the smoke can reach the fish.

• Season the fish inside and out with lemon juice, olive oil, salt and pepper.

• Put three or four sprigs of dill in the cavity and place the fish on the foil. Leave to stand for 20 minutes for the flavours to mingle.

• Cook over a hot fire. After five minutes, *carefully* turn the fish in the foil cradle, and repeat at 5-minute intervals. The fish should be cooked in 20–30 minutes in total, depending on how you like your salmon.

• Beat together the chopped dill, the butter (soften it in the microwave) and the mustard (add more to taste); this, and the lemon wedges, accompany the fish. Rather than trying to lift it out of the foil when it is cooked, just roll it onto the serving platter.

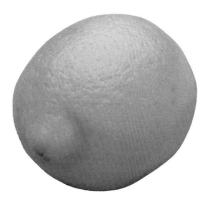

RIGHT **Whole salmon ready for cooking.**

SEA BASS WITH SHALLOTS
(Serves 4–6)

	US	Metric	Imperial
Bunch of shallots, trimmed			
Sunflower oil	3 tbsp	3 tbsp	3 tbsp
Lemons, sliced	2	2	2
Coriander, chopped	2 tbsp	2 tbsp	2 tbsp
Light soy sauce	4 tbsp	4 tbsp	4 tbsp
Bass, cleaned and scaled	3 lb	1.5 kg	3 lb

● Cut the shallots into 5 cm (2 in) lengths. Take a large sheet of double-thick foil and brush it with a little of the oil. Lay a third of the lemon slices on the foil. Sprinkle a third of the shallots over the lemon, then sprinkle a little of the coriander on top. Brush half of the soy sauce in the body cavity of the fish. Put half the remaining onoins and lemon in the cavity, then lay the fish on top of the onions and lemon on the foil.

● Top the fish with the remaining onions, lemon, coriander and soy sauce. Wrap the foil around the fish to enclose it completely. Placed the fish over medium heat and cover the barbecue. Cook for 15 minutes, then turn the fish over and cook for a further 15 minutes.

● Serve the fish in the foil, opening it along the top. Carefully lift away the skin, then remove portions of fish from the bones to serve. The fish will be well-flavoured with the aromatics which were enclosed in the foil package.

TUNA IN FRESH TOMATO MARINADE
(Serves 4)

	US	Metric	Imperial
Fresh tuna steak	2 lb	900 g	2 lb
Onion, finely chopped	1	1	1
Garlic clove, crushed	1	1	1
Olive oil	4 tbsp	4 tbsp	4 tbsp
Ripe tomatoes, chopped	1 lb	450 g	1 lb
Salt and fresh-ground black pepper			
Dried oregano	1 tsp	1 tsp	1 tsp

● Place the tuna in a dish. Cook the onion and garlic in the oil over a gentle heat for 10 minutes. Stir in the tomatoes and cook for a further 5 minutes. Press the mixture through a sieve. Add the oregano, plenty of seasoning and then leave to cool. Pour the cold marinade over the tuna, cover and chill for at least 2 hours.

● Lift the fish from the marinade and cook it over medium heat for 7–10 minutes on each side, depending on the thickness of the steak. Brush occasionally with marinade. Heat any remaining marinade to boiling point, then pour it over the grilled tuna before serving.

RIGHT **Fish and bacon kebabs on the grill.**

RIGHT **Tuna in fresh tomato marinade.**

FISH AND BACON KEBABS
(Serves 4)

	US	Metric	Imperial
Firm white fish	2 lb	900 g	2 lb
Lemon rind	1 tbsp	1 tbsp	1 tbsp
Chopped parsley	2 tbsp	2 tbsp	2 tbsp
Chopped thyme	1 tsp	1 tsp	1 tsp
Fresh-ground black pepper			
Bacon rashers	12	12	12

● Skin the fish if necessary – white fish such as bass, thick cod, halibut, swordfish, flake or monkfish are suitable. Cut the fish into 24 chunks and place them in a bowl. Add the lemon rind, parsley, thyme and pepper and mix well.

● Remove the rinds from the bacon, then cut each rasher in half. Wrap a piece of bacon around a chunk of fish. Thread the bacon-wrapped fish on four metal skewers. Cook over medium coals for about 15–20 minutes, turning twice, until the bacon is well browned and fish cooked through.

TUNA WITH THYME AND GARLIC
(Serves 4)

	US	Metric	Imperial
Fresh tuna steak	2 lb	900 g	2 lb
Fresh thyme leaves	2 tbsp	2 tbsp	2 tbsp
Garlic cloves	2	2	2
Olive oil	6 tbsp	6 tbsp	6 tbsp
Red wine	4 tbsp	4 tbsp	4 tbsp
Fresh-ground black pepper			
Lemon wedges	4	4	4

• Lay the tuna in a dish. Pound the thyme with the garlic, gradually adding the oil as the garlic is crushed. A heavy pestle and mortar is best for this. Alternatively, purée the mixture in a blender. Stir in the wine and add seasoning, then pour the marinade over the fish. Cover and chill for at least 2 hours. For a full flavour leave the fish overnight.

• Cook the tuna over medium heat for 7–10 minutes on each side, depending on the thickness of the steak. Brush with the marinade during cooking. Serve with lemon wedges for their juice.

SNAPPER IN VINE LEAVES
(Serves 4)

	US	Metric	Imperial
Large vine leaves	16	16	16
Butter	¼ cup	60 g	2 oz
Chopped parsley	1 tbsp	1 tbsp	1 tbsp
Salt and fresh-ground black pepper			
Snapper or red mullet, gutted and scaled	4	4	4

● Blanch the vine leaves in boiling water for 2–3 minutes, then drain them and pat them dry on absorbent kitchen paper.

● Cream the butter with the parsley, lemon juice and seasoning. Divide the butter between the fish, putting a knob in each body cavity. Overlap two vine leaves on a clean surface, lay one snapper on top, then wrap the leaves around the fish, leaving just the head and end of the tail showing. Repeat with another two leaves to enclose the body of the fish tightly in a neat parcel. Wrap the remaining fish in the other vine leaves.

● Cook the wrapped snapper over medium heat with the lid on the barbecue, allowing 8–10 minutes on each side, depending on the size of the snapper.

RIGHT **Swordfish on the grill.**

SWORDFISH WITH OLIVE AND PISTACHIO BUTTER
(Serves 4)

	US	Metric	Imperial
Black olives, pitted	12	12	12
Pistachio nuts	4 tbsp	4 tbsp	4 tbsp
Butter	½ cup	110 g	4 oz
Snipped chives	2 tbsp	2 tbsp	2 tbsp
Swordfish steaks	4	4	4

● Chop the olives and the nuts. Cream three-quarters of the butter with the chives, then lightly mix in the olives and nuts. Chill the butter, then shape it into a roll and wrap this in foil or plastic wrap and chill again. Remove the butter from the refrigerator and cut it into slices before cooking the fish so that it is at room temperature. However, do not allow the butter to become too soft or the slices will be difficult to manage.

● Melt the remaining butter and brush it over the fish steaks. Cook them over high heat for about 5–7 minutes on each side, until well browned and cooked through. Top each freshly cooked fish steak with a pat of olive and pistachio butter and serve at once.

FISH WITH WALNUTS
(Serves 4)

	US	Metric	Imperial
Trout or mackerel, gutted	4	4	4
Butter	¼ cup	60 g	2 oz
Salt and fresh-ground black pepper			
Walnuts, roughly chopped	1 cup	110 g	4 oz
Orange	1	1	1
Snipped chives	4 tbsp	4 tbsp	4 tbsp

● Trim all fins off the trout or mackerel, then rinse and dry the fish. Cut four oblongs of double-thick cooking foil, each large enough to enclose a fish. Grease the middle of a piece of foil with a little butter and place a fish on it. Fold the sides and ends of the foil up to form a neat package, leaving the top open but crumpling the ends to hold all juices. Repeat with the remaining foil and fish.

● Season the fish, then sprinkle the walnuts over them. Pare the rind from the orange. Squeeze the juice. Sprinkle the chives and orange juice over the fish. Cook the fish over low heat by the indirect method and place the orange rind on the coals just before putting the fish packages on the rack. Put the lid on the barbecue so that the smoke from the orange rind flavours the fish. Allow about 30 minutes cooking time, less for small fish and slightly longer for large fish.

● Serve the fish in their foil packages. New potatoes and Zucchini and Celery Salad (page 115) are excellent accompaniments.

Shellfish
● Prawns and mussels can both be cooked in foil packets. Scrub small mussels and remove the beards, and remove the heads and legs from prawns. Cook either type of shellfish in batches of half a dozen, forming a single layer in a foil pouch. Before sealing each pouch, add a knob (say 2 tbsp) of garlic butter, made as described on page 26.

● Prawns should be cooked over medium heat, and will be ready in 10–12 minutes. Cook mussels over medium-high heat, shaking the bundle every minute or two: they are cooked when they open of their own accord.

RIGHT **Fish with walnuts in foil.**

CHAPTER SIX

Ribs and fajitas

Pork ribs, popular in Chinese cooking, are one of the classic barbecue foods, and come in three types:

Spare ribs are cut from just behind the pork shoulder. A full set of ribs is a long, triangular cut made up of bone, cartilage, and a thin layer of meat which can be cooked to a crisp. Although some people regard them as awkward to cook and messy to eat, others rank them second to none in barbecue delicacies.

Back ribs are shorter and neater to eat, but have (if anything) even less meat.

Country-style ribs are cut from the loin, and have very much more meat than the other two cuts.

Many people pre-cook ribs before barbecuing them, which cuts down the time on the grill considerably. If you start with raw ribs, you can reckon on a minimum of 1 hour, with 1½ hours a realistic maximum. If they are pre-cooked, you can reckon on ½–1 hour on the grill over a medium-low heat for ribs of all kinds. A drip pan will reduce the chance of flare-ups.

To cook ribs, you can bake them in a foil packet on a hot grill for ¾–1 hour; steam them in a saucepan on the stove; or simply boil them. Plain boiling is surprisingly good for country-style ribs, which can be boiled until they are falling-apart tender, then crisped magnificently on a grill.

Baby back ribs can be cooked directly on the grill, or country-style ribs may be cooked on a rack in a closed barbecue.

Do not baste with thick barbecue sauces until 15 minutes or so before the meat is finally cooked, or the sauce will simply burn. Either cook the ribs without any basting, or use a thin marinade sauce and use that to baste (recipes for sauces are given on pages 21–26).

Determining the quantities for ribs (in terms of weight of meat per person) is all but impossible: it depends very much upon the quality of the ribs, the quality of the cooking, and the hunger (or gluttony) of the diners. As a

very rough guess, allow 225–450 g (½–1 lb) of ribs per person – you will need fewer of the meatier country-style ribs, but many a gourmand can demolish more than 900 gm (2lb) of spare ribs without really trying.

The traditional accompaniments for ribs are beer, beans (page 107), garlic bread (page 109) and salad.

Beef ribs

Beef ribs for barbecue are not always easy to find. You may have either to cultivate a butcher, or to buy a standard rib roast and remove the rib eye (for rib eye steaks!) yourself. You will need two sharp knives for this, one large butcher's knife and one small boning knife. You will also need practice and care.

Although you can use almost any barbecue sauce on ribs, some people prefer to eat them on their own, and others prefer to serve them with grainy Dijon mustard.

Allow 2 to 3 rib bones per person, up to about 450 g (1 lb) in uncooked weight. Pre-cooking of beef ribs is less important than with pork as many people prefer their beef rare.

Rare, crusty ribs

Over a medium-hot fire, brown the ribs first on one side, then on the other – at least 5 minutes on each side. When they are browned, brush with barbecue sauce or Dijon mustard, or simply continue to cook for another 5–10 minutes a side. This gives you rich, crusty ribs with rare meat sticking to them. They will not, however, be particularly tender: you can rely on getting a lot of meat stuck in your front teeth as you gnaw the bones.

Well-done ribs

Wrap the ribs in heavy-duty foil, and bake over a high direct heat for an hour. This will render out some of the fat, but (more importantly) it will ensure moist, tender, well-cooked meat on the inside.

Pour off the fat, and continue to cook over a medium-low indirect heat for at least 15 minutes on each side (or 30 minutes on a rack) with the lid on the barbecue. If you turn only once, you can coat the ribs liberally with barbecue sauce when you start this stage, without much risk of burning. Heat some extra sauce in a pan at the side of the grill, to serve with the meat.

This is the best way to cook beef ribs if you are a barbecue sauce addict. Serve with beer, beans (page 107), garlic bread (page 109), and salsa (page 109).

RIGHT **Beef ribs and salad.**

LEFT **Baby back pork ribs with rice.**

CRISPY LAMB RIBS
(Serves 4)

	US	Metric	Imperial
Breasts of lamb	2	2	2
Grated rind and juice of 1 lemon			
Garlic cloves, crushed	2	2	2
Dried marjoram	2 tsp	2 tsp	2 tsp
Tomato purée (paste)	2 tsp	2 tsp	2 tsp
Brown sugar	1 tsp	1 tsp	1 tsp
Cayenne pepper	⅛ tsp	⅛ tsp	⅛ tsp
Salt	¼ tsp	¼ tsp	¼ tsp

● Trim large areas of fat off the lamb, then chop the breast into ribs (or pairs of ribs). Alternatively, ask the butcher to chop up the meat for you. Place the ribs in a bowl.

● Mix all the remaining ingredients and stir in 2 tbsp water. Pour the mixture over the lamb. Mix the ribs thoroughly to ensure that they are all coated with seasoning. Cover and chill for 2–4 hours.

● Cook the lamb over medium, indirect heat with the lid on the barbecue. Take care to keep the lamb over the drip tray rather than over the coals, otherwise the fat causes the barbecue to flare into flames. Cook the ribs for about 40 minutes, turning occasionally, until they are well browned all over. Serve the ribs as an appetizer or with salad and crusty bread.

FIVE-SPICE PORK RIBS
(Serves 4)

	US	Metric	Imperial
Meaty pork spare ribs	2 lb	900 g	2 lb
Garlic clove, crushed	1	1	1
Five spice powder	1 tsp	1 tsp	1 tsp
Soy sauce	6 tbsp	6 tbsp	6 tbsp
Brown sugar	2 tbsp	2 tbsp	2 tbsp
Dry sherry	4 tbsp	4 tbsp	4 tbsp
Sesame oil	1 tbsp	1 tbsp	1 tbsp
Bunch of shallots, trimmed			

● Be sure to buy ribs that have a good covering of meat – reject some supermarket offerings that are scraped clean of all but a fine covering of fat and gristle. Ask the butcher to chop the pork into individual ribs. Trim off any large pieces of fat, then put the ribs in a saucepan. Pour in cold water to cover and bring slowly just to the boil. Skim any scum off the water, cover and simmer the ribs very gently for 30 minutes. Drain the ribs thoroughly, then put them in a bowl. The meat on the ribs will have shrunk during cooking but it should be tender – this method results in succulent ribs that are well worth the effort. Ribs that are grilled from raw tend to be disappointing and chewy.

- Mix all the remaining ingredients, then pour the mixture over the pork. Brush all the ribs to make sure they are evenly coated, cover and leave to cool.

- Cook the ribs over indirect, medium heat with the lid on the barbecue. Turn the ribs two or three times, until they are well browned all over – about 25 minutes. Brush with any remaining seasoning mixture during cooking.

- Cut the shallots into fine, diagonal slices and sprinkle them over the cooked ribs just before serving.

Note   Five spice powder is a Chinese seasoning. It has a strong flavour which is dominated by star anise but it also contains cinnamon, cloves, fennel and pepper.

BELOW **Five-spice pork ribs on the grill.**

CINNAMON SPARE RIBS
(Serves 4)

	US	Metric	Imperial
Meaty pork spare ribs	2 lb	900 g	2 lb
Salt and fresh-ground black pepper			
Small onion, grated	1	1	1
Vegetable oil	2 tbsp	2 tbsp	2 tbsp
Dried sage	1 tbsp	1 tbsp	1 tbsp
Ground cinnamon	1 tbsp	1 tbsp	1 tbsp
Honey	2 tsp	2 tsp	2 tsp
Grated rind and juice of 1 orange			

● Ask the butcher to chop the pork into individual ribs. Trim off any fat, then place the ribs in a saucepan and cover with cold water. Add a little salt and bring slowly to the boil. Skim off any scum, cover the pan and simmer the ribs very gently for 30 minutes.

● Meanwhile, cook the onion in the oil for 5 minutes. Remove from the heat and stir in the remaining ingredients, adding plenty of seasoning. Thoroughly drain the ribs, then put them in a bowl and pour the onion mixture over them. Make sure all the ribs are thoroughly coated in seasoning, brushing it over if necessary.

● Cook the ribs over indirect heat, with the lid on the barbecue, for about 25 minutes. Turn the ribs two or three times so that they brown easily and brush with any remaining seasoning mixture during cooking. A salad of sweet, ripe tomatoes and thinly sliced red-skinned onions goes very well with the slightly spicy ribs.

Fajitas

A *fajita* is a cut of beef (not a method of cooking, as sometimes thought), but opinions as to where 'fajitas' are cut from varies. Generally, though, it is accepted that they are cut from the area of the diaphragm, and are tough and fibrous with a layer of gristly membrane and a lot of surface fat. They therefore require careful stripping and tenderizing before cooking, which either the butcher will do for you, or which you can do at home.

Originally a field-hands' dish from the border of Texas and Mexico (hence the cheapness of the cut, which is also known as skirt steak), the sudden popularity of the dish in the 1980s means that it is now often cheaper to marinade and cook 'fajita-style' dishes using other cuts of meat.

To prepare real *fajitas*, lay the meat on a cutting board and carefully remove the fat with a very sharp knife. Next, remove the tough outer membrane by holding the steak while you slice away the membrane. Finally, puncture the meat repeatedly with a sharp, pointed knife, working both with the grain and against it. Using a fork to puncture the meat will help the marinades to enter. Do not use a meat mallet or bottled tenderizer, or the meat will be reduced to pulp.

If you are preparing other cuts 'fajita-style', you are saved much of this effort. Flank steak probably comes closest in flavour, but it must be sliced as soon as you take it off the grill or it will rapidly become tough and leathery.

Marinate the meat for at least 4 hours, and preferably overnight, using one of the recipes on page 17–20, the *fajita* marinades below or your own marinade. The usual rules apply: pawpaw and pineapple juice tenderize the most and fastest, citrus juices are next, and then come wines and beers or other liquids. Other ingredients are just for flavouring.

MARGARITA MARINADE

	US	Metric	Imperial
Tequila	½ cup	110 ml	4 fl oz
Lime juice	¾ cup	170 ml	6 fl oz
Triple Sec	¼ cup	55 ml	2 fl oz

LIME MARINADE

	US	Metric	Imperial
Beef stock (broth)	1 cup	225 ml	8 fl oz
Worcestershire sauce	3 tbsp	3 tbsp	3 tbsp
Garlic cloves, finely chopped	1–2	1–2	1–2
Chopped fresh coriander	1 tbsp	1 tbsp	1 tbsp
Juice of 1 lime			

● To serve *fajitas* as a steak (which used to be quite common), barbecue the meat over a medium heat for 6–8 minutes on each side. Brush with marinade while cooking, and just before serving.

To serve with *tortillas*, cook as above and then slice diagonally into thin strips about 10 cm (4 inches) long. Heat large flour *tortillas* (page 111) on the grill, and have the following garnishes available for those who want to make up their own *burritos*. If *tortillas* are a problem, use chapattis or pita bread instead.

Garnishes for *fajita burritos*
    Sour cream
    Salsa (page 109)
    Guacamole or sliced avocado
    Capsicum, raw, lightly fried or grilled
    Raw onion, sliced thinly
    Sliced tomato
    Shredded lettuce
    Refried beans

LEFT **Cinnamon spare ribs.**

FOLLOWING PAGE **Fajitas and salad.**

CHAPTER SEVEN

Cooking larger cuts of meat and game

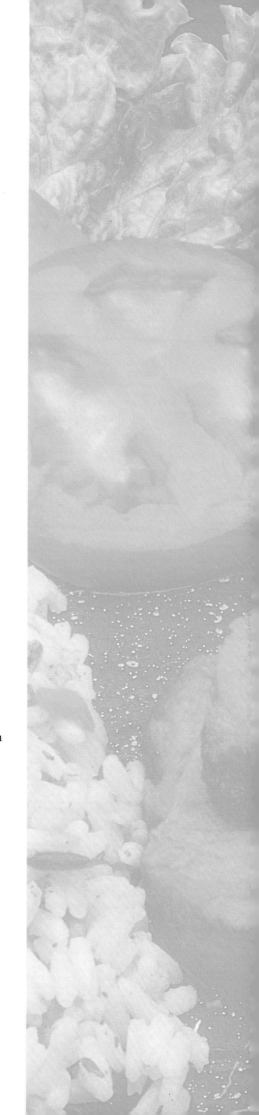

Chops, kebabs and meatballs have already been covered, but the great plus of owning a kettle barbecue is that larger cuts of meat can be cooked to perfection with less effort than using an open grill or rotisserie. As well as beef and pork, loin, shoulder and leg of lamb, chicken, turkey and ham are all equally suitable. Unless otherwise stated, all recipes in this section are prepared with the lid on the barbecue for the majority, if not all, of the cooking time.

Shoulder of lamb

Shoulder, as the fattiest cut, should be cooked for longest in order to render out the fat: it is not suitable to serve rare. Cook in the covered barbecue over a medium indirect heat.

To check when it is cooked, either use a meat thermometer (well-done at 75°C/170°F or medium at 70°C/160°F) or rely on time-and-temperature plus experience: allow 55 minutes per kg (25 minutes per lb) for well-done meat, and 50 minutes per kg (22 minutes per lb) for medium.

If you want to use a barbecue sauce, although the meat will taste perfectly good without it, this is the cut to use. The delicate, distinctive taste of lamb is all but wiped out by barbecue sauce, so you should use the cheapest cut.

Boneless loin of lamb

This is basically a row of chops with the bones removed, and is very good served rare (60°C/140°F on the meat thermometer). It should take no more than 44 minutes per kg (20 minutes per lb) at the most, cooked in the same way as a shoulder.

If you would like to experiment with taste, use a white wine marinade (page 18) and baste with that; most of the other barbecue marinades are too sweet for lamb. Garnish with mint, and serve with mint jelly, mint sauce or mustard dill sauce (see below).

Leg of lamb

A leg of lamb may be cooked on the bone. However, for even cooking and easy carving ask the butcher to bone out the meat. Once boned, herbs or garlic may be inserted in the cavity and the meat skewered to keep it in good shape. Alternatively the boned leg may be slit through to the middle and opened out flat. This gives a thinner joint which cooks quicker.

Heat the basting sauce before using it: equal quantities of oil and wine vinegar (or a one-to-two parts oil-to-vinegar mix), 2 crushed garlic cloves, and either a small handful of chopped fresh mint or 1 tsp dried mint flakes.

Cook over medium-hot coals, turning and basting fairly often. If you like your lamb rare, a 2½ kg (5–6 lb) leg of lamb should be fully cooked in 30–40 minutes; 1 hour for well-done lamb. Because of the taper of the leg, there will inevitably be less well-done lamb at one end and well-done lamb at the other, enabling you to serve all tastes.

Serve with rice, preferably in the form of a pilaf flavoured with saffron and garnished with fresh mint leaves; or alternatively, carve and serve in pita bread pockets, with or without accompanying salad.

LEFT Leg of lamb served with rice and salad.

REDCURRANT RACK OF LAMB
(Serves 4)

	US	Metric	Imperial
Rack of lamb	1	1	1
Rosemary, chopped	1 tbsp	1 tbsp	1 tbsp
Vegetable oil	1 tbsp	1 tbsp	1 tbsp
Salt and fresh-ground black pepper			
Redcurrant jelly	4 tbsp	4 tbsp	4 tbsp
Red wine	2 tbsp	2 tbsp	2 tbsp

● Ask the butcher to chine the lamb (sawing the bone which runs along the base of the ribs) and trim the bone ends. Remove any thick pieces of fat, then rub the rosemary all over the outside of the joint – rubbing the chopped herb well into the joint gives the meat a good flavour. Brush with the oil, keeping the chopped rosemary on the meat.

● Cook the lamb over medium, indirect heat with the lid on the barbecue. Start cooking with the fat uppermost, then turn the joint halfway through the cooking time. The lamb will be rare in the middle after 30 minutes, pink after 40 minutes and cooked through after about 50 minutes.

● While the lamb is cooking heat the redcurrant jelly and wine in a small saucepan until the jelly melts. Bring to the boil and boil for about a minute to reduce the glaze slightly. Brush this glaze generously all over the rack of lamb before cutting it into individual cutlets to serve.

RIGHT **Saffron-soaked lamb on the grill.**

SAFFRON-SOAKED LAMB
(Serves 6)

	US	Metric	Imperial
Leg of lamb, boned	3 lb	1.5 kg	3 lb
Saffron strands	½ tsp	½ tsp	½ tsp
Garlic clove, crushed	1	1	1
Salt and fresh-ground black pepper			
Grated rind and juice of 1 lemon			
Sunflower oil	2 tbsp	2 tbsp	2 tbsp

● Trim the lamb of any large pieces of fat, then place it boned side down in a large dish. Pound the saffron strands in a pestle and mortar until they are reduced to a powder. Add 2 tbsp boiling water and stir well. Mix the remaining ingredients into the saffron, then brush some of the mixture all over the meat. Turn the lamb over and brush the remaining saffron mixture over the boned side of the meat. Be sure to use every last drop on the meat. Cover and leave to marinate for a few hours or overnight.

● Cook the lamb over medium indirect heat, with the lid on the barbecue, for 1¼–1½ hours, or until the meat is cooked to your liking. During cooking turn the lamb two or three times and brush it with any juices left from marinating. Serve carved into thick slices.

● **Note** The lamb may be cooked on the bone, in which case increase the cooking time by 15–20 minutes. The thin end of the meat may need protecting if it becomes too brown before the main part of the lamb is cooked.

ALMOND-STUDDED LAMB
(Serves 6)

	US	Metric	Imperial
Leg of lamb, boned	3 lb	1.5 kg	3 lb
Blanched almonds	¾ cup	110 g	4 oz
Ground mace	1 tsp	1 tsp	1 tsp
Salt and fresh-ground black pepper			
Dry white vermouth	4 tbsp	4 tbsp	4 tbsp
Sunflower oil	2 tbsp	2 tbsp	2 tbsp

● Trim any large pieces of fat off the meat. Mix the almonds with the mace and seasoning, tossing them well so that they are all evenly coated. Use the point of a knife to make small cuts into the lamb, then insert an almond into each cut. Push the nuts right into the meat – if they stick out they will burn during cooking.

● Whisk the vermouth and oil together, then brush the mixture generously all over the joint. Cook the lamb over indirect medium heat, on the covered barbecue, for 1¼–1½ hours when the joint will be slightly pink in the middle. Turn the meat two or three times and brush it often with the vermouth mixture during cooking. Serve cut into thick slices.

BELOW Almond-studded lamb on the grill.

Summer chicken.

SUMMER CHICKEN
(Serves 4)

	US	Metric	Imperial
Chicken	3 lb	1.5 kg	3 lb
Butter	¼ cup	60 g	2 oz
Chopped parsley	2 tbsp	2 tbsp	2 tbsp
Chopped fresh thyme	2 tsp	2 tsp	2 tsp
Handfull of basil leaves, shredded			
Limes	2	2	2
Salt and fresh-ground black pepper			

● Trim the wing and leg ends off the chicken if necessary. Rinse it thoroughly inside and out, then mop it dry with absorbent kitchen paper.

● Soften the butter, then mix in the herbs. Grate the rind from the limes and cream it into the butter with plenty of seasoning. Squeeze the juice from one lime and gradually blend it into the butter.

● At the neck end of the bird, slide the point of a knife between the skin and the flesh, taking care not to break the skin. When you have established an opening, slide your hand between the skin and flesh up over the breast meat. Rub knobs of the herb butter under the skin, spreading it evenly over the breast meat. Put the remaining butter in the body cavity. Close the skin neatly in place using a metal skewer

● Cook the chicken over medium, indirect heat with the lid on the barbecue. Place the bird breast uppermost on the cooking rack. Cook for 30 minutes, then turn the chicken on one side and cook for a further 25–30 minutes. Turn the chicken on the other side and cook for a final 25–30 minutes. Check that the bird is thoroughly cooked by piercing the thick meat behind the thigh bone. If there is any sign of blood in the juices, continue to cook a little longer.

● During cooking, cover the wing and leg ends with small pieces of foil, if necessary, to prevent them from overbrowning.

SPRING CHICKEN WITH GRAPES
(Serves 4)

	US	Metric	Imperial
Spring chickens (poussin), about 350 g (12 oz) each	4	4	4
Dry white wine	½ cup	110 ml	4 fl oz
Sunflower oil	2 tbsp	2 tbsp	2 tbsp
Fresh marjoram sprigs	2	2	2
Salt and fresh-ground black pepper			
Seedless green grapes	¼ lb	110 g	¼ lb
Shallots, trimmed and chopped	1	1	1
Greek yogurt	½ cup	110 ml	4 fl oz

● Rinse the chickens in cold water, then dry them on absorbent kitchen paper. Place them in a dish. Heat the oil, wine, marjoram and seasoning slowly until just boiling. Remove from the heat at once and cool. Pour this marinade over the chickens, cover and chill for 2–4 hours.

● Drain the chickens, reserving the marinade, and cook them over medium, indirect heat for about 30 minutes, turning twice. Wash and dry the grapes, then place them in a pan with the marinade. Heat gently to simmering point. Stir in the yogurt and continue to heat gently but do not allow the sauce to boil or it will curdle. Remove the marjoram from the sauce, taste and adjust the seasoning, then serve it with the grilled chicken.

● The slightly tangy, fruity sauce is delicious with the very simple chicken. If you like, put some smoking fuel on the coals to flavour the chicken – soaked wood chips or some sprigs of dried rosemary twigs may be used.

SPATCHCOCK WITH PAWPAW
(Serves 4)

	US	Metric	Imperial
Chicken	2½–3 lb	1.25–1.5 kg	2½–3 lb
Bacon rashers, rinds removed and diced	4	4	4
Shallots, chopped	2	2	2
Pawpaw	1	1	1
Raisins	2 tbsp	2 tbsp	2 tbsp
Good curry powder	¼ tsp	¼ tsp	¼ tsp
Vegetable oil	1 tbsp	1 tbsp	1 tbsp
Small nob of butter			
Salt and fresh-ground black pepper			
Small bunch of watercress or flat-leaf parsley, trimmed			
Juice of ½ lemon			
Olive oil	1 tbsp	1 tbsp	1 tbsp

● Place the chicken breast down on a heavy board or stable surface. Split the bird down the back – either use a heavy chef's knife or strong poultry scissors. Cut out the back bone and trim off any flaps of skin. Remove any lumps of fat. Rinse and thoroughly dry the chicken on absorbent kitchen paper. Open the chicken out with the breast uppermost, then flatten it by pressing it firmly with the palm of your hand.

● Mix the bacon with the shallots. Halve the pawpaw and scoop out all the black seeds. Peel and dice one half, then add this to the bacon with the raisins and curry powder; mix well. Peel and thinly slice the remaining pawpaw, cover and set aside.

● Slide the point of a knife between the skin and flesh at the wing end of the spatchcock chicken, then slide your hand in to lift the skin away from the flesh. Take care not to split the skin. Spoon the bacon and pawpaw mixture into the pocket under the skin, then use a metal skewer to close the opening.

● Heat the oil and butter until the butter melts. Brush the bird all over with the mixture and season it well. Place the spatchcock breast uppermost on the barbecue over medium heat and cook, with the lid on, for 25 minutes, or until well browned underneath. Brush the spatchcock with oil and butter, turn it over and cook as before for 20–30 minutes, or until golden and cooked through.

● Meanwhile, mix the watercress and parsley, and toss in the lemon juice and oil. Add a little seasoning to this salad. Serve the chicken garnished with the salad and pawpaw.

HONEY-GLAZED TURKEY
(Serves 8–10)

	US	Metric	Imperial
Turkey	6–8 lb	2.75–3.6 kg	6–8 lb
Apple juice	½ cup	110 ml	4 fl oz
Honey	4 tbsp	4 tbsp	4 tbsp
Grated rind and juice of 1 orange			
Salt and fresh-ground black pepper			

BELOW **Honey-glazed turkey on the grill.**

● Before attempting to cook a whole turkey, check that your kettle barbecue is large enough to allow space for the bird between the grilling rack and the lid. If not, the turkey may be split in half through the breast bone – use a heavy kitchen knife and poultry scissors or meat chopper for this. Rinse the turkey inside and out under cold water and dry it thoroughly with absorbent kitchen paper. Heat the apple juice, honey, orange rind and juice to boiling point, then cool.

● Prepare the barbecue for indirect cooking and put some soaked hickory chips on the coals. Brush the turkey all over with the apple and honey marinade, sprinkle generously with seasoning, then cook it over low to medium heat. The bird will take about 2 hours to cook, depending on the heat of the coals. During this time turn the turkey every 20–30 minutes and brush it with the honey mixture.

● Keep the barbecue topped up with fuel adding hickory chips occasionally. After about 1½ hours, if the outside of the bird becomes too dark, wrap a piece of foil loosely around it. The wing and leg ends will need covering to prevent them from overcooking. Pierce the meat at the thickest part to check that it is cooked through: continue cooking if there is any sign of blood in the juices. At the end of cooking, the turkey should be a dark, rich red-brown, full-flavoured and succulent.

APPLE-GLAZED HAM

	US	Metric	Imperial
Boned and rolled joint of ham			
Onion, thickly sliced	1	1	1
Carrots, thickly sliced	1	1	1
Parsley sprigs	2	2	2
Apple juice	2 cups	450 ml	16 fl oz
Sage sprigs	2	2	2
Bay leaves	2	2	2
Cinnamon stick	1	1	1
Cloves	2	2	2

- Weigh the joint of ham and calculate the boiling time at 20 minutes per 450 g (1 lb) plus 20 minutes. Put the joint in a large saucepan and pour in cold water to cover the meat. Add the onion, carrots and parsley, then bring slowly to the boil. Skim any scum off the surface of the cooking liquid, cover and simmer for the calculated time.

- Put all the remaining ingredients in a saucepan and heat gently until boiling. Simmer the apple juice and spices uncovered until reduced to about 225 ml (1 cup/8 fl oz), then leave to cool.

- Drain the cooked ham. Remove any trussing string and cut off the rind – this will come off easily while the meat is hot, leaving a neat, even layer of fat. If necessary, put a couple of metal skewers through the joint to keep it in shape – most pieces of ham will retain their shape once boiled. Brush the ham all over with the cooled apple juice. Grill the joint for 5–10 minutes per 450 g (1 lb) over medium coals with the lid on the barbecue. Brush the joint with juice every 5–10 minutes and turn it often so that the outside browns and caramelizes evenly.

- Strain any remaining apple glaze into a pan and boil it until syrupy, then brush over the meat. Cut into thick slices, and serve with new or baked potatoes, crusty bread and crisp salad.

- **Note**   Smaller joints take slightly longer per 450 g (1 lb). The ham should be cooked through before it is put on the barbecue; the grilling gives the joint the distinctive flavour.

LEFT **A fillet of beef on the grill.**

Fillet of beef/pork tenderloin

These are basically the same cut of meat from two different animals and both are extremely tender. It is important to cook them as simply as possible and with the minimum of crisping and charring.

Both are expensive cuts, and the beef fillet is large: a whole beef fillet can easily weigh as much as 2.75 kg (5–6 lb) and can feed 10–12 people. A pork fillet or tenderloin, on the other hand, rarely weighs much more than 0.9–1.25 kg (2–2½ lb), but because it is so rich, it is usually enough for 6 people.

Beef fillet

Fold under the thinner end of the fillet in order to create a piece of meat of relatively uniform thickness (fillet tapers towards both ends: the narrower or head end can be as little as 4 cm (1½ in) across, while the wider butt end may well be 10 cm (4 in) thick) and cook with herb butter sauce (below).

HERB BUTTER SAUCE

	US	Metric	Imperial
Butter	½ cup	110 g	4 oz
Tarragon, fresh	1 tbsp	1 tbsp	1 tbsp
Chervil, fresh	1 tbsp	1 tbsp	1 tbsp
Shallots	1 tbsp	1 tbsp	1 tbsp
Dry white wine	2 tbsp	2 tbsp	2 tbsp
White wine vinegar	2 tbsp	2 tbsp	2 tbsp

If you are using dried tarragon and chervil instead of fresh, use *teaspoons* (tsp) not *tablespoons* (tbsp).

● Melt the butter in a saucepan, and add the herbs and onions. Cook over a very low heat, for a couple of minutes at most. Add the wine and vinegar slowly, stirring constantly. Brush the herb butter over the meat. Leave to stand at room temperature for at least an hour, brushing again at intervals of 15–20 minutes.

● When you are ready to cook the meat, pour any sauce that has dripped off back into the saucepan. This is the sauce which will be served, re-heated, with the cooked meat.

● Brown the meat on all sides, over a medium-high to high heat, turning frequently: this should take about 10 minutes. Then raise the grill (or move the meat towards the edge of the grill) and cook over a low heat for a further 15 minutes for rare meat, 20 minutes for medium-rare. If you don't like rare meat, don't eat fillet of beef: overcooking it is a waste.

Pork tenderloin

Purists would probably grill a pork tenderloin on its own, perhaps throwing a few sprigs of sage onto the fire from time to time, and basting occasionally with a little olive oil. Because pork is normally cooked for longer than beef, and because the initial searing would be over a medium rather than a high heat, total cooking time would be about the same for a 1 kg (2½ lb) pork tenderloin as for a 2 kg (5½ lb) beef fillet. For variety, though, try this:

ORIENTAL GINGER SEASONING

	US	Metric	Imperial
Fresh root ginger, grated	2 tsp	2 tsp	2 tsp
Garlic cloves, finely chopped	2	2	2
Soy sauce	⅓ cup	75 ml	3 fl oz
Sugar	2 tbsp	2 tbsp	2 tbsp
Water	2 tbsp	2 tbsp	2 tbsp
Sesame oil	1 tbsp	1 tbsp	1 tbsp

● These quantities can be varied. Some people might use half as much ginger, whereas others will prefer double the amount or more. The spicy effect of sesame oil cannot be duplicated with any other oil.

BELOW **Rib of beef.**

- If the meat is more than about 6 cm (2½ in) thick, slice it lengthwise into two thinner strips. Marinade in a plastic bag for at least 2 hours in the refrigerator; overnight is better still. Save the marinade for basting.

- Cook as for the beef fillet above, but use a drip pan. The total cooking time should include about 10 minutes browning plus 35 minutes slow cooking under a covered (or at least wind-shielded) barbecue. Baste every 5 minutes or so during the slow-cooking time.

Rib of beef and loin of pork

Majestic cuts, these, which might not seem particularly suitable for barbecuing – but they cook beautifully in a kettle barbecue. Use indirect heat to cook the joint with a drip tray under the meat, or flare-ups will be a constant problem.

Protect any exposed bones with aluminium foil, fixing it with a stapler if you have real trouble making it stick – but don't forget to remove the staples before serving!

Rib of beef

The meat should be well marbled (streaked with fat), as this will make it moist, tender and juicy, but you should trim all external fat to a maximum of about 12 mm (½ in). If you like garlic, make deep slits in the meat with a very sharp knife and insert whole or slivered cloves.

You will need heavy-duty tongs and a stout meat fork for the cooking. A half-cooked 2.75 kg (6 lb) beef roast is large, heavy, awkward and slippery.

Over a medium-to-high direct heat, brown the roast all over, turning frequently: this can take anything between 20–30 minutes.

Then, with the heat medium-to-low and the meat over a drip pan, cook with the lid on the barbecue for 26 to 33 minutes per kg (12–15 minutes per lb) for rare beef (internal temperature 60°C/140°F) or 33–40 minutes per kg (15–20 minutes per lb) for medium (internal temperature 70°C/160°F). Cooking with the bones upwards results in a better flavour, so favour this position when cooking. Small roasts cook disproportionately faster than large ones, so the rule of thumb translates to:

WEIGHT	RARE	MEDIUM
1.8 kg/4 lb	45 mins–1 hour	1–1¼ hours
2.75 kg/6 lb	1¼–1½ hours	1½–2 hours
3.6 kg/8 lb	1¾–2¼ hours	2¼–3 hours

The bigger roasts are also juicier, but unless you have a large family or a lot of meat-eating friends, you may end up with a lot of leftovers.

Leave any roast to sit for 15 minutes in a sheltered place before carving. After carving the rare meat, you may care to return the ribs to the grill for crisping.

Loin of pork

If your butcher bones, rolls and trusses the loin, it will be much easier to cook and to carve, but it will not look anything like so impressive – and in the opinion of many, it will not taste as good. The bones certainly add a flavour of their own.

Ask the butcher to chine the roast (cut through the bone) so that it can easily be carved into chops. If you can get the meat with the skin on, score it with a sharp knife and rub salt into the cuts to get good, crisp crackling. A loin on the bone cooks faster than a boned roast (bone is quite a good conductor of heat, at least when compared with meat), so a minimum cooking time of about 33 minutes per kg (15 minutes per lb), and a maximum of about 40 minutes per kg (18 minutes per lb), should be about right over a medium-to-low heat. Use indirect heat and keep the lid on the barbecue.

The heat should remain fairly constant throughout the cooking process, as searing the meat will toughen it. Cook the roast mostly bone-down, to give the crackling a chance to become really crispy.

LEFT **A loin of pork on the grill.**

RIGHT **Loin of pork with peaches.**

LOIN OF PORK WITH PEACHES
(Serves 8)

	US	Metric	Imperial
Boned and rolled loin of pork	3 lb	1.5 kg	3 lb
Paprika	1 tbsp	1 tbsp	1 tbsp
Dried sage	1 tbsp	1 tbsp	1 tbsp
Garlic clove, crushed (optional)	1	1	1
Salt and fresh-ground black pepper			
Peaches	4	4	4
Cloves	24	24	24
Ground cinnamon	1 tsp	1 tsp	1 tsp
Sugar	1 tbsp	1 tbsp	1 tbsp
Orange juice	2 tbsp	2 tbsp	2 tbsp

- Make sure the rind on the pork is well scored. Mix the paprika, sage, garlic (if used) and plenty of seasoning, then rub this all over the rind and the ends of the joint.

- Cook the pork over medium heat by the indirect method. Keep the lid on the barbecue and allow about 1½ hours, or until the joint is cooked through. Pierce the middle of the joint with the point of a knife to check that it is cooked. Alternatively, if using a meat thermometer it should read 85°C/185°F. Turn the meat three or four times during cooking, checking that the coals are hot enough to keep it grilling steadily but not too hot to overbrown the outside before the middle cooks.

- Meanwhile, place the peaches in a bowl and pour in boiling water to cover them. Leave for a minute, then peel and halve the fruit. Remove the stones and stud each peach half with three cloves. Place the fruit on double thick foil, large enough to wrap all the peaches in a neat parcel. Heat the cinnamon, sugar and orange juice in a small pan until the sugar melts, then brush this glaze all over the fruit. Wrap securely and put on the barbecue for 10–15 minutes before serving the pork.

- Cut the joint into thick slices and serve the hot peaches as an accompaniment.

Game

Because wild animals tend to be much less fatty than domesticated ones, you often have to supply extra fat when cooking game. The easiest ways to do this are by wrapping the game in sliced bacon before cooking (which also results in delicious, crispy bacon!) and by basting the birds or meat with fat: butter and olive oil are both good, but bacon dripping is best.

Opinions vary on how long game should be hung, but less than two days will often result in tough, flavourless meat, while more than seven days is excessive for most tastes.

Wild duck

Because ducks are bony, you do not get many servings per bird. Four would be miserly, three would be a reasonable limit, two is not excessive, and many people can eat a whole duck.

Dress and truss the duck and season with salt and pepper, but do not stuff. If you like, though, you can put a quarter of an onion, a quarter of an apple, or half a peach in the body cavity.

Ducks are fat enough that no extra barding or wrapping is required, but they should be basted frequently with melted butter. Place on the grill, with the breast up, over a low indirect heat. A small duck weighing about 1¼ kg) 1½ lb) dressed should be cooked in about 1 hour. If you use a meat thermometer, the temperature should reach 80°C/185°F.

Grouse

Grouse are generally cooked wrapped in bacon (as with pheasant), but they may also be spatchcocked like quail (see below). They are also very good spit-roasted. The method chosen will depend on the variety, and therefore size, of the grouse.

Pheasant

Servings for pheasant are much the same as those for duck. Two hundred years ago, it was not regarded as unusual for a well-to-do man to put away a brace of pheasant at a sitting.

Wipe the bird, season inside and out, and butter the skin generously. Wrap bacon all around the bird, and cook in a covered grill over a medium heat, using a drip pan. The bird should take just over 1 hour to cook, and after 50–55 minutes, remove the bacon to allow the pheasant to brown. Cook for a further 15 minutes. If the wings and legs start to look dry, protect them with foil. Meat thermometer readings for cooked meat should be as for duck, above.

DUCK WITH APRICOTS
(Serves 4)

	US	Metric	Imperial
Duck, thawed if frozen	4 lb	1.8 kg	4 lb
Fresh apricots	1 lb	900 g	1 lb
Red wine	1 cup	225 ml	8 fl oz
Cinnamon stick	1	1	1
Bay leaf	1	1	1
Brown sugar	3 tbsp	3 tbsp	3 tbsp
Soy sauce	2 tbsp	2 tbsp	2 tbsp
Button mushrooms	½ lb	225 g	½ lb

● Trim the leg and wing ends off the duck if necessary. Rinse the bird inside and out under cold running water, then pat it dry with absorbent kitchen paper. Cut away any lumps of fat from just inside the body cavity. Place the duck in a large bowl, then pour freshly boiling water from a kettle all over the outside of the bird. Drain it well and leave it to dry completely.

● Select firm, just ripe apricots – any that are too soft will fall during cooking. Cut the apricots in half, twist the halves apart and remove the stones. Place the halved fruit in a saucepan and pour in the wine. Add the cinnamon stick, bay leaf and sugar, then heat gently until the wine is just boiling. Remove from the heat at once and leave to cool. Do not cook the fruit any longer or it will be too soft. When the fruit is cold, strain off the liquor and add the soy sauce to it. Thread the apricot halves on metal skewers with the mushrooms.

- Prick the duck all over, then brush it with the apricot liquor. Cook over indirect medium heat, with the lid on the barbecue, for about 1½–2 hours. Brush the duck with the apricot liquor every 15 minutes or so and turn it three or four times during cooking so that it is evenly browned and crisp.

- About 15 minutes before the duck is fully cooked, brush the skewered apricots and mushrooms with liquor and cook them on the barbecue, turning once, for about 10–12 minutes.

- Boil any leftover cooking liquor until it is reduced to a syrupy glaze and brush it over the duck. Cut the bird into four joints and serve with the apricots and mushrooms.

PHEASANT WITH JUNIPER
(Serves 2–3)

	US	Metric	Imperial
Hen pheasant	1	1	1
Juniper berries	8	8	8
Dried oregano	1 tsp	1 tsp	1 tsp
Olive oil	2 tbsp	2 tbsp	2 tbsp
Port	4 tbsp	4 tbsp	4 tbsp
Salt and pepper			

- Tougher cock pheasants are better suited to braising or stewing than to roasting or grilling. Rinse the pheasant inside and out under cold water, then dry it on absorbent kitchen paper.

- Crush the juniper berries, then mix them with the oregano, oil, port and seasoning. Brush the mixture all over the pheasant, cover and leave to marinate for 2–3 hours. The pheasant may be chilled for several hours if preferred. Cook the bird over medium heat, with the lid on the barbecue. Put soaked hickory wood chips on the coals and brush the pheasant with marinade fairly frequently during cooking. Turn the pheasant about twice, until it is well browned, cooked through and tender: 45–55 minutes, depending on size. If any marinade remains, heat it in a small pan until boiling, then brush over the bird to glaze it before serving.

- The pheasant may be split into two for serving, or the legs may be removed and breast meat carved to serve three persons.

Quail
Quail are so small that they are more of an appetizer than a main dish. If they are served as the latter, then two or even three birds per person is about right.

Quail are normally spatchcocked, or split lengthways through the back, brushed with butter or melted bacon fat, and cooked over medium coals with no drip pan: they are not big enough to render enough fat for serious flare-ups. Allow 5 minutes at most for each side, cooking with the skin up first, and turning once.

If you like, marinate the quail in a mixture of olive oil and lemon juice, with a little finely chopped or grated onion and a pinch of nutmeg before cooking; if you do, you may also want to coat them with breadcrumbs.

A very traditional method of cooking quail is to wrap it in bacon and then in turn in vine leaves. Then roast the bird over medium-hot coals for 15–20 minutes.

Venison

Venison steaks or venison for kebabs should be marinated overnight, for example in a white wine or cider marinade (page 17), then cooked quickly over medium coals or until medium rare: 2 minutes on either side is plenty for a typical 2 cm (¾ in) steak. Alternatively the meat may be cooked through – just – but it must not be dried out.

The best cuts of venison for roasting are boned, rolled loin or haunch. Again, marinate overnight and wrap with bacon for the first half of the cooking time or lard the meat by threading fat through it.

SMOKY HERBED VENISON
(Serves 6–8)

	US	Metric	Imperial
Rolled haunch of venison	4 lb	1.8 kg	4 lb
Fresh thyme leaves	1 tbsp	1 tbsp	1tbsp
Chopped fresh sage	1 tbsp	1 tbsp	1 tbsp
Chopped parsley	2 tbsp	2 tbsp	2 tbsp
Chopped fresh rosemary	2 tsp	2 tsp	2 tsp
Pork fat (from belly) or bacon, cut in strips	¼ lb	110 g	¼ lb
Walnut or hazelnut oil	6 tbsp	6 tbsp	6 tbsp
Bottle of red wine			
Salt and fresh-ground black pepper			

• Trim every trace of fat off the venison. Use a meat skewer to pierce holes through the joint – these will be threaded with fat, a technique known as larding. Mix all the herbs, then roll the strips of fat in them. Use a larding needle to thread the strips of fat through the holes made by the skewer. The fat will keep the venison moist during cooking.

• Place the joint in a bowl, season it and pour the oil all over it. Pour the wine over the meat, cover and leave to marinate for 24 hours. Turn the joint a few times to make sure all sides are equally soaked in the wine.

• Drain the meat. Boil the marinade in an open saucepan until it is reduced by half. Brush some reduced marinade all over the venison, then cook it over indirect heat, on the covered barbecue, for about 2 hours, or until it is cooked to your liking. Put soaked hickory chips on the barbecue during cooking to give the venison a good, smoked flavour.

• After 1½ hours, the outside of the joint will be well browned and the middle will be pink. Cook for a further 30 minutes, until the venison is cooked through. Brush the venison frequently with marinade during cooking. If the outside of the joint becomes too dark, then wrap it loosely in a piece of foil. Any remaining marinade should be brought back to the boil and brushed over the joint before serving. Serve venison carved into thick slices.

CHAPTER EIGHT

Vegetables

Although barbecuing seems to be the meat-eater's domain, there are many ways of cooking vegetables.

Grilled corn

There are two ways to grill corn: with the husk and without. Grilling with the husks gives a tender, juicier ear, but grilling without results in a flavour and texture all its own.

To cook with the husk, first remove the silk (the threads between the husk and the corn). This means removing the husk, so do it as carefully as possible. You may need to secure the husk with florists' wire (but *not* the plastic-coated kind!) when you replace it.

Soak the corn in ice-water for at least 30 minutes – this chills and saturates it – then roast it over a medium, direct fire for about 20 minutes, turning frequently. To check if the corn is cooked, prick a kernel with a knife; if it spurts clear juice it is done.

Parched corn (cooked without the husk) is a roadside food in many countries, from Mexico to India. In Mexico, they usually parboil it first; in India, as in Egypt, it is just grilled.

To parboil, bring a large kettle or saucepan of water to the boil, and plunge the ears of corn into it for no more than a couple of minutes. Then finish the corn on a medium or medium-hot grill for another 3–5 minutes, depending on the heat, turning frequently.

For plain grilled corn, use a low heat for 10–20 minutes. Once again, turn frequently. Try serving with salt only instead of butter.

Grilled shallots

Shallots, spring onions, ciboes, chipples, *cebollitas* – whatever you call them — are surprisingly good grilled. Spread them 12–25 mm (1½–1 in) apart and cook them over a medium heat until they are soft, wilted, and golden-brown: at least 10–20 minutes. Allow three or four onions per person.

Grilled carrots

Parboil carrots until they are about half cooked (about 3–4 minutes), then finish cooking over a medium heat, turning frequently and basting with butter. Most people prefer their barbecued carrots to be slightly crunchy, rather than fully cooked. Sprinkle a pinch of parsley over the carrots before serving. To serve as a side dish for four you will need 450g (1lb).

Grilled potatoes

Whole potatoes can be cooked very successfully on the grill. Small potatoes (and sweet potatoes and Jerusalem artichokes) require 45–60 minutes; larger 'baking' potatoes take 1–1½ hours. Turn every 15 minutes or so until the potatoes can be easily pierced with a fork.

If you want a soft skin, oil the potato well before you put it on the grill: for a crisp skin, forget the oil.

Alternatively, cut large potatoes in thick, fairly uniform slices of about 12 mm (½ inch) and cook over a medium-to-hot fire. Baste repeatedly with melted butter, turning frequently. The potatoes should be golden and cooked in around 20 minutes. One large potato per person is adequate, but (as with so much barbecue food) many people may want more!

For a variation on this last recipe, crush a clove of garlic into a little pan of melted butter at the side of the grill and use for basting.

Cooking with a grill basket

A surprising number of vegetables can be cooked in a grill basket. Oil the basket to prevent them sticking and brush the vegetables liberally with melted butter or olive oil; turn frequently while cooking. Zucchini (courgettes) can be cooked this way, as can summer squash (halved) and even thickly sliced egg-plant (aubergines).

GRILLED EGGPLANTS WITH TOMATO
(Serves 4)

	US	Metric	Imperial
Large eggplants (aubergines)	2	2	2
Salt and fresh-ground black pepper			
Onion, finely chopped	1	1	1
Garlic clove, crushed	1	1	1
Olive oil	4–6 tbsp	4–6 tbsp	4–6 tbsp
Tomatoes, peeled and sliced	8	8	8

● Cut the eggplants in half lengthways, leaving their stalks on. Sprinkle the cut sides generously with salt, place the eggplants in a dish and leave for 30 minutes. Rinse off the salt and dry the eggplants on absorbent kitchen paper.

● Meanwhile, cook the onion and garlic in 2 tbsp of the olive oil for about 10 minutes, until the onion is thoroughly softened and just beginning to brown. Add plenty of seasoning and the tomato slices. Set aside.

● Brush the eggplants all over with olive oil, then cook them skin sides down over medium heat for 5 minutes, until well browned. Brush with more oil and turn the cut sides down, then cook for a further 5 minutes or so, until tender and browned.

● Place the cooked eggplants on a flat dish and slice them from the stalk outwards to make fan shapes. Quickly heat the tomato mixture, then spoon it between the eggplant slices. Serve at once with crusty bread as an appetizer or with grilled meat.

ABOVE **Grilled eggplants and tomato.**

Vegetable kebabs

Cooking both meat and vegetables on the same skewer is possible, but risky: all too often, the meat will still be half-raw when the vegetables are either burning or falling apart. A much better idea is to grill vegetable kebabs separately.

If you are using any vegetables which are notoriously slow-cooking, such as carrots, it is a good idea to parboil them first. Only experience will teach you exactly what sizes to cut the various vegetables that can be cooked together on a skewer, but you might care to try the following all-and-everything recipe to compare as many types of vegetables as possible.

ABOVE **Vegetable kebabs served with pasta.**

MIXED VEGETABLE KEBAB
(Serves 8)

	US	Metric	Imperial
2 marrows	¾ lb	350 g	¾ lb
1 large purple eggplant (aubergine)			
2 zucchinis	¾ lb	350 g	¾ lb
4 capsicums, red, green or yellow			
4 medium onions			
12 cherry tomatoes			
Olive oil	½ cup	110 ml	4 fl oz
Cider or wine vinegar	¼ cup	55 ml	2 fl oz
Dried basil	1 tsp	1 tsp	1 tsp
Dried thyme	½ tsp	½ tsp	½ tsp
Chopped fresh parsley	2 tbsp	2 tbsp	2 tbsp

- As an alternative to marrow you could try very tender young pumpkins, which can be cooked in the same way.

- Cut the marrow into 2.5 cm (1 in) cubes or slices, the eggplant into 2.5 cm (1 in) cubes and the zucchini into 2.5 cm (1 in) slices. Seed and core the capsicums, and cut into squares of the same size. Peel the onions and cut into quarters.

- Marinade all the vegetables in the oil/vinegar/herb mixture: a plastic self-seal bag is the easiest container to use. Shake the bag occasionally to ensure even coating, but be careful to avoid breaking up the onions.

- Then thread the vegetables onto a skewer, alternating the types. Cook over medium coals, turning frequently and basting with marinade, for 10–15 minutes. By this time, the tomatoes will be very soft indeed.

- If you want to add carrots, parboil them for about 3–4 minutse or they may be excessively crunchy for some people's tastes. Likewise, mushrooms should be steamed for a couple of minutes, or there is a real danger that they will split and fall off the skewer.

Vegetables in the embers

Scouts of both sexes will certainly remember baking potatoes in the embers of a fire – and then trying to eat the charred, gritty, half-raw result!

The technique *can* be made to work, though, for a variety of vegetables and to work deliciously. You need rather more patience than you had as a child, and you need the air-vent shut right down and the top closed so that the embers smoulder at as low a temperature as possible.

Potatoes cooked in the embers
Potatoes are the obvious choice for ember cooking. If you are not planning to use foil, oil the skin to reduce charring. A medium-sized potato should take between ¾–1 hour to cook fully. Turn often, using tongs.

The potatoes will require far less attention if you wrap them in foil before putting them in the embers but somehow, it isn't the same. They will take 5–10 minutes longer to cook, too.

Squash cooked in the embers
A less obvious choice, but arguably even more effective, is cooking pumpkin in the embers. Oil the outside, slash the skin *deeply* (to avoid the risk of explosion), and turn frequently during a cooking time of 45–60 minutes.

Onions cooked in the embers
The real surprise, at least until you try it, is onions cooked in the embers. Use large, sweet onions. Cut off the ends (which would otherwise burn), but do not peel them: just put them snugly into the embers and leave them for about 45 minutes, turning fairly frequently. The outer skin will be blackened and inedible and should be thrown away, but the onion inside is delicious.

Other vegetables in embers
You can cook almost any vegetable in this way, but you would be well advised to wrap it in heavy-duty foil first. With more delicate vegetables, such as zucchini (courgettes), use a double layer of foil to reduce the risk of charring. Corn will cook in the embers in 35–45 minutes; zucchinis, individually wrapped, in 30–40 minutes; and mushrooms, with butter, in about 30–60 minutes, depending on the size of the parcel.

Other ways to cook vegetables

Many vegetables can be cooked in a foil wrap on the grill, with only a partial foil covering. Potatoes and marrows, for example, can be halved, the cut side protected with foil, and then cooked on the grill.

Halved vegetables
Cutting potatoes and marrows in half, lengthwise, makes it easier to cook them evenly all the way through. Protecting the cut side with aluminium foil not only promotes moistness and prevents charring; it also slows down the rate of heat transfer, as the foil reflects a good deal of the heat, and makes even cooking easier, if longer. For either potatoes or pumpkin, the cooking time is about 60 minutes. Begin with the foil side downwards but after 35–40 minutes, turn and cook the uncovered side for the remaining time. The foil can be removed when you turn the vegetables over.

RIGHT **Vegetables can be cooked in the embers.**

GRILLED MUSHROOMS
(Serves 4)

	US	Metric	Imperial
Mushrooms	1 lb	450 g	1 lb
Butter	¼ cup	60 g	2 oz
Salt and fresh-ground black pepper			

• Wash and trim the mushrooms, and if they are really big, slice them. Divide the prepared mushrooms into four portions and place each on a large piece of doubled aluminium foil. Dot the mushrooms in each parcel with 15 g (1 oz) butter, and season to taste. Wrap the parcels securely and barbecue over hot coals for at least 15 minutes, turning every 5 minutes or so. The mushrooms are cooked when they are tender, but a little overcooking (even 5–10 minutes) will do no harm.

• Garlic lovers should slice a single clove of garlic into four pieces, lengthways, and add a slice to each parcel. For real luxury, substitute the heaviest cream you can find for the butter, using twice as much cream as butter (110 ml/½ cup/4 fl oz).

Parcelled mixed vegetables
Make foil parcels of any or all of the following vegetables, cut (if appropriate) into cubes of about 2.5 cm (1 in) square. Approximate cooking times for ¼ lb/110 ml/4 oz parcels are given beside each vegetable: remember that some vegetables are just as good underdone, while others do not suffer from a few minutes' overcooking. Those that can stand a little overcooking are marked with '+' after the cooking time. All times are for medium heat unless otherwise marked:

Eggplant (aubergine): 15+ minutes
Carrots, peeled or scrubbed, parboiled 3 minutes: 25 minutes
Cut corn (strip it off the ears with a knife: 20 minutes
Fresh green beans, sliced diagonally: 20+ minutes
Mushrooms: 20+ minutes
Soft-skinned squash and zucchini (courgettes): 15+ minutes
Tomatoes, cherry or halved: 30+

GERMAN POTATO SALAD
(Serves 4–6)

	US	Metric	Imperial
Potatoes, peeled	6–8	6–8	6–8
Onion, thinly sliced	1	1	1
Bacon, rashers	5	5	5
Vinegar	½ cup	110 ml	4 fl oz
Water	½ cup	110 ml	4 fl oz
Sugar	1 tsp	1 tsp	1 tsp

• Boil the potatoes, and cut them into slices 6 mm (¼ in) thick or less.

• Fry the bacon in its own fat until crumbly and sprinkle over the potatoes.

• Add the water, vinegar and sugar to the bacon fat and bring to the boil. Pour this over the potatoes and serve hot.

RIGHT **Mushrooms in foil.**

BAKED BUTTERNUT SQUASH

(Serves 4)

	US	Metric	Imperial
Butternut squash, each about ¾–1 lb in weight	¾–1 lb	350–450 gm	¾–1 lb
Cream cheese	½ lb	225 g	½ lb
Chopped parsley	2 tbsp	2 tbsp	2 tbsp
Snipped chives	2 tbsp	2 tbsp	2 tbsp
Mango chutney	2 tbsp	2 tbsp	2 tbsp

● Cook the squash whole, on the covered barbecue and over a medium, indirect heat. Allow 30–40 minutes, turning the squash once, until they are tender.

● Beat the cream cheese with the herbs. Chop any large chunks of mango in the chutney, then stir it into the cheese mixture. Hold the squash in a tea-towel and cut each one in half. Carefully scoop out the seeds from the middle. Serve each squash half topped with some of the cream cheese mixture.

SWEET POTATO WITH SAVORY CINNAMON BUTTER

(Serves 4)

	US	Metric	Imperial
Sweet potatoes, each about 1 lb in weight	1	1	1
Butter	¼ lb	110 g	¼ lb
Shallots, trimmed and chopped	6	6	6
Garlic clove, crushed (optional)	1	1	1
Ground cinnamon	1 tsp	1 tsp	1 tsp
Salt and fresh-ground black pepper			

● Scrub and prick the potatoes, then cook them over indirect heat on the covered barbecue for 50–60 minutes, turning occasionally. Pierce the potatoes with a pointed knife or fork to check that they are tender.

● Melt about a quarter of the butter in a small pan. Add the shallots, garlic (if used) and cinnamon and cook over moderate heat for 2–3 minutes. Leave to cool, then beat this mixture with the remaining butter, adding seasoning to taste.

● Hold the cooked potatoes in a tea-towel and cut them in half. Cut a criss-cross pattern into each potato half. Top each half with some butter and serve at once.

ABOVE Baked butternut squash.

RIGHT Zucchinis with blue cheese.

BELOW Sweet potato with savory cinnamon butter.

ZUCCHINIS WITH BLUE CHEESE
(Serves 4)

	US	Metric	Imperial
Large zucchini (courgettes)	4	4	4
Olive oil	2 tbsp	2 tbsp	2 tbsp
Blue cheese, crumbled	¼ lb	110 g	¼ lb
Shallots, trimmed and chopped	4	4	4
Soured cream	½ cup	110 ml	4 fl oz
Fresh-ground black pepper			

● Cut the zucchinis in half lengthways and brush them all over with olive oil. Mix the blue cheese with the shallots and soured cream, adding black pepper to taste.

● Cook the zucchinis over high heat for about 3 minutes on each side, starting with the cut side up. When they are browned and hot, transfer them to a serving platter, cut sides uppermost, and spoon the blue cheese mixture over the top. Serve at once – good as an appetizer with crusty bread or as an accompaniment to grilled chicken.

SKEWERED POTATOES WITH PRAWNS
(Serves 4)

	US	Metric	Imperial
Small new potatoes	32	32	32
Large uncooked prawns, peeled with tails on	16	16	16
Olive oil	2 tbsp	2 tbsp	2 tbsp
Good knob of butter, melted			
Grated rind and juice of ½ lemon			
Salt and fresh-ground black pepper			
Chopped fresh dill	2 tbsp	2 tbsp	2 tbsp

• Parboil the potatoes – about 5 minutes – then drain well. Mix the potatoes and prawns in a bowl with the oil, butter, lemon rind and juice, and seasoning. Toss the prawns and potatoes gently to coat them completely in the seasonings. When thoroughly coated, thread the ingredients on metal skewers.

• Cook over medium heat for 5 minutes on each side, until the potatoes have finished cooking and begun to brown and the prawns are cooked. Sprinkle with dill and serve at once.

FOILED MUSHROOMS
(Serves 4)

	US	Metric	Imperial
Button mushrooms	1 lb	450 g	1 lb
Cooked ham, cut in fine strips	¼ lb	110 g	¼ lb
Grated Parmesan cheese	4 tbsp	4 tbsp	4 tbsp
Shredded fresh basil	4 tbsp	4 tbsp	4 tbsp
Salt and fresh-ground black pepper			
Butter, melted	4 tbsp	50 g	2 oz

ABOVE **Foiled mushrooms.**

• Quickly rinse, dry and trim the mushrooms. Cut four squares of foil, each large enough to hold a quarter of the mushrooms. Divide the mushrooms between the foil. Sprinkle the ham, Parmesan cheese and basil over the mushrooms. Add seasoning to taste before spooning the melted butter over the top.

• Fold up the foil to enclose the mushrooms in neat packages. Cook over medium direct heat for 8–10 minutes. Serve the mushrooms in their foil wrapping, as an accompaniment to grilled meats or as an appetizer. Serve chunks of French bread to mop up the mushroom juices.

ABOVE **Stuffed capsicums.**

STUFFED CAPSICUMS

(Serves 4)

	US	Metric	Imperial
Green capscums	4	4	4
Onion, finely chopped	1	1	1
Chilli powder	1 tsp	1 tsp	1 tsp
Ground coriander	1 tbsp	1 tbsp	1 tbsp
Knob of butter			
Cooked pork or beef, chopped	1 lb	450 g	1 lb
Fresh breadcrumbs	6 tbsp	6 tbsp	6 tbsp
Chopped fresh thyme	1 tbsp	1 tbsp	1 tbsp
Beef stock	4 tbsp	4 tbsp	4 tbsp
Vegetable oil for brushing peppers			
Salt and fresh-ground black pepper			

• Cut the tops off the capsicums and retain them, then scoop out their seeds. Wash and dry the capsicum shells. Make sure they sit upright fairly neatly, taking a fine sliver off the base if necessary.

• Cook the onion, garlic, coriander and chilli in the butter until softened, for about 8 minutes. Remove from the heat and mix with the meat, breadcrumbs, stock and seasoning. Divide this stuffing between the capsicums, pressing it into the shells. Replace the capsicum lids and brush the vegetables all over with oil. Stand the capsicums on the barbecue over medium indirect heat. Put the lid on and cook for 35–40 minutes, or until the capsicum shells are tender and the filling hot through. Serve at once.

• If you like, offer a crisp salad and a bowl of soured cream with the spicy stuffed capsicums. Crusty bread or baked potatoes are also good accompaniments, or make a salad of canned red kidney beans tossed with diced avocado and spring onions – delicious!

FOLLOWING PAGE **Loin of pork with peaches.**

CHAPTER NINE

Accompani-ments and desserts

There are only a few recipes in this book which are not actually cooked on the barbecue: for example, German potato salad (page 100), beans and salsa. These are inseperably associated with Californian, Texan and New Mexico barbecues. Salsa (Spanish for sauce) usually refers to a mixture of tomatoes, onions and other ingredients, served cold; and the classic beans served with a barbecue are Santa Maria-style.

SANTA MARIA-STYLE BEANS

(Serves 8 as a side dish)

	US	Metric	Imperial
Dried beans	1 lb	450 gm	1 lb
Fresh hot green chilli (*serrano*)	1	1	1
Bay leaf	1	1	1
Olive oil or lard	1 tbsp	1 tbsp	1 tbsp
Tomato purée	4 tbsp	4 tbsp	4 tbsp
Mild chilli powder	1 tbsp	1 tbsp	1 tbsp
Bacon	¼ lb	110 g	¼ lb
Garlic clove, finely chopped	1	1	1
Small onion, finely chopped (optional)			

● For true Santa Maria style, the beans should be *pinquitos*, but small dried haricots will serve as well. Likewise, the chilli powder should be *pasilla* or *Nuevo Mexico*, but any mild chilli powder will do.

● Chop the fresh hot chilli (*serrano* or *jalapeño*) very finely. Sort the beans to remove any stones, and wash them carefully but do not soak them. Cover with plenty of water, add the chopped chilli and the bay leaf, and bring to the boil. DO NOT SALT as this will toughen the beans. Simmer gently, adding more water as necessary. When the bean skins begin to wrinkle, add the olive oil and continue to cook until the beans are soft (this can take several hours). When they are, add salt to taste and cook for another 30 minutes without adding any more water: these beans are not drained.

● Dice the bacon finely, and fry gently until it begins to render its own fat. Continue until the bacon is crisp, and then fry the garlic and the onion (if used) until soft. Add the beans, tomato purée and chilli powder, mix well and simmer (preferably in a pan at the side of a covered barbecue) until serving. Stir occasionally to help the barbecue flavour to permeate the beans.

● These beans can be frozen in heavy plastic bags, thawed naturally or in a microwave, and then re-heated on the barbecue.

LEFT **Salza and beans.**

SALSA
(Serves 8 as a side dish)

	US	Metric	Imperial
Can of tomatoes	28 oz	800 g	28 oz
Medium red onion, finely chopped	1	1	1
Fresh coriander, chopped	handful	handful	handful
Fresh hot chilli pepper	1–3	1–3	1–3
Garlic cloves, finely chopped	1–3	1–3	1–3
Olive oil (optional)	1 tbsp	1 tbsp	1 tbsp
Wine vinegar (optional)	1 tbsp	1 tbsp	1 tbsp
Oregano, dried	½ tsp	½ tsp	½ tsp

● Quantities can be varied: coriander, in particular, can range from a couple of tablespoons to a large handful. If you grown your own coriander, crush a few unripe coriander seeds under a heavy knife-blade for a superb aromatic flavour.

● Empty the tomatoes, undrained, into a large bowl. Add all the other ingredients, and mix together with your hand – not a very scientific procedure, but definitely the most effective. Leave for at least 30 minutes for the flavours to blend: 2–3 hours or more is even better.

● Use as a dip with corn chips, or spoon over beans, steak, hamburgers or anything else.

Breads

Of the many breads you can serve with a barbecue, garlic bread is probably the most popular. But you can also serve pita bread from the Near and Middle East; *nan* and *chapattis* from India; Mexican tortillas; or even bread cooked right on the barbecue. Keep cooked bread warm by wrapping it in a tea-towel and leaving it at the edge of the barbecue.

Garlic bread
Take a large French loaf and cut it almost through at intervals of 2–4 cm (¾–1½ in). Spread softened garlic butter (page 26) between the slices and wrap the loaf in foil. Grill for 20 minutes over medium-hot coals, and for the last few minutes, uncover the top of the bread to ensure a crisp, crusty finish. As a variation, try pounding two or three anchovy fillets into the garlic butter, and omit the parsley.

LEFT **Garlic bread**

Pita bread

Pita (or pitta) bread is a flat, oval sheet of bread eaten throughout Greece and in the Near and Middle East. Available in most large supermarkets, it is at its best re-heated over a charcoal grill: it should balloon out, making the pocket in the middle easier to fill. Give it 15–30 seconds on each side over medium-hot coals. Neither time nor temperature is particularly important, so long as you do not burn it.

BELOW **Pita bread.**

Nan

Nan is an Indian bread which looks like pita, but tastes rather different and rarely develops a pocket: this is a mopping up and dipping bread, rather than a bread for holding food. Reheat as for pita, or brush with garlic butter for an additional flavour.

Parathas

If you live near an Indian shop, you may be able to buy parathas – rich, buttered flat bread that is cooked by frying. Quickly re-heating over charcoal gives a delicious flavour and makes for a very different accompaniment to barbecued food.

Tortillas and chapattis
These are both thin, unleavened breads. Flour tortillas are very much like chapattis, while corn tortillas have a flavour all of their own. All are delicious when re-heated on a charcoal grill. Heat for 5–10 seconds on each side.

LEFT **Tortillas.**

Baked breads
Conventional bread recipes, including frozen ready-made breads or corn-breads made from a mix, can be cooked on a covered barbecue using indirect heat. Putting the bread over a drip pan, or an area of cleared coals, prevents the bottom of the bread from burning. Approximate cooking times are as follows:

Pan loaf, 450 g (1lb)	Medium, 15–20 minutes
Rolls, in baking pan	Medium/low, 15–20 minutes
Corn bread	Medium, about 35 minutes

With a covered barbecue and medium, indirect heat you can cook other baked delicacies such as gingerbread, although it is disputable whether this is a better idea than baking in the oven.

RIGHT **Baked bread.**

Salads

Salads are a natural accompaniment for barbecued food,
giving a welcome contrast in temperature and texture.
Because a barbecue is a usually fairly long-drawn-out affair
compared to a conventional meal, it is a good idea to make
salads which will not dry out or wilt unduly. This is why a
cabbage salad is a good idea, or one made with a heavier
lettuce, such as Romaine.

CABBAGE SALAD
(Serves 6)

To half a head of cabbage, shredded, add any or all of the
following:

> Almonds, whole or sliced, small handful
> Avocado(s), diced
> Beetroot (beet), sliced
> Carrot, shredded
> Celery, one or two sticks, sliced
> Cheese, 110 g (1 cup/4 oz)
> Coriander, chopped, up to a handful
> Raisins, small handful
> Red onion, thinly sliced
> Tomatoes, sliced
> Walnuts, 1–2 tbsp

Toss together with a dressing made of two parts olive oil
to one part lime or lemon juice. Instead of lemon juice alone,
you may care to use half lemon juice, half vinegar.

GREEK SALAD
(Serves 6)

	US	Metric	Imperial
Romaine lettuce, shredded	1	1	1
Feta (Greek) cheese, in small cubes	1 cup	110 g	4 oz
Tomatoes, quartered	3–4	3–4	3–4
Large black olives	12	12	12

• Toss together with the same dressing as for cabbage salad, above. Optional extras include chopped fresh dill, or fennel leaves, and capers.

FUL MEDAMES (Egyptian Bean Salad)
(Serves 6)

	US	Metric	Imperial
Beans, soaked overnight and drained	2 lb	900 g	2 lb
Garlic cloves, crushed and chopped	1–4	1–4	1–4
Hard-boiled eggs	6	6	6
Olive oil, to taste			
Lemon wedges			
Salt and pepper			

ABOVE **Greek style salad.**

• This Egyptian dish can be served hot or at room temperature. While it is not exactly a salad, it is a superb accompaniment to barbecued food. The correct *ful* beans can be found in Greek and Armenian stores and some delicatessens, but haricot beans will do at a pinch.

• Boil the beans until soft: 2–2½ hours in an ordinary saucepan or 30–45 minutes in a pressure cooker. (Newer beans cook faster than old ones.) When they are soft, drain them, add the chopped garlic, and divide into 6 bowls.

• Place a hard-boiled egg in the middle of each bowl, and offer olive oil, lemon wedges and salt and pepper.

• Egyptians would use *hamine* eggs, cooked for at least 6 hours in barely simmering water to which onion-skins have been added. The eggs are unusually creamy and delicately flavoured, while the whites are dyed a soft beige by the onion skins.

LEFT **Cabbage salad.**

POTATO, WALNUT AND OLIVE SALAD
(Serves 4)

ABOVE Potato, walnut and olive salad.

	US	Metric	Imperial
Small new potatoes	2 lb	900 g	2 lb
Salt and fresh-ground black pepper			
Walnuts, roughly chopped	1 cup	110 g	4 oz
Bunch of shallots, trimmed and chopped			
Stuffed green olives, sliced	1 cup	110 g	1 cup
Olive oil	4 tbsp	4 tbsp	4 tbsp
Cider vinegar	1 tbsp	1 tbsp	1 tbsp
Lettuce heart, shredded	1	1	1

• Scrub the potatoes, then cook them in boiling salted water until tender – 10–15 minutes, depending on size. Drain and place in a large bowl. Add the nuts, shallots, olives, oil and vinegar. Sprinkle in plenty of pepper and toss well, then cover and leave to cool.

• Line a bowl with the shredded lettuce. Toss the potatoes in their dressing before turning them into the lettuce-lined bowl just before serving.

ZUCCHINI AND CELERY SALAD
(Serves 4)

	US	Metric	Imperial
Celery sticks	6	6	6
Zucchini (courgettes)	3	3	3
Red onion, thinly sliced	½	½	½
Red capsicum	1	1	1
Honey	1 tsp	1 tsp	1 tsp
Cider vinegar	2 tbsp	2 tbsp	2 tbsp
Olive oil	5 tbsp	5 tbsp	5 tbsp
Chopped parsley	2 tbsp	2 tbsp	2 tbsp
Salt and fresh-ground black pepper			

• Cut the celery sticks lengthways into very thin slices, then cut them across into 5 cm (2 in) lengths. Put these fine sticks into a large bowl, cover with cold water and add a handful of ice cubes. Leave for about an hour, or until the celery is curled and really crisp. The celery may be left in the refrigerator overnight like this.

• Trim the zucchinis, then cut them into thin sticks about the same size as the celery. Drain the celery and dry it on absorbent kitchen paper. Mix the celery, zucchinis and onion. Trim the capsicum, discarding all seeds and pith, then cut it into small fine strips; add these to the salad.

• Mix the honey, cider vinegar, olive oil, parsley, salt and pepper in a screw-topped jar. Shake well until the dressing is thoroughly combined. Toss the dressing into the salad and serve.

RIGHT **Zucchini and celery salad.**

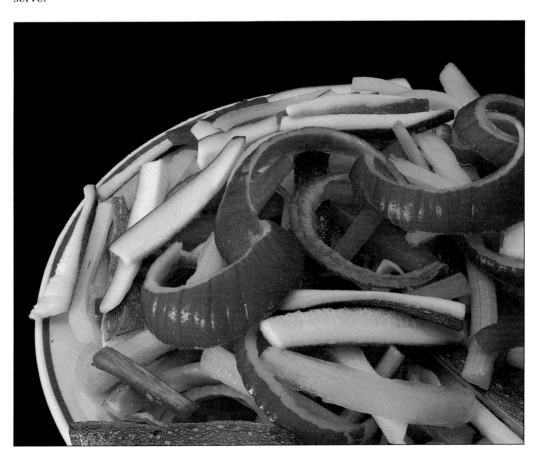

ROASTED EGGPLANT PURÉE
(Serves 4)

	US	Metric	Imperial
Large eggplants (aubergines)	2	2	2
Garlic cloves, crushed	2	2	2
Tahini (sesame paste)	2 tbsp	2 tbsp	2 tbsp
Olive oil	½ cup	110 ml	4 fl oz
Lemon juice	2 tbsp	2 tbsp	2 tbsp
Salt and fresh-ground black pepper			

- Roast the eggplants over medium heat on the covered barbecue until they are soft through and well browned outside – about 15–20 minutes, turning two or three times.

- Halve the eggplants and scrape all the soft flesh off the skin into a bowl. Mash the eggplant flesh thoroughly with the garlic until it is smooth. Alternatively, use a food processor. Beat in the tahini, then gradually beat in the olive oil, drop by drop at first. As the oil is incorporated it can be added a little faster. Beat well until smooth and creamy. Stir in the lemon juice, a little nutmeg and seasoning to taste.

- The purée is good served warm or it may be cooled and chilled lightly before serving. It makes a good appetizer, with pita bread, or it may be mounded on split baked potatoes. It also tastes good with grilled lamb chops or steaks.

LEFT **Roasted eggplant puree**

Desserts

Although there is something to be said for re-heating an apple pie on the barbecue, it is not really a barbecued dish, whereas the recipes given here are.

Fruit kebas
Many kinds of fresh fruit can be cooked on skewers. Cooking is not really a problem as what you are doing is warming the fruit through, and giving it a new kind of smoky flavour. Try any or all of the following, cooked over a low-to-medium heat:

Apples: Cut small apples in quarters, larger apples into 4 cm (1½ in) cubes
Bananas: Cut in slices up to 4 cm (1½ in) long
Oranges: Peeled or unpeeled, cut in quarters
Pineapples: Cut in 4 cm (1½ in) cubes.

For a sweet/savoury twist, intersperse the fruit with 2.5 cm (1 in) cubes of cheese: the kebabs are ready as soon as the cheese begins to melt.
Alternatively, baste the fruit kebabs with the brown sugar-cinnamon butter below. They are ready to eat when they are golden, but not caramelized.

ABOVE **Fruit kebabs.**

	US	**Metric**	**Imperial**
Butter	¼ cup	60 g	2 oz
Brown sugar, moist	¼ cup	75 g	2½ oz
Cinnamon	½ tsp	½ tsp	½ tsp
Nutmeg, preferably freshly-grated	¼ tsp	¼ tsp	¼ tsp
Grated lemon rind	½ tsp	½ tsp	½ tsp
Lemon juice	1–2 tsp	1–2 tsp	1–2 tsp

LEFT Baked apples in foil.

Baked apples

Core one large apple for each person and fill them with your favourite stuffing: raisins, brown sugar, cinnamon and butter are usual, but you may also want to try shredded coconut or chocolate pieces.

Wrap them in foil and bake over medium coals, with the lid on the barbecue, for about 20 minutes, or until soft.

Toasted marshmallows

The only way to do this properly is to have a bag of marshmallows beside the grill. Give each guest a long skewer or toasting fork and let them toast their own. If you want to *overdo* it properly, then you should also have to hand a bowl of whipped cream, and a bowl of hot chocolate sauce on the grill. You can also flavour toasted marshmallows by putting a cardamom seed in the middle.

SUMMER FRUIT PACKETS
(Serves 4)

	US	Metric	Imperial
Strawberries, hulled	½ lb	225 g	½ lb
Cherries, stoned	½ lb	225 g	½ lb
Peaches	2	2	2
Kiwi fruit	2	2	2
Unsalted butter	4 tbsp	60 g	2 oz
Brown sugar	2 tbsp	2 tbsp	2 tbsp
Grated rind and juice of 1 orange			
Mint sprigs	4	4	4

• Place the strawberries in a bowl with the cherries. Pour freshly boiling water over the peaches, leave them to stand for 1 minute, then drain and peel them. Cut the peaches in half, discard their stones and slice the fruit. Add to the strawberry mixture with the kiwi fruit.

• Cut four large squares of double-thick foil and divide the fruit between them. Heat the butter, sugar, orange rind and juice until the sugar has melted. Spoon this mixture over the fruit and top each portion with a sprig of mint. Fold the foil around the fruit to seal it in. Put the fruit packages over medium coals for about 10 minutes. Serve with cream or ice cream for a hot 'n' cold dessert.

HOT 'N' COLD BANANAS

(Serves 4)

	US	Metric	Imperial
Large bananas	4	4	4
Vanilla ice cream scoops	8	8	8
Maple syrup	4 tbsp	4 tbsp	4 tbsp
Chopped walnuts	4 tbsp	4 tbsp	4 tbsp
Grated chocolate	4 tbsp	4tbsp	4 tbsp

• Cook the unpeeled bananas on the barbecue until they are black all over, turning about twice. This takes about 7–10 minutes over medium heat, longer over dying embers.

• Slit the skin down both sides of the bananas, then half peel them. Place each banana on a plate with a couple of scoops of ice cream. Top with maple syrup, walnuts and chocolate. Eat immediately – take care, the bananas are very hot.

BELOW **Hot 'n' cold bananas.**

SPICED APPLES AND PLUMS
(Serves 4)

	US	Metric	Imperial
Juice of 1 orange			
Cinnamon sticks	4	4	4
Cloves	8	8	8
Honey	1 tbsp	1 tbsp	1 tbsp
Ginger wine	½ cup	110 ml	4 fl oz
Cooking apples, halved, cored and peeled	2	2	2
Plums, halved and stoned	1 lb	450 g	1 lb

● Put the orange juice, cinnamon, clove and honey in a small saucepan over very low heat and leave to infuse for about 15 minutes, or until steaming hot but not simmering. Off the heat, add the ginger wine (green ginger wine is best) and stir well.

● Cut four double-thick squares of foil and place an apple half on each. Divide the plums between the portions and fold the foil up around the edges to contain the spiced juice. Place a cinnamon stick and a couple of cloves on each apple, spoon the liquor over and fold up the foil to seal in all the liquid.

● Cook over medium heat, with the lid on the barbecue, for about 15 minutes, or until the apples are tender. Serve with whipped cream.

LEFT **Glazed pears in foil.**

GLAZED PEARS
(Serves 4)

	US	Metric	Imperial
Large, firm pears, peeled, cored and halved	6	6	6
Grated rind and juice of ½ lemon			
Golden syrup	4 tbsp	4 tbsp	4 tbsp
Vanilla essence (flavouring)	1 tsp	1 tsp	1 tsp
Red wine	4 tbsp	4 tbsp	4 tbsp
Chopped pistachio nuts	3 tbsp	3 tbsp	3 tbsp

● Cut four double-thick squares of foil and place three pear halves on each. Heat the lemon rind and juice, syrup, vanilla and wine until boiling, then spoon the mixture all over the fruit. Wrap the foil around the pears to enclose them completely.

● Cook the pears over medium heat for 5–8 minutes, until they are hot and tender but firm. Open each packet and brush the juices over the fruit. Sprinkle a few chopped pistachio nuts over each portion and serve.

GRILLED PINEAPPLE WITH COCONUT RUM CREAM
(Serves 4)

BELOW **Spiced apples and plums in foil.**

	US	Metric	Imperial
Medium to large pineapple	1	1	1
Unsalted butter	4 tbsp	60 g	2 oz
Honey	1 tbsp	1 tbsp	1 tbsp
Cream of coconut	¼ lb	110 g	4 oz
White rum	2 tbsp	2 tbsp	2 tbsp
Soured cream	1 cup	225 ml	8 fl oz
Icing sugar (confectioner's sugar) to taste			
Strawberries, hulled and sliced	¼ lb	110 g	¼ lb

● Peel the pineapple, removing all the spines, then cut it into eight thick slices. Remove the central core and place the slices on a large platter.

● Melt the butter with the honey, then brush the mixture all over the pineapple. Blend the cream of coconut in about 4 tbsp of boiling water. Stir in the rum and the soured cream, then add icing sugar to taste to sweeten the coconut cream.

● Grill the pineapple over high heat for about 2–3 minutes on each side, until lightly browned and hot. Overlap the slices on a platter, brush with any remaining butter and honey mixture and top with the strawberries. Serve with the coconut rum cream.

FOLLOWING PAGE **Grilled pineapple.**

A summary of cooking times

This 'quick reference' section will save you having to look up specific recipes. Large cuts and longer times, always require the lid on the barbecue. Thin foods, smaller cuts and items which cook quickly can be cooked on the open barbecue.

Beef

Fajitas
Medium: 6–8 minutes per side.

Fillet
Medium-high or high: brown, turning frequently, for 10 minutes. Then low: 15 minutes for rare, 20 minutes for medium.

Hamburgers

THICKNESS	FIRST SIDE	SECOND SIDE
	High	Medium-high
2.5 cm (1in)	2–4 minutes	Rare: 4–5 minutes
		Medium:6–8 minutes
		Well done: 10–15 minutes

Kebabs
Medium-high direct heat: 3–10 minutes, turning frequently

Korean Beef (page 32)
High: 1–2 minutes total

Ribs
Crusty rare ribs: medium-high coals, 20–40 minutes, turning 3 times.
Well done ribs: pre-cook in foil for 1 hour over direct heat. Finish over medium-to-low indirect heat for at least 15 minutes per side, turning once.

Rib Roast
Brown all over, medium-to-high direct heat, 20–30 minutes, turning frequently. Then with medium to low indirect heat, cook under cover for 26–33 minutes per kg (12–15 minutes per lb) for rare, 33–44 minutes per kg (15–20 minutes per lb) for medium.

Steaks: T-bone, Porterhouse, Sirloin & other tender steaks

THICKNESS	FIRST SIDE High	SECOND SIDE Medium-Low
2.5 cm (1in)	2–3 minutes	Rare: 2–3 minutes Medium: 5–8 minutes Well-done: 10 minutes or more
5 cm (2 in)	4–6 minutes	Rare: 8–10 minutes Medium: 12–15 minutes Well-done: 20 minutes or more

Steaks: Top Round, London Broil, etc. (Marinate first)

THICKNESS	FIRST SIDE High	SECOND SIDE Medium-low
2.5 cm (1 in)	5–6 minutes	Rare: 15 minutes Medium: 20 minutes
5 cm (2 in)	8 minutes	Rare: 20 minutes Medium: 23 minutes

Teriyaki (page 19)
High: 3–4 minutes total

Lamb

Chops

	FIRST SIDE Medium	SECOND SIDE Medium
1.2 cm (½ in)	3 minutes	3–6 minutes
2.5 cm (1 in)	6 minutes	6–9 minutes

Kebabs
Medium-low direct heat, 12–20 minutes, turning 3–4 times.

Leg
Butterflied, 2½ kg (5–6 lb): covered, medium-hot, direct heat, 30–60 minutes. Turn frequently.

Loin, boneless
Covered barbecue, medium indirect heat: 44 minutes per kg (20 minutes per lb) at most.

Shoulder
Covered barbecue, medium indirect heat: 50–55 minutes per kg (22–25 minutes per lb).

Meatballs

Kefethes (page 51)
Medium to low direct heat: 20–30 minutse. Turn frequently.

Seekh Kebab (page 52)
Medium-hot direct heat: 20 minutes. Turn every 3–4 minutes.

Pork

Chops

	FIRST SIDE	SECOND SIDE
1.2m (1½ in)	6 minutes	6–8 minutes
2.5 cm (1 in)	12 minutes	13–18 minutes

Kebabs
Medium-low direct heat: 15–25 minutes, turning 3–4 times.

Loin
Medium to low heat: covered barbecue, 33–40 minutes per kg (15–18 minutes per lb).

Ribs
From raw: Low heat, 60–90 minutes.
Pre-cooked: 30–60 minutes.

Tenderloin
Medium heat: 10 minutes, turning frequently, then low, 10–15 minutes.

Poultry

Chicken and domestic duck
Pieces: medium, direct heat, turn every 5–10 minutes

	COVERED BARBECUE
Breasts, boned	10–12 minutes
Wings or legs	30–35 minutes
Quarters	30–40 minutes
Halves	45 minutes or more

Spring chicken, Cornish Game Hen: whole bird, medium indirect heat, covered barbecue 25–30 minutes.
Whole chicken: covered barbecue, medium, indirect heat with drip tray, 75–90 minutes. Turn 3 or 4 times.
　　Spit: medium heat.
　　For small birds (700 gm/1 lb), minimum 1 hour; medium bird (1½ kg/3 lb) minimum 1½ hours; large bird (2½ kg/5 lb), minimum 2½ hours.
Whole, spatchcock: Medium, direct heat, skin side first, then favouring bone side: 35–45 minutes total. Turn 3 or 4 times.

Duck, wild
Low, indirect heat: about 1 hour for a 1¼ kg/1½ lb duck.

Pheasant
Covered grill, medium, direct heat: about 1 hour.

Quail
Split (spatchcocked): 5 minutes per side.

Turkey
Whole: covered barbecue, medium, indirect heat with drip tray. Turn every 15 minutes. Small bird (3½ kg/8 lb), 2 to 2½ hours; large bird (7 kg/15 lb), at least 4 hours.
Breast: spit roast, medium direct heat 2½–2¾ kg (5–6 lb), 2½ to 3 hours.

Seafood

Clams
Medium-high: cook until the shells begin to open, then turn and cook for 10–15 minutes or until shells are fully open.

Crabs
King Crab leg: medium coals, about 10 minutes. Turn occasionally.

Crayfish/rock lobster
Medium heat: shell-side down for 10 minutes, then flesh-side down, 5 minutes.

Fish & fruit kebabs
Hot coals, 15–20 minutes, turning frequently.

Lobster
Parboiled, split: 5–10 minutes total.
Parboiled, whole: as for crayfish.
Uncooked, split: shell-side down, 10–20 minutes, then shell up, 3–5 minutes. Finish claws in the embers, 2–3 minutes.

Lobster-Prawn-Scallop Kebabs (page 55)
Medium to low heat, 10–15 minutes, turning frequently.

Mussels
In foil, medium-high heat: ready when they open of their own accord.

Oysters
Cook as for clams.

Prawns
Butterflied: Low heat, 5 minutes.
Kebabs: Medium to hot coals, 10–15 minutes. Turn frequently.
In foil: medium, 10–12 minutes.

Fish
Small, whole: medium-low, 2–5 minutes per side.
Medium, whole (1¼ kg/3 lb): medium, 30–40 minutes total. Turn every 5–10 minutes.
Large, whole: hot, with foil cradle: 20–30 minutes total, turn every 5 minutes.
Steaks: low, 1–4 minutes per side.
In foil: medium-hot, 5–6 minutes per cm (12--15 minutes per inch of thickness).

Satay

Medium/high direct heat: 1–3 minutes, turning frequently.

Sausages

Black pudding, *blutwurst*, blood sausage, Bologna, *bratwurst* (cooked), salami, hog's pudding	Low, 5–10 minutes, turn frequently.
British 'bangers' *Chorizo* (thin)	Very low, 15–25 minutes, turn occasionally.
Chorizo (thick), *Linguisa*, Italian pork sausage, Polish smoked sausage	Low, 10–20 minutes, turn occasionally.
Frankfurters (canned)	Low, 5–10 minutes, turn frequently.
Weisswurst: boil first	Low, 5 minutes, turn frequently.

Vegetables

For additional vegetable recipes, see pages 00 and 00.

Carrots
Parboil 3–4 minutes, then cook over medium heat to taste (3 minutes or more).

Corn
Husked: low heat, 10–20 minutes, turning frequently.
Husked and parboiled for 2 minutes: medium heat, 3–5 minutes, turning frequently.
In husk, after ice-water treatment: medium direct heat, 20 minutes, turning frequently.

Mixed Vegetable Kebabs
Medium heat, 10–15 minutes, turning frequently.

Onions
In the embers, 45 minutes, turning frequently.

Potatoes
Small, whole: medium-low heat, 45–60 minutes.
Large, whole: medium-low heat, up to 1½ hours. Turn occasionally.
In the embers: 45–60 minutes (50–70 minutes in foil).
Sliced 1.2 cm (½ in) thick: medium-to-hot, about 20 minutes, turning frequently.

Shallots
Medium heat, 10 minutes or more.

Venison

For a 2 cm (¾ in) steak, 2 minutes per side over medium heat.
Rolled boneless loin, 1.5–1.8 kg (3–4 lb): low, indirect heat, 50–70 minutes, or on spit (medium-low heat), 55 to 75 minutes.

Index

Note: *References to captions to*
illustrations are indicated by italics

The Films of
GREGORY PECK

The Films of

Introduction by Judith Crist

Previous page: Gregory Peck, as Army Air Force General Savage, cracks up after pushing himself and his fliers beyond the limits of endurance, and is restrained by Gary Merrill and Dean Jagger. (*Twelve O'Clock High.*)

GREGORY PECK

by John Griggs

CITADEL PRESS   SECAUCUS, NEW JERSEY

With Greer Garson (*Valley of Decision*)... Ingrid Bergman (*Spellbound*) ... Joan Bennett (*The Macomber Affair*)...

Published by Citadel Press
A division of Lyle Stuart Inc.
120 Enterprise Avenue, Secaucus, N.J. 07094
In Canada: Musson Book Company,
A division of General Publishing Co. Limited
Don Mills, Ontario

Queries regarding rights and permissions should be
addressed to: Lyle Stuart Inc., 120 Enterprise Avenue,
Secaucus, N.J. 07094

Manufactured in the United States of America

Library of Congress Cataloging in Publication Data

Griggs, John.
   The films of Gregory Peck.

   1. Peck, Gregory, 1916-   2. Moving-picture
actors and actresses—United States—Biography.
I. Title.
PN2287.P35G74   1984   791.43′028′0924 [B]   83-26126
ISBN 0-8065-0897-3

Susan Hayward (*David and Bathsheba*)... Ava Gardner (*The Snows of Kilimanjaro*)... Ann Blyth (*The World in His Arms*)...

Jennifer Jones (*Duel in the Sun*)...

Dorothy McGuire (*Gentleman's Agreement*)...

Valli (*The Paradine Case*)...

Contents

Deborah Kerr (*Beloved Infidel*)...   Sophia Loren (*Arabesque*)...   and Tuesday Weld (*I Walk the Line*).

Foreword

The text of *The Films of Gregory Peck* has been researched and compiled from a wide range of sources over several years. These sources include published, broadcast and private interviews with some of the principals involved. Material has been included from trade press and general circulation newspaper accounts, magazine stories, published memoirs, histories and surveys, radio and television broadcasts, etc. Where facts, events and remarks are cited in the text, every effort has been made to identify and credit the origin of that information. Since a great deal of information processing and organization was involved, it is almost inevitable that there may be an instance or two in which such citation is missing. If that is the case, it is a result of oversight or human error and apologies are offered herewith for any unintentional slight in that regard.

Beyond the sources cited within, the author wishes to specifically acknowledge and express thanks to the following individuals and institutions whose encouragement, assistance and services were invaluable in the reseach and writing of this work:

Paul Meyers and the staff, especially Monty Arnold, of the Film and Theatre Collection at the Lincoln Center Library of the Performing Arts; Adrianne Mancia, Lillian Girard and the staff of the Film Department of the Museum of Modern Art; G. William Jones and the staff, especially Mary MacFarland, of the USA Film Festival at Southern Methodist University, Dallas; Ernest Parmentier and the staff of the late, lamented *Film-Facts* magazine; The Academy of Motion Picture Arts and Sciences.

Among the individuals to whom thanks should be expressed are (in no particular order): Patricia Newcomb, Mike Hutner, Lois Smith, Bill Werneth, Fred Skidmore, Lewis Archibald, Scott MacDonough, Judith Crist, Richard Christian, Ilene Wagner, Marshall Lewis, David Warlock, Barbara Russel, Olivia Singleton, and Myron. And there are undoubtedly others, overlooked, whose anonymity here should not be construed to diminish the importance of their contribution or my appreciation.

By far not least, there is Gregory Peck, to whom gratitude is expressed for his cooperation in granting interviews, providing guidance in the pursuit of research and supplying photos from his personal files.

Finally, deep gratitude is expressed for the generosity of director Henry King in making himself available for interview time in the midst of a busy schedule and personal discomfort (of which he never complained) while visiting New York with a couple of cracked ribs, at age 87.

A prolific craftsman, Henry King was one of a venerable generation of pioneering picture-makers whose own substantial and significant contributions to the history of Hollywood have received insufficient attention when legendary directors have been given their due. One need not reiterate this Virginia gentleman's many virtues to anyone whose life was enriched by knowing or working with him or even by a brief encounter. Suffice it that the term "gentleman" is itself enriched in the context of being applied to this gifted and generous individual.

It is, therefore, to the memory of Henry King that this work is respectfully dedicated.

J.G.
New York City

6

To the Memory of
Henry King
(1888-1982

Director Henry King takes a break with Joan Collins and Gregory Peck on location for *The Bravados* in Morelia, Mexico.

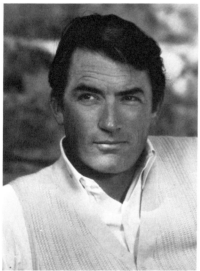

Introduction

They had faces then, the men who took over the still-silver screen during and after World War II, providing proper role models for the boys and romance for the girls and, in some cases, satisfying performances and rewarding, even enduring, portraits and perceptions for grown-ups. Like the idols who had their worshippers in the Thirties and Forties, that new generation of male movie stars (in contrast to our contemporary box-office stars) came—and went—with the final glory days of the great studios. Only a handful endured.

But it is not his durability—a continuing career that has yielded 49 films in 37 years—that has given Gregory Peck his stature. Neither is it the face—that handsome Abe Lincoln look in features and stance, that clean-cut "strength" in the matinee-idol countenance—that provides his timeless intergenerational appeal. Nor is it the vast variety of more than 40 different characters he has played that offers the major interest in Gregory Peck's film work.

Certainly there is that solidity—and stolidity—of personality that holds our confidence, that sense of integrity and righteousness that is inherent in his every portrait, be it of hero or of villain. Somewhere within that man we know is the best of us, in fact or aspiration. And as John Griggs's biography makes clear, it is a characteristic maintained on and off the screen.

What is interesting about his work, beyond its variety and scope, is that Peck created a series of prototypes or, indeed, role models and model roles that transcended, in some cases, the film itself and remain memorable beyond the context. These go beyond his being the Hemingway hero twice over, with *The Macomber Affair* and *The Snows of Kilimanjaro*; his bridging of time in *Captain Horatio Hornblower*; the wartime derring-doing of *Twelve O'Clock High* or *The Guns of Navarone*.

He came to his image of virtue early in his career, with Elia Kazan's *Gentleman's Agreement*, as the magazine writer exploring anti-Semitism among middle-class and professional folk. Given the naïveté the novel and film imposed upon the character, Peck nevertheless created the enduring image of the restrained and cool but obviously caring investigative reporter. Three years later, in Henry King's 1950 *The Gunfighter*, in what remains one of his great performances, he gave us the ideal and ultimate portrayal of the malaise of the professional gunslinger, of the inner turmoil of a man risking his life for a reunion with his estranged wife and child with a dream of a new life, making clear to us the tragedy of a "hero" whose time has gone. Peck showed us the end of a legend and gave posthumous grandeur to a wasted life.

Think of the romantic older-man-younger-woman escapade, of the charmer with ulterior motives losing his heart and knowing the futility thereof, and instantly there's the image of Peck in William Wyler's 1953 *Roman Holiday*, with Peck the American newsman and Audrey Hepburn, in her screen debut, the exquisite runaway princess. Peck set a standard for the romantic hero-heartbreaker who suffers the heartbreak, a model all-American (versus the Cary Grant) sophisticate. And after another three years, amid the suds-and-soap of Nunnally Johnson's 1956 *The Man in the Gray Flannel Suit*, Peck became the prototype of the man of sensibility and responsibility who finally says "shove Madison Avenue!" and asserts human values over those of the executive suite.

But it was in 1963, with the reverse coin of *The Gunfighter*, that Peck gave us his greatest role model, his portrait of Atticus Finch, in Robert Mulligan's *To Kill a Mockingbird*. As a widower and lawyer raising his two children in a small Alabama town in the Thirties, Peck faced the dual task of controlling his inner wrath in fighting racial injustice and of evidencing both that restraint and passion to the youngsters. Peck's portrayal of a man of compassion, of strength and of intelligence in both his public and private aspects is unforgettable—a triumph of performance, let alone of not letting the two children, and a third who joins them in their escapades, steal the movie right out from under him!

These are Peck's outstanding archetypical roles in my memory, crowded with other characters he made his own. The variety still astounds—but it is the "face"—in all its aspects—that endures.

—Judith Crist

Gregory Peck

Freedom fighter, priest, scion of wealth, mental patient, southern farmer, scoundrel, great white hunter, journalist, British barrister, bank robber, novelist, gunfighter, U.S. Air Force general, naval captain, cavalry officer, Biblical king, adventurer, military intelligence officer, pilot, ad man, sea captain, sports writer, rancher, infantry lieutenant, submarine commander, mountaineer, southern lawyer, gambler, partisan, psychiatrist, scientific researcher, professor, western marshal, Indian scout, biologist, government administrator, southern sheriff, Scottish outlaw, diplomat, U.S. Army general, Nazi arch-villain, British officer. These are the roles of Gregory Peck, a star with his very first picture, a uniquely American role-model, an archetypal hero.

In an outstanding career, spanning four decades and reflecting something of the history of the American film industry itself, Gregory Peck has carved out a screen persona that is mirrored as well in both his private life and his public concerns. If, as critic Richard Schickel has observed, there is "something Lincolnesque" in Peck's character (and in his stature) on screen and off, it is probably that integrity which we tend in our idealism to regard as quintessentially American: an ability to see a higher good and to place duty to that higher good above purely personal considerations; a dedication to nobler ideals by which we define our aspirations as individuals and as a nation. We tell ourselves that that sort of integrity is rewarded by society with success, and the celebrity it often brings, while the individual himself gains an inner satisfaction that derives from a job well done, a cause well served, a life well lived. Over the years, Gregory Peck has given both of his talents and of himself. And those rewards have been justly his, earned in a body of work deserving of our attention both for what it is and for what it represents.

A screen actor's life is in his pictures and it is that professional life of Gregory Peck with which we are primarily concerned in this survey; a personal biography of wider scope is left to others in another time and place. Even a professional biography, however, needs some background, some sense of origins, of what has gone into the man himself, of his own early experiences and aspirations which have inevitably molded his on- and off-screen character.

Eldred Gregory Peck was born to Gregory and Bernice Peck on April 5, 1916, in La Jolla, a gem of a beach village on the southern California coast near San Diego. His parents were divorced when young Greg was six years old and he was subsequently raised by his father and grandparents, attending La Jolla's Little Red Schoolhouse for his elementary education and completing his secondary school studies at San Diego High School and St. John's Military Academy in Los Angeles.

Gregory Peck, age 14 months, with mother and father, 1917.

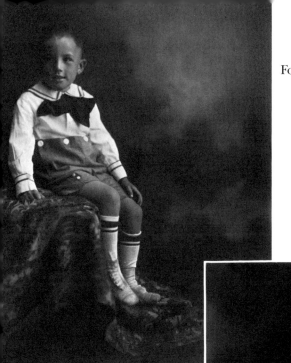

Four years old.

With mother and grandmother o[n]
an outing to Catalina Island, circ[a]
1924.

Nine years old, 1926.

As a student at St. John's Military
Academy, Los Angeles, 1930.

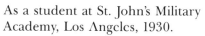
Member of St. John's baseball team, 1929.

Building a boat with boyhood friend
Johnny Buchanan, La Jolla, 1925.

Fourteen years old, with his dad.

Student at Berkeley, 1937.

As might be expected of a lad growing up in a seacoast town, Greg's earliest yearning was to become a boat builder and sailor. When he was nine, he single-handedly built a 12-foot sailboat which he dubbed *The Daisy*. Greg's maritime career was short-lived: two days after she was launched into the Pacific, *The Daisy* began taking on water and went rapidly to the bottom, leaving the young nautical engineer to swim to shore, where he was treated for exposure and the blistered hands that were the legacy of his labors.

The would-be seaman was so impressed by the kind and gentle doctor who tended his wounds that he decided then and there to forsake the sea for a career in medicine. Greg's father, a pharmacist, must have been pleased with his son's revised vocational intentions.

From high school, Greg went to San Diego State College for a year and, after a stint of oil-truck driving to earn tuition in between, transferred to the University of California at Berkeley, enrolling in its pre-med program. There, he also found an outlet for his athletic abilities and his interest in boating as well by becoming a member of the university's rowing team, with whom he distinguished himself as an oarsman.

It was, in fact, his rowing abilities that brought Greg on his first trip to New York, in 1928, when the Berkeley crew was invited to participate in the Poughkeepsie Regatta. The Berkeley team lost the race, but Greg discovered New York City, from the swinging Jazz

clubs of Harlem to the stone towers of the Brooklyn Bridge; saw his first Broadway play, *I Married an Angel*, at the Sam S. Shubert Theater, and found an interest in dramatics taking hold. When he returned to Berkeley, where he'd already discovered his interest in literature and switched his major from medicine to English, he joined the little theater group and decided to explore and develop his dramatic talents.

During this period, a spinal injury put an early end to Peck's athletic activities and his concentration became focused more and more on acting. Later, during his early days in Hollywood, some glamor-minded press agent had the idea of ascribing Greg's back problem to a rowing injury, but the actor has steadfastly maintained that the true story was much more prosaic: He was attempting a difficult stretching exercise in a dance class when the instructor, trying to be helpful, shoved her knee into his back. It helped at the time, but the next morning Greg found that he couldn't move. He spent a lot of time thereafter with osteopaths and other specialists who attempted to undo the damage.

The spinal injury also relegated Greg to a 4-F draft status, which turned out to be the silver lining of the affair, for he was later to arrive in Hollywood at the height of the wartime shortage of leading men, when the studios were frantically searching for draft-exempt, good-looking males to fill vacancies in the acting ranks left by the stars who were off

13

New York modelling job as telephone linesman for New Jersey Edison Company. Pay was $25 per day—not bad for 1939.

of a wooden bowl! Step this way folks!"

Greg alternated his spiel with another pitchman every half hour and the two of them worked until each had put in eight hours a day. According to reports, when he started out at the fair, Greg's voice was somewhat high-pitched; after a month he had a voice like a gravel mixer. The experience with his spinal injury was enough to make him acutely aware of the possibility of doing his voice permanent damage by the constant shouting, however, and for the sake of his vocal cords Peck applied for a job as a tour guide at Radio City in Rockefeller Center. He got the job and saved his voice but within a few weeks began to fear for his arches.

While at Radio City, Peck auditioned for and won a two-year scholarship to the neighborhood Playhouse School of Dramatics, one of New York's most renowned drama schools. At the Playhouse School, he studied the Stanislavsky method of acting and honed his talents under the guidance and inspiration of Rita Morganthau and Irene Lewishohn, the school's founders, and their associates Sanford Meisner and Martha Graham. Between semesters, Peck also won a scholarship to Robert Porterfield's famous Barter Theater at Abingdon, Virginia, for the summer of 1940.

An item in the June 1, 1940, *New York Times* reported that, "Carrying out the terms of her Barter Theater award, Dorothy Stickney yesterday selected two young actors, Gregory Peck and Evelyn Fargo, who will work with the Barter Theater this summer...."

Greg returned for his second term at the Neighborhood Playhouse that fall. During the term, his potential was recognized by Katharine Brown, movie-producer David O. Selznick's eastern representative. Miss Brown arranged to have him screen-tested for Selznick's consideration. Unfortunately the producer was not impressed with the results and Peck was not offered a contract.

At its commencement program in the spring of 1941, the Playhouse School held a final exercise for its graduating students and

on military service. For Peck, however, the road to Hollywood took a circuitous route via New York and the Broadway stage.

At U.C., the young actor had begun to shape his acting talents under the tutelage of Edwin Duerr. While appearing as Mat Burke in a university production of Eugene O'Neill's *Anna Christie*, Greg was spotted by George Marion, the actor who had played Chris, Anna's father, in the original New York production of the 1922 Pulitzer Prize winner. After the play, Marion talked to the aspiring college actor and encouraged him to pursue his career in the East, to aim for Broadway.

With that goal, Peck set out for New York in 1939. His step-father had provided him with a letter of introduction to a business acquaintance in the city and through it Greg was able to land a job—a show-business job of sorts—as a barker at a New York World's Fair concession. Located in the fair's amusement zone, the concession was an auto race where cars moved at terrifyingly high speeds around the inside of a gigantic wooden bowl, employing centrifugal force in defiance of gravity. The barker's job was to lure fairgoers to the ride; his "bark" went something like, "Step this way to the Auto Ride! Defy the laws of gravity in a car speeding like a bullet around the rim

Rehearsing Emlyn Williams's *The Morning Star* with Gladys Cooper, Guthrie McClintic directing, Morosco Theater, 1941.

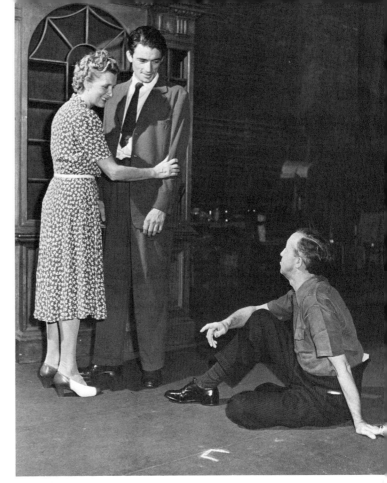

invited members of the New York theater establishment to attend. In the program, Gregory Peck read the Prologue and Epilogue to *Promenade*. Among the audience that day was famed Broadway producer Guthrie McClintic. McClintic was looking for a fresh young face for a small replacement part in *The Doctor's Dilemma*, a George Bernard Shaw play which he had produced in New York, starring his wife, actress Katharine Cornell. The play was to go on national tour in the fall.

The day after commencement, Greg was standing around near the school receptionist's desk when a phone call came in for the school director. The caller was Mr. McClintic.

"It's about you, Greg," said the receptionist, who apparently had overheard part of the conversation. McClintic was interested in engaging Peck for the tour.

"And that's all I needed to know," says Peck, recounting the event years later. "I took off—I knew where his office was—I took off, ran down four flights, ran half a block across 46th Street to Sixth Avenue. I ran four blocks up Sixth Avenue to 50th Street, plunged into the RKO building, there was an open elevator, pushed the button for the eighth floor, rocketed up there, walked through his door.

"His inner office was open and I walked right in...he was still talking to her and he dropped the phone and fell on the floor. And when he recovered, he said, 'You've got yourself a job.'"

The job amounted to eight lines in the third act of Shaw's light satire on the medical profession. Peck was to take over the role from David Orrick, who had opened in the Broadway production at, coincidentally, the Sam S. Shubert Theater where Greg had seen his first Broadway show. The play was to begin its national tour at the National Theater in Washington on September 22, 1941.

After four months on the road, *The Doctor's Dilemma* wound up its run at the Curran Theater in San Francisco in December. During the tour, Greg met and fell in love with Greta Rice, Miss Cornell's hairdresser. They were married in October 1942. It was typical of Greg's well-known disdain for pretentious press-agentry that a couple of years later in Hollywood he corrected a studio biography's assertion that Greta had been Miss Cornell's "secretary" by insisting, "She was her hairdresser...and a darn good hairdresser, too."

Peck was detoured off the road to Broadway by the folding out of town of his next vehicle, McClintic's production *Punch and Judy*, and spent the summer of '42 at the Cape Cod Playhouse in Dennis, Massachusetts. One day he received a call from McClintic, inviting him to visit the producer's house on Martha's Vineyard to discuss a new project.

When Greg arrived, McClintic handed him the script of British playwright Emlyn Williams's *The Morning Star*, which he intended to produce for American audiences. On the boards, the play itself met with mixed critical notices, but Peck was singled out by almost all of the critics as not only a good actor but "a new matinee idol." Even so, the play lasted for only 24 performances.

The Willow and I, Greg's next engagement,

which again garnered him good personal notices, ran but 28 performances. Although the young actor found himself out of work again sooner than he had expected, he was nevertheless steadily building a reputation as a credible and talented performer. Within a few months he was not only signed for another role but for one which would finally put his name on a theater's marquee with the play's title. Again, however, the long run proved elusive.

Irwin Shaw's *Sons and Soldiers* was the sort of drama that needed almost unanimous critical approval in order to attract sufficient audience to the Morosco Theater; when the unanimity was not forthcoming, neither were the ticket buyers. The show closed after 22 performances but Greg's luck took a good turn as a result.

Hollywood producer Casey Robinson, who had seen Peck earlier in *The Morning Star*, had meanwhile decided that he wanted the young actor to star in *Days of Glory*, a movie he

was producing which would also feature the screen dramatic debut of his own fiancée, ballerina Tamara Toumanova.

Although Greg's inclination was to remain in New York and continue to work on the legitimate stage, he found the thousand-dollar-a-week deal Robinson offered him difficult to refuse. It certainly seemed like a lot of money next to the $400 weekly salary he had been drawing at the Morosco, and, says Peck, "I thought *that* was a hell of a lot of money!"

Like many youngsters just starting out, Greg and Greta had just been squeaking by in New York and he had a few debts he wanted to pay off; with the end of the Broadway season also near at hand, ten weeks in Hollywood at those rates didn't seem at all like a bad idea. And the prospect of becoming a movie star undoubtedly carried a certain appeal of its own. Still, Greg's intention was to do the picture and return to New York. But fate intervened and, as far as anyone has been able to determine, Gregory Peck wound up becoming the first actor to begin his Hollywood career under contract to four studios: RKO (via Casey Robinson), 20th Century-Fox, The Selznick Studios and Metro-Goldwyn-Mayer. And for 16 pictures!

How did this happen to someone whose professed first love was theater, who had intended to make one picture and return to New York?

There were, according to Peck, two reasons why he stayed in Hollywood: "One was that I saw the rough cut of *Days of Glory* and I knew enough to know that the picture was bad. But I was intrigued by movies and I was reluctant to go back with one bad picture on the record."

Being associated with a bad picture and it being his only one, Peck felt, might prevent him from getting offers for others. His worries proved groundless.

"At the same time, Darryl Zanuck was offering me *The Keys of the Kingdom*. I'd loved the novel but in order for me to do it he

As *The Playboy of the Western World* at the Cape Cod Playhouse, Dennis, Mass., 1946. The girl is Beatrice Straight.

wanted me to sign for three additional pictures, one a year. After a lot of soul-searching, I decided to do that. The part in *The Keys of the Kingdom* and the story appealed to me more than anything that was being offered on the stage. So I stayed out there and now I was signed for four pictures with Fox.

"Meanwhile, Selznick got interested in me..." and in short order Peck found himself, courtesy of smart agentry on the part of Leland Hayward, signed with Selznick and with MGM for four pictures each, too. Hayward also counseled Peck that if he would take parts with three or four of the great screen leading ladies of the day, by the time he had made a half-dozen pictures he'd be known to *their* audiences all around the world.

"That sort of made some sense from his point of view," recalls Peck, "and I was getting more and more intrigued with movies. So it ended up with my being signed for sixteen pictures and I worked my way through them

one after another. And I was with Ingrid Bergman, Greer Garson, Ava Gardner, Jennifer Jones—all the top ladies of the Forties."

Hayward's ploy was indeed extremely successful for Peck: By October 1944, even before the release of *The Keys of the Kingdom*, Hedda Hopper reported in her "On Hollywood" newspaper column that, "Gregory Peck is the hottest thing in town. Some say he is a second Gary Cooper. Actually he's the first Gregory Peck."

Greg told Hedda that, among actors, he had great admiration for Edmund Gwenn, Barry Fitzgerald, Jimmy Cagney and Humphrey Bogart, as well as for Ingrid Bergman, Claudette Colbert and Teresa Wright. Having worked with Miss Bergman in *Spellbound*, he particularly admired her professionalism and lack of temperament on the set, noting that she "just goes into a scene and does a wonderful job without any fuss."

When Greg and Greta Peck arrived in

With Spencer Tracy and Father Jim Deasy, Phoenix, 1946.

With Hitchcock and Ingrid Bergman, contemplating some aspect of *Spellbound*, 1945.

Hollywood, they ran smack into the wartime housing shortage and wound up camping out in the Monterey Auto Court for several months while house-hunting. They finally located a comfortable house on a Hollywood hilltop. On July 20, 1944, their first son, Jonathan, was born. Greg and Greta later had two more sons, Stephen, born August 16, 1946, and Carey Paul, born June 17, 1949.

One proviso Greg insisted on in his studio contracts was that he be allowed some time off from film work to return to work in the theater in the East. He felt that a film actor, to keep in top form, needed the challenge the stage provided in bringing him into direct contact with a live audience.

In the summer of 1946, he journeyed back across country to the Cape Playhouse where he'd worked four years earlier. In part, it was Peck's gratitude for the earlier training he's received there under director Arthur Sircom that inspired his return as a highly publicized guest star. He was also drawn by the opportunity to play Christy Mahon in the title role of J.M. Synge's sardonic comedy, *Playboy of the Western World*, about a shy youth's development into a self-assured young man. Peck chose the classic Irish play for his vehicle especially because of the challenges it presented. For his trouble in struggling with an Irish brogue and Synge's poetic dialogue, however, Peck found himself the recipient of a

few less than approving words from some of the critics in attendance; but he was undaunted in the face of the negative criticism and took it all philosophically:

"I stuck my neck out and that's what happened," he told an interviewer. "I don't really care, though. I got what I came for. I wanted to try something I hadn't done before. I did. And I feel better for it and I think I'll go back to Hollywood and do better work because of it.... I think it's good to do things the hard way once in a while."

Returning to Hollywood, Greg carried his theatrical interests with him and he and his fellow performers Dorothy McGuire, Mel Ferrer, Jennifer Jones and Joseph Cotten founded the La Jolla Playhouse, through which they hoped to keep their feel for live-theater performing in full vigor while pursuing their careers in front of the cameras. From 1947 to 1952 the group produced ten plays in La Jolla every summer and each of them made at least one appearance during each season. They soon found that other Hollywood actors were interested in working at their playhouse, too.

"A lot of them come to us offering their services," Peck remarked to a reporter. "They realize it's a good chance to be seen and to gain experience with experienced casts and capable directors."

If Peck was fortunate in being able from

18

the outset to appear opposite some of the leading ladies of the time when he came to Hollywood, he was doubly fortunate in being able to work with some of the top directors; Clarence Brown, Alfred Hitchcock, Elia Kazan, Zoltan Korda, King Vidor, Raoul Walsh, William Wellman and William Wyler, among others. But it was his relationship with Henry King that early on meant the most to Peck, in both professional and personal aspects, and it is one which both men continued to cherish until King's death in 1982.

King guided Peck first through *Twelve O'Clock High* and then *The Gunfighter* and on through four more features. Working with Henry King was, for Peck, "a special relationship. He provided me with a one-man audience in whom I had complete trust. I think it was because of the kind of man he was, because I admired him so, because I wanted him to like what I did. And that was the best kind of direction. He was my kind of man. If I played to him and he liked it, then I was fairly confident I was on the right track. That can't be said of all directors."

Peck also counts himself fortunate to have been able to work for such producers as Darryl Zanuck, David O. Selznick, Nunnally Johnson, Sidney Franklin and Casey Robinson— and a good many others whom he admires.

As with any career, even the most successful, there are always those roles that one turns down and later regrets having done so. And there is always the concern about becoming stereotyped as an actor—in the eyes of both producers and the public. His roles in *Duel in the Sun*, *Yellow Sky* and *The Gunfighter* had led to Peck's being cited by exhibitors as "Cowboy Star of the Year" in 1950 and he began to worry about falling into the Western rut. So when another Western part was offered to him soon after, Greg declined it—but Gary Cooper took the job in *High Noon* and won the 1952 Best Actor Oscar for his performance.

Greg's departure from a 1959 project by producer Jerry Wald stirred up a considerable amount of movieland gossip. The picture's title was to be *The Billionaire* and Peck's co-star was to be Marilyn Monroe (both of them were hot box-office properties at the time). But on November 18, 1959, it was announced that

With director Lewis Milestone, discussing a sequence they're about to shoot for *Pork Chop Hill*.

Arriving at Cannes Film Festival, 1963, with Veronique and Alan Pakula.

With Fred Zinneman (*Behold a Pale Horse*).

With Stanley Donen in England for *Arabesque*, 1966.

Greg and Marilyn were not fated to be screen lovers after all; they had come to a parting of the cinematic ways even before the show had started.

The picture was to be made from an original script by Norman Krasna. Greg had been studying the script as well as learning to sing and dance for his part opposite Marilyn, when she, her husband Arthur Miller and her drama coach Paula Strasberg arrived in Hollywood to prepare for the production. Suddenly, Peck was leaving the picture.

According to gossip columnists, the problem was that, after everything had been set, script changes were abruptly being made at the request of Miss Monroe and her advisers Miller and Strasberg. Gossips also claimed that the changes were to her role's advantage and to Peck's loss. Although Wald denied that any important script revisions were being made, he did admit that "we are deepening the character a little for Marilyn and…writing in some special parts for others.…"

Peck and his press agent denied that he was dropping out of the picture because Marilyn's role was being fattened. The actor and 20th Century-Fox had agreed, said a spokesman, that he should be liberated from his contract because delays on the picture, which now appeared likely, would make it impossible for him to fulfill a previous commitment to appear in *The Guns of Navarone*, which was scheduled to begin filming in the Greek Isles in early 1960.

Peck had been so desirous of making the Monroe movie that, he noted personally, he had even learned to "croak" three songs and had taken tap-dancing lessons for his role. "Maybe I'll be able to do the dance some day at an actor's benefit," he observed.

As matters were resolved, French star Yves Montand assumed the Peck part and the picture, released as *Let's Make Love* in 1960, was the next-to-last in Miss Monroe's career.

Other projects also failed to jell: After their successful work together on *To Kill a Mockingbird* in 1962, Alan Pakula, Robert

Discussing a scene for *MacArthur* with director Joseph Sargent.

To Veronique and Gregory Peck — who added such beauty and talent to this dinner at the White House. with warm appreciation — Lady Bird Johnson   *[signature]*

At White House dinner with President Johnson and Vice-President Hubert H. Humphrey and wives, 1965.

Mulligan and Peck decided in 1965 to produce Ray Bradbury's celebrated science-fiction opus *The Martian Chronicles*, but a script couldn't be worked out to everyone's satisfaction and the picture was shelved and ultimately dropped.

Greg had experienced disruption in his personal life, too. A successful career can exact just as much of a toll on an actor's family and private life as an unsuccessful one, and, like many Hollywood first marriages, Gregory and Greta Peck's didn't survive the inevitable pressures to which it was subjected. They were divorced in 1954 and in December 1955 Greg married Veronique Passani, a beautiful French newspaper writer whom he had met in Paris in 1952. In October 1956, their son, Anthony, was born and a daughter, Cecilia, was born in May 1958.

Over the years of his career, Gregory Peck has devoted, often quietly and without much public notice, a great deal of his time and energy away from the cameras and sound-stages and locations to a wide range of charitable and humanitarian activities.

Though Greg has never sought public recognition for the good works in which he's been involved, by the 1960s he began to receive it anyway. In appreciation of his work on behalf of President John F. Kennedy's "New Frontier" programs, Greg and Veronique were invited to a White House luncheon scheduled for December 1963. Ironically, their invitation, postmarked in Washington on November 21, reached them the day after President Kennedy had been assassinated in Dallas, Texas. Later, Peck was chosen by the United States Information Agency to narrate *John F. Kennedy: Years of Lightning, Day of Drums*, a hauntingly beautiful and moving documentary tribute to the late president's life and his administration.

In 1964, President Lyndon B. Johnson, Kennedy's successor, appointed Greg to membership on the newly formed National Council

At the White House with American Cancer Society poster girl Julie Alice Dillard and President Lyndon B. Johnson, 1966.

With Robert F. Kennedy, who visited set of *Mackenna's Gold* while campaigning in Arizona, 1967.

on the Arts for a two-year term, during which he traveled about the country to promote regional theater programs. And in the White House Rose Garden on a summer afternoon in 1965, Peck stood only a few feet away from President Johnson, who had invited him to witness the ceremony affixing the presidential signature on the Arts and Humanities Act of 1965, which made the United States government, for the first time in history, an official patron of the arts. Reappointed to the National Council, Greg continued to serve tirelessly and without monetary compensation.

Peck undertook another commitment in 1964 when his friends and fellow actors William Lundigan and William Gargan, both cancer victims, persuaded him to accept the role of California Chairman for the American Cancer Society's statewide fund-raising activities. The reserved actor was reluctant at first, unsure of what he could contribute, but when he saw how his presence attracted throngs to rallies and was told by other volunteers how much he inspired them, he decided to devote as much time to the cause as he could. And when he was asked the next year to serve as National Chairman of the Cancer Crusade for 1966, he needed no coaxing, even though taking the job meant giving up his filmmaking activities for a considerable period of time. It turned out to be, he told friends, "the most rewarding work I've ever done."

From 1967 to 1970, Gregory Peck served as president of the Academy of Motion Picture Arts and Sciences, the organization founded by members of the industry in 1927 to raise the "cultural, educational and scientific standards" of film production. The Academy is most widely known, of course, as the presenter of awards, the Oscars, for achievements in filmmaking, but the Academy Awards are only the most readily visible aspect of Academy activities, which range from encouraging student filmmakers through various programs and competitions to operating a first-rate library and archives, where film history is preserved and filmmakers and scholars may study and conduct research. The Academy is also involved in various philanthropic and other works which benefit the film industry and the community at large.

The Academy presidency is an office of considerable prestige in Hollywood and elec-

Discussing *Guns of Navarone* with Queen Frederica of Greece on the island of Rhodes, 1960. Veronique looks on.

With Maurice Chevelier, Hope Lange and French Ambassador Herve Alphand, at the French Embassy, Washington, D.C., 1966.

tion to it is an indication of the high regard in which Academy members hold those called to serve. In addition to being its president, Gregory Peck has also served on the Academy's Board of Governors, the organization's directorate. But it was during his presidental tenure that the Oscar presentation ceremony, an internationally televised and highly attended event, was postponed for the only time in its history, from Monday, April 8, 1968, to Wednesday, April 10, in tribute to the memory of slain civil rights leader Dr. Martin Luther King, Jr., whose funeral was held on the afternoon of the 8th in Atlanta.

Greg was also a founder and first chairman of the board of the American Film Institute and continues to serve as one of its trustees.

Peck's additional contributions to the film industry include having served as chairman of the Motion Picture and Television Relief Fund Building and Endowment Campaign in 1966, to promote the care and housing of the industry's senior citizens, and as producer of the 50th Anniversary Gala of the Fund at the Los Angeles Music Center in June 1971. He has also served as a director of Los Angeles Public Broadcasting System affiliate station KCET-TV, of the Center Theater Group of Los Angeles, of the Salk Institute for medical research and of Capitol Industries, Inc.

Gregory Peck was nominated for a Best

With Goldie Hawn and Earl Mountbatten in London.

At mother's 75th birthday, Monte Carlo, 1969.

With Sophia Loren, with whom he was soon to be co-starred, after being presented with the Best Actor Oscar for 1962.

Actor Oscar four times (for *The Keys of the Kingom*, *The Yearling*, *Gentleman's Agreement* and *Twelve O'Clock High*) before winning on his fifth nomination, for *To Kill a Mockingbird*, in 1962. In 1968, the Academy board of governors honored Peck by bestowing upon him its prized Jean Hersholt Humanitarian Award for his distinguished community service, another indication of the esteem in which he is

The Gregory Pecks with George Burns and Mary Livingston (Mrs. Jack Benny) at March of Dimes dinner in honor of Jack Benny, 1978.

With fellow Oscar winners Patty Duke, Joan Crawford (accepting for Anne Bancroft) and Ed Begley, 1962.

held by fellow workers in the film industry.

In 1974, the USA Film Festival, in its fifth year as the only major festival in the world to celebrate exclusively American motion pictures, held its first "Great American Actor Retrospective," the beginning of an annual series designed to honor actors and actresses "whose large, varied and distinguished bodies of work have exhibited the genius of American film." As their first "Great Actor," the Festival's directors chose Gregory Peck, who traveled to Dallas, site of the festival, to appear in conjunction with a weekend-long retrospective showing of six of his films.

With Groucho Marx, 1966.

Presenting Scopus Award to Frank Sinatra and wife, 1978. Note *MacArthur* haircut.

The Gregory Pecks with Shirley MacLaine, Paul Newman and Bob Hope.

Peck himself selected the pictures which he thought provided a good cross-section of his career: *Twelve O'Clock High*, *Yellow Sky*, *Roman Holiday*, *The Gunfighter*, *Captain Horatio Hornblower* and *To Kill a Mockingbird*. Introducing them to the audience, he also commented: "I think I've inadvertently selected a sort of cross-section of the work of some of the great American directors." And indeed he had.

In his producer's hat and with his own still camera handy, Gregory Peck surveys a location for *The Dove*, the fact-based National Geographic adventure story of a lad who sets out to sail solo around the world.

Greg Peck's magnitude as a movie star is no less outside the boundaries of the United States; he is an internationally popular performer. During the Dallas retrospective he shared an anecdote about his worldwide following:

"I was in an Italian studio in Rome and walking by the dubbing room when I heard

With Laurence Olivier in Vienna during making of *The Boys from Brazil*, 1978.

25

Gregory Peck, family man, with Anthony, Paris, 1962.

With Veronique and Anthony (then four), Cecilia (two), and Stephen (14), La Turbie, France, 1960.

Daughter Cecilia focuses on stranger, Lisbon, 1978.

Clowning with daughter Cecilia, London, 1966.

Campaigning for Carey in Venice, California, 1978. Seated next to the candidate are Lillian Carter, Garson Kanin and Ruth Gordon.

the sound of my own voice, so I opened the door and peeked in. There was an Italian actor standing in front of a screen doing me in Italian. They'd play it in English first, then cut out my voice and he'd match lips with the Italian dialogue."

Peck stayed around and after the dubbing session the Italian was delighted to meet him. But he mystified Greg with an unusual interest in the American actor's health, asking, "Are you in good health? Do you stay in good shape? You exercise?"

Finally, Peck asked him, "What is all this interest in my health?"

"Well," replied the fellow actor, "I've dubbed your voice in 24 movies and I've raised five children doing your voice and I hope I'm going to go on doing it for a long time."

Peck laughed and promised his concerned new friend that he would do his best to stay in good shape and that, in fact, he would be even more inspired to take better care of himself than ever before, knowing that another family depended on him too.

A complete list of Gregory Peck's achievements and good works would run on and on, but perhaps the best summation of his career and life is found in the citation that accompanied an award he received personally from President Johnson on his last day in office in 1969.

The award was the coveted President's Medal of Freedom, the highest civilian award the United States bestows. President Johnson's citation read:

"An artist who has brought new dignity to the acting profession, Gregory Peck has enriched the lives of millions. He has given his energies, his talents and his devotion to causes which have improved the lives of people. He is an humanitarian to whom Americans are deeply indebted."

Dancing with Cecilia at the closing party for *Mockingbird*, 1962.

Gregory Peck, *bon vivant* and man of the world, with Veronique and the David Nivens at Ascot, 1960....

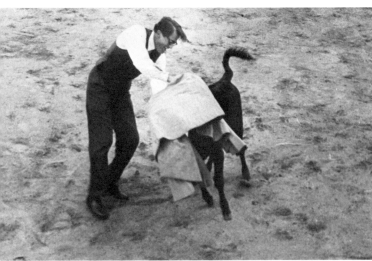

Strolling unrecognized through the Flea Market, Paris, 1963....

Testing the young bulls, Madrid, 1954....

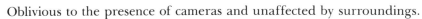

Oblivious to the presence of cameras and unaffected by surroundings.

The Films of
GREGORY PECK

With Claude Jarman, Jr., at his left elbow, Gregory Peck describes the courageous
deeds of a dog he hopes to sell, as neighbors Margaret Wycherly, Clem Bevans,
Donn Gift, Forrest Tucker and others pay rapt attention. A beautifully composed
shot from *The Yearling*.

Soviet partisans Lowell Gilmore, Tamara Toumanova, Hugo Haas and Gregory Peck share a meager meal in the hideout from which they launch their forays against the Nazi forces who constantly threaten their existence.

Days of Glory

RKO Radio Pictures   **1944**

Cast

Gregory Peck (Vladimir), Tamara Toumanova (Nina), Alan Reed (Sasha), Maria Palmer (Yelena), Lowell Gilmore (Semyon), Hugo Haas (Fedor), Dena Penn (Olga), Glenn Vernon (Mitya), Igor Dolgoruki (Dmitri), Edward L. Durst (Petrov), Lou Crosby (Johann Staub), William Challee (Duchenko), Joseph Vitale (Seminov), Erford Gage (Colonel Prilenko), Ivan Triesault (German Lieutenant), Maria Bibikov (Vera), Edward Licho (Anton), Gretl Dupont (Mariya), Peter Helmers (Von Rundholz).

Credits

Producer, Casey Robinson; *director*, Jacques Tourneur; *screenplay*, Casey Robinson, based on a story by Melchior Lengyel; *music*, Daniele Amfitheatrof; *cinematography*, Tony Gaudio; *editor*, Joseph Noriega; *production design*, Mordecai Gorelik; *art directors*, Albert S. D'Agostino, Carroll Clark; *set decoration*, Darrell Silvera, Harley Miller; *makeup*, Mel Berns; *special effects*, Vernon L. Walker; *assistant director*, William Dorfman. (86 minutes)

30

"It has always been considered daring to cast an important picture with newcomers to the screen," began an RKO press release dated May 26, 1944, "but *Days of Glory* will introduce no fewer than eleven new faces...."

Screenwriter-producer Casey Robinson was one who dared. Mindful of the failures and half-successes of others, Robinson determined to make his own picture of the harrowing, valiant resistance of the Russian people against the Nazi military machine which invaded their homeland in 1941 as realistic as possible. One way he could achieve this, he felt, was by going outside Hollywood to cast the film, finding fresh faces who would be unknown to American moviegoers, rather than using familiar Hollywood actors.

An extensive talent search was launched, in the course of which the diligent producer scouted Broadway and the New York theater scene for new talent. There he remembered seeing Gregory Peck, a young handsome actor playing opposite Gladys Cooper in Emlyn Williams's *The Morning Star*. Robinson now thought that Peck would be perfect as Vladimir, leader of a Russian resistance group—and the picture's male lead.

As female lead, famed prima ballerina Tamara Toumanova was persuaded to take a sabbatical from the Ballet Russe de Monte Carlo to portray Nina, a famous dancer from Moscow who becomes stranded behind Nazi lines and falls in love with the valiant partisan played by Peck.

Presumably to lend the production a stamp of quality and, it must be conceded, only befitting their stature as former inhabitants of the worlds of the legitimate theater and of dance, the leads were billed as "Mr. Gregory Peck" and "Miss Tamara Toumanova," an uncommon, though not unheard of, advertising ploy.

"It embarrassed me, really, to be given all the reverence due a great star of the theater, which I was not," Peck recalled years later. "That's the one and only time I ever got that billing."

As his director, Robinson chose Jacques Tourneur, son of the French director Maurice Tourneur whose silent films made in America

Stranded overnight in the woods after dynamiting a Nazi ammunition train, valiant partisans Gregory Peck and Tamara Toumanova discover their love for each other, a discovery which leads to the soon-to-be matinee idol's first on-screen kiss.

Gregory Peck interrogates Lou Crosby, playing a hapless Nazi soldier who wanders into the guerrillas' hideway, as Lowell Gilmore, Edward Durst, Hugo Haas and Alan Reed look on.

included *The Last of the Mohicans* and *Treasure Island*, both released in 1920. Jacques' own previous films included *Nick Carter, Master Detective* (1939), made at MGM, and the highly praised *Cat People* (1942) and *The Leopard Man* (1943), both among a series of low-budget but high-quality imaginative thrillers produced at RKO by Val Lewton.

When filming on *Days of Glory* commenced, Peck found that some of his theatrical habits and training did not mesh neatly with motion-picture technique. In the beginning, he had some difficulty making the transition from theatrical stage to soundstage.

"I'd just come from a lot of work in the theater ... had had a stage director who was a taskmaster. Guthrie McClintic used to listen to rehearsals from the rear of the balcony and wouldn't let an actor finish a sentence if he couldn't hear every syllable of every word."

"Can't understand it! Do it again! They pay to sit up here, too!" McClintic would shout down to his actors on stage.

Peck carried his stagecraft with him to Hollywood, but this theatrical style of projection was uncalled for there and director Tourneur worked to overcome the neophyte film actor's tendency to speak as if he had to be heard in the farthest reaches of the balcony.

"Greg," he'd say, "the microphone's right above your nose. It's two and a half feet from you just off camera range. Why are you shouting so? Common it up! Don't project!"

With Toumanova, accustomed primarily to performing just in terms of movement, the problem was exactly the opposite and Tourneur had to work constantly to get her to project and speak above a whisper.

Peck made the most of this direction, however, and found Tourneur a positive influence on a newcomer to motion-picture acting. "He was," says the actor, "a good teacher."

The performers adapted quickly to the demands of film-acting, and subsequently the production moved along in normal fashion, although one non-actor did disrupt the proceedings briefly: Toumanova had a miniature French poodle, Bella, who accompanied her to the set every day. The normally amiable pet became the company mascot and was a popular bystander with the crew until one day when she became hysterical with jealousy while watching her mistress and Greg enact a love scene. Shooting had to be halted while Bella was calmed and thereafter she stayed behind at home when Toumanova went to the studio.

Filming was completed, post-production work finished and the picture was readied for release on June 16, 1944, with RKO's press department stressing its neo-realistic approach. In the eyes of some beholders, though, Robinson's realism was strictly ersatz.

New York Daily News critic Kate Cameron, for example, attacked the film as "a bit of theatrical tripe that bears scant resemblance to the Russian films which have shown the Soviet's partisans in action...."

And while acknowledging some good action footage in general, critics complained about too much conversation among the guerrillas and too much lovemaking by the principals. Cameron further commented: "Love is beginning to take its place in the Soviet cinematic scheme, but that place is not yet on the front line...."

Archer Winsten, in the *New York Post*, reported that "during periods of fighting the action is commendably violent ... presented with a fair amount of realism and a fine volume of sound...."

Almost unanimously, the critics felt that Robinson the producer should have restrained Robinson the writer. Winsten also noted that "there is an ever-present danger when a successful writer of screenplays becomes a producer too. ... The guerrillas either talk themselves out of character or into an unlikely one ... the picture seems not to have been edited scarcely enough...."

In the *New York Herald Tribune*, Howard Barnes remarked, "The writing is eloquent, but it has too many purple passages about heroism, music, poetry and death...."

Giving the film perhaps its most favorable notice, Barnes went on to say, "The so-called new faces are a definite asset ... the picture has heart and artistry. ... Tourneur has staged both the talk and the doings ... with imagination and considerable force. ... The Hollywood touches are rarely offensive. ... Toumanova reveals herself as a fine actress. ... Peck is excellent. ... The picture has more than a little quality...."

Bosley Crowther, *The New York Times* critic, didn't exactly agree: "Robinson ... has tried something artful but daring. ... But less credit to him for loading his characters with dialogue rather than stirring deeds. ... Gregory Peck comes recommended with a Gary Cooper angularity and a face somewhat like that modest gentleman's, but his acting is equally stiff. ... Robinson has failed to provide a first-class script. ... Tourneur ... failed to make the best of what he had. As consequence, *Days of Glory* is more heroic in conception than effect."

Mr. Crowther's words about the overall effect of the picture were indeed perspicacious and the moviegoing public tended to agree with his assessment. *Days of Glory* garnered more yawns than applause. But other critics were perceptive too: John T. McManus wrote in *PM* that "Gregory Peck ... looks like a sure heart-throb for the postwar world...." And Kate Cameron forecast that "Peck ... is destined for screen stardom providing his next vehicle is an improvement on his first...."

In fact, his next vehicle netted Gregory Peck an Oscar nomination and established him firmly as a star.

Neophyte film actors Tamara Toumanova and Gregory Peck, as a Russian ballerina and a Soviet resistance fighter who fall in love in Nazi-occupied territory, were billed as stars in their very first movie roles.

The Keys of the Kingdom

20th Century-Fox   **1944**

Credits

Producer, Joseph L. Mankiewicz; *director*, John M. Stahl; *screenplay*, Joseph L. Mankiewicz, Nunnally Johnson, based on the novel by A.J. Cronin; *music*, Alfred Newman; *cinematography*, Arthur Miller; *editor*, James B. Clark; *special effects*, Fred Sersen; *art directors*, James Basevi and William Darling. (137 minutes)

Cast

Gregory Peck (Father Francis Chisholm), Thomas Mitchell (Dr. Willie Tullock), Vincent Price (Rev. Angus Mealy), Rosa Stradner (Mother Maria Veronica), Roddy McDowall (Francis as a boy), Edmund Gwenn (Rev. Hamish MacNabb), Sir Cedric Hardwicke (Monsignor Sleeth), Peggy Ann Garner (Nora as a child), Jane Ball (Nora), James Gleason (Dr. Wilbur Fiske), Anne Revere (Agnes Fiske), Ruth Nelson (Lisbeth Chisholm), Benson Fong (Joseph), Leonard Strong (Mr. Chia), Philip Ahn (Mr. Pao), Arthur Shields (Father Tarrant), Edith Barrett (Aunt Polly), Sara Allgood (Sister Martha), Richard Loo (Lt. Shon), Ruth Ford (Sister Clotilde), Kevin O'Shea (Father Craig), H.T. Tsiang (Hosannah Wang), Si-Lan Chen (Philomena Wang), Eunice Soo Hoo (Anna), Dennis Hoey (Alex Chisholm), Abner Biberman (Bandit Captain), J. Anthony Hughes (Ned Bannon), George Nokes (Andrew), Hayward Soo Hoo (Chia-Yu), James Leong (Taoist Priest), Moy Ming (Chinese Physician), Frank Eng (Father Chou), Oie Chan (Grandmother), Beal Wong (Captain), Eugene Louie (Joshua), Ruth Clifford (Sister Mercy Mary).

In September 1943 Darryl F. Zanuck, production chief at 20th Century-Fox, called Leland Hayward, Gregory Peck's agent, and offered Peck the coveted role of Father Francis Chisholm in Fox's film of A.J. Cronin's bestselling novel *The Keys of the Kingdom*, about a Roman Catholic missionary in China. The part would not only catapult Peck to stardom but also bring him the first of five Academy Award nominations as best actor. For another Hollywood titan, David O. Selznick, this would all be ironic indeed.

Selznick had bought the screen rights to Dr. Cronin's novel on its publication in 1941 for $100,000. His intention was to produce the picture as the prestigious first in a ten-year, twenty-picture production pact with United Artists.

Gregory Peck, as the young Francis Chisholm, bids goodbye to his sweetheart, Nora (Jane Ball), as he departs for school, unaware they will never see each other again.

As Father Chisholm, Gregory Peck disembarks from the barge which has brought him to the site of his mission assignment in China.

Father Chisholm and his assistants Benson Fong and Eunice Soo Hoo welcome Francis's old and dear friend Dr. Willie Tullock (Thomas Mitchell) to the mission.

One of the aspiring young actors who had come to Selznick's attention in 1941 was Gregory Peck. Katharine Brown, New York-based eastern representative for Selznick International Pictures, saw Peck in a stage production and arranged a screen test for the producer's consideration. He was not impressed.

In a memo to Miss Brown, who also brought Ingrid Bergman and Jennifer Jones, among others, to his attention, Selznick commented, "I am sorry to have to say that I don't see what we could do with Gregory Peck. ... He photographs like Abe Lincoln, but if he has a great personality, I don't think it comes through in these tests...."

Selznick thus passed up Peck and eventually *The Keys of the Kingdom* as well. After losing interest in making the film himself, he decided to offer it to other studios as a package, possibly with Dorothy McGuire, whom he had under contract, for the role of the love-lorn Nora, Father Francis's boyhood sweetheart. At one point, he also toyed with the idea of testing Phyllis Isley (a.k.a. Mrs. Robert Walker), another newcomer he was grooming for stardom, for the same part. But instead, he sold the novel to Darryl Zanuck, with no stars attached. He also loaned Miss Isley, whose name he meanwhile changed to Jennifer Jones, to the Fox studio for the saintly starring role in *The Song of Bernadette* (1943), which brought her the Academy Award for best actress. And it was the huge success of that Fox production that led to Zanuck's decision to make another religious picture and gamble again on a newcomer for the starring role.

Zanuck had also seen Peck on Broadway and found him interesting. While *Days of Glory* was still in production, he arranged to view Peck again, in some rushes. These convinced Zanuck that Peck was right for the Father Chisholm role and he offered it to the actor outright, without even the customary screen test actors frequently undergo for starring parts.

Father Chisholm shares a moment of thankful prayer with mission-adopted children under the supervision of nuns Sara Algood, Ruth Ford and Rosa Stradner.

Zanuck assigned the project to writer-producer Joseph L. Mankiewicz; John M. Stahl was engaged as director. Mankiewicz had been involved in movies since he joined his brother Herman on the writing staff at Paramount in 1929; a successful writer—*The Mysterious Dr. Fu Manchu* 1929), *Million Dollar Legs* (1932)—he had turned to producing in 1936, with *Fury* and *The Three Godfathers*, and began writing *and* directing with *Dragonwyck* in 1945.

John M. Stahl had been involved in motion pictures since 1914. He had worked both as a writer and as writer-director. As a director, his notable works included *Back Street* (1932), *Imitation of Life* (1934), *Magnificent Obsession* (1935), and *When Tomorrow Comes* (1939).

The script for *Keys* had been written for Fox by Nunnally Johnson shortly after the studio acquired the novel. Johnson was a talented, popular and widely respected member of the industry. He had already established himself as a journalist and successful writer of fiction when he took up screenwriting in 1933. His scripts included *Kid Millions* (1934), *Jesse James* (1939), *The Grapes of Wrath* (1940), *Tobacco Road* (1941), *Roxie Hart* (1942), and *The Moon is Down* (1943), which he also produced.

By the time the film came up for production, Johnson was no longer working at Fox, and when Zanuck turned the script over to producer Mankiewicz, writer Mankiewicz decided to make some revisions. Later, Johnson was surprised to hear that Mankiewicz had asked for sole screenplay credit and he was urged to challenge Mankiewicz's claim. He was not inclined to get into a personal argument over it, however, and the question was submitted to the Writers Guild for arbitration, since he didn't think Mankiewicz, who was also his friend, could have done enough work on the script to deserve sole credit for it.

Displaying what might be considered solomonic wisdom, the arbitration committee, a group established by the Guild to handle such

Vincent Price, a friend of Father Chisholm's during their seminary days, is critical of the way he finds the mission operated when he pays a visit as a church bureaucrat on inspection tour.

disputes, examined the script and ruled that the credit should go to both Johnson and Mankiewicz.

The production was budgeted at $3 million, making it one of the most expensive pictures of the year, with a shooting schedule of three months. Its photography by Arthur Miller later won the Fox cameraman an Academy Award nomination.

Though an atheist himself, Dr. Tullock is no less committed to helping mankind and, regardless of their different beliefs, a deep bond of mutual respect and tolerance exists between him and Father Chisholm.

Although the film was shot entirely on the Fox studio lot, its far-flung locales were rendered quite convincingly by art directors James Basevi and Bill Darling, who designed and supervised construction of the sets necessary in tracing the life of Father Chisholm from his Scottish boyhood through 33 years of service in China and back to his retirement in Scotland.

The picture was certainly a challenging one for the 27-year-old Gregory Peck, too, since his part required makeup changes for a character range from a college student of 19 (young Roddy McDowall played Francis as a boy) to an aged priest of 70. It was undoubtedly Peck's most demanding role to date as an actor, but a knowledgeable technical advisor was on hand to lend assistance.

"We had great help," Greg recalled later, "from a Catholic missionary, Father O'Hara, who spoke Chinese and had lived eight years in China. I remember particularly in one scene, where I had to preach in Chinese, how Father O'Hara was persuaded to act out the scene for me. I hadn't been able to catch the feeling of it somehow. I couldn't feel natural. So we asked him to try it. And he did, walking through that crowd of Chinese extras, ringing a little silver bell and talking to each one, in Chinese, after first bowing with the greatest courtesy. He did it as he must have done a thousand times in real life. Then I realized what I had missed in the scene: that grave courtesy and respect for each person as an individual."

Leonard Strong, as the wealthy Chinese unbeliever whose injured son's life is saved at the mission, offers to become a Christian but is initially turned down by Father Chisholm, who explains that he must come to God out of love, not gratitude.

The part meant a great deal to Peck, not only because it was his first chance, he felt, for a real characterization on screen—to develop a character and see him through life—but also because he was himself a great admirer of the Cronin novel. But he was afraid, too, that Dr. Cronin might object to the changes and omissions that were unavoidably necessary in transposing the book to film. When the picture was shown to Dr. Cronin, however, the author was not only satisfied with the result but praised both the adaptation and Peck's performance, to the actor's great delight.

On December 28, 1944, *The Keys of the Kingdom* was presented to an invited premiere audience at New York's Rivoli Theater, where it was warmly received and began regular performances the following day.

Critical reaction to the film was mixed, but *New York Daily Mirror* critic Lee Mortimer perhaps set the keynote for the picture by calling it "a gigantic opus—big in every way, including pathos, thrills, excitement, cast and celluloid. ... I was going to say it is the kind of picture whose appeal will be limited to the general public rather than to sophisticates and critics, so after mature consideration I think I will say so. ... Gregory Peck does a magnificent job...."

Alton Cook praised Peck in the *New York World-Telegram*: "There have been intimations of his forceful talent on stage and screen. Nevertheless there is astonishment awaiting everyone who sees *The Keys of the Kingdom*, with this fledgling movie actor tossing in one of the soundest and most intelligently presented performances of a year that has abounded in those merits. ... He has added to the picture a rich life and vitality that the novel did not have for a good many of its readers...."

Rose Pelswick reported in the *New York Journal-American* that the novel "has been brought to the screen with reverence, dignity and a deeply moving sincerity." She went on to say that Peck's "characterization of the tall and gaunt priest is a memorable one."

Bosley Crowther, in *The New York Times*, found the film "long and mellow ... but a surface shadow of the substance that was so finely wrought [by Cronin] ... and yet ... there is no question that the magnanimity of Father Francis is inspiringly conveyed. But ... one might reasonably expect a great deal more insight into character and its conflicts than is offered here. ... Gregory Peck ... gives a quiet and forceful performance ... carries a fine impression of godly devotion and dignity...."

Perhaps the most negative response came from Howard Barnes of the *New York Herald Tribune*, who said that "the translation itself is more episodic and contrived than dramatically convincing ... a bit fragmentary for comfort. ... Mankiewicz and ... Johnson have not succeeded in packing a rambling literary narrative into the exigent outlines of a satisfactory film entertainment. ... Peck is remarkably good as the good father. ... With such talent, one has a right to expect more than the scenarist and the director ... have made. ... Call it a valiant but disappointing try."

Peck's fellow actors, including Miss Stradner and particularly Edmund Gwenn and Thomass Mitchell, received good notices on the whole. But Crowther found Vincent Price's portrayal of a worldly canon "oddly distasteful" and felt that Miss Stradner was "constricted in her performance of a soul-wracked nun."

In the *New York Post*, Irene Thirer called the picture "a lengthy, highly dramatic, entrancingly photographed production. ... Stahl has captured a delicate spiritual quality, and at the same time managed to give the action sequences a biting tang; also he has preserved the wit and subtlety of the manuscript, with each and every performer expertly cast." She called Peck's performance "a personal triumph."

Kate Cameron awarded the film four stars (highest rating) in the *New York Daily News*, naming it "a must on any moviegoer's list." Peck's portrayal, she said, "is one of this year's outstanding character portraits. ... Peck carries the burden of the story with competence and artistry. A fine spiritual quality shines through his acting...."

"It must have been thrilling," Miss Cameron also commented, "for Gregory Peck ... to realize from the enthusiastic reception he received for his fine portrayal that he has reached top rank among the stars in his second appearance on the screen...."

And the members of the Academy of Motion Picture Arts and Sciences agreed with the critics regarding Peck's performance: he was voted an Oscar nomination for best actor. When the awards were given out, though, Ray Milland won for his equally fine performance in Paramount's *The Lost Weekend*. But for Gregory Peck, stardom so early in his career must have been more than adequate consolation. And it was not the last time he would know disappointment on Oscar night, before that ultimate Hollywood accolade was his.

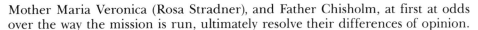

Mother Maria Veronica (Rosa Stradner), and Father Chisholm, at first at odds over the way the mission is run, ultimately resolve their differences of opinion.

With his father's steel mill belching fumes in the background, Gregory Peck and Greer Garson consider the different worlds each of them inhabits and the gulf (and mill) that lies between them as they find their friendship turning into love.

The Valley of Decision

Metro-Goldwyn-Mayer   **1945**

Credits

Producer, Edwin H. Knopf; *director*, Tay Garnett; *screenplay*, John Meehan, Sonya Levien, based on the novel by Marcia Davenport; *music*, Herbert Stothart; *cinematography*, Joseph Ruttenberg; *editor*, Blanche Sewell; *special effects*, A. Arnold Gillespie; *art directors*, Cedric Gibbons and Paul Groesse. (111 minutes)

Cast

Gregory Peck (Paul Scott), Greer Garson (Mary Rafferty), Donald Crisp (William Scott), Lionel Barrymore (Pat Rafferty), Preston Foster (Jim Brennan), Gladys Cooper (Clarissa Scott), Marsha Hunt (Constance Scott), Reginald Owen (McCready), Dan Duryea (William Scott, Jr.), Jessica Tandy (Louise Kan), Barbara Everest (Delia), Marshall Thompson (Ted Scott), Mary Lord (Julia Gaylord), John Warburton (Giles, Earl of Moulton), Mary Currier (Mrs. Gaylord), Arthur Shields (Callahan), Russell Hicks (Mr. Gaylord), Geraldine Wall (Kate Shannon), Norman Ollstead (Callahan's Son), Evelyn Dockson (Mrs. Callahan), Connie Gilchrist (The Cook), Willa Pearl Curtis (Maid), William O'Leary (O'Brien), Richard Abbott (Minister), Dean Stockwell (Paulie), Joy Harrington (Stella), Lumsden Hare (Dr. McClintock), Anna Q. Nillson (Nurse), Sherlee Collier (Clarrie), Mike Ryan (Timmie).

The Valley of Decision was Gregory Peck's first picture for Metro-Goldwyn-Mayer. Based on Marcia Davenport's best-selling 1942 novel about a Pittsburgh steel-family dynasty in the 1870s, it is a wholesome romantic drama, with socio-political undertones, that in both form and content epitomizes old Hollywood at its very best. Peck's role as a scion of the steel-mill-owning Scott family gave the young actor a sterling opportunity to be seen opposite one of Metro's—and the industry's—reigning box-office queens, but before he landed it Greg found himself in a startling confrontation with Louis B. Mayer, the benevolent dictator (some of his subjects would question the adjective) who reigned over the studio as its chief.

While Peck was being courted by Casey Robinson at RKO and Darryl Zanuck at 20th Century-Fox, Mayer too sensed the newcomer's potential and decided that he wanted to add him to the Metro stable of stars. One of Hollywood's most influential and powerful moguls, L. B. was in general accustomed to getting whatever he wanted and he told Leland Hayward, Greg's agent, that he wanted the actor, naturally on his own terms and exclusively. Peck was certainly interested in making pictures at MGM, but at that point in his career he still hoped to divide his acting time between Hollywood and the New York stage and he was adamant about not wanting to be under any sort of exclusive contract with a single studio.

"Neither of my two doctrines," he recalls, "particularly appealed to MGM, which wanted me to sign a long-term contract. Doing that would have meant I belonged to the studio and committed me exclusively to films."

Mayer must have been flabbergasted, not to mention annoyed, that a rank beginner would resist an overture from an industry giant. In any event, Peck was summoned to a personal meeting with L.B. in his office at the studio. There, the archetypal movie mogul intended to change this young upstart's mind and divest him of those silly notions about splitting his time between stage and pictures. Greg was ushered into the chief's imposing inner sanctum and brought before the stern gaze of the Metro patriarch.

"Initially, he used the fatherly approach," says Peck, "pointing out how he had sired the careers of numerous actors. When I declined to budge, he shifted his campaign to an attack against the legitimate theater, demeaning my career in it in the process."

Getting nowhere with this harangue, Mayer switched to another tactic: "He pulled

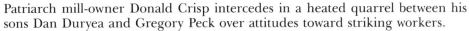

Patriarch mill-owner Donald Crisp intercedes in a heated quarrel between his sons Dan Duryea and Gregory Peck over attitudes toward striking workers.

Embittered Lionel Barrymore, crippled in a mill accident years before, aims for fatal revenge even as Gregory Peck tries to prevent strife in a tragic confrontation between striking workers and strike-breaking goons hired by his own brother.

out a handkerchief and began to cry, deeply saddened by my ingratitude which wouldn't allow him to make me the biggest movie star of all time."

The actor still stood his ground, but the mogul would not concede defeat. "His final ploy was to depict my refusal as an offense to motherhood, the American flag and family decency. I wondered why he stopped short of claiming it was also atheistic!"

Certainly this was one of the most extraordinary offscreen performances Peck had ever seen, but he assured Mr. Mayer that he was not about to sign an exclusive contract with anyone. It was a daring resistance; few people in the industry would ever think of defying this titan who was not known to have an easily forgiving nature. Did turning down one of the most powerful men in Hollywood hurt Peck's subsequent career at MGM?

"To the contrary," Peck replies, "I think Mayer gained a great respect for me as a result, because in the years to come he never once held it against me."

Accepting Greg's conditions, Mayer finally agreed to sign him to a four-picture, non-exclusive contract and immediately cast him with one of the studio's top female players—and one of Mayer's own personal favorites—Greer Garson, who would play the servant girl who falls in love with the son of the wealthy family for whom she works.

According to some of her contemporary industry pundits, Miss Garson was the epit-

ome of L.B. Mayer's fantasized image of womanhood: classically beautiful, genteel and self-sacrificing. In *Valley of Decision*, she followed in her noble grain of self-sacrificing femininity but, by this time, Garson was also tiring of the mold Mayer had shaped around her and in which he seemed content to keep her confined. She nagged him to let her alter her screen persona and try other sorts of roles. Eventually, Mayer acquiesced; Garson got her way. But in doing so she probably vindicated L.B., since *Valley of Decision* was her last huge hit and the subsequent change in her image brought on a decline in popularity.

Befitting her status, Greer Garson received top billing in the picture as Mary Rafferty, the bright Irish lass who finds a place in the Scott family's mansion and eventually in their hearts as well.

Peck plays Paul Scott, the son who is determined to carry on the family business in the tradition of his self-made father who built it.

Mayer assigned Edwin H. Knopf and Tay Garnett, the producer-director team responsible for *Mrs. Parkington*, to steer the Garson-Peck vehicle through its cinematic course.

MGM writers John Meehan and Sonya Levien wrote the script, following the main thrust of Mrs. Davenport's story but condensing the best-selling book as necessary to best-selling screen-story proportions.

On one level there is a Montague-Capulet aspect to *Valley of Decision*, with its would-be lovers coming from opposite sides of the tracks—or, more appropriately, of the mill. And the hatred Pat Rafferty feels for his daughter's employers ultimately results in a tragedy that keeps Mary and Paul apart for a very long time, even though Mary had tried honestly and valiantly to bridge the gulf reflected not only in their respective social positions but also in the conflicting passions arising from the budding labor union movement with which her father and friends are involved in their struggle to win concessions from the mill's managing owners.

The picture's supporting cast was assembled from among MGM's vast store of talent. Lionel Barrymore was in his crusty prime as the embittered Pat Rafferty, full of contempt, anger and distrust for the Scotts and anything having to do with them. The role was as if tailor-made for the 67-year-old Barrymore, who had been acting in a wheelchair since 1938 because of poor health resulting from both arthritis and two serious falls he had sustained and more recently complicated by a heart condition.

Within its absorbing and uplifting romantic drama, *Valley of Decision* makes some good and pertinent points about the spirit of the sort of individual entrepreneurship on which America's industrial sector was built, about the value of a commitment to meaningful, constructive work as opposed to mere self-indulgence as a way of life, and about the eternal conflict between ideals and greed in a materialistic society. Hard work, patience, perseverance and selfless love are virtues ultimately rewarded and the losers are those who think only of themselves and what they can take from life, rather than of what they can give.

Filmed entirely on the lot at MGM, the picture, with its roaring steel mill in the background, its workers' shanty town, its tree-shaded hills, its mansion-lined streets and imposing houses, is a tribute to the artfulness with which movie artisans such as Cedric Gibbons and Paul Groesse could create almost any locale, environment or effect believably within the confines of the studio itself.

The Valley of Decision opened at New York's Radio City Music Hall on May 3, 1945. In an unsigned review, the *New York Herald Tribune's* critic wrote: "A tale of an American dynasty has come to the screen with great feeling and some sense. ... Garnett's acute direction holds a tender romance in the shifty outlines of a politico-social period piece. ... John Meehan and Sonya Levien have saved the core of a best-seller ... in a script which is happily free

from most of the flaws of literary translations on the screen. ... The acting takes care of the essential entertainment values. ... Garson ... is sheerly brilliant. ... Gregory Peck rarely fails her ... [in] a motion picture of vitality and imaginative execution. It deserves to be a resounding hit."

In *The New York Times*, Bosley Crowther reported, "A great many liberties have been taken which alter the conceptions of the book. But the general movie audience should find the screen version to its taste, for this picture ... had many elements of dramatic appeal ... the early phases ... are rather studiously on the 'cute' side, with Greer Garson playing the young domestic with an abundance of her familiar charm ... the middle phases are also somewhat artificially contrived. ... But the final phase ... does have authority and depth. ... Gregory Peck is quietly commanding as the best of the Scott boys ... and Donald Crisp makes a pleasantly imposing Pittsburgh patriarch. ... Miss Davenport's fine American saga is barely perceived ... but there is here a full romantic show."

With Greer Garson, taking an anachronistic phone call on the set of *Valley of Decision*, 1946.

43

44

Spellbound

United Artists   **1945**
A Selznick International Pictures-Vanguard Films Production

Credits

Producer, David O. Selznick; *director*, Alfred Hitchcock; *screenplay*, Ben Hecht, based on the novel, *The House of Dr. Edwardes*, by Francis Beeding (a pseudonym of Hilary St. John Saunders and Leslie Palmer); *adaptation*, Angus MacPhail; *music*, Miklos Rozsa; *production designer*, James Basevi; *art director*, John Ewing; *dream sequence designed by* Salvador Dali; *cinematography*, George Barnes; *editor*, William Ziegler, *sound*, Richard De Weese. (111 minutes)

Cast

Gregory Peck (J.B.–John Ballentine), Ingrid Bergman (Dr. Constance Peterson), Leo G. Carroll (Dr. Murchison), Michael Chekhov (Dr. Alex Brulow), Rhonda Fleming (Miss Carmichael), Donald Curtis (Harry), Jean Acker (Matron), John Emery (Dr. Fleurot), Norman Lloyd (Garmes), Steven Geray (Dr. Graff), Paul Harvey (Dr. Hanish), Erskine Sanford (Dr. Galt), Janet Scott (Norma), Victor Kilian (Sheriff), Wallace Ford (Stranger in hotel lobby), Bill Goodwin (House Detective), Dave Willock (Bellboy), George Meader (Railroad Clerk), Matt Moore (Policeman at railroad station), Harry Brown (Gateman), Art Baker (Lt. Cooley), Regis Toomey (Sgt. Gillespie), Clarence Straight (Secretary at police station), Joel Davis (J.B. as a boy), Teddy Infuhr (J.B.'s Brother), Addison Richards (Police Captain), Richard Bartell (Ticket Taker), Edward Fielding (Dr. Edwardes), Alfred Hitchcock (Man carrying a violin).

When he saw that almost every major studio in town was trying to hire Gregory Peck, the man who had given him his initial Hollywood rejection reconsidered his action and decided to offer the rising new star a contract himself. Years later, Kay Brown, who had first brought Peck to David O. Selznick's attention, observed, "It cost him about four times what he would have had to pay originally."

The legendary producer, whose outstanding screen achievements included *Dinner at Eight, David Copperfield, A Tale of Two Cities, A Star Is Born, Gone With the Wind, Intermezzo* and *Rebecca*, rarely, however, let cost stand in the way of getting what he wanted. And Selznick wasted no time in casting his handsome new leading man opposite his beautiful leading female player in a suspense picture directed by a master of the genre and concerning a subject close to the producer's own heart.

Selznick had gone through a long period of psychoanalysis, which he found to be of immense help and comfort. As a result of his positive experience, he became a strong advocate of psychiatry and analysis and decided that he wanted to share his discovery with moviegoers around the world, introducing the general public, he hoped, to the wondrous healing possibilities of this relatively new branch of medicine. Out of this desire came *Spellbound.*

Selznick purchased the screen rights to *The House of Dr. Edwardes,* a novel by Francis Beeding, which was a pseudonym for Hilary St. George Saunders and Leslie Palmer. Their novel was a bizarre and melodramatic story

Afraid that their true identities will be discovered, Ingrid Bergman and Gregory Peck stand by anxiously while Michael Chekov, who is sheltering them, attempts to throw detectives Regis Toomey and Art Baker off course.

about a psychopath taking over an insane asylum where even members of the staff were lunatics. It was the perfect project for director Alfred Hitchcock, whom Selznick also had under contract and who was also interested in psychiatry. As they discussed the project, Hitchcock and Selznick were determined to make a sensible picture about psychoanalysis that would work both as a thriller, to attract and hold its audience, and as a conduit to relay some reasonable information about psychotherapy. And of course the picture must also have all the class the public had become accustomed to expect in a David O. Selznick film: the Selznick touch on which the producer had built his studio's reputation and which promised audiences both quality entertainment and excellence of production.

Hitchcock had been nominated for an Academy Award for his direction of *Rebecca*, his first picture for Selznick, in 1940, and the picture itself had won an Oscar as best production and received additional nominations as well. During the four years between *Rebecca* and *Spellbound*, the prolific British director had made *Foreign Correspondent* (1940), *Mr. and Mrs. Smith* and *Suspicion* (1941), *Saboteur* (1942), *Shadow of a Doubt* and *Lifeboat* (1943).

Before he could begin work on *Spellbound*, Hitchcock returned to England in 1944 to direct a pair of short films for the war effort in France. While working in London, he re-encountered Angus MacPhail, a writer he had first met when he was directing *The Lodger* at Gaumont-British studios in 1926. In the interim MacPhail had gone on to become head of the script department at Gaumont. Hitchcock

asked his old acquaintance to collaborate on fashioning a screenplay from the Beeding novel, which he did; but the MacPhail adaptation turned out to be too rambling and unwieldy to produce.

Back in Hollywood, Selznick and Hitchcock asked veteran screenwriter Ben Hecht to try his skilled hand at turning the novel into a workable script. Since Hecht had worked on the screenplay for *Foreign Correspondent* (without screen credit), a rapport already existed between him and Hitchcock and, more important, Hecht was himself not only fascinated by psychoanalysis but also friendly with several of its leading practitioners. He seemed to be the ideal person for the job; certainly, his credentials were in order.

In the Hecht script, Gregory Peck plays John Ballentine, a young man who arrives at a mental hospital and is at first assumed to be its new director. But he is soon discovered to actually be an amnesiac who even suspects himself of being a murderer—and who may indeed have murdered the man who was to be the real new director. The core of the plot is the parallel unravelling, through careful psychoanalysis, of both the murder mystery and the mystery of John Ballentine's true identity, the discovery of the cause of his amnesia and the true nature of his personality that has been obscured by his illness. Peck reflects very well the troubled man who must confront the possibility that curing his psychosis may reveal an even more troubling reality—one that is all the more painful to face because he has meanwhile fallen in love with the doctor who wants to help him.

Opposite Peck, Selznick cast his top star, Ingrid Bergman, as Dr. Constance Peterson. Selznick had brought Miss Bergman to the United States from Sweden in 1938 and made her an international star in her first Hollywood picture, *Intermezzo* (1939).

Leo G. Carroll and Michael Chekhov were cast respectively in the supporting roles of Dr. Murchison, the asylum's retiring direc-

Prompted by Ingrid Bergman, a bewildered Gregory Peck tries to recall his earlier life and events that led to his amnesia.

tor, and Dr. Brulov, an analyst who is a friend of Dr. Peterson's.

When production got underway, Peck found working with Hitchcock "a remarkable experience. ... I admire him greatly. He is the greatest of the film technicians and all directors learn from him."

Commenting on Hitchcock's well-known reputation for the amount of preparation work he puts into a picture before shooting begins, Peck observed, "Almost like an architect, he doesn't start erecting the building until the plan is perfect and he has it so very well calculated that very little can go wrong.

"I do think that as far as actors are concerned, that Hitchcock is at his best with 'technical' actors—like Cary Grant, for example—who have an accomplished technique of producing effects. They've worked very hard on their techniques and it's very facile—and they can turn it on like that. That pleases Hitch because he likes to control the performance and the actor's expression and emotion just as he can control the preparation of the script and the sets and the camera. He likes to eliminate the intangibles, if possible. So I think he's best with technical actors. As for actors who have to find the truth inside themselves, who have to delve around and find an emotional reality in a situation before they can produce the right external effect, he tends to be a bit impatient with those. That's not his kind of actor." But, adds Peck, "I never saw him browbeat or humiliate an actor. ... He's far too wise and too human...."

Of course, no David O. Selznick production was ever completed without Selznick's personal touch liberally applied and Selznick was known as a producer who frequently visited the set during shooting, offering advice wherever and whenever he felt it was necessary. Some of his directors and production personnel found this sort of involvement—which could range from merely helpful to obsessive—annoying, not to mention a hindrance to work, and in some situations it undoubtedly was. But during the production

of *Spellbound*, Selznick hardly ever visited the set and, in fact, later asserted that he had gone there only twice during the entire course of shooting. Selznick kept his own involvement to the post-production stages, apparently supervising editing and scoring extensively. He later recalled, in another memo, that he had voluntarily given Hitchcock double credit on the picture, advertising it as "Alfred Hitchcock's *Spellbound*," as a gesture of his pleasure at Hitch's efficient working style and the "remarkable quality" he achieved on the picture, "and without the slightest set supervision on my part either as to quality or efficiency...." Yet, in a 1947 letter to Ingrid Bergman, Selznick reminded her that following the first preview of *Spellbound* he had "completely re-edited the picture ... taking out two reels, without collaboration...."

Central to *Spellbound* and any consideration of it are the fascinating and unforgettable dream and fantasy sequences designed by artist Salvador Dali, to depict symbolically on screen the jumbled and confused content of John Ballentine's amnesiac mind and subconscious.

Hitchcock asked Selznick to hire Dali to create the all-important sequences because he wanted something distinctive to break with the hackneyed Hollywood tradition of misty, gauzy scenes and blurred, hazy photography to which filmmakers had commonly resorted in depicting dreams and fantasies. Dali's razor-sharp imagery was what Hitch envisioned for the movie, with, as originally conceived,

47

dream sequences that would be visually sharper than even the film's real-life scenes.

Dali's particular brand of surrealistic art was itself "psychoanalytical," projecting symbols and images from his own dream life, from hallucinations and from fetishes. The artist had previously collaborated with Spanish director Luis Buñeul on two films of unusual power, *Un Chien Andalou* (1928) and *L'Age d'Or* (1930), that became classics of the avant garde cinema. Their imagery so touched the fears and taboos buried deep within the collective unconscious of their audiences, and the films were so disturbing, that they in fact were totally banned for a number of years by various nervous paranoid governments and authorities.

The Dali-designed sequences for *Spellbound* are a bewitching and exciting blend of sensual and psychological symbolism, including one beautiful moment (not only of symbolism but also of cinematic double entendre) when Bergman and Peck come together for their first kiss: As the pair merge, the camera sweeps past them into a shot through seven doors opening one after the other toward infinity, in a romantic evocation of both the spiritual and the sensual exhiliration of two lovers' first embrace. It is visually stunning and emotionally exciting, but unfortunately in post-production a gush of lush romantic movie music was scored for the sequence, apparently at the insistent behest of Selznick, and the visual richness is almost entirely overwhelmed by the heavy-handed surging of massed violins.

Dali did have some strange ideas that did not wind up in the picture. One of them involved having an ant-infested statue crack apart and, as the pieces fell away, an ant-covered Ingrid Bergman would be revealed underneath. It turned out to be quite impossible, as did Hitchcock's idea of shooting the dream sequences outside in direct sunlight, instead of on a soundstage, to increase the sharpness of the images. That plan was vetoed by Selznick who felt, at least for once, that the additional expense couldn't be justified.

The photography of *Spellbound* presented a number of challenges to the craftsmen who produced it. Perhaps the most notable was the near-to-last scene in the picture where, in a

subjective shot from his own point of view, Dr. Murchison aims a revolver threateningly across his desk at Ingrid Bergman, who has just informed him that she knows the identity of the real murderer of Dr. Edwardes. Murchison's hand, holding the revolver, looms in large menacing foreground close-up, with the mortally imperiled Bergman in the background facing him (and the audience).

When Bergman calls Murchison's bluff, turns her back on him and walks out of the room, Murchison's hand slowly turns 180 degrees until the gunbarrel is pointing directly at himself, off-screen (and therefore at the camera and the audience); he squeezes the trigger, shooting himself. In the original release prints of this black-and-white picture, a single solid red frame was inserted at this point, with the on-screen effect of a sudden and very unexpected red flash accompanying the gun shot. It was an effective audience-jolter. Unfortunately, in the years since *Spellbound*'s initial release, its distributors have ceased making this single colored-frame insertion in prints and the original effect is rarely seen anymore as Hitchcock intended it.

Shooting the sequence was problematic in terms of then-current cinema technology. Getting both Murchison's hand and the revolver in focus in the foreground and Bergman in focus in the background of the shot was well beyond the depth-of-field capabilities of the camera unless the set was flooded with much brighter than normal lighting and the aperture of the camera lens reduced to a very small opening.

George Barnes, Hitchcock's cameraman, who had also worked on *Rebecca*, claimed that he couldn't stop down to that extent, however, because it would be bad for Miss Bergman's face. Barnes was known for being particularly conscious of how unflattering lighting and exposure would detract from an actress's "look," so the normal method of securing such a shot was ruled out.

In one attempt to solve the problem, Bergman's action was filmed separately and projected onto a rear projection screen while the doctor's hand and the revolver were filmed in front of it in a composite shot. The result was not satisfactory. Finally, Hitchcock and Barnes had the prop department construct a

Spellbound marked the motion picture debut of Rhonda Fleming, as a sanitarium patient about to be helped back to her quarters by Donald Curtis. Note the "outside" lighting Hitchcock hoped to achieve.

giant hand and a revolver four times life-size. These "props" were held close enough to Bergman to be in focus with her for the camera. And·their enlarged size and the fake perspective made the hand and gun appear to be of normal size but merely closer to the audience than Bergman. On screen it all looks very simple—and it works!

When the advertising and promotion strategy for *Spellbound* was being plotted by Selznick and his staff, there was a feeling that mystery pictures might be undergoing a slump in popularity, and it was decided, therefore, to stress the love-story angle in the picture's advertising and play down the mystery-melodrama aspects. One "romantic" ad featured Greg and Ingrid embracing under a double headline:

"Irresistible their love!
Inescapable their fears!"

The message in another ad was equally vague regarding the nature of the movie:

"The magnificence of its cast...the intensity of its emotions...will hold you SPELLBOUND!"

Whatever the slant of the ad campaign, previews confirmed for Selznick the romantic appeal of his new leading man. In a later memo to Neil Agnew, one of his organizational vice-presidents, the producer reported on how excited the preview-goers had been by Peck's presence in the picture: "We could not keep the audience quiet from the time his name first came on the screen until we had shushed [them] through three or four sequences and stopped all the dames from 'ohing' and 'ahing' and gurgling...."

Spellbound opened on November 1, 1945, at New York's Astor Theater. Selznick's and Hitchcock's perception of the general public's ignorance (and perhaps unacknowledged fear?) of psychoanalysis was reflected somewhat in the lead sentence of *The New York Times* critic Bosley Crowther's November 2 review:

"This writer has had little traffic with the

practitioners of psychiatry or with the twilight abstractions of their science.... This story...has relation to all the faith-healing films ever made, but the manner and quality of its telling is extraordinarily fine.... Bergman is Hitchcock's chief asset...but Mr. Peck is also a large contributor. His performance, restrained and refined, is precisely the proper counter to Miss Bergman's exquisite role.... Selznick has a rare film...."

Howard Barnes, in the *New York Herald Tribune*, said, "The secret recesses of the mind are explored with brilliant and terrifying effect.... With Ben Hecht's crafty scenario and compelling performances by Ingrid Bergman and Gregory Peck, the work is a masterful psychiatric thriller...irresistibly engrossing.... Bergman and Peck make the most of it under Hitchcock's inspired staging.... Peck's portrait of the mentally ill ex-army doctor is ably modulated and utterly convincing.... *Spellbound* is in the great tradition of such films as *Private Worlds*. It is the best of the lot."

Psychiatric expert Albert Deutsch, in New York's *PM*, remarked, however, that the film contained so many psychiatric distortions that practicing Freudians might well tear their hair on seeing it. According to Deutsch, the film's chief violation seemed to be allowing the analyst (Bergman) to become emotionally involved with her patient (Peck), a fundamental professional taboo. But Deutsch went on to say that "despite these and other flaws, I regard *Spellbound* as the most mature movie treatment of the delicate subject of psychoanalysis I've ever seen…besides being one of the dozen best Hollywood films that have come my way."

Variety's critic reviewed the film favorably and reported that "some of the concluding action takes place on a ski run where the suspense and accompanying musical score create such a tension that the audience at the preview was literally bound as if by a spell…. Peck handles the suspense scenes with great skill and has one of his finest screen roles to date…." Bergman, Chekhov, John Emery and Carroll were also praised, and *Variety* predicted, "Top grosses should be assured."

Filmgoers turned his prognostication into truth: world-wide grosses for *Spellbound*'s initial release totaled $7.9 million, the equivalent of perhaps a $40 million gross in terms of 1980s admission prices. The picture had cost only $2 million to produce.

Spellbound received an Academy Award nomination for Best Picture, as did Hitchcock for his direction, Michael Chekhov for best supporting actor, and George Barnes for his photography. Miklos Rosza won an Oscar for his haunting musical score, spellbinding in its own right. Miss Bergman, who had received an Oscar nomination for her performance in *The Bells of St. Mary's*, was honored by the New York Film Critics' Circle with their "best feminine performance" award for *Spellbound* and *The Bells*.

In a November 11, 1945, followup to his earlier *New York Times* review of *Spellbound*, Bosley Crowther commented that for the past several years some critics had felt that Hitchcock's American films had lacked the excellence of his British works, but "…now we are put in the position of having to revise that estimate. Mr. Hitchcock's accomplishment with *Spellbound* is the rock upon which our minds are split….."

While Gregory Peck sleeps peacefully, Ingrid Bergman confronts the possibility that the man she loves is not only very seriously ill but may also be an extremely dangerous individual.

Claude Jarman, Jr., Jane Wyman and Gregory Peck, a family trying to make a go of farming in the Florida hinterlands, find that they must defend their crops from a variety of four-legged foraging marauders.

The Yearling

Metro-Goldwyn-Mayer   **1946**

Credits

Producer, Sidney Franklin; *director*, Clarence Brown; *screenplay*, Paul Osborn, based on the novel by Marjorie Kinnan Rawlings; *music*, Herbert Stothart; *cinematography*, Charles Rosher, Leonard Smith, Arthur Arling; *second-unit direction*, Chester Franklin; *editor*, Harold F. Kress; *art directors*, Cedric Gibbons, Paul Groesse; *set decoration*, Edwin B. Willis; color by Technicolor. (134 Minutes)

Cast

Gregory Peck (Pa Baxter), Jane Wyman (Ma Baxter), Claude Jarman, Jr. (Jody Baxter), Chill Wills (Buck Forrester), Clem Bevans (Pa Forrester), Margaret Wycherly (Ma Forrester), Henry Travers (Mr. Boyles), Forrest Tucker (Lem Forrester), Donn Gift (Fodderwing), Daniel White (Millwheel), Matt Willis (Gabby), George Mann (Pack), Arthur Hohl (Arch), June Lockhart (Twink Weatherby), Joan Wells (Eulalie), Jeff York (Oliver), B. M. Chick York (Doc Wilson), Houseley Stevenson (Mr. Ranger), Jane Green (Mrs. Saunders), Victor Kilian (Captain), Robert Porterfield (Mate), Frank Eldredge (Deckhand).

His son, Claude Jarman, Jr., is thrilled when farmer Gregory Peck agrees to let him keep and raise a motherless fawn they have found in the forest.

Gregory Peck's second picture for Metro-Goldwyn-Mayer actually went into production two years before Peck arrived in Hollywood. And when *The Yearling* finally opened at Radio City Music Hall on January 23, 1947, the occasion marked the happy ending of a head-ache that had pained producer Sidney Franklin and MGM for some five years since the movie first started shooting in Florida in 1941. In sum, it actually had taken eight years to bring the project from the purchase of the novel's screen rights to the Music Hall stage.

Marjorie Kinnan Rawlings' novel about a Florida backwoods lad's relationship with an orphaned fawn and his coming to the respon-sibilities of manhood in the late 1870s was published in 1938. It was almost instantly hailed as a "classic" of American literature and by the time Ms. Rawlings received the Pulitzer Prize for fiction for it in 1939, MGM had already purchased the screen rights.

Metro decided to make the picture one of its most important film projects, with Sidney Franklin producing and playwright Marc Connelly, himself a Pulitzer Prize winner, as-signed to turn the novel into a workable screenplay.

From his days as a director, Franklin had gained a reputation as a perfectionist; he carried it with him as a producer. A decision was made to film *The Yearling* in the forests of central Florida, using as near as possible the actual locations where the story was laid. This was unusual in film production in the early 1940s, when Hollywood's army of artists and skilled technicians had perfected the process of believably recreating almost any location in the world on the backlots and soundstages of the studios. For this picture in 1940, however, the studio leased a farm in Florida's Ocala National Forest and dispatched a crew to plant crops and get the locations into shape for shooting to begin.

Another crew rounded up local animals to meet the production's menagerie require-ments. Pigs, chickens, hounds, deer, bears, a bobcat, raccoons, foxes, squirrels, quail, doves, buzzards, snakes and an owl were shipped back to Hollywood for training. When every-thing was ready for shooting to begin, they were transported back to their natural habitat with the cast and crew, apparently having fared nicely by their Hollywood experience, since they appeared very well groomed and photogenic when they arrived back in the Florida forest.

The animals had not returned home right away, however; their Hollywood sojourn had been extended somewhat when production was postponed while a search was conducted for a boy between the ages of ten and eleven years to fill the crucial role of Jody Baxter.

Launched in February 1940, the canvass undertaken by MGM became the biggest and most publicized talent hunt since the search for an actress to play Scarlett O'Hara in that other Southern-set picture. Scouts fanned out all over the southeastern states; several thou-sand boys from all over the region were inter-viewed. More than 200 youngsters were actually screen-tested before the quest came to an end in Atlanta, Georgia, where a lad named Gene Eckman was found and seemed to be perfect for the part.

"You *are* Jody!" Mrs. Rawlings was said to have exclaimed on meeting young Gene for the first time.

Finally, in May 1941, after more than a

While his son Claude Jarman, Jr., dreams in his arms, Gregory Peck appears to have daydreams of his own in *The Yearling*.

year had been spent in the search for Jody and in training the animals, a location troupe of 275 actors and technicians with 40 tons of equipment departed Hollywood for Ocala. In the group were Spencer Tracy, cast as Jody's father, and Victor Fleming, whose extensive credits included both *Gone With the Wind* and *The Wizard of Oz* (1939), as well as a superb *Treasure Island* (1934), as director.

After only three weeks of shooting in Florida, the cast and crew returned unexpectedly and mysteriously to Hollywood, several weeks earlier than scheduled. Rumors of production difficulties and of differences of opinion and temperament among the filmmakers circulated throughout the industry.

On May 28, it was announced, without official explanation from MGM, that King Vidor would take over direction of the picture from Fleming. After reading the script, Vidor decided that because of his general unfamiliarity with the story, its milieu, its characters and with the production's logistics in general, he could not possibly begin to work on it and resume shooting right away.

MGM's management grew more and more disturbed over the picture's problems. It had already cost more than $500,000 (no small sum in 1941 production-dollar terms) and any further delays would mean that, among other things, the troupe of carefully trained fawns would outgrow their roles and the animal trainers would have to begin their arduous work all over again. Since the picture dealt with a fawn at various stages of its life over a year (and the shooting schedule was to involve far less time, or so it had been hoped), a number of lookalike fawns at various stages of growth had been found and trained. And since the animals grew very fast during their first year, matching them from shot to shot would clearly be an extremely complicated affair.

In addition, young Eckman's authentic Southern accent contrasted too greatly with Tracy's ersatz drawl and made him difficult to record and understand. An additional period of voice coaching seemed inevitable if Eckman was to be intelligible, but the studio wanted very much to retain him for the role.

A few days after the announcement that Vidor would take over the directorial reins, Metro released another official statement saying that the project was being shelved "in the best interests of the company."

A few months later, plans were quietly made to salvage the picture and early in 1942 a revival of the project was announced. Under the new plan, the picture was to be filmed entirely in Hollywood and 14-year-old British child actor Roddy McDowall was being tested for the role of Jody. But it soon became apparent that the Hollywood trend in 1942 was toward war—rather than animal—pictures and, after careful consideration, studio chiefs decided to leave the project on its shelf.

The passage of time, as we know, salves wounds, veils memories and befogs minds. In 1944, when the tribulations and trials of 1941-42 seemed remote and diminished,

Claude Jarman, Jr., and Gregory Peck pay a business call on general store-owner Henry Travers.

MGM and Sidney Franklin announced plans to revive *The Yearling* project with another cast and crew and another assault on the swampy Florida forest and farmland. The new production would star Gregory Peck and Jane Wyman, as Penny and Ma Baxter, Jody's parents, and would be directed by Clarence Brown.

Some of the animals, including a group of dogs, a raccoon, a raven and a deer, engaged for the original production contingent, had been kept under contract when it was shut down but practically an entire new zoo had to be rounded up. Ultimately, the studio found itself with a collection of some 469 animals, including 126 deer.

Unfortunately for him, young Eckman had meanwhile outgrown his role and a search for a new Jody had to be undertaken. Clarence Brown personally took over the job of finding a child for the new production. He and an assistant toured the South, surveying hundreds of school classrooms in the process and interviewing more than 12,000 youngsters. Finally, as Brown stood in the doorway of a schoolroom at the Eakin Grammar School in Nashville, Tennessee, one day, his eye fell on a tow-headed ten-year-old.

"That's my Jody," he thought, then had Claude Jarman, Jr., called to the principal's office. The search was ended and filming could at last commence.

With the cream of MGM's stable of craftsmen and artisans engaged to contribute their talents to the production, Franklin once again led an expeditionary force of filmmakers, actors and animals to Florida, hopeful that the problems which had thwarted him before would now be overcome. But even the best plans...

"Never again," swore Clarence Brown after the last shot of the film was in the can. Although he had survived years of dealing with the temperamental whims of actors, coping with trained deer and a growing field of corn proved to be more than he had reckoned on.

"You have to direct a deer or a stalk of corn to understand my problems," Brown told a newspaper reporter. And although shifting the Florida shooting schedule to winter had reduced exposure to the steamy heat that had plagued the earlier company working there in Florida's early summer, many of the problems of shooting in the forests there, including insects, sand, unpredictable weather and oppressive humidity, still had had to be faced and endured.

When the location work was completed in February 1946, a relieved crew returned to California to shoot some additional exterior scenes at Lake Arrowhead and interiors at the studio.

Once the film was edited and assembled, Herbert Stothart composed the score. Stothart based his lilting music for the film on pastoral themes by English composer Frederick Delius, deftly capturing the mood of the Florida backwoods, the simultaneously primitive and fragile atmosphere of that subtropical wilderness, of the swamp and the joyous freedom of its natural inhabitants, delicately underscoring a boy's love of nature.

The Yearling opened in Los Angeles before the end of 1946, to qualify for that year's Academy Awards; the New York premiere was scheduled for Radio City Music Hall on January 23, 1947. A minor snag with that booking developed when Music Hall managing director Guy Eyssell previewed the picture and afterward told MGM that the Technicolor blood of a pig which had been mauled by a bear was too vivid for the Music Hall's screen and he convinced the studio that the scene had to be cut. As a result, it was dropped from some 200 prints then being prepared at Technicolor's labs but was left in 90 prints that had already been completed.

Considerable fanfare accompanied the picture's release and one of Metro's ad lines for it read: "This is the year of THE YEARLING... and it's worth waiting for!" Perhaps the studio was trying to convince itself as well as the public. In any event, the critics tended to agree:

"It isn't very often," wrote Bosley Crowther in *The New York Times*, "that there is realized upon the screen the innocence and trust and enchantment that are in the nature of a child or the yearning love and anxiety that a father feels for his boy.... [*The Yearling*] provides such a wealth of satisfaction as few pictures ever attain...vitality and zest flow through the whole film.... There's no denying that the fitness of the picture is due in large measure to the incredibly fine performance which little Claude Jarman, Jr., gives.... Equally important, however, is the performance of Gregory Peck, the warm and gentle father.... Although he measures several inches taller than Mrs. Rawlings original...he fills out every one of them with simple dignity and strength.... Jane Wyman...compels credulity and sympathy...."

Crowther's only reservations were for those moments "when the Aurora Borealis is turned on and the heavenly choir starts singing" and he felt that Jody's hysterics were overlong toward the end, but he summed it up as "a cheerful and inspiring film."

Life magazine reported that "Although *The Yearling* tends to become tediously sentimental toward its conclusion and its beautiful scenery sometimes dares to improve on reality, it is nevertheless a stunning production. The photography, the musical score...and the acting of young Claude Jarman, Jr., Gregory Peck and Jane Wyman are beyond reproach."

"Gregory Peck is excellent," said *The New Yorker*, while *Cue* magazine called the film "...a

brilliant masterpiece of technique and photography, a gem of sympathetic writing...."

No summations of the film surpassed the eloquence of John Mason Brown in *The Saturday Review*: "*The Yearling*," he wrote, "has a quality most other films cannot claim. It is something born of the open air; of fields and rivers and forest; of the primal issues of life and survival as they are there encountered; of the poverty of humble, hard-driven people; and of man's courage and patience in his endless struggle with nature ... in Gregory Peck's and young Claude Jarman's admirable playing of father and son it comes through with dignity."

In the *New York Herald Tribune*, Howard Barnes said that the picture ranked "among the fine achievements of the cinema...a motion picture of beauty, artistry and deep feeling...a piece of universal experience has been spread across the screen.... Peck is particularly appealing...gives a superb portrayal."

The members of the Motion Picture Academy evidently agreed. Gregory Peck received his second Oscar nomination as best actor (but the award went to Fredric March for *The Best Years of Our Lives*). *The Yearling* was also nominated for best picture, Jane Wyman received a best-actress nomination and Harold Kress was nominated for film editing. Oscars were won by Cedric Gibbons, Paul Groesse and Edwin B. Willis for their art direction and set decoration, however, and Charles Rosher, Leonard Smith and Arthur Arling won Oscars for their Technicolor photography. An honorary Oscar was bestowed on Claude Jarman, Jr., as "outstanding child actor of 1946." Although he missed the Oscar, Peck could at least console himself with the Hollywood Foreign Press Association's Golden Globe award, bestowed on him as Best Actor.

The Yearling was a solid commercial success as well as a critical one, returning more than $5.2 million to MGM in domestic film rentals alone, a huge sum in 1947 dollars.

Claude Jarman, Jr., in a tender moment with one of the fawns who comprised a substantial part of the menagerie MGM collected and trained for its production of *The Yearling*.

Hassan Said, Robert Preston and Gregory Peck use extreme caution in approaching the thicket where they suspect their wounded quarry is waiting to charge them.

The Macomber Affair

United Artists 1947

Credits

Producers, Benedict Bogeaus, Casey Robinson; *director*, Zoltan Korda; *screenplay*, Casey Robinson, Seymour Bennett, based on Ernest Hemingway's story "The Short Happy Life of Francis Macomber"; *adaptation*, Seymour Bennett, Frank Arnold; *music*, Miklos Rozsa; *cinematography*, Karl Struss; *African cameramen*, O. H. Barradaile, John Wilcox, Fred Francis; *editors*, James Smith, George Feld, *art director*, Erno Metzer; *set decoration*, Fred Widdowson; *sound*, William Lynch; *assistant director*, Joseph Depew. (89 minutes)

Cast

Gregory Peck (Robert Wilson), Robert Preston (Francis Macomber), Joan Bennett (Margaret Macomber), Reginald Denny (Police Inspector), Earl Smith (Kongoni), Jean Gillie (Aimee), Carl Harbord (Coroner), Martin Wilkin (Bartender), Vernon Downing (Reporter Logan), Frederic Worlock (Clerk), Hassan Said (Abdullah), Darby Jones (Masai Warrior).

•

Despite its deviant ending and some other minor embellishments, among all the films that have been based on works by Ernest Hemingway, the Casey Robinson-Benedict Bogeaus production of "The Short Happy Life of Francis Macomber" comes closest, perhaps, to successfully translating Hemingway's terse literary style into the medium of motion pictures.

Released as *The Macomber Affair*, this was Gregory Peck's second picture under his contract with producer-writer Robinson. And it is undoubtedly Robinson's involvement that accounts for the felicitous transition of Hemingway's short story from printed page to its sight and sound embodiment on film.

Director Zoltan Korda's principal screen works had been made in association with his producer-director brother, Alexander, one of the titans of the British film industry during the 1930s and 40s. Zoltan himself had a reputation not only as a skilled director of spectacular action-adventure pictures set in exotic locales, but also as one who had a genuine liking and respect for writers and literature. His Hollywood-produced pictures included *The Jungle Book* (1942) and *Sahara* (1943).

Gregory Peck's rugged and lean good looks must have made him seem a natural for the role of the white hunter, even though Hemingway's Robert Wilson was of British, rather than American, background. As a "great white hunter" he is the pivotal character in the playing out of a domestic drama to its tragic end and in witnessing a 35-year-old sportsman's triumph over cowardice and transition to true manhood.

Robert Preston, a generally stalwart type, was cast as Francis Macomber, the American hunter of definite wealth and dubious courage, who employs Wilson as his hunter-guide. Preston, under contract to Paramount, was making the film for release by United Artists on loan-out; it was his first picture after war service in the Army Air Force.

Joan Bennett's attention appears unwavering as Gregory Peck and her husband Robert Preston discuss the various thrills and rewards of big-game hunting.

With the body of the late Francis Macomber on a litter in the ambulance, coroner Carl Harbord discusses his death with hunter-guide Gregory Peck.

In happier days, Gregory Peck, Joan Bennett and Robert Preston discuss their impending hunting safari in a Nairobi gun shop.

Gregory Peck, Robert Preston and supporting cast members amid the realistic African safari campsite constructed on a Hollywood soundstage for *The Macomber Affair*.

Joan Bennett was the ideal embodiment of Hemingway's "extremely handsome and well-kept woman," Margaret Macomber, Francis's wife. Although she was only a few years older than her co-stars, Miss Bennett already had the major portion of her film career behind her and had been an established and very popular star for many years.

The Macomber Affair's interiors and safari encampment scenes were shot on soundstages in Hollywood. Backgrounds and African animals were filmed in Africa itself by three cameramen who were sent there, but the cast never left North America. The hunting scenes with Peck, Preston and Bennett were shot across the Mexican border in the northern part of Baja, with some wild variegated countryside there standing in—and admirably so—for the Dark Continent.

"So we were rolling along in our four-wheel-drive jeeps and safari cars and running through the brush firing our rifles at animals we never saw," said Peck. "They were cut in later. And it all got monotonous. We were there for about six weeks, 80 men and only two women, Joan Bennett and her hairdresser.

"Well, we were all kinda stir crazy. Joan would always go to bed at around 8:30 at night

and her hairdresser lived in the bungalow with her, so there was just a big stag party every night. Most of the fellows stuck it out but there were a few who couldn't stand the tension and they would drive about 80 miles at night to Tijuana, where there were bars and brothels where they could have some fun. But it was a long pull from this place we were in, called Rosarito Beach, and the road to Tijuana was so terrible they called it 'Dead Man's Highway.' All the curves were graded the wrong way and right along cliffs above the sea.

"For the rest of us there was a marimba band of particularly rough-looking piratical Mexicans. I remember most of them had all-gold teeth and they would drink tequila and beer and so would we all. And we'd sing with the band, play poker, shoot pool, talk and carry on. Later on, when we'd finished the picture at the studio in Los Angeles, we tried to import this marimba band for a party, for the sake of sentiment. And the leader and two others couldn't come across the border because they were wanted for murder in San Bernardino. They'd been involved in some shoot-out and were fugitives. But nevertheless, they were great fellows down there.

"One particular night, we stayed up all

night and drank and sang. Bob Preston and I were there and the whole crew, except the director Zoltan Korda—he went to bed at 10 o'clock—and Joan Bennett and her hairdresser, who had gone to bed at 8:30. It was just about 6 A.M., just about time for us to climb into the cars and go on this hour-and-a-half drive over these terrible mountain roads to this terrain that looked like Africa, when somebody said, 'The cars are leaving in 20 minutes.' And we were still carousing in the bar with the marimba band.

"So we all went down to the beach and stripped and ran into the surf to try to sober up, got out and got into our clothes, swallowed some black coffee and got into these cars— drunk. We got to the location and were ready to shoot at 8:30."

Korda's demanding attitude as a director did not in the least diminish Greg's respect and regard for him: "Zoltan Korda," he says, "was one of my favorite directors. He could be very bad-tempered—not with me because he liked me and I liked him, but he was short-tempered with phonies and hypocrites and types like that—and there was a producer on this film, Benedict Bogeaus, who was not Zolly's type. And we had a little title problem.

"It was decided that Hemingway's title, 'The Short Happy Life of Francis Macomber,' was too long for the marquee and we'd been discussing alternate titles for several weeks. I remember one day at lunch at the General Service Studio, this little old-fashioned Hollywood studio, Aldous Huxley, who was doing some writing in an office there, heard us discussing our title problem and also talking about a mechanical buffalo that was to charge down a track at Bob Preston at a certain point, while he stood his ground and fired away at it. And it was to fall right at his feet while I was standing there with him.

"This thing was under construction and had a hide made of rubber and hair and had pistons in it and was very life-like. They'd invested about $30,000 in this contraption. Huxley was very amused by all this discussion and he put the two things together and said, 'Why don't you call it "The—ah—Rubba Buffalo"?'

"Well, that didn't go down too well and so one day in the middle of a tense scene on the

After overcoming his cowardice, Robert Preston appears pleased with his kill, Peck is satisfied with his pupil's progress and Preston's wife, Joan Bennett, seems to be definitely troubled by the ramifications of her husband's new-found courage.

At their safari campsite, Robert Preston and Gregory Peck talk about Preston's triumphant emergence into manhood.

set—pressure was mounting, we had to have a title to get the ads in, make announcements, et cetera—Bogeaus appeared. he was a kind of man with a lot of cologne and a lot of gold jewelry and elegant tailoring, a nice enough fellow, but just not Korda's type.

"Anyway, he just burst onto the set right in the middle of a heavy rehearsal and said, 'Zolly, listen to this! I've got it—and it's great!'"

Everything stopped. Korda turned to the intruder, regarded him briefly, then asked, "Well, what the hell is it, Benedict?"

Bogeaus, Peck recalls, raised his arms triumphantly and shouted: "Congo! ... Congo!!"

"Well, Korda just stared at him for a moment, then he took out a pocket knife he always carried. He unfolded this thing, it had a long, mean-looking blade to it, and walked over to Bogeaus and stuck it right close into his upper-abdominal region and said, 'You stupid son-of-a-beech! You get off my set and if you ever come back here again, I cut your leever out!'

"And he backed him right off the set, right out the door. The producer of the picture! And we never saw him again.

"He was really something, Zolly Korda, a tough guy but also a very sensitive, very good man. I always got along well with those fellows. We had a good working partnership."

The aspect of the production which perhaps caused the filmmakers the most trouble was the picture's ending; they even petitioned author Hemingway for assistance in resolving their dilemma when they realized that some

changes would have to be made to the ending he had provided.

As close as the picture hews to the Hemingway lines, some changes invariably became necessary to bring it to screen, and criticism has been leveled at the picture because of some of the screenwriters' embellishments to the Hemingway plot, chief among them the attenuation of a romantic angle between Robert Wilson and Margaret Macomber that really doesn't exist in the original (beyond a one-night stand) and the addition of some scenes at the beginning and end. The early scenes serve basically to introduce the characters and give us information conveyed originally by Hemingway in literary methods which have no simple cinematic equivalent. Both the movie and the short story, however, employ flashback to get into the narrative.

In Hemingway's version there was no doubt that Margaret Macomber had deliberately shot and killed her husband when she realized that he had come into his manhood, would no longer be subject to intimidation by her, and might very well leave her. Wilson, into whose tent she had crept one night after her husband had fallen asleep, told her that he would report the shooting as an accident, even though he clearly doesn't believe that it was. He clearly has no affection for Margaret. The story ends shortly thereafter and it is clear that Wilson will have nothing further to do with her; they will go their separate ways and she will not be punished for her ignoble deed.

This sort of denouement was not allowable to the filmmakers. The old Hollywood Production Code (the industry's self-applied morality guide) required that wrongdoers must be punished for their evil deeds by picture's end. Clearly the Hemingway ending was in conflict with the code, so the filmmakers tried to find a compromise that would be true to Hemingway's intent and still satisfy the requirements of the Hays Office (so-called after Will H. Hays, the Code's author and chief enforcer).

"So," Peck recalls, "we sweated and

Earl Smith, Robert Preston, Joan Bennett, Gregory Peck and Hassan Said have mixed emotions about their impending confrontation with a wounded water-buffalo they have tracked into a thicket.

grunted and strained and wrote and re-wrote. We all had a go at it. I was not a real producer but I sat in on things and opinionated. And we cabled Hemingway.

"We told him exactly what trouble we were in and that we didn't want to corrupt his story. He never answered one of our cables. We'd paid him $80,000 for the screen rights for this story. He endorsed the check, all right, deposited it. But when we tried to get him to help us out of that dilemma, we couldn't even get a reply. The upshot of the whole thing was that we did the best we could."

The movie ends outside a jury room, before a coroner's inquest, with a confrontation between Wilson and Margaret during which she lays much of the blame for what has happened on the unhappiness of her marriage, on Maçomber's bad treatment of her, etc., and indicates that she may be ready to accept a degree of guilt and pay for it with a jail term. Wilson, who had previously admitted to Macomber that he was in love with Margaret (the screenwriter's twist), seems to fall out of love with her in the course of their argument about her motives and the killing itself. The picture ends with uncertainty over whether Wilson will be waiting for Margaret when she emerges from the inquest. Hemingway's clean-cut fiction thus becomes muddled in the end.

"That was the best we could do," says Peck, "to try to preserve the hard unsentimental nature of the story and at the same time placate the Hays Office. And of course it screwed up the entire picture. The last ten minutes we had to devote to wrapping up those loose ends and suddenly the picture dissipated."

Contemporary critics were in agreement with that assessment: Otis L. Guernsey, Jr., in the *New York Herald Tribune*, called it "...a confused and shapeless screen translation...it is both adapted and performed in a vague, indecisive manner, as though...Robinson and ...Bennett were hiding their meanings from the censors...the whole thing ends up in the air in a muddle of motives and excuses."

Of the actors, Guernsey wrote, "Except for some difficulty with English slang phrases, Peck's portrayal of Wilson is assured...the actor does a good job of mirroring a sort of masculine independence of manner toward both women and wealthy cowards...."

In *The New York Times*, Bosley Crowther was more tolerant and indicated that if one would overlook the fore and aft sections, "you will find a quite credible screen telling" of Hemingway's story. "It is not," Crowther did hasten to point out, "a romantic story...and the producers have not improved it by trying to make it so...."

Crowther thought the film "a tight and absorbing study of character. Joan Bennett," he said, "is completely hydrochloric as the peevish, deceitful dame.... Robert Preston is patently the victim ... the measured performance of Gregory Peck ... implies the distrust and cynicism of the latter toward the unsporting dame...." Crowther also noted that "the hunting scenes, incidentally, are visual knockouts...."

Within three weeks of its opening at the Globe Theater in New York, on April 20, 1947, *The Macomber Affair* was eclipsed by the hoopla surrounding Selznick's opening of *Duel in the Sun*, and the unpretentious little black-and-white picture paled in comparison to the lurid spectacular. But it is a gem to rediscover, and, its embellishments aside, still seems perhaps the best screen rendition to date of Hemingway's simple, eloquent and uncluttered prose.

62

Duel in the Sun

Selznick Releasing Organization   **1946**
A Vanguard Production

Credits

Producer, David O. Selznick; *director*, King Vidor; *screenplay*, David O. Selznick, suggested by the novel by Niven Busch; *adaptation*, Oliver H. P. Garrett; *music*, Dimitri Tiomkin; *song*, "Gotta Get Me Somebody to Love" by Allie Wrubel; *cinematography*, Lee Garmes, Hal Rosson, Ray Rennahan; *second unit directors*, Otto Brower, B. Reeves Eason; *special effects*, Clarence Lifer, Jack Cosgrove; *supervising editor*, Hal C. Kern; *editors*, William Ziegler, John Saure; *art director*, James Basevi; *associate art director*, John Ewing; *production design*, J. McMillan Johnson; *technical director*, Natalie Kalmus; *choreography*, Lloyd Shaw, Tilly Losch; *costumes*, Walter Plunkett; color by Technicolor; *narrator*, Orson Welles. (138 minutes)

Cast

Gregory Peck (Lewt McCanles), Joseph Cotten (Jesse McCanles), Jennifer Jones (Pearl Chavez), Lionel Barrymore (Senator McCanles), Lillian Gish (Laura Belle McCanles), Walter Huston (The Sin Killer), Herbert Marshall (Scott Chavez), Charles Bickford (Sam Pierce), Joan Tetzel (Helen Langford), Harry Carey (Lem Smoot), Otto Kruger (Mr. Langford), Sidney Blackmer (The Lover), Tilly Losch (Mrs. Chavez), Scott McKay (Sid), Butterfly McQueen (Vashti), Francis McDonald (Gambler), Victor Kilian (Gambler), Griff Barnett (The Jailer), Frank Cordell (Ken), Dan White (Ed), Steve Dunhill (Jake), Lane Chandler (Captain of U. S. Cavalry), Lloyd Shaw (Caller at Barbecue), Thomas Dillon (Engineer), Robert McKenzie (Bartender), Charles Dingle (Sheriff Thomson), Kermit Maynard (Barfly, Presidio Bar), Hank Bell (Ranch Hand), Johnny Bond (Hand at Barbecue), Bert Roach (Eater), Si Jenks, Hank Worden, Rose Plummer (Dancers at Barbecue), Guy Wilkerson (Barfly), Lee Phelps (Engineer).

"The way I see it," David O. Selznick once said, apropos of the role of a producer, "my function is to be responsible for everything."

....

David O. Selznick to scriptwriter Oliver H. P. Garrett and director King Vidor: "I want this to be an artistic little Western. You take it over and if you need any help, let me know. But it's your baby."

....

King Vidor, on location near Tucson, Arizona, to David O. Selznick: "You can take this picture and..."

....

From humble beginnings—and, allegedly, intentions—*Duel in the Sun* grew into a blockbuster of epic proportions, becoming one of the most lavish and spectacular, not to mention highest-grossing, Westerns of all time. The transition was not an easy one—nor calm.

"Everything that had ever happened west

A lavish and lively party (David O. Selznick style) at the Spanish Bit ranch is the occasion for a lineup of Walter Huston, Joseph Cotten, Jennifer Jones, Gregory Peck and land baron Lionel Barrymore on the hacienda's veranda.

of the Rocky Mountains was considered for the script," observed director Vidor several years later in his autobiography, *A Tree Is a Tree.*

When Vidor's epic film *The Big Parade* was released to critical and popular acclaim in 1925, bucking the industry notion that the public didn't want to see war pictures, his reputation as a director was made. In a few years, he confirmed his range and talent as he segued from the gritty turmoil of war to the pathos and delicacy of *La Boheme* (1926), to comedies such as *Show People* (1928), to sentimental successes like *The Champ* (1931) and to deeply felt social commentaries like *Our Daily Bread* (1934).

As *Duel*'s script took on epic proportions, so did the cast Selznick was assembling. And he seemed to take special delight in casting Gregory Peck, who had heretofore appeared only in "hero" roles as a noble and stalwart type, as the low-down, mean-spirited but somewhat likable Lewt McCanles; taking him,

as Peck noted some years later, "from *The Keys of the Kingdom*, where I had played this saintly maverick priest, and making me a rapist, a forger, a killer, a liar, a thoroughly rotten no-good but with a certain likability. I played a very bad boy and I played the part for fun."

Joseph Cotten was cast as Lewt's brother, his complete opposite in morals and demeanor. And Jennifer Jones, who had won an Oscar for her first major screen role, as the French peasant girl who saw a holy vision at Lourdes in *The Song of Bernadette*, and in whom Selznick had a special personal interest, was cast as Pearl Chavez, the hot-blooded half-breed who came between the two brothers. The casting against previously established type inspired one newspaper of the time to comment, "It will be quite a sight to see the erstwhile Father Chisholm leering at the onetime Saint Bernadette."

Lionel Barrymore was to play the land-baron patriarch of the McCanles clan and Lillian Gish was persuaded to make one of her

64

rare (since the 1920s) screen appearances as his wife. For the role of the revivalist preacher, "The Sin Killer," Selznick wanted Walter Huston. As originally scripted, Huston's role would have required him for only a few days of shooting, but his minimum fee per picture was then $40,000. Selznick protested, but Huston's agent was adamant and the only concession the producer could get was an agreement that the actor would be available for ten weeks at $4,000 per week. It was typical of the way the production grew that by the time Huston's work on the film was finished, the ten-week period had expired and he was being paid overtime.

The physical aspects of *Duel in the Sun* kept pace with the inflation of the script: Sets were designed, then re-designed, always bigger than before; ranch houses became haciendas, a little cantina became a roaring dance-hall and gambling casino. And everything—every piece of 1880 period architecture, every piece of furniture, every prop and every costume—was checked and re-checked for authenticity by an army of consultants. Experts on Western folklore, dancing and customs were likewise called upon to verify details. No single item was too small to be double-checked.

One day when Vidor got to the set for a sequence in a saloon, he noticed a stranger hanging around. When he questioned the man, he found out that he was a bartender Selznick had met the night before at a party and had hired on impulse to supervise the scenes where liquor was poured and to make sure it was done properly and was the correct color. Vidor, who was fairly keen when it came to details himself, was not fond of this sort of uninvited interference and told the bartender to leave.

As scenes were expanded, estimates for the number of livestock, horsemen and extras (some 2500) were constantly revised upward. So was the production budget, which ultimately mushroomed to nearly $6 million, exceeding the cost of *Gone With the Wind* by

As Lewt McCanles, Gregory Peck takes Jennifer Jones for a few spirited dance turns around the patio during his family's big barbecue.

more than a million dollars. In all, the film was in various stages of production from March 1945 until November 1946—and wasn't released until May, 1947.

Director Josef von Sternberg was engaged as a special visual and color consultant to supervise Jennifer Jones's scenes and impart to her the sort of glamorous look he had achieved for Marlene Dietrich in such films as *The Blue Angel* and *Morocco* (1930) and *Shanghai Express* (1932). Von Sternberg later claimed that his contributions to *Duel* weren't visible in the finished product. Beyond Vidor and Sternberg, veteran Selznick cinematographers Lee Garmes, Hal Rosson and Ray Rennahan worked with second-unit directors Reeves Eason and Otto Bower to create some of the film's spectacle.

In general, however, the production did not go smoothly and many of the difficulties and delays were undoubtedly attributable to Selznick's own constant revisions of the work in progress, his frequent decisions to reshoot scenes that had already been shot, his almost never-ending expansion of the "artistic little Western."

"David," recalled Vidor, "would spare neither expense nor effort if he felt a scene could be improved by redoing it, no matter how infinitesimal the changes might be."

Of course, Selznick's revisions were not the only cause of delays. On one occasion, Gregory Peck's relative inexperience as a young gunslinger (this was, after all, his first Western) slowed down the proceedings.

According to the plot, Charles Bickford, playing Sam Pierce, the kindly foreman of the Spanish Bit ranch, the McCanles baronial spread, was to be shot and killed by Lewt on the night before Pierce was to marry Pearl Chavez.

When it came time to shoot the scene,

there was a small problem: Bickford, who had been an actor since 1929 and had done his share of Westerns, was much more experienced at gunplay and easily outdrew the less-experienced Peck. Every time they attempted the scene, Bickford drew first and "plugged" the man who was supposed to shoot him. Vidor at first urged Peck to draw faster, but when it became apparent that Peck was drawing as fast as he could the director asked Bickford to slow down and let Peck outdraw him. Bickford demurred.

"It won't look right," he told Vidor. "Let Peck go and practice."

"But we don't have time, Charlie," the director pleaded. "Let's finish the shot."

Bickford, though a thorough-going professional, had something of a reputation for occasional cantankerousness and could not be persuaded to slow his draw. Peck, he continued to insist, must speed up his. So Greg retired to practice and when he felt sufficiently fast enough to challenge Bickford again, Vidor called for another go at filming the scene. But it still required nine takes before Peck outdrew Bickford and the older actor bit the dust.

"When Vidor called 'Print that!' I could hear the relief in his voice," remembers Peck.

Whatever the various causes, there were many delays on the picture. David O. Selznick's memos to the production crew alternated between requests for more retakes and reshooting and castigations for the slow pace at which the project was proceeding.

Publicity stunts during the course of a production were not unusual. As a part of *Duel's* advance promotion the Hollywood

trade papers carried numerous ads quoting various pundits praising Selznick and the film, even though it was not in release; indeed since it was still in production it could not even have been seen. As a retaliatory joke, director Billy Wilder ran an ad for his own current picture-in-progress, *Double Indemnity*, which read:

"*Double Indemnity* is the greatest picture I have every seen...." and was signed, "George Oblath." Oblath was the proprietor of a small Hollywood restaurant. Although Hollywood chuckled, David O. Selznick was not amused and, infuriated, threatened to cancel his ads if the trade press accepted any further material ridiculing his picture.

Whatever was stirring Selznick's psyche, the conflict between him and director Vidor came to a climax one day during the shooting of the picture's somewhat lurid finale, wherein Lewt and Pearl, having mortally wounded each other, crawl painfully across the rock-strewn terrain toward a final dusty and bloody embrace.

Selznick had worked meticulously on this crucial emotional—not to mention melodramatic—scene to which the entire picture had to build; he was adamant that it be shot according to his idea of it, just as he had written it. Vidor may have had second thoughts about it, but they could hardly have mattered.

While Greg and Jennifer lay on the ground waiting to play out their death scene under Vidor's direction, David himself called a halt. He had decided that they were not bloody enough, so he grabbed a container of make-up blood and began to splash it over the actors.

Vidor sat looking on with his script in hand. Then, he closed the script, stood up and handed it to Selznick with a succinct comment: "You can take this picture and shove it."

The cast and crew stood and gaped silently as Vidor strode to his limousine, got in and told his driver to take him back to Tucson. In silence they watched as the car headed onto the road stretching eight dusty miles across

After her father's death, half-breed Jennifer Jones comes to live on the Spanish Bit ranch, as the ward of land baron Lionel Barrymore and his wife, played by Lillian Gish.

the desert until it vanished over a hill. They watched it all the way. Glaciers advanced and retreated, mountain chains rose and fell. An eternity later, when the limousine was gone from sight, everyone turned to look at Selznick.

"Well," he said matter-of-factly, "that's all for today." Then he asked an assistant director to dismiss the company.

When it became clear later that Vidor would not return to the production, Selznick called William Dieterle, who had directed *I'll Be Seeing You* (1944) for him, to come out from Hollywood and wind up the location work. Additional second-unit work was directed by Otto Bower, Chester Franklin and William Cameron Menzies, but it was Dieterle who guided the picture through its later stages.

The Directors Guild arbitrators supported Vidor, however, and awarded him sole director credit. Brower and B. Reeves Eason received second-unit credits but neither Dieterle, nor Sternberg, nor Chester Franklin nor William Cameron Menzies received any official credit at all.

Eason's exciting train-wreck sequence was added after principal photography on the picture had been completed. In the script, as Selznick added it, Lewt sabotages the railroad and causes a fatal train wreck out of pure maliciousness. To further emphasize Lewt's meanness, Selznick had Peck merrily singing "I've Been Workin' on the Railroad" as he rode away from the scene of devastation.

"At that moment," Peck has recalled, "I just kind of imitated a cousin of mine who was a bit of a rascal, a black sheep in the family, but likable."

Vidor saw an early preview of the picture and felt that the scene destroyed what little sympathy the audience had felt for Peck's character in the first place and damaged the picture. Despite their difference of opinion earlier, Vidor and Selznick had remained on relatively friendly terms and Vidor went to David's home to plead with him to remove the scene. When Vidor found him, Selznick was in the bathroom shaving; he went right on shaving while Vidor used every conceivable argument against retaining the train wreck.

After Vidor had stated his case, Selznick turned to him and said, "I want to make Lewt the worst son-of-a-bitch that's ever been seen on a motion-picture screen, and I believe the train wreck scene will prove my point." It stayed.

Obtaining a satisfactory music score proved to be no less troublesome than any other facet of the production of *Duel in the Sun*. By the time Dimitri Tiomkin called on Selznick to discuss the possibility of his doing it, seven other composers had tried and failed to come up with music that approached David's idea of what the score should be.

Finally the long production siege was drawing to a close and Selznick began to turn his attention to the details of the film's release and its publicity campaign. He announced the formation of the Selznick Releasing Organization to distribute *Duel* and all subsequent D.O.S. productions.

Film industry observers meanwhile looked upon David's latest venture as the greatest screen gamble of all time because of the high production costs and the fact that it was based on a novel of limited circulation, without the "pre-sold" characteristics of a film made from a best-seller, like *Gone With the Wind*, for example, which might justify such lavish expenditures. In its April 29, 1946, issue, *Time* magazine reported that the picture "at $6 million will outcost any other film ever made."

The publicity budget alone, which added up to almost $2 million by the time the picture

Jennifer Jones in a less than receptive attitude toward the attentions of Gregory Peck, who has become a fugitive wanted for the murder of her fiancé.

was in full release in June 1947, was remarkable: for a single picture, Selznick was spending an amount equal to the entire annual advertising budgets studios like Columbia and Universal spent for the release of 50 films.

Among the stunts used to promote the picture was the dropping of thousands of war-surplus weather parachutes on sporting events around the country, even including the Kentucky Derby. The chutes contained not only promotional material for the film but also, in some cases, bets on the sporting events in progress.

The picture not only ran afoul of the Roman Catholic Legion of Decency, but was also denounced for its immorality in the U.S. House of Representatives in Washington. The denunciation prompted Paul MacNamara, S.R.O.'s publicity chief for advertising and promotion, to write to Rep. Everett M. Dirksen explaining that the Breen Office (formerly known as "the Hays Office, but still the industry's self-censorship agency) had been consulted more than 25 times during the course of production and that a number of changes had been made at the suggestion of industry Production Code chief Joseph I. Breen. The changes, MacNamara reported, had cost over $200,000.

When the Legion's moral guardians finally did see the movie, they too demanded several cuts. Selznick reluctantly made the deletions ("They can make me cut it," he reportedly said, "but they'll never make me like it") and *Duel* was subsequently rated "B"— the same rating that had been given such then-current films as *The Best Years of Our Lives*, *The Sign of the Cross* and *Blue Skies*—which classi-

fied it as "Morally Objectionable in Part for All (films in this category are considered to contain elements dangerous to Christian morals or moral standards)."

Thirty-odd years later, *Duel*'s "lurid" scenes would hardly cause a raised eyebrow, let alone a brouhaha. But it was widely criticized when it was released.

Even Jennifer Jones came in for criticism. After her Oscar-winning role in *The Song of Bernadette*, she was so closely identified with that saintly maiden that many religious-minded moviegoers and quite a few clergymen were aghast when she assumed the persona of Pearl Chavez, an antithetical role to say the least. So strong did the criticism become that Miss Jones felt obliged to respond, pointing out, "I was never Bernadette, nor was I Pearl Chavez. Each was simply a role I as an actress tried to interpret." Presumably Father Chisholm was held to a much less strict code of subsequent moral conduct.

Duel in the Sun's release and distribution were carefully planned. When the picture was finished, Paul MacNamara had taken a look at it and told David that in his considered opinion it was "lousy." Although he was pained by this blunt and honest assessment, Selznick listened as MacNamara advised that he thought the only way to salvage the project was to play the picture off as fast as possible in every situation to negate the effects of inevitably bad reviews and possibly equally bad word-of-mouth.

With Selznick's approval, MacNamara devised a saturation booking and advertising campaign for New York City, based on opening the picture in all five boroughs simultaneously instead of in only one Manhattan theater initially, which was the traditional and time-worn method of opening a new release. Selznick's pride was stung, but pragmatism carried the day and he agreed to test MacNamara's plan.

It worked. The unprecedented promotional campaign MacNamara waged thoroughly whetted moviegoers' appetites and in its first five days of release in New York *Duel* raked in $750,000. Based on that strategy, Selznick opened the picture in 300 theaters around the country on May 7, 1947, and wound up taking in some $17 million on its initial release. The lesson of this success was not lost on the other studios, who learned from David O. Selznick the benefits of saturation booking and nationwide exploitation—a new way of releasing pictures.

MacNamara's prognosis regarding critical reaction to the picture was fairly accurate. Bosley Crowther, in *The New York Times*, said the film "has some flashes of brilliance in it," but called it "a spectacularly disappointing job...a clutter of clichés worn thin in a hundred previous Westerns....Selznick...seems to have been more anxious to emphasize the clash of love and lust than to seek some illumination of a complex of arrogance and greed...." Crowther conceded that the picture had "some eye-dazzling scenes" but lamented, "if only the dramatics were up to the technical style! But they're not. Nor are the performances, which are strangely uneven....The best and the most consistent is that of Mr. Peck, who makes of the renegade brother a credibly vicious and lawless character.... The final scene...is one of those chunks of theatrics that ranks with Liza crossing the ice," said Crowther, but *Duel* "is still something to see...."

Variety's reviewer wrote that "the familiar Western formula reaches its highest commercialization.... The star lineup is impressive. Vastness of the western locale is splendidly displayed.... Rarely has a film made such frank use of lust and still been cleared for showings.... Miss Jones...proves herself extremely capable in quieter sequences but is overly meller in others. Same is true of Peck. ... The role has no audience sympathy but will call a great fascination for the femmes...."

In the *New York Herald Tribune*, Howard Barnes called the picture "a more or less conventional horse opera...extravagant in treatment, performance, color and exploitation." He remarked that it had "interludes of arresting cinematic action...passages of straight pictorial composition which are sometimes stunning.... For all that, it is more ponderous and tasteless than cumulatively entertaining.... Vidor's touch is evident in more than one scene, but it is fumbling in the overall staging.... For every passage of comparatively convincing period reconstruction, lovemaking or violence...there are half a dozen exaggerated sequences to match. Walter Huston has a fine passage.... The acting is as hamstrung by the script as the direction. Jennifer Jones plays...with no more conviction than some heavy make-up contributes to the portrayal. She over-acts at every turn.... Peck is not much better...and Joseph Cotten merely looks mournful...a top-heavy and trying motion picture."

It may have been *Time* magazine which best put the picture in perspective, calling it "...a knowing blend of oats and aphrodisiac... the costliest, most lushly Technicolored, the most lavishly cast, the loudest ballyhooed, and the sexiest horse opera ever made...rip-roaring gunplay, overheated histrionics.... The audience eventually learns...that Illicit Love doesn't really pay in the long run, but for about 134 minutes it has appeared to be loads of fun.... Millions of moviegoers will feel that the mere opulence of *Duel's* color, music, noise and activity is good enough value for the price of admission.... Mr. Selznick may well be Hollywood's smartest businessman...."

Whatever the critical response to *Duel in the Sun*, moviegoers flocked to see what all the hoopla and commotion and moralizing and sermonizing had been about, making it one of the most successful Westerns ever made—and an ironic tribute to the power of would-be censors to pack the theaters. And in 1970, when *Action*, the official magazine of the Directors Guild of America, polled a cross-section of newspaper and magazine film critics for their choices of the best dozen Westerns of all time, *Duel* made the consensus list.

"THE PICTURE OF A THOUSAND MEMORABLE MOMENTS," as one ad line touted it, did not, as its producer might have hoped, outdo *Gone With the Wind*. But apropos of that obsession, *Newsweek* magazine observed, in its July 5, 1965, obituary of David O. Selznick, that, "Try as he might, he could not find anything to top *Gone With the Wind*. But neither could anyone else."

Gregory Peck, as magazine writer Phil Green, discusses his proposed series on anti-Semitism with Dorothy McGuire, Jane Wyatt and Curt Conway.

Gentleman's Agreement

20th Century-Fox   **1947**

Credits

Producer, Darryl F. Zanuck; *director*, Elia Kazan; *screenplay*, Moss Hart, from the novel by Laura Z. Hobson; *music*, Alfred Newman; *cinematography*, Arthur Miller; *editor*, Harmon Jones; *art directors*, Lyle Wheeler, Mark-Lee Kirk; *set decoration*, Thomas Little, Paul S. Fox; *costumes*, Charles Le Maire, Kay Nelson; *special effects*, Fred Sersen; *assistant director*, Saul Wurtzel. (118 minutes)

Cast

Gregory Peck (Phil Green), Dorothy McGuire (Kathy), John Garfield (Dave), Celeste Holm (Anne), Anne Revere (Mrs. Green), June Havoc (Miss Wales), Albert Dekker (John Minify), Jane Wyatt (Jane), Dean Stockwell (Tommy), Nicholas Joy (Dr. Craigie), Sam Jaffee (Professor Lieberman), Harold Vermilyea (Jordan), Ramsom M. Sherman (Bill Payson), Roy Roberts (Mr. Calkins), Kathleen Lockhart (Mrs. Minify), Curt Conway (Bert McAnny), John Newland (Bill), Robert Warwick (Weisman), Gene Nelson and Robert Karnes (Ex-G.I.'s in restaurant), Marion Marshall (Guest), Louise Lorimer (Miss Miller), Howard Negley (Tingler), Victor Kilian (Olsen), Frank Wilcox (Harry), Marilyn Monk (Receptionist), Wilton Graff (Maitre d'), Morgan Farley (Clerk), Mauritz Hugo (Columnist), Jesse White (Elevator Starter), with Olive Derrring, Jane Green and Virginia Gregg.

One warm day in mid-February 1947, Gregory Peck received a telephone call from Darryl F. Zanuck of Twentieth Century-Fox. The call came between takes during the filming of a courtroom scene on the elaborate set constructed for David O. Selznick's *The Paradine Case*. In his English barrister's robe and powdered wig, Greg took the call and listened while Fox's production chief told him about an important and unprecedented picture he was planning to make.

Zanuck had just finished reading the galleys of Laura Z. Hobson's soon-to-be-published novel, *Gentleman's Agreement*, and he wanted it to be Peck's second picture for Fox, with the actor starring as Phil Green, a magazine writer who pretends to be Jewish while researching and writing a series of articles about anti-Semitism in America. It was certain to be a controversial picture and those involved would have to be a courageous lot to broach a subject many people wanted to ignore.

The climate for controversial films in post-war Hollywood was certainly not the best. As the "cold war" competition between the Western democracies and the Communist-bloc nations spread its chilling brand of paranoia and suspicion across the country, the film industry found itself coming under increasing scrutiny and even attack by anti-Communist zealots and their minions, chiefly embodied by the House Un-American Activities Committee, which was cooking up subpoenas and pre-heating its witness chair. As the inglorious days of the Red Menace hysteria, interrogations and witch-hunts proceeded, the noose of paranoia slipped around the neck of Hollywood led all too often—there as elsewhere—not to a strengthening but to a retrenchment of ideals.

Anything even mildly critical of American society became suspect. Even so fine and patriotic a work as *The Best Years of Our Lives* was accused of harboring subversive thoughts. And the unfortunate part of it all is, of course, that more than 30 years later it doesn't seem bizarre in the least that there were citizens who really believed—and would have others believe—that a Hollywood mogul like Samuel Goldwyn, the film's producer, was in reality a tool of Josef Stalin! Such is the corrosive effect of fear on rational thought.

An incident of anti-Semitism sparks a tense confrontation between Gregory Peck, John Garfield, Celeste Holm and a couple of strangers (Gene Nelson and Robert Karnes) in a New York restaurant.

The announcement that Zanuck would produce a picture from the Hobson book created a considerable uproar among the wealthy Jewish citizens of Hollywood. Although none could deny that anti-Semitism did exist in the United States and found its expression not only in the overt rantings of such traditional hatemongers as the Ku Klux Klan but also in far more subtle and thereby more pernicious ways, many people in the industry did not want the picture made. A meeting was called at Warner Brothers, some say by Harry Warner himself, where Zanuck was pressured to cancel the project.

One can imagine that the scene was similar to one in the picture itself in which a Jewish industrialist hears about Phil Green's impending series of articles and argues against their publication:

"I think it a very bad idea ... the worst, the most harmful thing you can possibly do now ... because it will only stir it up more. Leave it alone. We'll handle it our own way.... You can't write it out of existence. We've been fighting it for years and we know from experience the less talk there is about it, the better."

"Sure," comes the reproachful reply, "pretend it doesn't exist and add to the conspiracy of silence...."

The conversation must have gone much the same way as the committee pleaded with

Having fallen deeply in love, Gregory Peck and Dorothy McGuire share a tender moment, little suspecting that the controversial nature of writer Peck's assignment will threaten their future happiness.

Zanuck: "Why make that picture. ... why raise the whole subject."

They were still very close to the eternally horrifying discoveries of the Nazi death camps in Europe, to the frightful examples of anti-Semitism unleashed and carried to its dreadful barbarous extreme. Better to keep the evil djinn darkly bottled up out of view, Zanuck was told. After listening to the objections, Zanuck, in a reportedly polite—and uncharacteristic, when faced with opposition—way, told them to mind their own business. And when Catholic churchmen told him that he couldn't make the picture because the leading lady, Kathy Lacey, was a divorced woman, Zanuck told them where to get off, too.

Even Peck felt some pressure as a result of a general—and not altogether unfounded—superstition among actors that involvement in a controversial movie could be detrimental to one's career.

"Some well-meaning friends," Greg recalled in a magazine article later that year, "fear that my screen popularity might be affected by such a role, but I feel that an actor can't go wrong in a good picture, no matter how controversial its subject."

Undaunted by the naysayers, Zanuck forged ahead, taking personal charge of the production and staying on it from start to finish. He persuaded playwright Moss Hart to forsake the lights of his beloved Broadway long enough to come to Hollywood and write the screenplay. Hart's only previous screenwriting credit was for Zanuck's production of *Winged Victory* (1944), based on Hart's stage play. He had left to others the writing of the screenplays based on his other successful plays, among them, *Once in a Lifetime* (1932), *You Can't Take It With You* (1938) and *The Man Who Came to Dinner* (1942).

Elia Kazan, the young stage director who had made *A Tree Grows in Brooklyn* (1945) and *Boomerang* (1947), successful Fox productions, was picked to direct. While Kazan was finishing his directorial job on the Broadway debut of Tennessee Williams's *A Streetcar Named Desire* in the East, Zanuck and Hart worked on the script in Hollywood, possibly with some advice from Miss Hobson herself, who was at the studio during the time the picture was made.

For Zanuck and Hart and Kazan, the picture presented a double challenge: they must adhere to the story and remain true to the theme of the book and at the same time avoid, above all, making it a dull picture. As Zanuck put it in a letter to Hart, there was "the subject on one side and the utter necessity for an exciting lively drama on the other side." He knew from experience that the success of a picture dealing with a serious subject depended on its not boring the audience.

Peck's character, Phil Green, was a young California writer, a widower who had come to New York City with his mother and young son to work for *Smith's Weekly* magazine. The three form a closely knit family, with Anne Revere, as the mother, serving from time to time as a sounding board as the writer tries out various angles to find one that will fittingly tell his story.

Miss Revere, a superb character actress, had appeared in many movies, including *The Keys of the Kingdom* and *National Velvet* (1945), for which she won an Academy Award as best supporting actress. Later, she would be black-listed as a communist sympathizer and be out of movie work for many years.

Dorothy McGuire was cast as the divorcee, Kathy Lacey, with whom Phil Green falls in love. She was, like Peck, also under contract to David O. Selznick and had once been considered by Selznick for the role of Nora in *The Keys of the Kingdom*, even before Greg came into the Hollywood scene. She played Kathy, a niece of the magazine publisher, as a liberal of some complex contradictions, a socially aspiring, somewhat insecure and snobbish woman but nevertheless attractive to Phil. Though it is Kathy who suggests the series of articles to her father, her particular brand of liberalism is such that after their engagement to be married, she asks Phil's permission to tell her upper-crust friends that her fiancé is not really Jewish.

In contrast was Celeste Holm's vivacious and appealing fashion editor, Anne Detrie, who also develops a romantic interest in Phil, who seems oblivious to it throughout most of the picture. Miss Holm had made her film debut only a year before in *Three Little Girls in Blue* (1946); *Gentleman's Agreement* was her third picture. In Miss Hobson's novel, Anne has an affair with Dave Golden, Phil Green's Jewish buddy who has come to New York for a new job and to find an apartment to which he can bring his wife and children. Since any kind of adulterous relationship was strictly forbidden by the Production Code in those days (unless, of course, the participants wound up dead, or worse) it was eliminated from the scenario. There is only the barest suggestion that Anne is interested in Dave but she clearly carries the torch for Phil, ultimately revealing her feelings to him in an emotionally charged scene near the picture's end. It was, perhaps, Miss Holm's skillful playing of that scene that led her industry peers to subsequently honor her performance.

The important role of Dave Golden went to John Garfield, the remarkably talented, versatile and forceful actor who had made his film debut in 1938 in *Four Daughters* and gone on to success, stardom, heroics and anti-heroics in such pictures as *They Made Me a Criminal* (1939), *The Sea Wolf* (1941), *Air Force* (1943), *Pride of the Marines* (1945), *Humoresque* and

Body and Soul (1946) before *Gentleman's Agreement*. As Dave, he played a war veteran and Phil's best friend, with a lot of insight into the varieties of anti-Semitism, its subtleties and its not-so-subtle expressions. And, he makes it clear, he cares not only about anti-Semitism and its effect on the Jews but about "the whole thing" of bigotry and discrimination regardless of who the victims are.

Gentleman's Agreement was shot by Arthur Miller, one of Fox's top cinematographers, who had also filmed *The Keys of the Kingdom*. Miller, a native of New York, had been involved in pictures since before he reached his teens, shortly after the turn of the century. His political beliefs might be described as "conservative," like those of several of the industry pioneers, and he talked about *Gentleman's Agreement* with Charles Higham for Higham's book, *Hollywood Cameramen*, some 20 years later: "It was a way-out Left picture, most of the cast were to the Left, Celeste Holm, Anne Revere, John Garfield, the whole damn lot, Jesus!"

A reasonable summary, perhaps, of the opinions of some segments of the population toward any movie with a pronounced idealistic social slant or any which suggested that American society was anything less than perfect. But Miller went on to tell an ironic story of how, while on location for the film at a popular Jewish resort in upstate New York, he was discouraged from seeking accommodations at a particular hotel because he was obviously a gentile!

Some location work was also done in Darien, Connecticut, on scenes having to do with, among other things, those "gentleman's agreements" between landowners by which Jews were excluded from buying property in their vicinity. This led to a report by Bennett Cerf in *Saturday Review* noting that "the *Darien (Conn.) Review...* finally has taken official note of Miss Hobson's best-selling blast against bigotry—particularly in Darien. In a front-page story, the on-the-ball *Review* reports:

" 'Hollywood came to Darien on Monday when the tall, handsome Gregory Peck and slender and pretty Dorothy McGuire enacted a scene at the Darien railroad station. Elia Kazan, who directed *Boomerang*, which was filmed in Stamford recently, was in charge of the proceedings. The scene is a minor one for the film *Gentleman's Agreement*, a story of real-estate dealings.'"

However serious in their work, the film-makers were under no delusion that their project would eradicate a prejudice so historically entrenched. Moss Hart didn't expect the film to change the hearts and minds of confirmed anti-Semites, but he did hope it would say, "Look, this is what happens to the person who accepts a label. This is the irrationality and idiocy of social prejudice in terms of the label".

Hart also saw the movie as demonstrating that the motion picture medium, "if it gets courageous and grown-up, can be a wonderful medium. We were able, at any rate," he further remarked in an interview in the November 17, 1947, *Christian Science Monitor*, "to do a love story in which two people break up over an idea."

There was also the hope that audiences would come away realizing, above all, that the worst aspect of discrimination is the unfair attack of bigoted and cruel adults on innocent children. Indeed, the most agonizing injustice of anti-Semitism comes most acutely home to Phil Green at a time when he thinks he's experienced just about every aspect of it. Some neighborhood children refuse to play with his son, Tommy, and shout insults at him because they think he is a Jew. Later Phil tells Dave about the incident and Dave responds, "Now you know it all! There's the place they really get at you—your kids!"

This is reinforced later when Phil's mother reads aloud from his finished article in which he describes one facet of anti-Semitism as "an unending attack by adults on kids of seven and eight and ten and twelve...."

These exchanges, important and pointed as they are, also point to what some critics consider the film's major weakness. For example, in *Saturday Review*, John Mason Brown generally praised the picture for its "audacity" and its ambition and significance and said Hart's adaptation has "sharpened, hence bettered, Mrs. Hobson's story." Brown did feel, though, that for a supposedly experienced journalist, Phil Green seemed somewhat naive about anti-Semitism and its various manifestations.

Bosley Crowther remarked likewise in *The New York Times*: "...it is amazing that the writer ...should be so astonished to discover that anti-Semitism is cruel...."

On one level, this is valid criticism of the movie. "But," said Kazan, years later, "try to put yourself back in American films in 1946 when the word 'Jew' was never mentioned before. For the first time someone said that America is full of anti-Semitism...." For this reason, it was felt necessary that the film had to—in a sense— "discover" and express shock and surprise at what was common knowledge to many moviegoers, particularly those "sophisticated" enough to be critics. To that extent, some of the movie's "revelations" did indeed seem naive.

There was, in fact, another picture about anti-Semitism released in 1947: RKO's *Crossfire*, which involved the murder of an ex-G.I. who is killed merely because he is a Jew. While *Crossfire*, too, was considered a good work, *Gentleman's Agreement* had both a more specific and, simultaneously, a wider relevance, as Max Lerner pointed out in *PM* (November 12, 1947). "The violence in *Gentleman's Agreement* as opposed to *Crossfire* is not that of the killing of the body, but of the mutilation of the spirit. It is the violence of the thousands of daily slurs, insults, repulses, exclusions, condescensions, discriminations to which Jews are subjected...."

Although the film deals in a specific sense with the more "polite" forms of social and economic discrimination against Jews, in the larger sense it deals with intolerance and bigotry of all kinds. Passing over the obvious lunatic fringe of haters, racists and murderers, it points a finger at the subtle wagers of the war of discrimination, addressing its arguments to the inherently good people who victimize themselves and others by their indifference to the issue, by their silence in the face of bigotry and, thereby, their tacit acceptance of it.

This is exemplified in a scene where Kathy, while disavowing any anti-Semitism on her own part, relates to Dave how she had been sickened and disgusted at a dinner party when someone had told an anti-Semitic story.

"What did you do, Kathy?" Dave asks, "What did you say when he finished?"

Dorothy McGuire helps Gregory Peck comfort Dean Stockwell, as his son, Tommy, after the lad himself has encountered a particularly insidious sort of anti-Semitic attitude.

Kathy admits that as much as she wanted to speak out, as ashamed as she and everyone else around the table felt, they just sat there, lacking the courage and too polite to confront the bigot, not wanting to make an unpleasant scene, however justified.

"That's the trouble..." says Kathy, in a moment of realization, "we never do."

In this way, the movie raised the issue of "unconscious" anti-Semitism (the implicit "gentleman's agreement" by which politesse requires bigoted remarks to go unchallenged), saying, as Max Lerner pointed out, "that the anti-Semitism of the people on the sidelines, who abet bigots by their silences and inaction even while they scorn them, is more dangerous than ... violence.

"In America," Lerner continued, "the anti-Semitism of the lunatic fringe can thrive

only when it is nourished in the soil of the anti-Semitism of the 'respectable' people ... who have formed a conspiracy of silence about the whole issue. And in a real sense the soil of cowardice and blindness is more dangerous than the flower of evil that sends its roots down into it ...." A better summation of the movie's major point cannot be found.

Gentleman's Agreement opened on November 11, 1947, at the Mayfair Theater on Broadway and played there for 28 weeks, a resounding success. Having cost $2 million to produce, it became Fox's top-grossing film for 1948 and returned $3.9 million in net rentals (profits) to the studio. Fox executives were particularly surprised when the picture turned out to be the company's second largest all-time grosser in the American South, usually a weak area for social-problem and message pictures. Fox's all-time Southern box-office champion by 1948 was 1945's *Leave Her to Heaven.*

On the whole, *Gentleman's Agreement* was as popular with the critics as with the public. Bosley Crowther, *The New York Times* (November 12, 1947) comparing the film to the book, said that "...every point about prejudice... has been made with superior illustration and more graphic demonstration in the film, so that the sweep of Miss Hobson's moral indignation is not only widened but intensified.... A sizzling film," said Crowther, with "a fine cast, brilliant direction ... realism and authenticity...." As already mentioned, he was bothered by Phil Green's apparent ignorance regarding anti-Semitism, saying, "although the role is crisply and agreeably played by Gregory Peck, it is, in a careful analysis, an extraordinarily naive role...."

"Brilliant and powerful...," said *Variety's* reviewer. "One of the most vital and stirring and impressive [films] in Hollywood history. ... Peck gives unquestionably the finest performance of his career to date. He is quiet, almost gentle, progressively intense and resolute, with just the right suggestion of inner vitality and turbulence...."

Cue magazine called it "...an extraordinary achievement...a mature, honest and well-balanced drama...."

In the *New York Herald Tribune*, Howard Barnes called the picture "a brilliant blow against racial and religious intolerance...irresistible entertainment.... Peck...and the...cast act as though they knew what they were up to and meant every minute of it.... Persecution of the Jews has been noted before ... notably in *Crossfire*, but never so ideologically and emotionally stirring as it is in this account...."

Of course, you can't please everyone. *The New Yorker's* film critic derided the film and sniffed that "...the problem ... is quite a bit bigger than Mrs. Hobson and Mr. Hart make it out to be...."

Some took an even dimmer view. In Spain the picture was banned altogether because, according to the president of the Spanish censor board, anti-Semitism was not a problem in that country.

"There is no racial problem in Spain," said Garcia Espinia. "We do not know here the conflict of Semitism or anti-Semitism. And precisely because of the beautiful and traditional Spanish idea of human freedom, these anguishing racial differences...are alien to us and we want them to continue being alien to us.... The film speaks to us in a spiritual language so hard and so lacking in charity that we neither understand it, nor would we want to understand it, ever."

But let us not smile too quickly or cluck too knowingly over the Spanish censor's words. Around the same time, the Motion Picture Association of America joined a court battle against censorship American-style in Memphis, Tennessee, where the local censor board had banned a picture because it showed Negro children attending the same school with white children!

No reasonable person would have expected *Gentleman's Agreement* to put an end to prejudice but it was honored probably as much for its intentions as for its excellence.

The New York Film Critics' Circle voted it best picture of the year and gave Elia Kazan their best-director award, as did the National Board of Review, which also included the picture on its list of the ten best movies of the year. Both *The New York Times* and *Time* magazine included it in their ten-best lists. The Hollywood Foreign Press Association voted Golden Globe awards to the picture, the director, Celeste Holm as supporting actress and to Dean Stockwell as best juvenile actor.

At the Academy Awards, *Gentleman's Agreement* and *Crossfire* were both nominated in the best-picture, direction, supporting-actress and screenplay categories. Gregory Peck and Dorothy McGuire were also nominated for best-actor and best-actress awards respectively; Anne Revere and Celeste Holm were both nominated for their supporting roles.

Accepting the Oscar for the best picture, Zanuck thanked the members of the Academy but commented, "I should have won it for *Wilson.*" Zanuck's personally prized biographical epic about Woodrow Wilson had been nominated three years earlier but lost, a fact which had pained Zanuck greatly. Kazan was named best director and Celeste Holm also carried home an Oscar. The screenplay went to George Seaton for *Miracle on 34th Street*.

The success of *Gentleman's Agreement* exploded the long-standing myth that controversial topics were box-office poison at the very time when Hollywood, intimidated by the HUAC and other axe-grinding groups, seemed ready to settle for producing purely escapist entertainment. It bolstered the position of those people in the industry who were resisting that intimidation and who felt that pictures with meaningful adult themes and controversial subjects should be tackled with courage and boldness rather than timidly avoided.

For those reasons as much as for its message, *Gentleman's Agreement* is an honorable achievement in filmmaking; it fearlessly held up a mirror and asked a nation to consider carefully the unflattering reflection.

The obligatory happy ending has Gregory Peck re-united with Dorothy McGuire, but their relationship still seems a troubled one.

As barrister Anthony Keane, Gregory Peck finds himself falling under the bewitching spell of his beautiful client Maddalena Paradine, an accused murderess played by Valli.

The Paradine Case

Selznick Releasing Organization
A Vanguard Films Production

1948

Credits

Producer, David O. Selznick; *director*, Alfred Hitchcock; *screenplay*, David O. Selznick, based on the novel by Robert Hichens; *adaptation*, Alma Reville, James Bridie; *music*, Franz Waxman; *cinematography*, Lee Garmes; *editor*, Hal C. Kern; *associate editor*, John Faure; *art director*, Thomas Morahan; *production design*, J. McMillan Johnson. (131 minutes)

Cast

Gregory Peck (Anthony Keane), Charles Laughton (Lord Horfield), Charles Coburn (Sir Simon Flaquer), Ann Todd (Gay Keane), Ethel Barrymore (Lady Horfield), Louis Jourdan (Andre Latour), Valli (Maddalena Paradine), Leo G. Carroll (Sir Joseph Farrell), Joan Tetzel (Judy Flaquer), Isobel Elsom (Keeper at the inn), Alfred Hitchcock (Man with cello).

The Paradine Case was Gregory Peck's third picture for David O. Selznick and the last Peck picture Selznick himself would produce. Al-

though Greg remained under contract to Selznick for several more years, his remaining work under that contract would be on a loan-

In a sumptuous Selznick-style drawing-room setting, Ann Todd, Joan Tetzel, Gregory Peck, Ethel Barrymore and Charles Coburn listen as Lord Horfield, played by Charles Laughton, shares some of his views on human folly while obviously attracted to Gay Keane's elegantly bared shoulder.

out basis, working at other studios at Selznick's behest. Although this picture was shot before Peck began work on *Gentleman's Agreement* early in 1947, post-production work and editing delayed its release until after that of the later-made film. And *The Paradine Case*, like all of Selznick's later productions, had its own share of problems.

This was Alfred Hitchcock's third—and last—Selznick-produced film, too, under the terms of a seven-year contract. The Hitchcock-Selznick association had begun around 1937, with Selznick's plans for a picture about the ill-fated luxury liner *Titanic*, which never came to fruition. Just possibly, *The Paradine Case* sank their relationship.

Selznick had originally become interested in making the movie around 1933 while he was a producer at MGM. At his bidding the studio purchased the rights to the Robert Hichens novel as a possible vehicle for Greta Garbo. It remained in limbo until some twelve years later when Selznick, now self-employed and with a studio of his own, bought it from MGM for $60,000, for Alfred Hitchcock to direct. At the time, Selznick was paying Hitchcock $5,000 a week to do nothing and *The Paradine Case* looked like good Hitchcock material.

The first work on adapting the novel for the screen was done by Hitchcock and his wife Alma Reville. Then the director persuaded Selznick to hire Scottish playwright James Bridie, whose works included successful dramatizations of well-known criminal cases in the 1930s, to write the actual screenplay from the adaptation the Hitchcocks had prepared. Selznick had Bridie fly to the United States from England, but when the writer arrived at the airport in New York and found no one there to meet him, he turned around and flew right back to London. Though both producer and director pleaded with him, Bridie refused to make the trip again and subsequently worked on the script in England and sent it to Selznick in Hollywood. On reading it, David decided

he didn't like Bridie's version and set about rewriting it himself, under the most difficult conditions.

Another factor that required script revisions was the casting of the role of Maddalena Paradine, the leading lady. Despite her earlier refusal, Hitchcock and Selznick made another overture to Garbo, attempting to persuade her to come out of a well-publicized retirement and take the part. When she declined again, Selznick decided to use the picture to "create" another new star, as he had done with Ingrid Bergman in *Intermezzo*. He had seen screen tests of a beautiful Italian actress, Alida Valli, and decided to bring her to Hollywood from Italy, where she had already appeared in several films.

When Alida Valli arrived in California, Selznick immediately set about glamourizing her in the traditional Hollywood fashion, in the course of which he came up with the idea that she would seem somehow more exotic if she dropped her first name and was billed simply as "Valli."

With this casting, it now became necessary to change Mrs. Paradine in the script from a working-class Swede to an elegant Italian—an ex-prostitute, to be sure, but one with class. And Selznick undertook the script-revision job at a time when he was having considerable difficulties not only in his personal life—his marriage to Irene Mayer had broken up and his relationship with Jennifer Jones was frequently turbulent as he attempted to manage both her life and career—but at the studio as well.

There was the matter of the unreleased

Duel in the Sun, with the myriad problems it presented. There was also the nagging realization that his company and operations needed drastic overhaul to remain profitable. At a time when the business of making motion pictures was changing rapidly and other studios were in the process of reorganizing their methods of working and making maximum use of new production technology, the Selznick studios were, as Hitchcock himself told David, "twenty years behind the times."

Thus Selznick was under a great deal of strain as he attempted to complete the script during the latter part of November and in early December 1946. He apparently received some assistance on it from Ben Hecht, who was at the studio around that time, but Hecht had to leave for another project before the work on *The Paradine Case* was finished.

Dissension arose between Hitchcock and Selznick over the casting of Gregory Peck and Louis Jourdan. The director felt that Peck was wrong for the part of Anthony Keane, the successful middle-aged English barrister who falls in love with his client. He had hoped to get Laurence Olivier or Ronald Colman for the role, but Selznick insisted on using Peck, who was undeniably a star and a big box-office draw by this time.

David had also brought over Jourdan, an exceedingly handsome young European actor, from France, to make his American screen debut as Andre Latour, Colonel Paradine's valet—and Mrs. Paradine's illicit lover. Hitchcock thought this was another mistake in casting. It was his feeling that the lover should be a rough, coarse type of man, a stablehand, perhaps, with, as Hitch put it, a nuance of manure about him; this, he felt, would emphasize Mrs. Paradine's wantonness. Her nymphomania, to Hitchcock's way of thinking,

should be such that she would be driven to seek a liaison even with a man of a decidedly unsavory nature. Given the advanced age and blindness of her husband versus Jourdan's youth and irresistible good looks, audiences could only find Mrs. Paradine's infidelity completely understandable, instead of shocking and repulsive. Hitchcock thought the part called for the sort of earthiness that could be projected by an actor like Robert Newton. Selznick insisted on Jourdan and, since he was the producer, had his way; but Hitchcock ever after considered that bit of casting the worst mistake in the entire picture.

There seems to have been no disagreements, however, over the remaining cast. British actress Ann Todd came over to play Gay Keane, barrister Peck's wife who saw her husband's growing obsession with Mrs. Paradine destroying not only what had seemed to be a satisfactory marriage but his fine career as well. Charles Coburn was properly fatherly in the role of Peck's adviser and associate, Sir Simon Flaquer; Joan Tetzel, another British actress, played Coburn's daughter, Judy, who was also Gay Keane's best friend and confidante.

The inimitable Charles Laughton was cast as the eminent jurist, Lord Horfield, playing him as a leeringly sadistic tyrant of near-reptilian viciousness, who seems to have terrorized his heartbreakingly vulnerable and apparently completely intimidated wife, Ethel Barrymore, into premature dotage. Laughton is superb as a character who is simultaneously repellant and fascinating. And Miss Barrymore, who was nominated for a best-supporting-actress Oscar for the role, perfectly projects the fright of the victim who has become so accustomed to her victimization that it seems, to her, to be the natural way of life, inescapable but nevertheless painful. As Lady Horfield, she seems to exist in a perpetual state of awe—and fear.

Screen newcomer Louis Jourdan, the late Lord Paradine's valet, who is himself also a victim of Mrs. Paradine and accused of being her adulterous lover, is subjected to excruciating questioning during her trial.

Barrister Gregory Peck, hopelessly enthralled by his client, intensely argues her case in Old Bailey.

With his usual zeal for authenticity, Selznick sent Hitchcock to London during early stages of production planning to photograph and measure Old Bailey, the bar before which many of England's famous criminal trials have been played out, for the actual trial sequences. When Hitchcock returned with the photos and measurements, art director Thomas Morahan and production designer J. McMillan Johnson supervised the reproduction of the courtroom exactly, according to Selznick's specifications, to the point of even having the walls made "permanent" rather than removable, as sets were usually constructed for convenience in getting certain camera angles during shooting. This later became a factor in the escalation of the film's production costs, which headed for the roof once filming began.

When the photography of *The Paradine Case* actually did get underway the last week in December 1946, there still was no finished script. This situation must have been particularly vexing for a director like Hitchcock, who is legendary for the amount of careful pre-production planning he did in working out just exactly how he wanted each scene in the entire script shot before the cameras began rolling on the first one. In fact, in describing his work style, Hitchcock had said that all of the work is in the preparation and that once filming begins it's merely a matter of "driving the cattle into the corral." This time, he arrived with his cattle only to find that the corral hadn't been built yet. Nevertheless, the cameras began to roll.

In charge of photography was Lee Garmes, veteran of several Selznick pictures, including *The Garden of Allah, Gone With the Wind* (uncredited) and *Duel in the Sun*. Once, when Hitchcock challenged his cameraman's ingenuity by asking for a particularly tricky bit of camera movement during a scene, Garmes and three of his associates on the film came up with an idea and designed and built a device that later came to be known as the "crab dolly," a mobile camera mount which granted much more freedom of movement to the camera and became one of the standard tools of the industry. One of the inventors, not Garmes, refined their design and went into business manufacturing the equipment.

After the first four days of shooting. Selznick found the production already two days behind schedule; after six days, he estimated it to be three days behind what he had expected. He complained in a memo to his general manager, Daniel O'Shea, that Hitchcock, with his reputation for extraordinary efficiency (to which David could testify first-hand), had unaccountably slowed down. Neither the pace nor, undoubtedly, Hitchcock's disposition were improved when what script that had been written had been filmed within a few weeks, and cast and crew then found themselves shooting scenes as they were sent to them by Selznick each morning.

In an attempt to save time (and, thereby, money) during the filming of scenes on the Old Bailey set, four cameras were used simultaneously to record the action. One was focused on the judge, one on the witness box and one each on the prosecution and defense counsels; two of the cameras were fixed and two were on cranes that could be raised and lowered. The stationary walls of the set did restrict the filmmakers options in terms of camera placement, but talent and determination triumphed over adversity. Critic Bosley Crowther, in *The New York Times*, compared the camerawork in the courtroom to "an accomplished trial lawyer, droning quietly along with routine matters and suddenly hitting you dramatically in the face...."

The Paradine Case has all the hallmarks of Selznick-style mid-forties movie classicism, glossy-textured, opulent and elegant. There is also throughout the picture a remarkable visual emphasis on the eyes of its characters, as time and again Hitchcock's camera lingers on them in close-up: the eyes of Mrs. Paradine as she hears, for the first time, the door of her jail cell close with a resounding clang; Tony Keane's eyes studying his beautiful client; the prurient eyes of Lord Horfield as he fixes upon Gay Keane's bare shoulder after a dinner party and proceeds with a not-at-all subtle sexual overture while her husband, his wife and their friends are engaged in conversation only a few feet away from the sofa where he has cornered her; the nervous and terrified eyes of Lady Horfield; the defeated eyes of Andre Latour on the witness stand, caught up in the inescapable horror of a situation he has been forced into against his will; the sneering disgust with which the eyes of Lord Horfield look down from his bench upon the ill-starred mortals whose lives are disintegrating in his courtroom; the pain in Gay Keane's eyes as she sees her marriage dissolving.

Despite its complexity and complex personalities, *The Paradine Case* unfolded too slowly and ponderously on screen and perhaps was much too talky for a mass audience whose tastes in movies were changing after the war years. The final production costs were close to $4 million and, despite the box-office lure of Gregory Peck, it was an unmitigated financial disaster. An extensive advertising campaign was mounted but the public apparently found the picture boring—and maybe confusing. Hitchcock himself admitted later that the script was unclear about exactly how Mrs. Paradine had committed the crime she

ultimately confesses to, and courtroom testimony about it is merely confusing rather than explanatory. It all has to do with the administration of poison in a glass of wine, but the logistics of precisely how the crime was accomplished are somewhat muddled, even in the confession of the poisoner. Hasty script-writing seems to have been one of the production's more acute problems.

When *The Paradine Case* opened at Radio City Music Hall on January 8, 1948, critical reaction was mixed: Bosley Crowther called it "a slick piece of static entertainment. ... It isn't," said Crowther, "a too-well-written story—for the purposes of cinema, that is. ... Courtroom action tends to weary. ... Gregory Peck is impressively impassioned as the famous young London barrister. ... Ann Todd ... is attractively anguished. ... Alida Valli ... makes the caged Mrs. Paradine a compound of mystery, fascination and voluptuousness. ... Louis Jourdan ... is electric as the badgered valet...."

In the *New York Herald Tribune*, Howard Barnes was more praiseful and specific: "Alfred Hitchcock has brought all his directorial cunning to a screen tour de force. ... The show is generally stunning. ... There is scant lack of artistry ... merely too much David O. Selznick production. ... With extraordinary imagination ... Hitchcock has projected his story on two planes simultaneously. On the one hand ... the sordid jigsaw puzzle of a homicide. ... On the other ... Mrs. Paradine's evil fascination for men. ... To have realized the psychological overtones of a typical whodunit with such double-barreled force is no mean achievement. ... Peck is handsome and properly befuddled ... adding still another striking portrayal to what is becoming an impressive list...."

A rare shot of David O. Selznick with some of the help. From the left: Alfred Hitchcock, Louis Jourdan, Selznick, Charles Laughton, Charles Coburn, Gregory Peck. Seated: Joan Tetzel, Ann Todd, Ethel Barrymore. All from *The Paradine Case*, 1948.

Desperadoes John Russell, Gregory Peck, Richard Widmark, Charles Kempner and Henry Morgan ride across parched salt flats.

Yellow Sky

20th Century-Fox   **1948**

Credits

Producer, Lamar Trotti; *director*, William A. Wellman; *screenplay*, Lamar Trotti, based on a story by W. R. Burnett; *music*, Alfred Newman; *cinematography*, Joe MacDonald; *editor*, Harmon Jones; *art directors*, Lyle Wheeler, Albert Hogsett. (98 minutes)

Cast

Gregory Peck (Stretch), Anne Baxter (Mike), Richard Widmark (Dude), Robert Arthur (Bull Run), John Russell (Lengthy), Henry Morgan (Half Pint), James Barton (Grandpa), Charles Kemper (Walrus), Robert Adler (Jed), Victor Kilian (Bartender), Paul Hurst (Drunk), William Gould (Banker), Norman Leavitt (Bank Teller), Chief Yowlachie (Colorado), Eual Guy (Woman in Bank), Harry Carter (Lieutenant), Hank Worden (Rancher), Jay Silverheels (Indian).

———◆◆———

Don't look for this Gregory Peck movie on anyone's ten-best list. It has also been overlooked or given scant attention in just about every book written about Westerns, but its relative obscurity is no reflection on its quality.

The band discover a treasure of gold in an apparently abandoned mine.

Peck's third picture for 20th Century-Fox, written and produced by Lamar Trotti and directed by William A. Wellman, is an unpretentious little Western that has nothing going for it beyond a taut story line, some fine performances, superb outdoor photography, bank robbers, Indians, a ghost town, a girl, her grandpa, a horde of gold and lots of action and flyin' bullets. And it all adds up to a mighty good show and a good morality tale about the wages of greed, to boot.

Arriving in theaters about a year after the release of *The Paradine Case, Yellow Sky* gave Greg a change of pace, not to mention character, from England's Old Bailey to the badlands of the American Southwest, and put him decidedly on the opposite side of the law. But although Peck played an outlaw named Stretch—a moniker definitely suggestive of a nasty disposition and evil deeds—he was not without a conscience and a personal code of honor that a pert woman could bring to the fore.

The screenplay by Trotti was based on a story by William Riley Burnett, a novelist and screenwriter himself, who was a leading exponent of the American School of hard-boiled fiction. Trotti had written the screenplay for and produced *The Ox-Bow Incident* (1943), which William Wellman had wanted so badly to direct that he had himself bought the screen rights to the Walter Van Tilburg Clark novel. The film, about three innocent men who are hanged for a crime that later turns out not even to have been committed, was a *succès d'estime* for its collaborators, but audiences of the day were not in the mood for a sombre

tale. Savvy filmmakers like Trotti and Wellman must surely have suspected that such a serious and downbeat picture might not fare well at the box office, but they obviously felt that the film's social significance and what it had to say about lynch-mob mentality was a more important consideration than its financial potential (although they undoubtedly hoped that it would be a profit-making project).

William A. Wellman, an adventurer who had been a Foreign Legionnaire and had flown as a pilot with the Lafayette Escadrille in World War I, and who was known affectionately and endearingly (and with good reason) to his legion of friends as "Wild Bill," had made a sensational splash in 1927 with *Wings*. An exciting epic of wartime romance and aerial combat, the tremendously successful picture had given Gary Cooper a large boost on the ladder to stardom and also won the first Academy Award ever given for Best Picture.

Wellman's varied personal experience, not to mention his zest for living, served him well as a versatile director who was as adept at making big masculine adventure films like *Public Enemy* (1931) and *The Light That Failed* (1939) as he was at handling a touching, moving show-business story like *A Star Is Born* (1937), which he also wrote. Wellman's films are shining examples of the best sort of commercial moviemaking: entertaining and, more often than not, with valid social points to make as well.

Having started his career in the days of silent films, Wellman was, as Gregory Peck himself puts it, "another master of the art of telling a story with pictures. Words are important but of secondary importance to these pioneer directors."

Certainly, the visual elements and dialogue in *Yellow Sky* are expertly blended, with an emphasis on action rather than talk. And what we see tells us as much as what we hear.

Anne Baxter plays the female lead with just the right touch of tough self-assurance and the proper amount of femininity. Miss

Baxter, who made her film debut at age 17 in the Western *Twenty Mule Team* (1940), was a versatile actress, equally at home playing romantic types, as in *Sunday Dinner for a Soldier* (1944), as well as such schemers as in the title role of *All About Eve* (1950). Her other films included *The Magnificent Ambersons* (1942), *North Star* (1943) and *The Razor's Edge* (1946), for which she won an Academy Award as Best Supporting Actress for her portrait of a wife whose life is shattered by the deaths of her husband and children. Lamar Trotti had written the screenplay for that film as well, based on W. Somerset Maugham's 1944 novel.

Making his debut as a Western villain was Richard Widmark, who had previously proved himself an eminently evil type, playing a vicious killer in *Kiss of Death*, his first film, which was followed by *Road House* and *The Street with No Name* (all 1948). Widmark's callous cynicism is established early in the picture while the gang is making its weary way across the parched salt flats they traverse before reaching the ghost town.

Trotti and Wellman make some powerful points about honor and redemption but on the whole opted for a good show rather than for profundity. Their movie is, above all, a jim-dandy entertainment. And it is not without a sense of humor—and irony: When Peck and his sun-roasted compadres arrive at the outskirts of the deserted town that's slowly settling into the dust of the surrounding badlands, they are greeted by a sign that reads: "YELLOW SKY... fastest growing town in the territory." There is also an encounter with Indians—Apaches—who stage an attack but who are nevertheless, Stretch thinks, "fine people, if you understand them."

Yellow Sky opened at New York's Roxy Theater on February 1, 1949. Danny Kaye headed the stage show, with assistance from Georgia Gibbs, Calvin Jackson and the Roxyettes. And the critics seemed to enjoy the movie as much as the moviegoers did:

In *The New York Times*, Bosley Crowther wrote that "in this scorcher ... the guns blaze, fists fly and passions tangle in the best realistic Western style. ... Wellman has directed for steel-spring tension from beginning to end. ... Trotti ... and Mr. Wellman have kept their [movie] on the surface level of action and partly contrived romance. And on this popular level they have made it tough, taut and good. ... Of course, it is all unlikely. And it works out conventionally. ... But it's classy and exciting while it lasts."

Howard Barnes, in the *New York Herald Tribune*, called the picture "an utterly implausible and vastly exciting horse opera ... with such stars as Gregory Peck, Richard Widmark and Anne Baxter giving more than a touch of sincerity and compunction to conventional material. ... Wellman ... makes one realize very clearly that the Western is one of the most substantial commodities of the screen. ... Peck is the bulwark of this Wild West epic. ... He acts quietly. ... Like the brilliant *Treasure of Sierra Madre*, the offering adds meaning to an oft-repeated tale. The dialogue is crisp and economical. The characters are always drawn in proper stature. ... There is a somewhat corny climax ... but there is melodramatic substance to sustain the central theme...."

Yellow Sky found favor in other quarters, too: the Writers Guild of America gave Lamar Trotti and W. R. Burnett an award for the "Best Written American Western" of 1949.

Although their relationship gets off to an antagonistic start, the winsome Anne Baxter and ultimately reformed bank-robber Gregory Peck wind up resolving their differences.

Ava Gardner tries to entice her father, Walter Huston, away from the gaming tables, as Gregory Peck and casino habitués look on.

The Great Sinner

Metro-Goldwyn-Mayer   **1949**

Credits

Producer, Gottfried Reinhardt; *director*, Robert Siodmak; *screenplay*, Ladislas Fodor and Christopher Isherwood, from a story by Ladislas Fodor and Rene Fulop-Miller; *music*, Bronislau Kaper; *musical director*, Andre Previn; *cinematography*, George Folsey; *editor*, Harold F. Kress; *special effects*, Warren Newcombe; *art directors*, Cedric Gibbons, Hans Peters; *set decoration*, Edwin B. Willis, Henry W. Grace; *sound*, Douglas Shearer, Conrad Kahn; *costumes*, Irene Valles; *assistant director*, Marvin Stuart. (110 minutes)

Cast

Gregory Peck (Fedja), Ava Gardner (Pauline Ostrovsky), Melvyn Douglas (Armand de Glasse), Walter Huston (General Ostrovsky), Ethel Barrymore (Grandmother), Frank Morgan (Aristide Pitard), Agnes Moorehead (Emma Getzel), Frederick Ledebur (Secretary), Ludwig Denath (Doctor), Curt Bois (Jeweler), Ludwig Stossel (Hotel Manager), Erno Verebes (Valet).

•

In recognition—and promotion—of its 25th anniversary year, MGM's publicists dubbed some of the studio's 1949 releases, particularly the more lavish ones, "Silver Jubilee Productions." Gregory Peck's third picture at Metro was one of those so dubbed but, whatever its production merits, and it has some, it was far from a shining success.

Although Feodor M. Dostoevski's name appeared nowhere in the credits for *The Great Sinner*, it was based in large part on the Russian author's short novel *The Gambler*, which was published in 1866, the same year as his classic *Crime and Punishment*. Writers Ladislas Fodor and Rene Fulop-Miller, using *The Gambler* as a point of departure, fashioned a story incorporating material from *Crime and Punishment* as well as biographical events from the novelist's life itself. The final screenplay was written by Fodor and English novelist and playwright Christopher Isherwood, who had lived in Germany during Hitler's rise and emigrated to the U.S. after the outbreak of the European war.

The title was obviously inspired by Dostoevski himself, who began work in the late 1860s on a massive project which he planned to spread over several novels inspired by his own early years, the religious problems that were the center of his thoughts for much of his life, his political radicalism, his falling away from his father—and his ultimate redemption. It would be, in the writer's own words, "the life of a great sinner."

Producing the film for Metro was Gottfried Reinhardt, son of Max Reinhardt, the great Austrian theatrical producer and renowned impresario of stage spectacles.

Director Robert Siodmak, although born in Tennessee, also had a European background. Taken abroad as a small child, he grew up there and received his early moviemaking experience in France and Germany. The day Hitler came to power, Siodmak left Germany and returned to the United States to work in Hollywood, where he directed, among others, *West Point Widow* (1941), *Son of Dracula* (1943), *Phantom Lady* and *The Suspect* (1944), *The Killers* and *The Dark Mirror* (1946). In the process, he established himself as a master of suspenseful melodrama and developed a reputation for having a central-European flair.

Fashionable 19th-century Wiesbaden is the setting for an *haute MGM* period piece in which Ava Gardner and Gregory Peck are struck by both love and gambling fever.

Metro's justifiably famous art department produced the handsome and opulent settings for the picture, including the fashionable resort at Wiesbaden, its hostelries, gaming rooms and grand salons, sumptuously recreated in all their mid-nineteenth century splendor.

Peck's character, Fedja, as noted, bears relation to both Dostoevski's gambler, Aleksei Ivanovich, and to the author himself.

His romantic interest and would-be nemesis, Pauline, is played by Ava Gardner. This was the first of three pictures she and Peck would make together and the actor has said that Miss Gardner is one of his favorite leading ladies (he might say "favorite" without qualification were it not for his well-known gallantry).

The ravishingly beautiful Miss Gardner had made her film debut with a bit part in MGM's *Joe Smith, American* (1941) and appeared in small parts in other Metro pictures

Gregory Peck's romance with Ava Gardner becomes a family affair as he encounters her father, General Ostrovsky, played to the aristocratic hilt by the inimitable Walter Huston.

such as *Pilot No. 5* and *Reunion in France* (1942) before her first substantial role, in *Three Men in White* (1944). She had previously worked with Siodmak when he made *The Killers* at Universal, then made *The Hucksters* (1947) with Clark Gable, at Metro, returned to Universal for *Singapore* (1947) and *One Touch of Venus* (1948), before reporting back to MGM for *The Great Sinner*.

Her character was based in part on the real-life Polina Suslov, the young student who became Dostoevski's mistress in 1862. Polina later left the writer for a young Spaniard in Paris, but she nevertheless served as the prototype for several heroines in his later works.

Supporting players included Walter Huston as Pauline's father; Ethel Barrymore, as Pauline's grand-mama, who makes a grand entrance into the casino complete with retinue and a silver casket containing the family fortune, which she proceeds to lose; Melvyn Douglas, as the rascally casino owner who all

but has a lien on poor Pauline herself; Frank Morgan, as an old gentleman whose losses drive him to suicide; Agnes Moorehead, as a pawnshop proprietress.

Huston and Peck had previously worked together on *Duel in the Sun*. The younger actor was an unabashed admirer of the veteran and enjoyed talking with him, mostly about baseball and boxing, between takes. "He'd never talk about ordinary stuff, like acting," says Peck. "He didn't have much patience with it."

But once Peck did ask Huston if he had any advice for a young actor like himself. Huston thought for a moment, then said, "Well, sonny ... give 'em a good show and always travel first class."

Despite the first-class nature of its cast, costumes and settings, *The Great Sinner* was a downbeat story with so much suffering and anguish amid its opulence that moviegoers found it less than compelling entertainment. Critics were inclined to agree:

Gregory Peck watches as casino-owner Melvyn Douglas applies a bit of flattery to the lovely Ava Gardner.

Howard Barnes (*New York Herald Tribune*, June 30, 1949) called it "a topheavy period piece ... [that] goes around and around like the wheel of fortune which dominates the show. ... Aside from the brilliant interludes in which Miss Barrymore, Walter Huston, Frank Morgan and Agnes Moorehead appear, it is a pompous and dull entertainment. ... Peck has the arduous title role ... plays with what might be termed a steady charm ... handles the romantic moments easily but he is far from persuasive when he calls upon religion for a preposterous regeneration. Ava Gardner is attractive and doleful ... although ... scarcely the type for the role. A happy ending ... is contrived by having the pale reflection of a Dostoevski character dash off a masterpiece in a fit of some sort...."

In *The New York Times*, Bosley Crowther pointed out the too familiar nature of the picture's theme, saying, it "follows the course of all fables in which love and gambling are romantically and tragically confused. ... Peck plays the fellow with sideburns and a Continental leer and Ava Gardner plays the lady with her emotions and her chest well exposed. ... Happily, Walter Huston ... is permitted to clown his performance and he comes close to doing a W.C. Fields. ... But for all the romantic ostentation and the hovering tensely over clicking roulette wheels, ... [it] is a dreary picture. And the actors, entrapped by a weak script and fustian direction, are more sinned against than sinning, on the whole. ... Everyone gets taken to the cleaner, including Metro-Goldwyn-Mayer."

The public agreed, and this was one Silver Anniversary special that rang like pewter at the box office.

A stunned Ethel Barrymore, as Pauline Ostrovsky's grandmother, realizes she has wagered her way into bankruptcy, as Ava Gardner, Walter Huston, Gregory Peck, fellow-gamblers and family retainers look on.

Gregory Peck and Gary Merrill, as Air Force commanding officers and longtime friends, discuss their difference of opinion regarding bombing tactics and how much additional pressure already battle-fatigued airmen can endure.

Twelve O'Clock High

20th Century-Fox   **1949**

Credits

Producer, Darryl F. Zanuck; *director*, Henry King; *screenplay*, Sy Bartlett, Beirne Lay Jr., based on their novel; *music*, Alfred Newman; *cinematography*, Leon Shamroy; *editor*, Barbara McLean; *art directors*, Lyle Wheeler, Maurice Ransford; *technical advisers*, Col. John H. de Russy, Maj. Johnny McKee. (132 minutes)

Cast

Gregory Peck (Gen. Frank Savage), Hugh Marlowe (Lt. Col. Ben Gately), Gary Merrill (Col. Keith Davenport), Dean Jagger (Maj. Harvey Stovall), Millard Mitchell (Gen. Prit-chard), Robert Arthur (Sgt. McIllhenny), Paul Stewart (Capt. "Doc" Kaiser), John Kellog (Maj. Cobb), Robert Patten (Lt. Bishop), Lee MacGregor (Lt. Zimmerman), Sam Edwards (Birdwell), Roger Anderson (Interrogation Officer), John Zilly (Sgt. Ernie), William Short (Lt. Pettinghill), Richard Anderson (Lt. McKessen), Lawrence Dobkin (Capt. Twombley), Kenneth Tobey (Sentry), John McKee (Operations Officer), Campbell Copelin (Mr. Britton), Don Guadagno (Dwight), Peter Ortiz (Weather Observer), Steve Clark (Clerk in antique shop), Joyce MacKenzie (Nurse), Don

Hicks (Lt. Wilson), Ray Hyke (Bartender), Harry Lauter (Radio Officer), Leslie Denison (R.A.F. Officer), Russ Conway (Operations Officer).

———— ◆ ————

Now and again, the many diverse elements that go into the making of a motion picture—writing, casting, acting, direction, photography, editing, and scoring, to mention the more obvious—meet and blend in such a way as to produce a truly outstanding and timeless work. In the production of movies, such a propitious conjunction is as rare as in any field of manufacture and, in the history of film, *Twelve O'Clock High*—dealing, as it does, with men in war, with intelligence, perception and obvious affection for the human spirit—is as fine an example of that rarity as there is to be found.

That one can tell within the first ten minutes of a picture whether or not it will be any good is one of those apocryphal tenets so dear to the heart of the sophistic mentality, but about six-and-a-half minutes into Gregory Peck's twelfth film we feel that particular rise of excitement that hints that we are in the presence of something very special. And whatever the merits of his earlier works, *Twelve O'Clock High* stands tall as indisputably one of the more distinguished pictures of Peck's career. It begins with disarming—and deceptive—simplicity....

It is 1949. We are in London. American businessman Harvey Stovall is passing a small curio shop when he notices—and instantly recognizes—a small battered Toby mug in the window. After purchasing the mug, he catches a train out to an English country village and bicycles from the station into the peaceful countryside on a bright, sunny day.

Bicycling along a country lane, he is flanked by shrubbery, trees and tall grasses waving in gentle breezes. He leaves the bike propped against a fence and makes his way on foot through a field of nearly shoulder-high grass, obviously looking for something. Then, we see the dilapidated remains of a wind-sock hanging from a thin wooden pole and stirred by the breeze. We find ourselves on the frac-

Hugh Marlowe waits to be upbraided by a rigid Gregory Peck following a report of less than satisfactory performance by the bomber group Peck has taken under his personal command.

tured tarmac of an abandoned airfield runway, grass and weeds having long ago pushed up through the cracks, seeking the sun.

As Harvey looks around he remembers something. Suddenly the light pastoral music on the soundtrack is broken by a dark and ominous chord, dramatic music replaces the country air, then gives way to the mingled voices of a men's chorus raised in the comraderie of song, familiar tunes but far, far away: first the liltingly remonstrative romanticism of "Don't sit under the apple tree with anyone else but me, anyone else but me, anyone else but me..." giving way to a more rousing drinking song, "Bless 'em all ... bless 'em all..." then to a more dramatic instrumentation that is in turn supplanted by the melancholia-tinged strains of "We're poor little lambs who have lost our way; baa, baa, baa; we're little black sheep who have gone astray; baa, baa, baa...." The gentle, haunting song is cut short by the sudden mechanical sound of a piston-engined airplane motor turning over, then more of them cranking up, then taking off, until the sounds of many planes fill our ears. The camera pans across the sky and then we see them: American B-17 bombers! The air

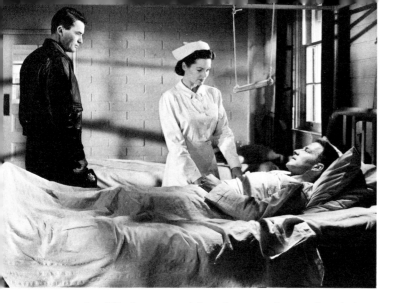

Gregory Peck visits the wounded Hugh Marlowe who has proved his bravery in battle. Nurse Joyce MacKenzie is the sole female member of the picture's cast.

is filled now with planes, planes in droves returning from a mission, coming home. And we are suddenly in an earlier time, so subtly taken back that the exact moment of our time-shift is virtually imperceptible. ... We are somewhere in England, 1942. ... And we are in the grip of something very compelling....

"I would say Zanuck chose him for the part," said director Henry King about 30 years later, "because Zanuck told me about him and said, 'I think we can get Greg Peck for this. If we can, don't you think he'd be great for it?' I had seen him in one other picture and I said 'Yes, I do. I don't know of anyone who'd be better. It's either he or Burt Lancaster and I prefer Peck.' Lancaster's a totally different type of actor—and a fine actor, but a different type."

Darryl Zanuck had purchased the screen rights to a World War II novel, by Sy Bartlett and Beirne Lay Jr., about the pioneers of precision daylight bombing and the effect of the strain of aerial warfare on the fliers and their commanders. The novel had its basis in reality. The central character, General Frank Savage, played by Peck, was based on Air Force Major General Frank A. Armstrong, who had directed the first American daylight precision-bombing air raids against the German military machine. The nervous break-down suffered by General Savage in the movie had, in fact, been suffered by General Armstrong, who told the story to Bartlett and Lay while they were serving under him in the factual equivalent of the film's 918th Bomber Group. Although they had joined the group after the central events of the story took place,

Armstrong's story and their own wartime experiences provided the material for their popular novel. The title of the novel and the picture is from the Air Force system, based on the clock face, for locating approaching enemy planes.

Leading up to *Twelve O'Clock High* there had been a series of postwar Hollywood dramas dealing with combat, including, notably, *Fighter Squadron* and *Command Decision* (1948), *Task Force, Battleground,* and *The Sands of Iwo Jima* (1949). Even though they dealt with warfare in much more realistic terms than had the propaganda and morale-boosting pictures made during the war itself, there was still a tendency to glamourize the facts of combat life. Then there was *The Best Years of Our Lives* (1946), which had dealt meaningfully and in exemplary fashion with servicemen's problems in re-adjusting to postwar civilian life after the welcome-home kisses and parades were over.

Although *Twelve O'Clock High* does include powerful scenes of aerial combat, it concerns itself chiefly with the physical and mental stress suffered by the combatants, examining particularly the emotional conflict of an "iron-tail" general who whips a disintegrating group of fliers into shape and renewed self-respect, sends them off to possible death, and finally breaks under the strain. This is a story, according to Henry King, "exploring the responsibilities of officers to their men rather than merely a phase of aerial warfare."

Henry King, himself an avid aviator, was a natural choice to direct the picture; his experience was extensive. He had started out as an actor, first on stage and then in silent pictures, from around 1913. Three years later he became a director and over the course of a long and prolific career this versatile gentleman from Virginia became something of an expert in dealing with Americana themes, with a decided touch of romanticism, in such films as *State Fair* (1933), *Alexander's Ragtime Band* (1938), *Jesse James* (1939), written by Nunnally Johnson, *A Yank in the R.A.F.* (1941), *Wilson* (1944), *A Bell for Adano* (1945), and *I'd Climb the*

Highest Mountain (1951). Associated with 20th Century-Fox for the major part of his professional life, King was a close friend of Darryl Zanuck and was to direct six pictures starring Gregory Peck. *Twelve O'Clock High* was, for King and Peck, the beginning of a long-term relationship.

From the time he purchased the novel for his studio, Darryl Zanuck, who also had a long-standing relationship with the military, had taken a particular personal interest in the picture's production. Initially, he had assigned producer Buddy Lighton to the project but when Lighton left the studio, Zanuck decided to produce it himself and the project was shelved until Henry King was available for it. There was a rumor that he had asked William Wyler to direct *Twelve O'Clock High* (he had directed *The Best Years of Our Lives*), but that Wyler had turned it down.

"I heard that he wanted Willy Wyler to direct it," said Henry King, "but I never heard Willy say anything about it. ... I heard Willy turned it down but I've talked with him many times and I've never asked him directly, because since it's been a successful picture, he wouldn't want to tell me he turned it down. But Zanuck says, no, he saved it for me.

"I was in Europe doing *Prince of Foxes* [1949] and when I came back, Zanuck told me, 'I have a story that I have kept for you.' He said he'd worked with the writers on it. Of course, Sy Bartlett and Beirne Lay had been doing the writing. They had developed the story well but Zanuck said, 'I have taken three scripts and put it into one and I'm so tired of it. If you like it, do it. If you don't like it, I'm gonna throw it in the wastepaper basket.' Well, now whether that was true or not I don't know, anyway, I read it and said I liked it.

" 'Then make it your next production,' said Zanuck. 'I'd like for you to take Bartlett and get the hell away from the studio, someplace where nobody can bother you, and get the script the way that you want it, then I'd like to read it again.'"

After getting a satisfactory script, King went to work immediately on research and pre-production work. In securing the necessary cooperation of the U.S. Department of Defense and scouting for locations, he personally flew more than 16,000 miles in his own plane. Leaving Hollywood, King flew to an air base in New Jersey, then down to the Pentagon in Washington for a couple of days. There, he saw the head of Air Force Intelligence, Air Force chief General Vandenburg and other military intelligence officials, explained the nature of the project and received their assurances of assistance. Eglin Air Force base in Florida was chosen as the shooting location, with additional sites in southern Alabama.

As King recalled, "Everything went through in beautiful shape. I had beautiful support, beautiful help, everything. And as it happens, today the Air Force uses the picture as a training film about stress, the human stress on men under these circumstances. And the British do the same thing."

Henry King had long before combined his avocational interest in aviation with his professional life and had, in fact, been influential in 20th Century-Fox's being the first film company to purchase its own aircraft. To get *Twelve O'Clock High*'s cast, crew and four tons of equipment to the Florida location in the spring of 1949, King also had Fox charter a United Airlines DC-4, the civilian equivalent of the legendary Douglas C-54 twin-engined military aircraft.

"It was an amazing thing," said King. "We had the company bring this DC-4 down to Santa Monica to load the stuff. We put 50 people in it and all the camera equipment, all the grip equipment, electrical equipment, sound recorders, etc."

After the plane was loaded, the pilot looked at King. "Is that all?" He asked. King nodded.

"And with that, he had the gas tank-trucks come up and put in another couple of thousand gallons of fuel, took off, went non-stop to Eglin, unloaded everything and then took off and flew to Chicago without putting any more gas in it. They had long range," King remarked, in praise of the dependable DC-4.

Gregory Peck flew with the rest of the cast on the charter trip, but King flew his own plane back to Florida. He later estimated that the company had saved at least ten days of the travel time which going to Florida by train— the usual mode of long-distance location transportation in those days— required.

For King and Peck, working together on *Twelve O'Clock High* proved to be a great mutual pleasure. King's first impression of Peck, when they met to discuss the project, was a very good one, in part because the actor told him right at the outset that he'd had no military experience that might help prepare him for the role.

"Well," said King, "you're going to live on a military base. You're going to live a military life. It's very easy. I'll give you a man who will instruct you in saluting and all the things you'll need to know. There's just one thing: try to act like a general and not like a second lieutenant."

"What's the difference?" Asked Peck.

"A second lieutenant," replied the director, "is always trying to act like a general, like he thinks a general should be, and everything is very stiff. A general's more relaxed."

Since he was going to be playing a general who was having a nervous breakdown, Peck also asked King about the symptoms he might display. What are the symptoms of a nervous breakdown, he wanted to know. King told him that he had only observed one man who had a nervous breakdown and he used to see him sitting and pulling his knees up with his hands and rocking back and forth at different times and moving his feet around a lot. That was all he told Peck about symptoms and the talk moved on to other things.

"About two months after that," remembered King, "we were doing a scene with Gen. Savage at his desk prior to his breakdown and Peck was sitting there pulling on his knees. I'd forgotten all about our talk and I said, 'Peck, what in the world are you doing?'

"Well, you told me this is the symptom," the actor responded.

"And he had worked it out until he had

really made something of it," remarked King. "Peck is a very dedicated man, dedicated to learn and to know. He's seeking information every minute. When he has a part to do, he is the part, even at home, he's so dedicated to do the best job with it."

King's admiration of Peck is mirrored in Peck's warm regard for King. When asked if there was one director or other individual whom he felt had made the most significant contribution toward helping him develop his skills as an actor, Peck replied without hesitation.

"Yes. I've worked with so many fine men—Kazan, Hitchcock, Zinnemann, Huston and the whole list of them—and I don't mean any disrespect or lack of regard for them when I say that the fellow who meant the most to me was a fellow named Henry King."

Peck talked about the special relationship between a motion picture actor and his director, comparing it to the relationship between stage players and their audience. The film actor plays to *one* man, the director, on whom he must rely to be objective about the performance he's giving. "He becomes," said Peck, "a kind of confidante, a kind of brother, a father. *He's* your audience.

"I did have a special relationship with Henry. He formed a kind of older-brother-younger-brother relationship with me, provided me with a one-man audience in whom I had complete trust. And he didn't direct me very much. I think it was because of the kind of man he is. Because I admired him so, I wanted him to like what I did and that was the best kind of direction. He used to say something now and then but very often he wouldn't say anything at all. We didn't have to talk very much. He was just my kind of man and I wanted him to be pleased with my performance and that made it relatively easy. It really came out of his character and my character that we had such a good rapport. And that's very special. If I played to him and

Director Henry King discusses a scene from *Twelve O'Clock High* with Gregory Peck and Dean Jagger. It was the first work together for Peck and King and the beginning of a long professional association and friendship.

Unaware that he too is near the breaking point, Gregory Peck prepares to fly a bombing mission himself, although Gary Merrill, Hugh Marlowe and Dean Jagger sense his inner tension.

he liked it, then I was fairly confidant that I was on the right track."

Supporting Peck were a number of capable performers. Beyond Dean Jagger's warm portrait of the very humane, compassionate and understanding group adjutant, Maj. Harvey Stovall, there was Gary Merrill's Col. Keith Davenport, whose very deep concern for his men not only undercut their efficiency but, ironically, did them more harm than good; Hugh Marlowe's Lt. Col. Ben Gately, whose initial cowardice turns to performance beyond the call of duty; Millard Mitchell's Gen. Pritchard, Gen. Savage's own superior, who provided the overview of the entire situation and whose reponsibility extended to the entire bombing operation.

Holding off the actual combat sequences until relatively late in the picture seems to heighten their effectiveness and dramatic intensity, while concentrating attention on the men, whom we get to know very well before actually taking to the air with them.

The aerial warfare sequences themselves were a combination of process shots, using the B-17s provided by the government, and actual aerial combat footage photographed not only by American forces but also by Luftwaffe cameramen as well.

When King and his editor Barbara McLean looked at the footage that had been collected, they discovered a peculiar thing: In some of the American films they had spotted a B-17 that had had a stabilizer shot off and turned continually in a circle, out of control. In the Luftwaffe footage they discovered they had the exact same airplane, photographed by the Germans, missing the same stabilizer, the same airplane turning in a circle. The skillful intercutting of American, German and re-enacted combat film footage produced some of the most exciting aerial warfare sequences ever seen.

The only sequence in the picture that caused any worry was the wheels-up belly-landing that takes place near the beginning, as Harvey Stovall is remembering the planes returning from a mission. Although the Air Force was very cooperative in many ways, that cooperation did not extend to participating in a dangerous stunt. Even so, there were 20 Air Force pilots at Eglin who wanted to do it. But it was absolutely against Air Force rules and regulations. So King put in a call to Paul Mantz, in Hollywood; Mantz had not yet come down to Eglin to do his own aerial formation flying for the film. King asked him to do the stunt.

"Mantz wanted a terrific figure of money to do it," recalled King. "I called the studio and told them to tell Mantz that I'd do it if he didn't want to. I'd do it. And he immediately cut his price in half and said, 'Tell Henry I'll come on down and do it.'"

Post-production work on the picture in Hollywood occupied the summer and fall of 1949, but it was ready to open in December to qualify for the Academy Awards, with actual release planned for January. The formal world premiere was held at New York's Roxy Theater on January 26, 1950, in recognition and celebration of both the eighth birthday of the 8th Air Force and the seventh anniversary of the first daylight precision bombing raid on Germany at Wilhelmshanen.

The picture—and Peck—drew widespread critical and popular praise. *Variety* found it "a topflight drama, polished and performed to the nth degree. ... Peck gives the character much credence as he suffers and sweats with his men. ... We can mark it down as just about his best work to date...."

Time magazine called the film "the freshest and most convincing movie of the current cycle about World War II. It successfully blends an artistry all too seldom shown by Hollywood and the high technical skill only Hollywood commands. ... Nothing about ... Zanuck's painstakingly made film is better than its performances. ... If Hollywood had no star system, the difficult central role would call for an actor of more physical maturity than Gregory Peck. Nonetheless, star Peck rises above the handicap with a strong, beautifully modulated performance that never lets the role down."

The New York Times critic Bosley Crowther found in the picture "a strong feeling of affection for the comradeships and heroism of war, only slightly tinged with reflections of war's terrible tragic irony" and noted that even though it didn't make "aerial warfare a particularly enviable delight," it is "an affectionate recollection of high gallantry inspired by the pressure of war. ... The general ... beautifully played by ... Peck, is magnificently, unselfishly heroic, even in his breakdown at the end."

Twelve O'Clock High was nominated for a best-picture Oscar, Peck received his fourth nomination as best actor, Dean Jagger was nominated for best supporting actor, and Thomas T. Moulton for his sound recording.

Jagger and Moulton won, but it was the year of *All the King's Men* and Broderick Crawford in the best-picture and best-actor categories respectively. Peck must have found partial consolation, however, when the New York Film Critics Circle voted him their best-actor award for 1950.

In more recent times, modern weaponry and advanced technology have so changed the nature of large-scale warfare as to make it nearly unthinkable, if not improbable, and in our recent military involvements we have found ourselves blessed with the luxury of debating our very participation rather than finding our backs against the proverbial wall. *Twelve O'Clock High*'s heroics may seem dated to some, even naive to generations who have not found their very survival at stake, who have no personal awareness of a time when the question of survival left little, if anything, in the way of choice, other than to fight.

It sounds cliché-ridden and platitudinous to say that *Twelve O'Clock High* presented men in the very worst of times and that it probed men's souls in the time of their greatest trial. But there is no banality in saying that in its probe it revealed something awesome about human beings. There were heroes—however "human"—then....

A near-catatonic Gregory Peck "flies" with his group, as Paul Stewart, Dean Jagger and Gary Merrill show their concern.

In a demonstration of alcohol-induced barroom bravado, young (and foolish) glory-seeking upstart Richard Jaeckel goads the reluctant gunfighter Gregory Peck into a fatal contest.

The Gunfighter

20th Century-Fox   **1950**

Credits

Producer, Nunnally Johnson; *director*, Henry King; *screenplay*, William Bowers, William Sellers, from a story by Mr. Bowers and Andre de Toth; *music*, Alfred Newman; *cinematography*, Arthur Miller; *editor*, Barbara McLean; *art directors*, Lyle R. Wheeler, Richard Irvine. (84 minutes)

Cast

Gregory Peck (Jimmy Ringo), Helen Wescott (Peggy Walsh), Millard Mitchell (Marshal Mark Strett), Jean Parker (Molly), Karl Malden (Mac), Skip Homeier (Hunt Bromley), Anthony Ross (Charlie) Verna Felton (Mrs. Pennyfeather), Ellen Corby (Mrs. Devlin), Richard Jaeckel (Eddie), Alan Hale, Jr. (First Brother), David Clarke (Second Brother), John Pickard (Third Brother), D. G. Norman (Jimmie), Angela Clarke (Mac's wife), Cliff Clark (Jerry Marlowe), Jean Inness (Alice Marlowe), Eddie Ehrhart (Archie), Albert Morin (Pablo), Kenneth Tobey (Swede), Michael Branden (Johnny), Eddie Parkes (Barber), Ferris Taylor (Grocer), Hank Patterson (Jake), Mae Marsh (Mrs. O'Brien), Credda Zajec (Mrs. Cooper), Anne Whitfield (Carrie Lou).

The essentially friendless life of a professional gunfighter is exemplified by Gregory Peck's Jimmie Ringo, who travels alone, dogged both by his reputation as a killer and by revenge-seekers.

As *Twelve O'Clock High* is regarded as a "classic" picture of men at war, so *The Gunfighter* has come to be regarded as one of the "classic" Westerns. And although *High Noon* (1952) is entrenched in the popular mind as the landmark Western that marked the turning of the genre from shoot-'em-ups to psychological drama (with Shakespearean undertones), this Nunnally Johnson-Henry King production actually got there first—complete even with the wall-clock ticking away the minutes to heighten the suspense and reinforce the tension with its unrelenting countdown to a fateful rendezvous. The picture also includes a moustache reputed to have cost a million dollars.

Gregory Peck's thirteenth film involved him again not only with Henry King but also with Nunnally Johnson, co-author of the screenplay for *The Keys of the Kingdom*. The prolific writer had begun producing pictures as well at 20th Century-Fox in 1936, and was responsible for such films as *Cafe Metropole* (1937), *Roxie Hart* (1942), *The Moon Is Down* (1943), *Casanova Brown* (1944), *The Senator Was Indiscreet* (1947) and *Three Came Home* (1950).

This story of a professional killer's last hours introduced to Westerns a motif that has since been repeated to the point of cliche: that of a young punk out to make a reputation for himself by gunning down an older outlaw, with whom the audience's sympathy usually lies. It also bears in part a thematic relationship to *Twelve O'Clock High* in that its hero is also an essentially isolated individual cut off by circumstance, by necessity and, to an extent, by his own nature from the people who sur-

round him and with at least some of whom he seeks rapport. There is, too, an element of Greek tragedy in the character of an outlaw who is as much a prisoner of his own reputation as if he were locked away in an actual jail cell; his character is inexorably his destiny, and his fate, sealed a long time ago, is closing in fast.

The original story was written by William Bowers and Andre de Toth with John Wayne in mind for the lead role. When it was finished, Bowers took the script to its intended star; Wayne read it, liked it very much and told him he wanted to make the picture. He then reportedly offered Bowers $10,000 for it but the writer thought his screenplay worth a great deal more and told Wayne so.

"Well," said Wayne, "you said you wrote it for me. Don't you have any artistic integrity?"

"No," replied Bowers, who then took the script to Nunnally Johnson at Fox, where he sold it for $70,000. And, according to Bowers, Wayne forever after accused him of selling the picture out from under him.

At Fox, Nunnally Johnson gave the script to Gregory Peck, thinking that it would be a good picture for Peck and Henry King. After he read it, Peck went looking for King, who was still editing *Twelve O'Clock High*. "Have you read *The Gunfighter*?" Peck asked the director when he found him.

"No," replied King.

"Well," said Greg, "it's a story about just one thing and it's the first time I've every seen a story that's about just one thing and I think it's great. If you'll direct it, I want to do it."

"Well, I'm anxious to read it if you feel that way about it," King responded.

"About an hour later," King recalled, "I saw Nunnally Johnson and he said, 'When you have time I wish you would read *The Gunfighter*.' And I said, 'I certainly will. Why don't you send it up to my office and I'll read it as soon as I can.'

"Between then and the following day, I read it," said King, "and I had the same opinion: that it was just about one thing and it

Sporting the moustache that Fox president Spyros Skouras claimed cost $1 million in lost revenues, Gregory Peck cuts a lonely figure in *The Gunfighter*, one of the best Westerns of all time.

was great. So I told Nunnally, 'If you get Greg Peck to do this (I didn't want to tell him what Greg had told me), I'll do it.'"

"Greg wants to do it if you'll do it," Johnson announced.

"All right," said King, "that makes a good team."

Johnson also sent King a copy of a book called *Trigger-nometry*, which contained the true story of every Western bad man who had actually lived. The Jimmy Ringo character in *The Gunfighter* had really existed and the book proved to be a valuable research tool. King decided he wanted an authentic look to this Western, not the usual frontier-according-to-Hollywood version, and he called Peck in to talk about it.

"You know," King told the actor, "a man in those days who was over 21 had a moustache. You didn't see people running around with clean upper-lips and, furthermore, when they got a haircut, they put a pot on their heads and shaved way up close all around it."

"We talked about the character in general," the director recalled, "about clothes, the way they dressed and about things that wouldn't be the sort of 'one-two-three, kick' stuff you saw in every Western picture in those days."

They were aiming for—and succeeded in capturing—what has been dubbed "the Remington look," not after the firearms manufacturer but after Frederic Remington, the American painter and sculptor (1861-1909) who traveled the frontier and accurately depicted Western life in his paintings, illustrations and sculptures.

"About two days later, Greg came into the studio and there his hair was cut way up to here! He'd been to the studio barber—and had had a time getting him to cut it that way. And he had a two-day growth of moustache and his sideburns came down just a little bit. And I said 'You're on the right track.'"

It so happened that Darryl Zanuck, Fox's production chief who normally oversaw every aspect of the company's output, and Spyros

Skouras, Fox's president, were in Europe at the time and not around for consultation. No one around the studio paid any attention to Peck's moustache or haircut; once the moustache reached a certain length, King assigned make-up man Ben Nye to keep it that way.

They were getting ready to start the picture when one day Johnson said to King, "I don't think Darryl is going to like that moustache."

"Well, Nunnally," King responded, "what are you gonna do? I can't just take the man out of uniform and change his clothes and call him a general and then a gunfighter. We've got to have some difference somewhere."

Johnson agreed, "I know it and I'm just as concerned about it as you are, but I'm telling you Darryl's not going to like it."

"Well, I'm sorry, but if Darryl were here I'd give him the same argument," King told his producer.

"You may have to," warned Johnson.

As Peck himself recalls it, shooting had been underway for a little more than two weeks when Zanuck returned, looked at the rushes and, sure enough, hit the roof. He called in King and Johnson.

"You can't show Peck with a moustache like that!" he exclaimed. "It will ruin him! He looks just terrible! You don't take the best-looking man in the whole world and put him in a funny hat and a funny moustache. Peck has a youthful following, a large teen-aged following and this may just lose it!"

"Well, Darryl, what are you gonna do?" asked King. "Are you just going to take the uniform off a man and put a pair of blue jeans on him? He's the same guy. He was a general yesterday and he's a gunfighter today."

"Henry, let me tell you," said Zanuck, "this is a Rembrandt. Rembrandt couldn't have done a greater job of characterization than you've done, but I'm just thinking about the audience. I'd give twenty-five-thousand dollars out of my own pocket if I could take that moustache off of Peck."

"Well, let's let the audience take care of itself," King remarked.

"That's all right for you to say. You're not responsible for selling it," Zanuck replied. He was thinking of what Skouras, who oversaw the sales division of the company at the front office in New York, was going to say.

According to Peck, Zanuck sent for the production manager and asked him to estimate how much it would cost to re-shoot the work to date without the moustache. The man was in cahoots with King and Peck and Johnson, however, and told them what Zanuck had requested; they wanted to know what he was going to tell the chief.

"It would actually cost us about $175,000," he told them.

"Why don't you tell him $300,000?" they suggested, and although the fellow protested that he'd surely be fired if Zanuck discovered he was inflating the figure, they persuaded him to do just that. And the ploy worked; Zanuck and Skouras decided that the cost of re-shooting would be a little too high and the picture continued with Peck's moustache intact.

Their aim for authenticity did not go unnoticed; As *Life* magazine reported later, "It is not only in its portrait of the melancholy murderer that *The Gunfighter* differs from the ordinary Hollywood Western. Director Henry King has made his actors wear the authentic drab clothes and handlebar moustaches which decorated males of the Old West."

Zanuck objected to another aspect of the picture too: its original ending, in which Hunt Bromley, the young punk who has shot Jimmy Ringo in the back, was merely led away under arrest. Throughout the film, audience sympa-thy slowly builds for the gunfighter, and the more the suspense mounts, the more we hope he will succeed in getting away, escaping his past and starting a new life with his wife and child. When he's killed, our hopes are crushed.

For the hero to die at the end of the picture was, according to Henry King, "sacrilegious in making pictures at that time as far as people like Mr. Skouras were concerned: 'The hero cannot die!' I'd gone through that so many times—on *Jessie James* (1939), on *White Sister* (1923)—that I didn't pay any attention to it.

"Zanuck tried to find a new ending for both *Jessie James* and *The Gunfighter*, but he finally gave up and said 'It's no use, we might as well just swallow the pill. It's there, it's happened.'"

Whatever his feelings about having the hero die at the end of the picture, Zanuck, says King, was obviously moved by the picture's climax when it was screened for him.

"It was the only time I ever saw Zanuck really hot. When the boy shot Jimmy Ringo in the back ... and the sheriff grabbed him, Zanuck was so mad he yelled at the picture: 'Take that son of a b—— out and kick the living hell out of him!'"

Then Zanuck turned excitedly to the director: "Henry, you've got to do something! You can't just let him get away with arrest and all, like that!"

King and Johnson huddled to discuss Zanuck's reaction and what they might do about the sequence that left him so obviously emotionally unsatisfied.

"I think Zanuck was right," observed Johnson, "but I thought we had enough with him caught and arrested. It seemed all right."

Zanuck's outburst about the killer gave them an idea, however: "Have the sheriff," Johnson suggested, "drag him into the barn and then just have him beat him up."

"So," remembered King, "I had him drag him into the barn and throw the revolver down to see if he'd pick it up. And the fellow jumped and I had the sheriff kick him under the chin—and that was the only time in my life that I ever did actual brutality in a picture, but it was justified. Emotionally it had upset Zanuck so much that he just yelled out 'Kick

Gregory Peck lends a sympathetic ear as Jean Parker, a late buddy's girlfriend, relates the lonely life and heartbreak that is the gunfighter's only legacy to those who love them.

the living hell out of him!' He was a good audience. It hit him."

As Bosley Crowther pointed out in his *New York Times* review: "Through ... Peck's fine performance, a fair comprehension is conveyed of the loneliness and the isolation of a man with a lurid name."

For him, Peck has said, the role was "like putting on a suit of clothes that hangs right the moment you try it on. It fits."

Although the original screenplay had been written for Wayne, Nunnally Johnson, whom Henry King says wrote the shooting script, may well have altered the tailoring a bit to Peck's dramatic dimensions. And although King had been accustomed to doing a lot of uncredited script work on his movies himself, he said, "Here's a script I don't think I changed, I think I did less work on it than I ever did on any. I never saw anyone who wrote a script as good as Nunnally Johnson."

The Gunfighter opened at New York's Roxy Theater on June 23, 1950; critical reaction to the picture was very good: Howard Barnes commented in the *New York Herald Tribune*, "It is difficult to pull a screen Western out of rutted paths, but Nunnally Johnson has done quite a job. ... It has Gregory Peck giving a brilliant performance ... it drives its points home with hammer-stroke precision. ... the dialogue is crisp and the action unfolds with extraordinary power. ... Henry King has done an excellent job ... keeping a delicate balance between acts of violence and the underlying morality of a changing society...."

Bosley Crowther, in *The New York Times*, called Jimmy Ringo "one of the most fascinating Western heroes as ever looked down a six-shooter's barrel ... played shrewdly by Gregory Peck...." Crowther called the picture "one of the tautest and most stimulating Westerns of the year. ... King and Mr. Johnson have fetched an intriguing film which actually says a little something about the strangeness of the vainglory of man ... an arresting and quite exciting film."

In a second article on the movie, Crowther further remarked that "...thanks to Henry King's fine direction of a tangy and crisply written script ... the film gives a poignant demonstration that the lonesomest man in the world is an old, glory-trailing gunfighter...."

It was for Peck, said *Life* magazine, "one of the best roles of his career."

Dwight MacDonald, in his 1969 book *On Movies*, commented "I think John Huston's *The Maltese Falcon* is the best crime picture ever made in Hollywood for the same reason I think *The Gunfighter* (the Gregory Peck, not the William S. Hart version) is the best Western; because each shows movie types behaving realistically instead of in the usual terms of romantic cliché."

In 1970, *Action*, the magazine of the Directors Guild of America, surveyed some 250 film critics to determine "The Best Dozen Westerns of All Time." *The Gunfighter* was among those chosen and Judith Crist wrote in an article for the magazine that the picture "stands as the classic study of the malaise of the professional gunslinger. Henry King's remarkable humanistic approach gives every aspect of this 1950 film an emotional impact that does not lessen in the face of countless imitations. ... King's triumph is in bringing heartbreak to the end of a legend, in giving posthumous granduer to a wasted life."

After *The Gunfighter*, Peck was asked to do the equivalent of the role at least half a dozen times, but he always said no out of a feeling that one should not repeat himself. One of the roles offered to him was that of an ex-marshal in a picture to be called *High Noon*. Peck turned it down because he thought the film would be too much like *The Gunfighter*; Gary Cooper took the part and won the Academy Award as best actor in 1952 with it.

William Bowers and Andre de Toth received award nominations for their story from both the Motion Picture Academy and the Writers Guild, but the awards went to others.

Although the picture received generally good-to-excellent reviews when it was released, it performed poorly at the box office; Darryl Zanuck's instinct that the public didn't want to see Gregory Peck in a funny hat and moustache apparently proved (as his instincts usually did) correct. But the picture has since acquired a large number of fans and continues year after year to bring revenue into the Fox coffers from revival houses and television showings.

Certainly Spyros Skouras blamed the moustache—and, by extension, producer Nunnally Johnson—for the film's financial failure. "For a year or two after that," Johnson told William Froug in an interview, "Skouras, when he had occasion to introduce me to somebody, would say, 'Nunnally's the man who put a moustache on Gregory Peck. ... You know, you cost that picture a million dollars.'

"I thought it was nonsense," said Johnson, who got the blame, but the idea for the moustache was "Mine," says Henry King.

"And Mr. Skouras," says Gregory Peck, "maintained to his dying day that 'that damned moustache' cost him a million dollars. But it's one of the pictures that I like best of all that I've done."

Marshal Millard Mitchell tries to help Gregory Peck escape a possible ambush as Peck's wife, Helen Wescott, declares her love and pleads with him to be careful.

In a rather fake-looking canyon (or is it a cavern?), Gregory Peck and his gang of Cavalry misfits prepare to hold off an Apache raiding party.

Only the Valiant

Warner Brothers 1951

Credits

Producer, William Cagney; *director*, Gordon Douglas; *screenplay*, Edmund H. North, Harry Brown, based on a novel by Charles Marquis Warren; *music*, Franz Waxman; *cinematography*, Lionel Linden; *editors*, Walt Hannemann, Robert S. Seiter; *production design*, Wiard Ihnen; *set decoration*, Armor E. Marlowe; *sound*, Leslie G. Hewitt; *assistant director*, William Kissel. (105 minutes)

•

Cast

Gregory Peck (Captain Richard Lance), Barbara Payton (Cathy Eversham), Ward Bond (Corporal Timothy Gilchrist), Gig Young (Lieutenant William Holloway), Lon Chaney Jr. (Trooper Kebussyan), Neville Brand (Sergeant Ben Murdock), Jeff Corey (Joe Harmony), Warner Anderson (Trooper Rutledge), Steve Brodie (Trooper Onstot), Dan Riss (Lieutenant Jerry Winters), Terry Kilburn (Trooper Saxton), Herbert Heyes (Colonel Drumm), Art Baker (Captain Jennings), Hugh Sanders (Captain Eversham), Michael Ansara (Tucsos), Nana Bryant (Mrs. Drumm).

David O. Selznick's production company was seriously hurt by the financial damage resulting from the commercial flop of *The Paradine Case* and the damage was further compounded by the poor public reception accorded his next expensive project, *Portrait of Jennie* (1949); twilight was settling over the Selznick empire.

Although he had no new productions planned, Selznick did have under contract a sizeable stable of actors whom he now made readily available to other studios which desired their services. Selznick had done this all along but usually with careful consideration as to what sort of production his stars were going into, since he didn't want his talent seen in pictures that might detract from the "class" status for which he liked them to be known. But the standards were, of necessity, slipping. Thus Gregory Peck was informed one day that he was being loaned out to Warner Brothers for a Western entitled *Only the Valiant*, based on a novel by Charles Marquis Warren.

When Peck read the script for his proposed new picture, he found it to be an obvious potboiler, a routine cavalry-and-Indians story. It was a far cry from the type of material the star was by now accustomed to being offered; and, not only that, but he also found that his co-star was to be Barbara Payton, a young blonde bombshell who, though not entirely untalented, certainly owed her career more to her luscious pulchritude than to her acting abilities. This would clearly be a comedown for someone whose leading ladies had included the likes of Ingrid Bergman, Jennifer Jones, Greer Garson and Jane Wyman.

Hugh Sanders, Barbara Payton and Gregory Peck listen as Gig Young discusses an impending mission into Indian territory.

Peck protested to a Selznick aide that he deserved a classier vehicle, but his protest was waved aside: "David needs the money," he was told. "He won't discuss it." The actor himself received $60,000 for making *Only the Valiant*, while Selznick collected $150,000 from Warner Brothers for loaning him out.

Essentially, the screen story is of a U.S. Cavalry captain and a small detachment of Army and social misfits who hole up at a burned-out desert fort to fight a delaying action designed to hold off an Indian attack on their main post until a relief column can arrive with reinforcements.

No one sets out deliberately to make a bad picture, or so it is said (or so it *was* said in the Hollywood of *that* period), and certainly everyone's intentions in the case at hand must have been honorable—and just as certainly, *Only the Valiant* dishonors no one, whatever its shortcomings.

The picture's problems were more basic than obviously faked scenery, however, and it was, some felt, only the presence of a strong leading man like Peck that saved it from total failure. As Thomas M. Pechter noted in his *New York Times* review, after the film opened at the Strand Theater on April 13, 1951, "Thanks to Gregory Peck's physical authority and his ability as an actor to imbue a synthetic character with a degree of conviction that would be lost to a lesser performer, the spectator is not, at least, overwhelmed by the banality of the plot...."

Could be the script writers were impressed by *Twelve O'Clock High.* Certainly Gregory Peck's Cavalry Captain Lance bears a resemblance to his Air Force General Frank Savage. Here again Peck plays a stern disciplinarian, a competent but unpopular officer faced with transforming a poorly disciplined group of men—in this case roughnecks and misfits all—into a reliable fighting unit. Again, he is at first perceived as a martinet and hated by the men he has to command, but finally is revealed as a human being with real feelings whom even some of his worst enemies will wind up admiring. But even tenuous compari-

Captain Gregory Peck, U.S. Army, takes charge of Apache Michael Ansara from Corporal Ward Bond and Indian Scout Jeff Corey.

sons with *Twelve O'Clock High* end there.

Barbara Payton proves to be an attractive woman and a so-so actress, at least when not called upon to do much more than look in the opposite direction every time Peck appears after she suspects that out of jealousy he had sent Gig Young on a deadly mission in his place. Miss Payton's films included *Trapped* (1949), *Kiss Tomorrow Goodbye* (1950), *Dallas* (1951), *Bride of the Gorilla* (1952) and *The Great Jesse James Raid* (1953). Ultimately her suspicions of Capt. Lance are proved unfounded and they are reconciled at the end.

Among the character actors, Ward Bond is worth noting, playing the alcoholic Corporal Timothy Gilchrist. So is Lon Chaney Jr., clearly his father's son. While Chaney Jr.'s career otherwise consisted in large part of playing monsters, as in *The Ghost of Frankenstein* (1942); mummies, as in *The Mummy's Tomb* (1942); and full-moon mutants, as in *The Wolf Man* (1943), here he made one of his rarer appearances as an ordinary—and almost recognizably human—miscreant, in this case a homicidal Arab (usually referred to by other characters as "the A-rab". There is no explanation of what a homicidal Arab is doing in the post–Civil War U.S. Cavalry, and from the rolling eyes and grunts and groans and generally violent demeanor of his character, it seems that Chaney may have thought he was still playing the wolf-man.

With its major action concentrated largely around this crew's attempt, under Peck's command, to prevent the Apache force from getting through a narrow mountain pass to attack the main Army outpost in the territory, the scope of the picture was rather narrow, but it does build to a bang-up finish when a relief column arrives with a Gatling gun just as the Indians are about to make their final assault on the three lone survivors.

Most of the critical complaints directed at *Only the Valiant* centered on the contrived Peck-Payton love affair at the outset and the attenuated emotional complications it generated. As Otis L. Guernsey, Jr., noted in the *New York Herald Tribune*, "…it is a pity it wastes time

on long and trivial opening sequences. … Once it gets down to the business of defending an outpost with a handful of soldiers … the screenplay … the direction … combined with the acting in a most exciting cat-and-mouse situation … big in aching cross-currents of suspense. … It is worthwhile disregarding the first half of this picture in order not to miss the second. … Peck gives a strong performance…."

In sum, Guernsey thought the picture "…finally, a good cavalry-and-Indians melodrama which might be much better if the first thirty minutes were cut down to five." A kind assessment, perhaps, for what would have been, without its major star, a rather routine grade-B Western more befitting the Monogram or Republic studios than Warner Brothers.

The New York Times's Pechter also praised director Douglas for "creating and sustaining an atmosphere of threatening danger. This does much to cushion the absurd impression of soldiering…created by the actions of Ward Bond, Lon Chaney, Neville Brand and Steve Brodie in particular. But don't blame the actors: they just read dialogue…."

There is one coincidence of plotting in *Only the Valiant* that is interesting to note: In this picture Peck is unjustly suspected of having sent his rival for the hand of Cathy Eversham off to his death on a suicide mission; in his next film, as King David, he does indeed deliberately send Uriah the Hittite, the husband of Bathsheba, the woman he loves, off to certain death in a dangerous battle in order to take his wife.

Having sent Bathsheba's husband to his certain death, Gregory Peck now takes his widow, Susan Hayward, in marriage, with James Robertson Justice in processional attendance close behind.

David and Bathsheba

20th Century-Fox   **1951**

Credits

Producer, Darryl F. Zanuck; *director*, Henry King; *screenplay*, Philip Dunne; *music*, Alfred Newman; *cinematography*, Leon Shamroy; *editor*, Barbara McLean; *art directors*, Lyle Wheeler, George Davis; *costumes*, Charles LeMaire, Edward Stevenson; *dances*, Jack Cole; *color consultant*, Leonard Doss; *special effects*, Fred Sersen; Technicolor. (153 minutes)

Cast

Gregory Peck (David), Susan Hayward (Bathsheba), Raymond Massey (Nathan), Kieron Moore (Uriah), James Robertson Justice (Abishai), Jayne Meadows (Michal), John Sutton (Ira), Dennis Hoey (Joab), Walter Talun (Goliath), Paula Morgan (Adultress), Francis X. Bushman (King Saul), Teddy Infuhr (Jonathan), Leo Pessin (David as a boy), Gwyneth Verdon (Specialty Dancer), Gilbert Barnett (Absalom), John Burton (Priest), Lumsden Hare (Old Shepherd), George Zucco (Egyptian Ambassador), Allan Stone (Amnon), Paul Newlan (Samuel), Holmes Herbert (Jesse), Robert Stephenson, Harry Carter (Executioners), Richard Michelson (Jesse's first son), Dick Winters (Jesse's second son), John Duncan (Jesse's third son), James Craven (Court announcer), Shepart Menken (Police guard), John Dodsworth (Ahithoplel).

If the Bible had never existed, Hollywood would very likely have had to invent it. The Old and New Testaments have proved time and again to be a rich, easily mineable and almost always profitable story lode, made all the more attractive to the studios by the absence of any original authors—or their agents—to haggle over screenrights and payments, and by the reluctance of censors to venture where angels fearlessly tred.

Inasmuch as Hollywood had always been alert to lusty love stories in biblical settings, it is somewhat surprising that so well known a story as this one had apparently not been filmed before.

But regarding *David and Bathsheba*, Henry King was emphatic about the filmmakers' artistic intentions: "We never went out for spectacle, never had it in mind. That picture was done purely. Everything was from the Bible."

Zanuck declared that the production objective was to strike a fine balance between the intimate and the panoramic because, he said, he preferred that 20th Century-Fox "be known as a filmer of great dramas instead of a maker of mere spectacle." Whether this was a sly dig at Paramount's Cecil B. DeMille, whose name is practically synonymous with resplendent and wonderfully overblown spectacle, is purely conjectural.

Screenwriter Philip Dunne said that he suspected that the story of David and Bathsheba hadn't been done before because the Bible's account of the two lovers has no satisfactorily dramatic ending. With the inspiration of the 23rd Psalm, however, Dunne thought he had found one: although the Second Book of Samuel clearly indicates that a vengeful God will punish David and his paramour for their sins ("...therefore the sword shall never depart from thine house; I will raise up evil against thee out of thine own house...," etc.), Dunne interpreted the 23rd Psalm, with David's praise therein of a merciful, forgiving God, to indicate that the sinners could in time be forgiven.

Jayne Meadows plays the vengeful and unforgiving Michal to Gregory Peck's equally determined and obstinate King David.

Kieron Moore, as Bathsheba's husband Uriah the Hittite, refuses Gregory Peck's entreaty to pretend that he is the father of Bathsheba's son by King David.

Gilbert Barnett, as the young Absalom anxious to do battle with Israel's enemies, meets with Gregory Peck and Kieron Moore on the eve of a fateful military confrontation.

Properly imposing as the prophet Nathan, Raymond Massey comes to King David's court to warn him that he risks the wrath of God if he continues his unholy relationship with Bathsheba.

Great emphasis was placed on authenticity, and Zanuck hired Dr. Chester C. Mc-Cown, an international authority on biblical archeology and history, as a technical adviser for the picture, which was budgeted at $3 million.

David and Bathsheba was the first of two pictures Gregory Peck would make with Susan Hayward, the vivacious auburn-haired actress who might easily turn any king's head. As Bathsheba, she is an indeed alluring enchantress.

According to Henry King, more than a year was spent on the picture from preparation to completion. It opened at New York's Rivoli Theater on August 14, 1951.

Variety's Abel Green called *David and Bathsheba* "...a big picture in every respect. It has scope, pageantry, sex (for all its biblical background), cast names, color—everything. ...a surefire boxoffice entry.... The emotional impacts are highlighted by sterling splashes of drama and vivid scenes of conflict...projected excitingly on a broad canvas. ... Peck is a commanding personality. ...He shades his character expertly. His emotional reflexes are not as static as the sultry Miss Hayward's...."

Look magazine's report must have pleased Messrs. Zanuck, King and Dunne, not to mention Leon Shamroy, whose photography, said *Look*, "brings to life the panoramic poetry and realism in a way that suggests colored Sunday School illustrations." And Dunne "was successful in capturing the essence of biblical speech." Summing up the picture, *Look*'s article went on to say "It does not have the blustering showmanship of *Samson and Delilah*, but it is certainly a more creditable attempt to bring biblical history to the screen in a reverent, poetic and tasteful manner."

Saturday Review's critic saw things differently, calling the film " ...a misguided effort to beat Cecil B. De Mille at his own game," but said that "Gregory Peck lends dignity and his virile good looks to the role of David...."

Joe Pihodna agreed in the *New York Herald Tribune*: "The producers have obviously intended to follow in the footsteps of...De Mille, but they have failed to come up with the eye-filling mass movements of men and material which such an extravaganza requires. Here and there...the film picks up some steam. But the many long scenes of dull dialogue keep [it] in low gear. ...Peck is properly dignified...though there is less fire in his acting than is indicated in the heroic legends. Susan Hayward...photographs well ... is hardly as convincing as she should be. ... Massey...at least remains in character. ... Visually...as handsome as Hollywood's production opulence could make it...while it fills the eye, it only partially serves to hold the attention...."

Abe Weiler took a more admiring view in *The New York Times*, however: "...a reverential and sometimes majestic treatment...avoids to a great extent the pagentry and over-whelmingly concocted spectacles of some biblical productions. ... In concerning itself with an ageless romance, *David and Bathsheba* admirably achieves its goal. ... There is no attempt made—to the credit of all concerned—to make David a titan without faults. He is human...in Gregory Peck's delineation the producers have an authoritative performance. ... Unfortunately...the rest of the cast is entirely overshadowed by this role. ... For all its verbosity and occasional slickness and sensuality [the picture] makes its point with feeling and respect."

The Protestant Motion Picture Council named *David and Bathsheba* "The outstanding film of 1951." Philip Dunne and Leon Shamroy received Academy Award nominations for their work, and the picture, returning some $7 million in domestic rentals alone to 20th Century-Fox, was the industry's top moneymaking film for the year.

With the weight of his sinfulness full upon him, Gregory Peck walks beside the Ark of the Covenant as its procession enters the city of Jerusalem.

Captain Horatio Hornblower

Warner Brothers   **1951**

Cast

Gregory Peck (Captain Horatio Hornblower), Virginia Mayo (Lady Barbara Wellesley), Robert Beatty (Lieutenant Bush), James Robertson Justice (Quist), Dennis O'Dea (Admiral Leighton), Moultrie Kelsall (Lieutenant Crystal), Terence Morgan (Second Lieutenant Gerard), Richard Hearne (Polwheal), James Kenney (Longley), Ingeborg Wells (Hebe), Alex Mango (El Supremo).

•

Credits

Producer, Warner Bros.; *director*, Raoul Walsh; *screenplay*, Ivan Goff, Ben Roberts, Aeneas MacKenzie; *adaptation*, C. S. Forester, from his novels; *music*, Robert Farnon; *cinematography*, Guy Green; *editor*, Jack Harris; *art direction and costumes*, Tom Morahan; *makeup*, Tony Sforzini; *sound*, Harold King; *special effects*, Harry Barndollar, Arthur Rhodes, George Blackwell, Cliff Richardson; *Technicolor consultant*, Joan Bridge; *assistant director*, Russ Saunders; *technical advisor*, Commander I. T. Clark, R.N.; filmed in Technicolor in Great Britain and France. (117 minutes)

———— ◆•◆ ————

Close on the heels of *David and Bathsheba* came the release of Warner Brothers' and Raoul Walsh's stylish swashbuckler *Captain Horatio Hornblower*.

"Just the thing for these hot nights," said Arthur Knight, extolling its virtues in the July 7, 1951, issue of *Saturday Review*.

Gregory Peck's first picture to be shot overseas, it also brought him the opportunity to work with another member of Hollywood's directorial pantheon, play opposite one of Hollywood's more talented blonde bombshells and to portray one of the more popular characters in contemporary historical fiction.

Mindful of the millions of Hornblower fans assumed to be eagerly awaiting the motion picture about their hero, the writers made particular effort to remain as faithful to the original material as the dictates of screen adaptation would allow. Although Hornblower as a character could not be treated in the same depth on screen as in the novels, neither was

he turned into simply a swashbuckling hero; the less-than-heroic nuances of his character were respected, to the filmmakers' credit and the picture's benefit. This approach to the protagonist appealed to actor Gregory Peck:

"I thought Hornblower was an interesting character. I never believe in heroes who are unmitigated and unadulterated heroes, who never know the meaning of fear. I just don't believe that. I think it's inhuman. I like a hero, particularly a sea-going hero, who gets seasick, who gets nervous before every battle, because I think people are like that and I don't really subscribe to the hard-nosed guy who's afraid of nothing. That's a cinematic cliche. I'd rather play someone who's like the rest of us."

Director Raoul Walsh, who time and again had proved his skill in handling masculine action-adventure pictures as well as demonstrating an ability to deal with complex characterization, seems to have been the perfect man to helm the Hornblower saga.

While his crew readies their cannon for battle, Gregory Peck, as Captain Horatio Hornblower, surveys the situation from the deck of the frigate *HMS Lydia*.

The luscious Virginia Mayo was cast as Lady Barbara Wellesley, the ultimate object (in spite of himself) of Hornblower's affections. A ravishing blonde with what has been accurately (for once at least) called a "peaches-and-cream" complexion, Miss Mayo made her film debut in the early 1940s and appeared in such pictures as *Up in Arms* and *The Princess and the Pirate* (1944), *The Best Years of Our Lives* (1946) and *The Flame and the Arrow* (1950).

Having previously worked for Raoul Walsh in *White Heat* and *Along the Great Divide* (1949), Virginia Mayo was very much at home with the director and in many respects epitomizes the lusty "Walsh woman" who manages to project both a toughness and vulnerability at the same time.

Because Warner Brothers had some money tied up in England that could not be exported to the United States, it was decided to produce the film there, using the "frozen" funds. The result is that the supporting cast is largely a British one.

The production was headquartered in London at Sir Alexander Korda's extensive Denham Studios, one of the finest motion-picture-making complexes of its time. For sequences taking place at sea, cast and crew moved to the south of France, to Villefranche on the Riviera between Nice and the principality of Monaco.

Although the movie didn't open at Radio City Music Hall until September 13, *Variety* reviewed it on April 18, 1951, saying, among other favorable comments, that "...*Captain Horatio Hornblower* has been brought to the screen as effervescent entertainment with action all the way. ... In his interpretation of the title role, Gregory Peck stands out as a skilled artist, capturing the spirit of the character and atmosphere of the period...."

Arthur Knight commented in *Saturday Review*, "All the gusto, sweep and color that endeared the Hornblower series to millions of readers has been preserved in...Walsh's rapid and muscular direction...the producers have spared no expense in staging the great sea battles...."

Cue magazine reported the film to be "a swashbuckling tale of adventure and love, written and unfolded in the best motion picture idiom...."

"Don't look for any frills and fancies of a literate or artistic sort in this bright-colored sea-adventure picture," wrote Bosley Crowther in *The New York Times*. "...Hornblower himself, as represented by handsome Gregory Peck, is a much more conventional type for romance than the squat "sundowner" of Mr. Forester's tales. ... What he goes through in this fable ... is a well-calculated register of all the standard business in a square-rigged film. ... Mr. Walsh and the Warners have put plenty of action on the screen...it should please those mateys who like the boom of cannon and the swish of swords. The conduct of those who made it will be brought to the attention of the Admirality. A portion of rum all around!"

"Peck cuts a fine figure as the capable, laconic and embarrassed captain, but..." said Otis L. Guernsey, Jr., in the *New York Herald Tribune*. "Hornblower's self-doubt and constant worry about court-martial are hardly noticeable here, and his skill in handling the ship must be conveyed by the awkward mechanics of having someone else talk about it. ... Miss Mayo is good to look at. ... Walsh...has put on a good visual show with his sea fights and land distresses and has let only two scenes become sugary. ... It is a good job, fun to watch for the most part, respectful of its source and presenting a colorful sequence of romantic sea events...."

Captain Horatio Hornblower was a great popular success, returning nearly $3 million in domestic rentals alone to Warner Brothers (enough in 1951 terms to make it one of the 20-odd top money-making films of the year).

The picture remains one of Gregory Peck's personal favorites.

The faint Virginia Mayo, having proved her own selflessness in battle and won both his admiration and affection, is carried below by Gregory Peck.

Aboard the *Lydia*, Gregory Peck receives Virginia Mayo, as Lady Barbara, the Duke of Wellington's sister but nevertheless an unexpected, uninvited and definitely unwanted passenger.

Gregory Peck and Robert Beatty, as Lieutenant Bush, review their situation during a lull in battle in Raoul Walsh's rousing seagoing adventure picture.

A patiently caring Susan Hayward tries to rally resentful writer Gregory Peck out of his fatalistic obsession with death and what he considers a failed career as he suffers from an injury sustained on an African safari.

The Snows of Kilimanjaro

20th Century-Fox

1952

Credits

Producer, Darryl F. Zanuck; *director*, Henry King; *screenplay*, Casey Robinson, based on the short story by Ernest Hemingway; *music*, Bernard Herrmann; *cinematography*, Leon Shamroy; *second-unit photography*, Charles G. Clarke; *editor*, Barbara McLean; *art directors*, Lyle Wheeler, John De Cuir; *sets*, Thomas Little, Paul S. Fox; *choreography*, Antonio Triana; *special effects*, Ray Kellogg; Technicolor. (117 minutes)

Cast

Gregory Peck (Harry), Susan Hayward (Helen), Ava Gardner (Cynthia), Hildegard Neff (Countess Liz), Leo G. Carroll (Uncle Bill), Torin Thatcher (Johnson), Ava Norring (Beatrice), Helene Stanley (Connie), Marcel Dalio (Emile), Vincent Gomez (Guitarist), Richard Allan (Spanish Dancer), Leonard Carey (Dr. Simmons), Paul Thompson (Witch Doctor), Emmett Smith (Molo), Victor Wood (Charles), Bert Freed (American Soldier), Agnes Laury (Margot), Monique Chantel (Georgette), Janine Grandel (Annette), John Dodsworth (Compton), Charles Bates (Harry, age seventeen), Lisa Ferraday (Venduse), Maya Van Horn (Princess), George Davis (Servant), Ivan Lebedeff (Marquis), Martin Garralaga (Spanish Officer), Julian Rivero (Old Waiter), Edward Colmans (Clerk), Ernest Brunner and Arthur Brunner (Accordian Players).

More than five years elapsed between the release of *The Macomber Affair*, Gregory Peck's first picture based on a story by Ernest Hemingway, in 1947, and the release of his second in 1952.

The Snows of Kilimanjaro, by contrast, is a big Technicolor production that expanded an even shorter Hemingway story into a 117-minute picture that covered—for good reason and to reasonably good effect—a great deal more territory geographically, chronologically and literarily.

The film of Hemingway's 1938 story was 20th Century-Fox production chief Darryl F. Zanuck's only personally produced picture of the year. The script and the expansion of the story was the work of Casey Robinson, the writer-producer who had given Gregory Peck his start in motion pictures and who had also written the screenplay for *The Macomber Affair*.

"And on his writing on this," said Henry King, who was directing his fourth film with Peck, "you couldn't tell where Hemingway's quit and Robinson's began. He developed a Hemingway style…drew a little bit on everything Hemingway had written…."

In the film, Peck's character, Harry, is given two love affairs: one with Cynthia, played by Ava Gardner, who was apparently suggested by the story. Henry King said that Robinson patterned the character, with Miss Gardner in mind for the role, somewhat after Lady Brett Ashley in Hemingway's novel *The Sun Also Rises* (1926), the character Miss Gardner would also portray in the Zanuck-King movie from that work five years later.

The *Kilimanjaro* role was to be, according to Miss Gardner, one of her own favorites: "I really felt comfortable in that part," she said later, "I could understand the girl I played so well. … She was a good, average gal with normal impulses. I didn't have to pretend."

The second love affair is with Countess Liz, portrayed by German actress Hildegard Neff, an *objet d'amour* during Harry's middle period, on the French Riveria.

One segment of the film industry, the

Marcel Dalio and Gregory Peck have a friendly reunion as Monique Chantel and Janine Grandel watch with a mixture of amusement and impatience.

Leo G. Carroll, as Gregory Peck's Uncle Bill, offers some familial and manly advice in front of a French Riviera background.

Hildegard Neff played Countess Liz, a love object in the earlier life of writer Gregory Peck.

Gregory Peck in a flashback Spanish Civil War battle scene.

theatre owners, who were already prematurely graying from the effect of television on ticket sales, voiced an ironic reservation about one crucial aspect of the production being advertised as "Ernest Hemingway's *The Snows of Kilimanjaro.*" It was the title itself, which so worried some exhibitors that Robert A. Wile, executive secretary of the Independent Theatre Owners of Ohio, wrote to Fox distribution chief Al Lichtman, saying that "several exhibitors in this state have asked me to convey to you their apprehension over the box-office possibilities of 'Snows' because of the picture's title. It is felt that people will not go to see a picture whose name they cannot pronounce. They hope that you will see fit to change this title before the picture is released...." To buttress his suggestion, Mr. Wile cited the fate of MGM's recent *Scaramouche*, a box-office loser.

In reply, Fox assistant sales head W. C. Gering admitted that it was indeed an "odd title, but it is a very famous one...." He went on to reassure the nervous exhibitors that company executives, including Mr. Skouras, "are sure that the title is just right, the picture is great and...will be a huge box-office success...."

Interviewed for a newspaper story a few weeks before the picture's opening at New York's Rivoli Theater on September 18, 1952, director Henry King, probably not unmindful of the power of positive suggestion, called it "the best picture I have ever made, because the locations (East Africa, France, Spain) are something amazing, Hemingway's story is vital and the performances are magnificent. Greg plays an age span from 17 to 40, and you'll believe the 17."

Critics, on the other hand, are a bit more exacting and are rarely pleased with the translation of literature into film; their response was mixed. Some, such as *Newsweek's* critic, came down hard on the script changes: "This Technicolor feature is currently being touted as 'Ernest Hemingway's greatest love story'; but as a matter of fact the film represents a considerable perversion of Hemingway's famous tale...might properly be advertised as producer Darryl F. Zanuck's 'greatest love story,' or screenwriter Casey Robinson's. ... The succinct and vivid qualities associated with Hemingway are rarely evoked, and what has been substituted is for the most part meandering, pretentious and more or less maudlin romance."

Otis L. Guernsey, Jr's *Herald Tribune* review referred to the movie as "...a lumpy grab bag of adventurous thrills and soul-searching loosely tied together by the wisps of Hemingway's original tale. ... The quality of the different episodes...differs almost as widely as their subject matter...but it sometimes succeeds as spectacle whenever the sporting melodrama runs high or the glances over the cigarettes become more than unusually warm. ... Peck's performance is a good one: he gives off a lot of the interior doubts and exterior hardness of a Hemingway hero and manages to hold himself together even while hanging intoxicated over a bar. ... Miss Gardner is sultry, Miss Hayward self-possessed and Miss Neff irritating as is required...."

The New York Times's Bosley Crowther seemed to be more tolerant, finding the picture, "...thanks to a skillful combination of some sensational African hunting scenes, a musical score of rich suggestion and a vivid performance by Gregory Peck...a handsome and generally absorbing film. ... But a stubbornly analytic viewer will still be moved to inquire what all this chasing about...proves." Although Crowther thought Zanuck and Robinson had not made a completely clear and convincing film, he said "they have made a picture that constantly fascinates the eye and stimulates the emotions in small, isolated ways.

Ava Gardner and Gregory Peck in flashback to an earlier safari. Gardner's character Cynthia was actually based by writer Casey Robinson on a Hemingway character in *The Sun Also Rises*.

... Mr. Peck, by the very force and vigor of his physical attitudes, suggests a man of burning temper and melancholy moods. ... And the music of Bernard Herrmann...helps one sense the pathos of dead romances and a wasted career...."

And in a later comment Mr. Guernsey also noted that "...within the limits of such films, Mr. Peck's performance is a fine one. His version of a frustrated man is presented in a well-controlled style—there is not a sign of the breast-beating type of acting in it—and his moments of excitement are all the more effective in contrast to the calmness with which he plays through most of the scenes."

Contrary to the dire warnings of the Ohio distributors, *The Snows of Kilimanjaro* was a success at the box office and was one of the top moneymaking films of 1952.

Gregory Peck and Anthony Quinn in what looks distinctly like a bit of posed derring-do in Raoul Walsh's period adventure for Universal-International.

The World in His Arms

Universal-International 1952

Cast

Gregory Peck (Jonathan Clark), Ann Blyth (Countess Marina Selanova), Anthony Quinn (Portugee), John McIntire (Deacon Greathouse), Andrea King (Mamie), Carl Esmond (Prince Semyon), Eugenie Leontovich (Anna), Sig Ruman (General Ivan Vorashilov), Hans Conreid (Eustace), Bryan Forbes (William Cleggett), Rhys Williams (Eben Cleggett), Bill Radovich (Ogeechuk), Gregory Gay (Paul Shushaldin), Henry Kulky (Peter).

Credits

Producer, Aaron Rosenberg; *director*, Raoul Walsh; *screenplay*, Borden Chase, based on the novel by Rex Beach; *additional dialogue*, Horace McCoy; *music*, Frank Skinner; *cinematography*, Russell Metty; *editor*, Frank Gross; *art directors*, Bernard Herzbrun, Alexander Golitzen; Technicolor. (104 minutes)

Gregory Peck had a second picture which wound up with *The Snows of Kilimanjaro* among the 20-odd top moneymaking movies of 1952, due undoubtedly as much to director Raoul Walsh's sure hand in guiding sea adventures skillfully to profitable berths as to actor Peck's admirable status as a top salt at the box office. In the case of *The World in His Arms*, they were abetted by a veteran character actor recently attracting attention as a top supporting player and by a beautiful brunette who had herself been an Oscar nominee, but the action-packed story was the real star and the performers themselves were upstaged by a couple of beautiful schooners.

Peck was cast as Jonathan Clark, a.k.a. "the Boston man" (even though he actually hailed from Salem, Massachusetts), the tall, handsome, self-assured and courageous captain of a seal-hunting schooner, a hero to the roustabouts and denizens of San Francisco's Barbary Coast, circa 1850, and the scourge of the Russian seal-hunting interests monopolizing the harvest from the seal-rich Pribilof Islands off Alaska's Aleutian chain.

Ann Blyth is the lovely royal lady whose head is turned and heart taken with Peck's dashing seaman.

Jonathan Clark's chief seagoing rival is a Portuguese seal-poacher and seaman-of-fortune played by Anthony Quinn and named, appropriately, Portugee. This was the first of three pictures in which Quinn and Peck would work together and marked the second collaboration between Quinn and director Walsh, the Mexican-born actor having appeared in Walsh's Western epic *They Died With Their Boots On* (1941).

The World In His Arms was not only a second collaboration between Peck and Walsh and Walsh and Quinn, but also between the director and screenwriter Borden Chase. Walsh had, in fact, directed Chase's first-produced screenplay, *Under Pressure* (1935), co-authored with Edward J. Doherty and based on their novel, *Sand Hog*.

Ann Blyth plays Russian Countess Marina Selanova and Eugenie Leontovich her chaperone in *The World in His Arms*.

Anthony Quinn and Gregory Peck get down to competitive business as a pair of rival seal-hunters who ultimately join forces to thwart their Russian competitors and rescue Ann Blyth from their clutches.

The World In His Arms went into production in the Fall of 1951 on the Universal-International lot in Hollywood.

When the picture opened at New York's Mayfair Theater on October 9, 1952, Otis L. Guernsey, Jr., *New York Herald Tribune*, called it "a brawling, colorful tale of adventure…and romance…displayed by director Raoul Walsh in the bold and swashbuckling manner which one expects of heroes operating in Technicolor in an 1850 period piece. … The whole thing is as stereotyped as the sea language of command, but it is delivered with a flair and a laugh that makes it irresistible. … The sailing scenes…are among the best of their kind." In sum, Guernsey thought the movie "as simple as it is enjoyable…a rousing show.…"

Guernsey's *New York Times* counterpart, Bosley Crowther, reported, "A couple of handsome down-east schooners…pretty much steal a robust show from Gregory Peck, Ann

Blyth and other mortals. ... And this is no whit of discredit to the mere actors in a lively film; they are faced with uneven competition. ... Walsh has staged this brave confusion so that the screen never stops quivering and the watcher...never has time to spot the story's seams. ... The characters ... make more motion and color than they make sense. ... Peck ...is only a shade more restrained than Anthony Quinn, who plays a Portuguese captain as though he were animated by hot-feet and rum. Miss Blyth is lady-like and subdued. ... It is really that race between the schooners that you'll go to this picture to see...."

The World in His Arms was not an award-winning movie but it did score at the box office, bringing Universal some $3 million in rental earnings, a modest amount, perhaps, by current standards, but a respectable return in 1952.

A captive but hardly subdued Gregory Peck is subjected to the lash by cruel, ambitious and ruthless Czarist prince Carl Esmond, for the apparent edification of Ann Blyth.

Gregory Peck invites pal Eddie Albert, who just happens to be a news photographer, along to share his and Audrey Hepburn's Roman holiday.

Roman Holiday

Paramount Pictures   1953

Credits

Producer and director, William Wyler; *screenplay*, Ian McLellan Hunter, John Dighton, from a story by Ian McLellan Hunter; *music*, Georges Auric; *cinematography*, Franz F. Planer, Henri Alekan; *editor*, Robert Swink; *art directors*, Hal Pereira and Walter Tyler; filmed at Cinecitta Studios, Rome. (119 minutes)

•

Cast

Gregory Peck (Joe Bradley), Audrey Hepburn (Princess Anne), Eddie Albert (Irving Radovich), Hartley Power (Mr. Hennessy), Laura Solari (Hennessy's Secretary), Harcourt Williams (Ambassador), Margaret Rawlings (Countess Vereberg), Tullio Carminatie (General Provno), Paolo Carlini (Mario Delani), Caludio Ermelli (Giovanni), Paola Borboni (Charwoman), Heinz Hindrich (Dr. Bonnachoven), Gorella Gori (Shoe Seller), Alfredo Rizzo (Taxi Driver).

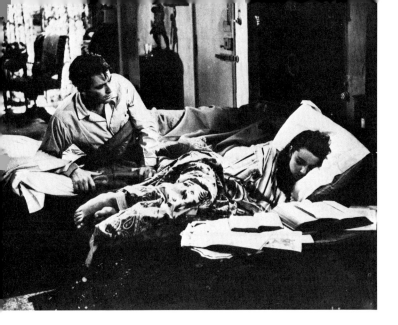

After a long string of action-adventures, *Roman Holiday*, the charming light-hearted story of an American newspaperman's encounter with a royal princess, brought a distinct change of pace to Gregory Peck's career. And it gave him an excellent opportunity to display his heretofore rarely seen talent for romantic comedy, which may well account for the picture's being one of Peck's personal favorites, an irony considering that he at first turned the part down. The project itself had dubious parentage and considerable trouble getting off the ground at all, but it made a virtually unknown young actress an overnight star and was so popular that it even affected hair styles in Japan.

At the end of World War II, directors Frank Capra, George Stevens and William Wyler and Capra's business associate Sam Briskin formed a partnership, Liberty Films, as an independent production company and made a deal with RKO to make nine films, which were to involve expenditures of over $15 million. One of the properties purchased for Capra was the story for *Roman Holiday*, which he planned to film with Elizabeth Taylor and Cary Grant.

The late forties were years of financial turmoil in the movie industry, however, and the young company soon found itself in difficulty as Hollywood was assaulted by the House Un-American Activities Committee and by U.S. Department of Justice lawsuits that forced the studios to divest themselves of their theater chains. The latter merely soured the entire financial situation in film production and dealt the studio system a devastating economic blow, making it doubly vulnerable to the effect of television's siphoning off of its audience and which ultimately all but wrecked the industry.

After the disappointing financial performance of Capra's first Liberty production, *State of the Union* (1948), the partners assessed the economic adversity they faced and decided to sell Liberty, lock, stock and literary properties, to Paramount, with Capra planning to make *Roman Holiday* under that studio's aegis. But no sooner had Capra checked in there than he ran smack into Paramount president Barney Balaban's 1948 cost-controlling decree that no Paramount Picture could cost more than $1.5 million. Presented with what he considered an impossible financial stricture, Capra abandoned the project.

Paramount then offered the picture to William Wyler, who wanted very much to make it and agreed to on the condition that he be allowed to shoot it in Rome.

"You can't build me the Colosseum, the Spanish Steps. I'll shoot the whole picture in Rome or else I won't make it," he told the Paramount moguls.

Prevailing in this manner was consistent with Wyler's reputation for almost always getting what he wanted as a director, regardless of how long it took. *Roman Holiday* was the first American feature film to be made entirely in Europe after World War II.

Wyler sent the script to Gregory Peck, whom he wanted for the part of the American journalist. Peck read it, concluded that the princess was the real star of the picture, and turned the role down.

This was an unexpected turn of events and Wyler was astonished: "You surprise me," he told Peck. "If you didn't like the story, okay, but because somebody else's part is a little better than yours...that's no reason to turn down a film. I didn't think you were the kind of actor who measures the size of the roles."

That was a crafty appeal to an actor who is

While his princess-on-the-lam, Audrey Hepburn, enjoys a gelato on the Spanish Steps, reporter Gregory Peck muses on the sure-money exclusive story he will write about their escapades in the Holy City.

widely known and well regarded for his lack of egotism. And it worked. Peck thought it over, changed his mind, and signed for the picture, satisfying Paramount's insistence that the film have a star with marquee value if Wyler was to be allowed to fulfill his desire to cast an unknown girl, without an American accent, as the princess. A lengthy search began.

In order to satisfy Paramount that he had exhausted every local possibility, Wyler had considered and rejected most of the obvious Hollywood beauties. At one point he decided he could use Jean Simmons. Miss Simmons, however, was under contract to Howard Hughes at the time and the negotiations for her release to Paramount became protracted. Finally, Hughes's asking price for her services was considered too high and Miss Simmons also had several other commitments that would unreasonably delay the start of the production, so Wyler dropped her from consideration.

On his way to Rome for some pre-production work the director stopped in London to interview several prospects. One of the girls he met there was a Brussels-born dancer whose parents were Dutch and English-Irish. She had appeared in bit parts in several British films, including *The Lavendar Hill Mob* (1951), in which she appeared briefly as a cigarette girl in a scene at the beginning of the picture. Wyler was impressed by her delicate good looks and graceful bearing and arranged to have her screen-tested in London, with the test to be forwarded to him in Rome. When it was screened there, he was convinced that Audrey Hepburn would be perfection as Princess Anne.

There was only one hitch: Miss Hepburn had been signed to appear on Broadway in the title role of the stage production of *Gigi*. She had, in fact, gotten the part when she was spotted by *Gigi*'s creator, Colette herself, quite by accident in the lobby of the Hotel de Paris in Monte Carlo, while she was working as an extra in a movie with the fetching title of *Monte*

Carlo Baby (1952). Apprised of this commitment, Wyler and Paramount decided to sign her anyway, even if it meant a delay in production. Their hunch was that the play would last only a month; but the month stretched into six, while audiences packed New York's Fulton Theater to see a new enchantress.

Actual shooting in Rome began in June, 1952. Gregory Peck recalled the first day: "On the opening day of the picture, in fact, on the opening day of *all* his pictures, Willy Wyler calls the cast together and says, 'Now, boys and girls, there's just one prima donna on this picture and I'm the one. And I'll have that understood from the beginning.'

"Wyler's a taskmaster and he's known for, among other things, hardly ever being satisfied and for having you play a scene forty or fifty times. Some people are restless with that because he doesn't always tell you what he wants on the 41st take. But I always knew what he wanted: to have everybody at their best at every moment. And with Willy you always had a pretty good shot at being your best. I always loved working with him for that reason.

"I wouldn't mind doing it a hundred and forty times because he had a purpose. He was not always able to explain what it was that he'd like you to do differently, but when you did it right, he knew it and that gave you great confidence that you'd give a good performance. And that's a great thing for an actor, to know that the director recognizes a scene and a performance when it's at its peak."

For Peck, who is in almost every scene, the shooting schedule was a demanding one, from the day work began in June until it was completed in October. His typical day would begin at 6:30 in the morning and rarely ended before 8:30 at night. On one occasion, during the shooting of a sequence in the Colosseum, he worked for 22 straight hours without letup. Nevertheless, he found the change from Hollywood routines exhilarating.

Peck recalled one occasion when William Wyler's toughness in demanding exactly what he wanted from an actor was turned on Audrey Hepburn: "There was a sad little scene in the Roman Forum and Willy wanted her to shed some tears. And Audrey was very good at everything but that, I think because her greatest talent is as a comedienne. At the time, she'd done a lot of ballet, been in a couple of musicals in London and hadn't been deified on screen yet. She was really pretty wacky and funny, a very lovable girl who would make faces and do back-flips and clown. She was really marvelous at that, it was her strong point. And when it came to playing a poignant scene, she couldn't quite find it within herself.

"The makeup man was blowing menthol in her eyes to get a few tears and we did the scene about thirty times and it just wasn't there. She wasn't able to call up the right kind of emotion. And Willy really startled me; he just changed into this sort of character and said, angrily, 'God-dammit Audrey, it's lousy! I don't believe a god-damned word of it! Now get into it and give me something!'

"He really just came out strong and in front of everybody on the set. It *was* embarrassing and frightened her and shook her up but she did it perfectly the very next time. It wasn't exactly from the situation in the picture, but nevertheless it was a very genuine feeling and it served. On screen it looked like it was because she was parting from me, but actually it was because Wyler had just scared the wits out of her."

When *Roman Holiday* opened at Radio City Music Hall on August 27, 1953, Gregory Peck's perception that it was a star vehicle for the actress playing the princess was thoroughly validated.

The escapades of errant princess Audrey Hepburn and avaricious reporter Gregory Peck, who finds his affection for the princess taking precedence over his need for plane fare back to the States, ultimately bring them to Rome police headquarters.

For Eddie Albert and Gregory Peck the affair with the princess begins as strictly a business matter, but romantic feelings soon push purely pecuniary considerations out of the picture.

Time magazine devoted the cover of its September 9 issue to Audrey Hepburn, whose portrait, painted by Boris Chaliapin, featured her against a background of Rome's Fontana de Trevi, one of the film's locations, with a strawberry ice cream cone floating above it. And *Time's* adulatory article began with a gush: "Amid the rhinestone glitter of *Roman Holiday's* make-believe, Paramount's new star sparkles and glows with the fire of a finely cut diamond...." It was merely the beginning of the acclaim. Moviegoers fell in love with Audrey just as Joe Bradley had fallen for Princess Anne. Wyler's "unknown actress" would be unknown no longer.

Newsweek reported, "What Wyler has done is to fashion one of the gayest, most original and endearing comedies to be credited to Hollywood in recent years."

Writing for vacationing Otis L. Guernsey, Jr., in the *New York Herald Tribune*, Paul V. Beckley called *Roman Holiday* "...a rather remarkable film. There is absolutely nothing uncommon about its plot...yet...a capable director and a remarkable young actress have made one of the better pictures of the year, certainly one of the brightest comedies. ... Hepburn ... makes the sad skylarking of a princess...lovely and carries off the finale with a nicety that leaves one a little haunted. ... Gregory Peck portrays the...reporter with alternate abandon and thoughtfulness...."

In Bosley Crowther's stead at *The New York Times*, A.H. Weiler dubbed the movie "...a royal lark in the modern idiom...a bittersweet legend with laughs that leaves the spirits soaring. ... Wyler and his associates have fashioned a natural, tender and amusing yarn... have sensibly used the sights and sounds of Rome to dovetail with the facts in their story. ... Audrey Hepburn...is a slender, elfin and wistful beauty, alternately regal and childlike. ... Peck makes a stalwart and manly escort and lover, whose eyes belie his restrained exterior. ... Eddie Albert is excellent...."

The movie was an instant hit. The New York Film Critics Circle voted Miss Hepburn their Best Actress award, the Writers Guild of America bestowed their award for Best Written American Comedy on Hunter and Dighton and the Directors Guild cited William Wyler for an "Outstanding Directorial Achievement." The members of the Academy of Motion Picture Arts and Sciences nominated *Roman Holiday* for awards in eight categories, including Best Picture, Best Director, Best Supporting Actor (Eddie Albert), Best Screenplay and Black-and-White Cinematography. But 1953 was also the year of the powerful and moving drama *From Here to Eternity*, which took most of the Oscars in those categories. Still, Audrey Hepburn received the prize for Best Actress, Ian McLellan Hunter received an Oscar for his story, and Edith Head was honored for costume design in a black-and-white picture.

Among *Roman Holiday's* millions of fans was John F. Kennedy who is reported to have had it screened for himself and his guests several times in the White House theater when he was president, almost a decade later. And the movie's popularity knew no national bounds: While on a tour of Japan in 1955, William Wyler was startled to discover, when alighting from a train one day, that Audrey Hepburn's *Roman Holiday* hairdo had become the rage of young Japanese women and he and Mrs. Wyler found themselves surrounded by a sea of lovely oriental Audreys.

125

At a Berlin nightclub, Gregory Peck explains to Broderick Crawford why obtaining his son's release is a complicated affair and that former Gestapo agents, now in cahoots with the Russians, want to trade the boy for a German ex-general who has plotted against Hitler.

Night People

20th Century-Fox 1954

Credits

Producer and director, Nunnally Johnson; *screenplay*, Nunnally Johnson, based on a story by Jed Harris and Thomas Reed; *music*, Cyril Mockridge; *musical director*, Lionel Newman; *cinematography*, Charles G. Clarke; *editor*, Dorothy Spencer; *art directors*, Hanns Kohnert, Theo Zwierski; *costumes*, Ursula Maes; *makeup*, Raimund Stangl, Fritz Seyfried; *sound*, Hans Wunschel, Roger Heman; *associate producer*, Gerd Oswald; *assistant director*, Lutz Hengst; *Technicolor color consultant*, Leonard Doss; color by Technicolor. (93 minutes)

Cast

Gregory Peck (Col. Steve Van Dyke), Broderick Crawford (Leatherby), Anita Bjork (Hoffy), Rita Gam (Miss Cates), Walter Abel (Foster), Buddy Ebsen (Sgt. McColloch), Casey Adams (Frederick S. Hobart), Jill Esmond (Frau Schindler), Peter Van Eyck (Petrechine), Marianne Koch (Kathy), Ted Avery (Johnny), Hugh McDermott (Burns), Paul Carpenter (Whitby), John Horsley (Stanways), Lionel Murton (Lakeland).

126

proclaimed an ad for 20th Century-Fox's *Night People*, a fast-paced and topical tale of international skullduggery between super-powers, set in one of the world's most prominent tension spots. The picture marked the directorial debut of one of Hollywood's most accomplished screenwriters, who produced it as well, and provided Gregory Peck yet another role as a tough military man.

That *Night People* was to be a Cinema-Scope production indicated to some degree the studio's high regard for the project. The screenplay for this story of a U.S. Army counter-intelligence officer who pulls a fast one on his Soviet counterparts in Berlin was written by Nunnally Johnson, who was also slated to produce it, as he had *The Gunfighter* four years earlier. Johnson's script was written from a story by Jed Harris and Thomas Reed.

Since the picture was to be filmed in Germany, primarily in Berlin itself, but with some work in Munich, Johnson asked studio head Darryl F. Zanuck if he could also direct it. Zanuck was agreeable but reminded Johnson that Peck, as the picture's star, had a contractual right to approve or veto the studio's choice of director. Peck and Johnson had at that point been friends for several years, however, and when the actor's approval was sought, he quickly assented.

The international flavor of the militarily sectored postwar city was reflected in *Night People*'s cast, which included, beyond its American principals, Swedish, Scottish, German, Canadian and English members and bit players and extras of even more international complexion.

The result of all of this is a good, fast-moving entertainment politically akin to both the genre of anti-Nazi propaganda pictures the Hollywood studios turned out by the

Unaware that Anita Bjork, as Frau Hoffmeyer, is both an impostor and a double agent, Gregory Peck confides in her and seeks her assistance in thwarting the Russians.

As his aide, "Sgt." Buddy Ebsen, and his American secretary, played by Rita Gam, stand by, Army Intelligence "Col." Gregory Peck queries a German contact about the kidnapping of a G.I. by Soviet agents in Berlin.

Gregory Peck and Peter Van Eyke, U.S.-U.S.S.R. liaison officer, listen without much patience as assertive U.S. businessman Broderick Crawford complains about the slow pace of efforts to free his abducted son.

scores during the World War II period and to the sort of foreign-intrigue melodramas that followed close on the war's heels.

The film opened at New York's Roxy Theater on March 12, 1954, and, as Otis L. Guernsey, Jr., put it in the *New York Herald Tribune*, "*Night People* has many assets. Johnson's script is slashingly written and his action is paced like a rapier duel. Gregory Peck does one of his dominant, towering 'Command Decision' jobs. ... The ending alone is disappointing; the story paints itself into a corner from which there is no escape except the kind of deceit which ought to be the exclusive property of the villains. Except for this, *Night People* has the mysterious air and staccato performance of a good spy thriller. ... Peck issues his commands and crushes interference in the very personification of authority. He is hard-boiled and sarcastic, yet sympathetic with the underdog...."

The New Yorker magazine reported, "The title...is based on the notion that the Russians do all their dirty work after dark, which, of course, makes things difficult for the Americans, sun-lovers to a man. ... If you should happen to be worried about the possibility that the operatives of the Kremlin are proving too wily for the lads who look after our interests in Berlin, *Night People* should ease your mind. ... As the colonel, Gregory Peck is every inch a heroic defender of democracy and as the troublesome businessman, Broderick Crawford is a zealous blusterer...."

Bosley Crowther, in *The New York Times*, said the picture "...is first-rate commercial melodrama—big, noisy, colorful and good. ... The skillful and wily Mr. Johnson manipulates his pieces with such speed and such trickery in some places that you may well be confused. ... But that's okay...he keeps his melodrama mounting...works in plenty of mystery, romance, tension, sex and comedy...directs a film head-on. He does not resort to such devices as character and mood subtleties. He has Mr. Peck play a 'fixer' with no more refinement or finesse than the big, booming, blundering, bumptious magnate that Broderick Crawford plays. ... Johnson has brought forth a picture that is plenty of fun to watch. It may be the sheerest piece of fiction, and a reckless piece at that, but it is fun."

After U.S. security officers haul Anita Bjork in for questioning, Gregory Peck, by now aware of her duplicity but planning to use her in his own plot, and Buddy Ebsen obtain her release from Hugh McDermott.

Proving that the mere appearance of wealth is as good as its true possession, Gregory Peck trades his shabby tatters for Savile Row finery and acquires Reginald Beckwith as a gentleman's gentleman.

Man With a Million

United Artists   **1954**
A J. Arthur Rank Organization Presentation

Credits

Producer, John Bryan; *director*, Ronald Neame; *screenplay*, Jill Craigie, based on Mark Twain's short story "The Million Pound Bank Note"; *music*, William Alwyn; *cinematography*, Geoffrey Unsworth; *editor*, Clive Donner; *art director*, Jack Maxsted; *set decoration*, Ario Simoni; *costumes*, Margaret Furse; *sound*, Dudley Messenger, Gordon K. McCallum, Winston Ryder; *makeup*, George Blackler; *Technicolor consultant*, Joan Bridge; *assistant director*, Bob Asher; filmed in Technicolor at Pinewood Studios, London. (92 minutes)

Cast

Gregory Peck (Henry Adams), Jane Griffiths (Portia Lansdowne), Ronald Squire (Oliver Montpelier), Joyce Grenfell (Duchess of Cromarty), A. E. Matthews (Duke of Frognal), Reginald Beckwith (Rock), Hartley Power (Hastings), Brian Oulton (Lloyd), Wilbur Evans (American Ambassador), Maurice Denham (Mr. Reid), John Slater (Parsons), Wilfrid Hyde-White (Roderick Montpelier), Hugh Wakefield (Duke of Cromarty), Bryan Forbes (Tod), Ann Gudrun (Renie), George Devine (Chop House Proprietor), Ronald Adam (Mr.

Young, penniless, and friendless American-marooned-in-London Gregory Peck receives a million-pound banknote from wealthy wagerer Wilfrid Hyde-White that will change his life.

London society types who formerly sneered at pauper Peck are soon all-too-anxious to make the acquaintance of the young handsome millionaire in their midst.

Clements), Hugh Latimer (Bumbles Receptionist), Ernest Thesiger (Bank Director), Eliot Makeham (Consulate Official), Richard Caldicott (James), James McNaughton (Williams).

———— •=• ————

"Once upon a time, when Britain was very rich…"

An elegant and bouyant waltz underscores the credits at the beginning of this frothy fable, Gregory Peck's 21st film, but at credits' end, *Man With a Million* slows down to an amble. The company is so good and genial and the production so lavish in its turn-of-the-century London settings and costuming, however, that one doesn't object too much to the reduced pace, a pleasant one nevertheless.

Peck's second encounter with film comedy doesn't quite measure up to the romantic ideal of *Roman Holiday*, nor did it equal its success, but it is a fable of a different time and place and subject, and of an altogether different mood. Based on Mark Twain's 1893 short story "The Million Pound Bank Note," and released in Britain and elsewhere overseas as simply "The Million Pound Note," *Man With a Million* is a charming satire on human vanity, avarice, British manners and on the effects of the illusion, as opposed to the reality, of wealth.

The film's production staff is as totally British as, excepting Gregory Peck, its acting contingent. Peck's performance as Henry Adams, the down-and-out American who finds fame and unexpected responsibility when he comes into possession of a million-pound note, is a dignified, almost reserved one, perhaps too much so, for comedy roles generally call for a more relaxed approach than he seems to take here. But the style of playing is clearly the responsibility of the director, and Greg is genuinely engaging and likeable as young Adams.

Man With a Million opened at New York's Sutton Theater on June 28, 1954, but the

Though besieged by anxious and collapsing creditors when word that his banknote has vanished gets around, Gregory Peck tries to remain outwardly unperturbed as he reviews the situation with Reginald Beckwith and Hugh Wakefield.

A lovely and demure Jane Griffiths provides the romantic interest opposite Gregory Peck in *Man With a Million*.

good-mannered nature of its very British brand of satire was not generally very well appreciated by the critics in the former colonies, where the custom is toward more raucous satirical approaches.

Otis L. Guernsey, Jr., in the *New York Herald Tribune*, called it "...a production shimmering with the Technicolor elegance of the horse-and-carriage era. After the first few surprises, though, its humor becomes laborious because it cannot quite make up its mind whether it wants to be a breezy satire on human vanity or a fancy period romance. ... Gregory Peck looks like a man of promise even in rags. ... His touch with comedy is light but guarded, almost suspicious; but no one really throws himself into this affair...."

Bosley Crowther, of *The New York Times*, thought that "the lack of cleverness, we fear, is the film's one weakness. ... Peck is skillful and handsome. The rest of the cast is refined. The production in color is delicious... direction ... smooth. ... Indeed, there is everything about it that renders it apt and amiable—everything except bounce and bouyance, which are matters of cleverness. ... The picture doesn't spark with humor...doesn't flash the satire on money-madness that is lodged in the yarn...."

In *Saturday Review*, however, a different view was set forth: "That rare and remarkable quality of complete accord, of deft interplay not merely between the actors but between the entire production team on a film, is again visible in a delicious comedy. ... Peck reveals unsuspected comic gifts. ... Twain's story has been extended and elaborated...with a keen appreciation of the intrinsic humor of the situation and just how far a point can be pushed. Indeed, the film derives its basic strength, grace and richness from the knowledgeable craftsmanship lavished upon every phase of its production...."

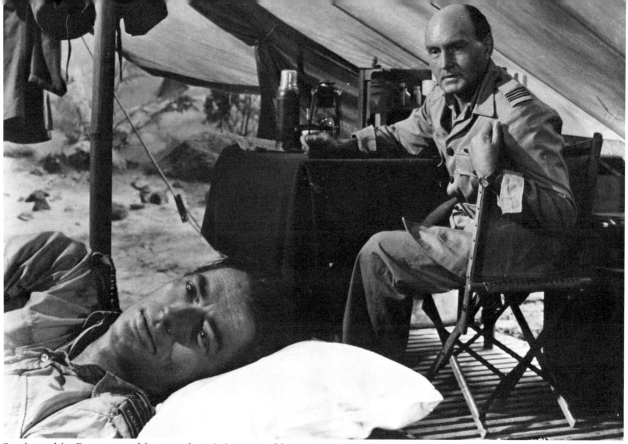

Stationed in Burma and haunted and depressed by memories of his bride's death in the blitz of London, Gregory Peck is taunted to the point of explosion by the unsympathetic, self-assured and garrulous Maurice Denham.

The Purple Plain

United Artists   **1955**

Credits

Producer, John Bryan; *director*, Robert Parrish; *screenplay*, Eric Ambler, based on the novel by H.E. Bates; *music*, John Veale, conducted by Muir Mathieson; *photography*, Geoffrey Unsworth; *editor*, Clive Donner; *art director*, Jack Maxsted; *set decoration*, Dario Simoni; *camera*, James Bawden; *sound*, Dudley Messenger, Gordon K. McCallum, Harry Miller, Eric Boyd-Perkins; *makeup*, Geoffrey Rodway; *hair*, Iris Tilley; *continuity*, Joan Foster; *assistant director*, David Orton; *special effects*, Bill Warrington, Charles Staffell; *optical effects*, S. Guidobaldi; *Technicolor consultant*, Joan Bridge; *executive producer*, Earl St. John. (100 minutes)

Cast

Gregory Peck (Forrester), Win Min Than (Anna), Bernard Lee (Dr. Harris), Maurice Denham (Blore), Ram Gopal (Mr. Phang), Brenda De Banzie (Miss McNab), Lyndon Brook (Carrington), Anthony Bushell (Aldridge), Jack McNaughton (Sergeant Brown), Harold Siddons (Navigator Williams), Peter Arne (Flight Lieutenant), Mya Mya Spencer (Dorothy), Josephine Griffin (Mrs. Forrester), Lane Meddick (Radio Operator), John Tinn (Burmese Jeweler), Soo Ah Song (Old Woman in Jeweler's Shop), Dorothy Alison (Nurse).

•

Gregory Peck's second picture for British producer John Bryan, *The Purple Plain*, is a good survival story of wartime derring-do and romance, with the emphasis primarily on the former but with clear perception of the latter's role in motivating heroics, not to mention survival. Although it also has something vital to say about coming to terms with the hard knocks life may deal us, it is an unpretentious work that exemplifies as much as any of his films the stalwart-hero character Peck has come frequently to personify.

With the cooperation of the British Air Ministry and the Royal Air Force, *The Purple Plain* was filmed at London's Pinewood Studios and on locations in the former British Crown Colony of Ceylon (Sri Lanka), an island off the southeast coast of India, that served as stand-in for Burma, the Asian country on the eastern shore of the Bay of Bengal where the fictional story is actually set. In this steamy tropical land, the actors had no need to draw upon their craft or the makeup man to suggest that their characters were suffering from the unrelenting heat and humidity, to which their perspiration unmistakably attests.

"Gregory Peck has pulled himself through lots of trouble and many tough situations on screen," observed Bosley Crowther in *The New York Times*, after *The Purple Plain* opened at the Capitol Theater on April 10, 1955, "but he seldom has had to take a physical ordeal as rough as the one he undergoes. ... He shows the stuff of which heroes are made ...plays his role with stolid drive...."

The supporting players all enhance the film's credibility and, as William Zinsser put it

While Brenda De Banzie leads Bernard Lee and Mya Mya Spencer in a spirited singalong, Gregory Peck's attention is diverted by the beauty and warmth of Win Min Than, with whom he soon falls in love.

Although chronic and cowardly whiner Maurice Denham is solely concerned with saving his own neck, Gregory Peck insists that they carry the injured Lyndon Brook with them to safety after their plane crashes in enemy-held territory.

in the *New York Herald Tribune*, Win Min Than, the lovely green-eyed Burmese actress who plays Anna, and who apparently has not graced American screens since, "would beguile any man away from his troubles."

Brenda De Banzie, the British character

After Maurice Denham commits suicide in despair, a heroic and determined Gregory Peck hauls Lyndon Brook on alone.

actress who had made a memorable impression on American audiences and critics a year earlier as the strong-willed daughter of tyrannical father Charles Laughton in *Hobson's Choice* (1954), brings to the character of Mrs. McNab a particularly spirited and spiritual quality. "She gives," said Archer Winsten in the *New York Post*, "a performance so extraordinarily good that you would believe it was type-casting if you hadn't seen her in another entirely different role last year."

As Carrington, the injured navigator, Lyndon Brook, son of famed British actor Clive Brook, had not much to do beyond register agonizing pain, but he did it well. And fans of the James Bond movies may recognize Bernard Lee, who, as Dr. Harris, is as attuned to wounded souls as he is to injuries of the flesh.

But, after Peck, it is perhaps Maurice Denham, as Blore, who makes the major impression. According to critic Zinsser, "the prize performance is that of Denham. Pompously lecturing Peck at the air base, he is an objectionable bore. Grounded in the jungle, he is at first methodical, then querulous and finally panicky, as he...cracks pitiably under the strain. All the irony of war is in his downfall.. ."

"You can almost feel the humid, oppressive heat of the jungle," said Zinsser. "Much of the fascination of the film lies in the conflict between these two men, so unlike each other but trapped in the same desperate situation. ... Ambler's sardonic script makes the characters real. Peck is his old competent self. ... *The Purple Plain* is too slow to be a rousing adventure but it is mature and thoughtful...."

"Mr. Peck," reported Mr. Crowther, "has a terrible, tedious time working his way out of the jungle. And the extent of his agony is impressively transmitted to the audience in vivid and unrelenting scenes...one suffers with him as he doggedly sweats and strains to save himself and his ineffectual companions. ... A slight rationalization of wartime tensions and the endurance of hopeless strains may be got from Ambler's screenplay...but the bulk of the picture is that ordeal in the jungle, and that's a sheer demonstration of blood and guts."

Gregory Peck and Keenan Wynn in one of *The Man in the Gray Flannel Suit*'s flashbacks to World War II battle action.

The Man in the Gray Flannel Suit

20th Century-Fox   **1956**

Credits

Producer, Darryl F. Zanuck; *director*, Nunnally Johnson; *screenplay*, Nunnally Johnson, based on the novel by Sloan Wilson; *music*, Bernard Herrmann; *cinematography*, Charles G. Clarke; *editor*, Dorothy Spender; *art directors*, Lyle Wheeler, Jack Martin Smith; filmed in CinemaScope and De Luxe Color. (153 minutes)

Cast

Gregory Peck (Tom Rath), Jennifer Jones (Betsy Rath), Fredric March (Hopkins), Marisa Pavan (Maria), Lee J. Cobb (Judge Bernstein), Ann Harding (Mrs. Hopkins), Keenan Wynn (Caesar Gardella), Gene Lockhart (Hawthorne), Gigi Perreau (Susan Hopkins), Portland Mason (Janie), Arthur O'Connell (Walker), Henry Daniell (Bill Ogden), Connie Gilchrist (Mrs. Manter), Joseph Sweeney (Edward Schultz), Sandy Descher (Barbara), Mickey Maga (Pete), Kenneth Tobey (Mahoney), Geraldine Wall (Miriam), Jack Mather (Police Sergeant), Frank Wilcox (Dr. Pearce), Nan Martin (Miss Lawrence), Phyllis Graffeo (Gina), Dorothy Adams (Mrs. Hopkins' Maid), Dorothy Phillips (Maid), John Breen (Waiter), Mario Siletti (Carriage Driver), Roy Glenn (Master Sergeant Mathews), Robert Boon (First German Soldier), Jim Brandt (Second German Soldier), Otto Reichow (Third German Soldier), Harry Lauter (Soldier), William Phipps (Soldier), De Forrest Kelley (Medic).

Marisa Pavan played Maria, the Italian girl with whom Gregory Peck's Tom Rath had an extra-marital though meaningful affair in war-torn Italy.

Gregory Peck had hoped that *The Man in the Gray Flannel Suit* would turn out to be something on the order of *"The Best Years of Our Lives*, ten years later," exploring what had happened to those former G.I.'s in the years after their return to civilian lives and occupations.

The presence of Fredric March in both these films does perhaps give them a tenuous link, but the consensus of opinion is that this latter work, estimable as it is, falls short of that goal Peck enunciated. But this survey of the corporate workplace and suburban living is no less a sincere and relevant examination of an important aspect of American life and morality at a particular point in time.

This was Peck's fifth picture to be personally produced by Darryl F. Zanuck and, as the last project on Zanuck's schedule as production chief at 20th Century-Fox, before his resignation became effective and he left the studio, it gave him the satisfaction of leaving with a hit. It was also Peck's second picture with Nunnally Johnson as director, his third with a Johnson screenplay and his second with Jennifer Jones as leading lady.

Although "Suit" went into production after Peck had finished his work on *Moby Dick*, post-production on that film took so long that *The Man in the Gray Flannel Suit* was released before the John Huston epic was finished.

Two weeks before shooting began in october 1955, Peck visited New York, took a stroll down Madison Avenue, observing its denizens; visited several advertising agencies; and paid a call at the executive offices of the NBC television and radio network in Rockefeller Center, where he had once worked as a tour guide. He also took an afternoon commuter train to Larchmont, New York, observing attentively all the while everything that went on around him. During all of this reconnaisance, Peck camouflaged himself so well, as the very model of the young business executive, that few of the people he was observing recognized him or were aware of a star's presence.

Two days were subsequently spent shooting scenes around the Westport, Connecticut, station of the New Haven Railroad, with Peck, as Tom Rath, ad man and commuter, being driven to the station by his wife. At that time, however, Jennifer Jones was still not firmly lined up for the role of Betsy, so Christine Linn, a willowy blond actress from the nearby town of Norwalk, was chosen from the ranks of the extras as a stand-in for Mrs. Rath. For the scenes, Miss Linn's head was be-kerchiefed so that from a distance she could pass for either a blonde or a brunette.

Peck may have been inconspicuous on Madison Avenue, but his presence with a crew of 145 filmmakers and extras did not go unnoticed in Westport, as housewives, some of them with infants in their arms, deserted their kitchens to join the teenagers somehow out of school and the town businessmen somehow neglecting their shops to gather around the train station and watch the goings-on.

A reporter from the *New York Herald Tribune* asked Greg whether the crowds of onlookers disturbed their work. They didn't, he responded, pointing out that "In Rome, where we were making *Roman Holiday*, we had everywhere from five to fifteen thousand people watching while they were shooting."

After this preliminary work, the company returned to Hollywood. An agreement for Jennifer Jones's services was finally reached with the actress and her husband, David O. Selznick, who was at the time managing her career. After Miss Jones began work on the film, Nunnally Johnson found himself bombarded by memos from Mr. Selznick, telling him how he thought Jennifer should be

Distraught on learning of Gregory Peck's wartime infidelity, his wife Jennifer Jones reacts with neither understanding nor compassion and the stability of their marriage is severely threatened.

treated and photographed, etc. The memos were undoubtedly an annoyance to Johnson, but his reply was always polite: "Thank you very much, David," he wrote back. "I passed your notes on to Mr. Zanuck," Mr. Zanuck's response is not on record.

The Man in the Gray Flannel Suit opened at New York's Roxy Theater on April 12, 1956, with a successful benefit premiere for the March of Dimes. Although critical reaction was varied, the top-drawer cast and first-class production combined with the novel's popularity to make it a solid hit at the box office.

Bosley Crowther of *The New York Times* called the picture "a mature, fascinating and often quite tender and touching film.... In Mr. Wilson's novel," said Crowther, the "problems were rather awkardly mixed, but Mr. Johnson has managed to arrange them in a seemingly scattered yet clear and forceful way. He has also managed to work in very nicely the tragic domestic problems of the hero's boss... some intimations of the harried life of other people...in a full, well-rounded film. To do this he has had to take his sweet time...except for two somewhat long war flashbacks, every minute is profitably used...all the actors are excellent. Mr. Peck is a human, troubled Tom Rath. ... Mr. Zanuck's expensive production gives proper setting to this intelligent film...."

William Zinsser, of the *New York Herald Tribune*, felt that "there are enough people here for two or three movies, and each scene is an emotional crisis...a series of tiny soap operas laid end to end. It has almost no unity or satiric bite. But let's face it: it's entertaining ...there are many scenes that are rich in human detail. ... Peck is sincere and natural ...but very docile. ... March ... steals the show. ... Johnson...has molded some excellent performances, and he keeps every scene spinning on its emotional way. The two and a half hours pass surprisingly quickly...."

Not everyone agreed: In *Saturday Review*, Arthur Knight noted that Johnson had adapted Wilson's book "not only with fidelity to the original but with considerable dexterity as well. ... As a director, however, Johnson falls short...permits Jennifer Jones and Ann Harding to overplay...draws merely competent performances from Gregory Peck, Lee J. Cobb, Keenan Wynn and Arthur O'Connell. Only Fredric March...and Marisa Pavan... give a strong, personal modeling to their roles. The result is a film that is intelligent and able, but lacking in sufficient dramatic fire to sustain an entire two hours and a half."

In *The New Yorker*, John McCarten concurred in a generally negative review: "In its diffuse aggregate, the movie...has quite a few scenes that aren't at all badly constructed, and if it were an old-fashioned serial, I'm sure we might be able to tolerate it. In one massive dose, though, it's just too damned much...."

In a sneeringly sarcastic report, *Time* magazine complained that "the movie...relentlessly envelops every idea, obscures every issue in a smug smog of suburbanity. ... It was a virtue of the book that, while it conceded that publicity men may sometimes be intellectually dishonest, it showed them as human beings too. It is a vice of the picture that it can't tell a human being from an overage Boy Scout. Greg is presented as a red-white-and-blue wonder boy just because he tells the boss man...a smart truth rather than a dumb lie...."

Kate Cameron, in the *New York Daily News*, however, called the picture "a work well done ...a deeply moving domestic drama. ... The various roles are so realistically acted that the audience becomes absorbed in the action. ...

Gregory Peck's honest ambition and obvious integrity attract the attention of executive Fredric March, who warns him that life at the top can be lonely and filled with regrets.

Peck gives a full-bodied, well-rounded characterization. ... Jennifer Jones...adds another impressive role to her list. Fredric March is brilliantly right...."

Cue magazine agreed: "This movie... may well turn out to be the best dramatic film to come out of Hollywood this year. ... The dozen or so reels are jampacked with enough action, humor and solid drama to support half a dozen ordinary pictures. ... Johnson and a fine cast...combine their distinguished talents to help make this an eminently satisfying, full-bodied, honest and mature drama of real people and real situations...a firm, fully packed drama with...some of the best acting we've had from the three principals mentioned...."

Gregory Peck's own feeling is that the picture didn't live up to that potential he saw in the book. "It was spotted," he has said, "with some good sequences," but he feels that the Madison Avenue side of it "was not very interesting" and that the domestic problems turned indeed into soap opera. Peck's own favorite sequences and the ones he felt were most successful were the flashbacks to the war, to the romance with Maria in Italy, the battles and the wartime relationships. Although he feels the picture was not a complete success, there are "good sequences" here and there and "some good acting."

For the *Gray Flannel* family man, success often comes down to a choice between family duties and professional concerns.

With a determination that has long since crossed the line of obsession, Gregory Peck, as the mysterious and possessed Captain Ahab of the *Pequod*, pursues the elusive white whale—and his own rendezvous with fate.

Moby Dick

Warner Brothers
A Moulin Picture

1956

Credits

Producer and director, John Huston; *associate producer*, Lehman Katz; *screenplay*, Ray Bradbury, John Huston, based on the novel by Herman Melville; *music*, Philip Stainton; *photography*, Oswald Morris; *second unit photography*, Freddie Francis; *film editor*, Russell Lloyd; *art director*, Ralph Brinton; *special effects*, Gus Lohman; *sound recording*, John Mitchell, Len Shilton; *costumes*, Elizabeth Haffenden; *assistant director*, Jack Martin; color by Technicolor; *narrator*, Richard Basehart. (116 minutes)

Cast

Gregory Peck (Captain Ahab), Richard Basehart (Ishmael), Leo Genn (Starbuck), Orson Welles (Father Mapple), James Robertson Justice (Captain Boomer), Harry Andrews (Stubb), Bernard Miles (Manxman), Noel Purcell (Carpenter), Edric Connor (Daggoo), Mervyn Johns (Peleg), Joseph Tomelty (Peter Coffin), Francis De Wolff (Captain Gardiner), Philip Stainton (Bildad), Royal Dano (Elijah), Seamus Kelly (Flask), Friedrich Ledebur (Queequeg), Ted Howard (Blacksmith), Tamba Alleney (Pip), Tom Clegg (Tashtego), Iris Tree (Lady with Bibles).

139

British actor Leo Genn, as the *Pequod*'s chief mate Starbuck, is rational and quietly courageous in contrast to the monomaniacal Ahab, whose obsession he rightly sees as a threat to all the crew's lives and is compelled to oppose.

"Call me Ishmael...."

When Richard Basehart spoke those words, perhaps the most famous three-word sentence in all of literature, at the beginning of the world premiere of *Moby Dick* in New Bedford, Massachusetts, it was the culmination of a twenty-year-old dream for writer-producer-director John Huston and the official end of an ordeal that some involved have compared to Captain Ahab's own insanely driven and vengeful pursuit of the monstrous white whale. In any event, the production story tends toward the epic itself.

In retrospect, Gregory Peck has commented that, "Huston was more Ahab himself than any actor could be. I always thought he should have played that part. His intense desire to make this picture without any compromise is certainly comparable to Ahab's relentless quest to kill the whale."

Huston's original intention had been to make the film with his father as Captain Ahab, but Walter Huston died in 1950 before the project could be undertaken. Huston also had discussions with novelist-critic-screenwriter James Agee about a screenplay while he was shooting *The African Queen*, which Agee had written. The director liked Agee's ideas and asked him to come to his County Kildare, Ireland, base and work on the script with him in 1953. Agee agreed and Huston thought the matter was settled. Then, Agee was offered the chance to direct a movie himself, which would be the fulfillment of a lifetime dream. But he would have to choose between writing *Moby Dick* and making his own film. He chose the latter, sealing the production agreement with a handshake. Informed of this development, Huston was not only angered by Agee's desertion but astonished that he had reneged on his promise to write *Moby Dick* on the basis of a handshake deal. Unfortunately for Agee, his own project later fell through and Huston had already found another co-writer, Ray Bradbury.

Huston encountered Gregory Peck at a party in London one day and asked the actor to join the project. Peck was surprised when he found out that Huston wanted him for the role of the captain; he personally felt that he would be better suited for the role of Starbuck, one he had, in fact, played in a college production based on the novel. But Huston convinced him to play Ahab, whom Peck says he initially came to see as "a kind of champion of the human race, a symbol of mankind's struggle for fulfillment. He dares to go farther than most people in exploring the mysteries of life, and so he resents mankind's restrictions and limitations. He rebels against being the helpless pawn of fate. There aren't a lot of men like this. And Ahab, like many people with a stroke of genius, is almost equally good and evil...." By the time shooting ended, Peck's assessment of Ahab's character, as drawn by Bradbury and Huston at least, had changed.

With script generally completed and casting in progress, Huston set out on a worldwide search in February 1954 for a sailing vessel to be converted into the *Pequod*, as Melville had described it. The search was a long one but finally, in the harbor at Scarborough, on the English coast, Huston came across the *Hispanola*, a vessel Walt Disney had used in his film of Robert Lewis Stevenson's *Treasure Island*. The ship was purchased and carpenters set to remodeling her to Melville's specifications.

In addition to finding a vessel to play *Pequod*, Huston also had to find a stand-in town for New Bedford, the Massachusetts

Ocean spray and foam wash the decks of the *Pequod* as Leo Genn and Gregory Peck urge their crew onward in the grip of the madness that will carry them to the brink of disaster.

coastal village where the film's opening sequences take place (even though Melville's whaling port was actually Nantucket). He settled on the little town of Youghal on the south Irish coast.

The filmmakers also needed, of course, a white whale and for Moby Dick himself no living creature would suffice. With the assistance of British whale expert Robert Clarke, special-effects technicians set to work in England designing and constructing a monster to Huston's specifications. The result was a 90-foot-long hulking beast made of a plastic-and-rubber skin over a steel frame and weighing many tons. Electronic controls would allow it to dive, surface, spout and slap its tail against the side of a boat. The creature was so huge and heavy, however, that it constantly broke the cables—even the largest ones available—used to tow it in the open sea.

The company assembled to begin filming sea sequences in the South Irish Sea, in St. George's Channel, off the coasts of Ireland and Wales. In these waters they encountered some of their most vexing problems.

"Every day we went out," Peck recalled later, "but we had only ten good weather days. The boat was top heavy because of the mast and when it got too stormy we were chased in."

People were constantly getting seasick as storms battered the unlucky company. Actors Richard Basehart and Leo Genn were injured and in one hair-raising episode, Peck himself was nearly lost with Moby Dick.

The crew was filming off Fishguard, Wales, with the actor on the giant beast's back, when, as Peck remembers, "a sudden squall blew up and a fog bank rolled in with it just about the time I lost sight of the motor launch that was towing the whale with an underwater line.

"The towline snapped and I was in the fog in a squall in waves that were 10-15 feet high, alone on a slippery rubber whale. And I thought, 'What a way to go!' But I yelled and they were able to find me in the fog. I got off that whale in a hurry. The whale itself was

never found. We searched for it but never found it. We were just glad to get out of there ourselves and made for shore."

The climactic scenes with Gregory Peck lashed to the whale's side as it dives and rolls over in the water were shot in a large tank at London's Elstree Studios. Ordinarily such scenes would be done by a stunt double for the actor, but Peck did these scenes himself, which he actually hadn't expected to do: "I thought it would be a trick shot in miniature, but [this] was a little treat Huston had been saving for me."

According to Huston, "Peck spent half the movie in the water. ... He did things that most stunt men won't do. For instance, the final scene where Ahab is killed by Moby Dick ... everytime the whale turns over the ropes get tighter and the man goes underwater again. Peck was half-drowned but when the

Realizing the imminent danger Ahab's unrelenting rage for revenge poses to every man among them, Starbuck challenges Captain Ahab in the midst of a storm and has to defend himself against a murderous response.

Ahab approaches his final encounter with the white whale—assisted by the equally mysterious harpooner Queequeg, played by Friedrich Ledebur.

scene was finished, he wanted to do it again in case we missed anything."

When it was all finished, John Huston personally brought the film to the United States for a gala premiere in New Bedford on June 27, 1956. Warner Brothers pulled out all the stops for an occasion to remember. A "Moby Dick Special" plane flew celebrities, press people and a large entourage from New York City to the Massachusetts town where thousands of citizens turned out to greet them at the airport and along the road to their hotel.

More than 100,000 people showed up for a parade on the afternoon of the premiere; nothing was overlooked that might add to the event.

The New York opening of *Moby Dick* took place on July 4, 1956, at the Criterion and Sutton theaters. *The New York Times* critic Bosley Crowther was unequivocal in his praise: "...a rolling and thundering color film that is herewith devoutly recommended as one of the great motion pictures of our times. ... The clean dramatic structure...sound and pictorial elements...are composed like a symphony...to build up a mighty harmony of spiritual striving and failing, of hope and despair. ... Space does not possibly permit us to cite all the things...brilliantly done or developed. ... Peck gives Ahab a towering, gaunt appearance that is markedly Lincolnesque, and he holds that character's burning passions behind an unusually mask-like facade."

"A classic of the American screen..." said William K. Zinsser in the *New York Herald Tribune*, "...may just be the finest film that this country has achieved." Zinsser praised Huston for preserving "much of Melville's writing. The stately phrases march by, rising to sheer poetry when Capt. Ahab muses on the demons that goad him. ... The final encounter with Moby Dick is one of the most sensational episodes ever filmed. ... Peck plays Ahab with a scarred cheek and a scarred soul, a somber man hag-ridden by black furies. ... His voice is a deep rumble, his eyes are heavy except when he hears of the white whale…and then they blaze with lust. … He builds his role with mounting fervor…a fine adventure movie. … Beneath a mortal tale Huston has dared to hunt its immortal meanings, and he has found them.…"

In *Saturday Review* (July 7, 1956), Arthur Knight called the film "…a masterful production," cited its "skillfully compressed and synthesized screenplay, superb direction and performances. … There have been few films to use color so dramatically. The cast is…as exciting as the colors, the bearded, brooding Peck a demon possessed.…"

Not everyone agreed with these overwhelmingly favorable assessments. For example, *The New Yorker* magazine's critic labeled the picture "a fine, big, elementary job that misses the mystical Melville by several nautical miles but affords us an almost completely satisfactory tour of the bounding main. … Mr. Peck resembles Abraham Lincoln even more than usual and…has the further handicap of portraying Capt. Ahab not as a man who is merely hipped on the white whale but as an all-round lunatic. … Still, if we overlook Mr. Peck and forget all the profundities of Melville, we have here a simple epic of the briny that is a hell of an exciting piece of moviemaking."

Peck himself admits to finding the picture ultimately a bit of a disappointment, lacking the sense of action and forward drive vital to motion pictures. Perhaps, he says, because "Huston approached the project with an overly reverential attitude toward Melville. Those great dollops of Melville's purple prose," made for, the actor feels, "a pedestrian script. I'm not sure that it's possible to make a good movie script out of *Moby Dick*."

Peck also says that "I never liked myself" as Ahab. "I thought I was miscast in it. … But I've never regretted having done it. It was a try, a risk.…

"I got to thinking Ahab was just a damned old fool…screaming that if there is a God he's a malevolent God and he's chasing the whale because to him it signifies a fate and a destiny that he cannot control, that he's just a bit of flotsam cast onto this earth without any control over his own destiny and he resents it and he's angry about it. Well, I thought, he's just an old nut, that's all. And I certainly found out that that was not my cup of tea. But I don't regret having done it or having done other things that didn't turn out as well as I would have liked."

While filming scenes on the back of the white whale off the Irish coast, a sudden fog and storm at sea threatened the actor Peck with the fate of his fictional character.

Fashion designer Lauren Bacall shows off some of her sketches to New York sportswriter Gregory Peck as their romance blossoms in a Southern California marina.

Designing Woman

Metro-Goldwyn-Mayer   1957

Credits

Producer, Dore Schary; *director*, Vincente Minnelli; *screenplay*, George Wells, from a suggestion by Helen Rose; *music*, Andre Previn; *musical numbers and dances*, staged by Jack Cole; *photography*, John Alton; *editor*, Adrienne Fazan; *art directors*, William A. Horning, Preston Ames; *set decoration*, Edwin B. Willis, Henry Grace; *gowns*, Helen Rose; *special effects*, Warren Newcombe; *assistant director*, William Shanks; CinemaScope and Metrocolor. (118 minutes)

Cast

Gregory Peck (Mike Hagen), Lauren Bacall (Marilla Hagen), Dolores Gray (Lori Shannon), Sam Levene (Ned Hammerstein), Tom Helmore (Zachary Wilde), Mickey Shaughnessy (Maxie Stulz), Jesse White (Charlie Arneg), Chuck Connors (Johnnie "O"), Edward Platt (Martin J. Daylor), Alvy Moore (Luke Coslow), Carol Veazie (Gwen), Jack Cole (Randy Owen).

•

144

When *Designing Woman* came along, after the intense dramatic work *Moby Dick* and *The Man in the Gray Flannel Suit* had required, Gregory Peck found another opportunity to play a comedy role, a welcome respite and a delightful exercise of his comedic talents with another classy leading lady.

The story for this glossy comedy about a dress designer and a sports writer who fall in love, marry after a four-day courtship in Hollywood and then return to New York to try to reconcile their incompatible backgrounds was based on an idea by long-time Metro-Goldwyn-Mayer costume designer Helen Rose, who, according to press releases, also designed some 132 gowns for the production. That's at least more than a gown-a-minute in this 118-minute picture, but the entertainment's so diverting only a dedicated spoilsport would bother counting gowns.

Miss Rose, winner of Academy Awards for her costumes for *The Bad and the Beautiful* (1952) and for *I'll Cry Tomorrow* (1955), took her idea to MGM's head of production, Dore Schary, and writer Geroge Wells, who turned it into an Academy-Award-winning screenplay. Schary himself produced the picture and chose Vincente Minnelli to direct it.

(*Designing Woman* turned out to be Schary's last project at the studio and he had not yet completed it in late 1956 when Joseph Vogel, newly designated president of the financially troubled company, summoned him to New York and told him his services were no longer required.)

Director Minnelli is most readily associ-

After the perils of *Moby Dick* and the Irish Sea, scenes like this one with Lauren Bacall around the pool of the Beverly Hills Hotel in *Designing Woman* must have seemed a godsend to Gregory Peck.

Meeting unsuspecting old flame Dolores Gray in a posh New York eatery, Gregory Peck prepares to break the news to her that their relationship has been extinguished by his sudden marriage.

ated with such lavish MGM musicals as *Meet Me In St. Louis* (1944) and *An American in Paris* (1950). Many of his films are notable for a particular lushness of production look and quality associated with what has been termed "the MGM look," and the present case is no exception. For him, Minnelli says, this project "was great fun because Betty Bacall and Gregory Peck were wonderful to work with...."

Designing Woman was Peck's fourth picture under his Metro contract and his star-status also gave him the right to leading lady approval. Schary and Minnelli were delighted when Peck agreed with them that Lauren Bacall would be terrific playing opposite him.

Schary and Minnelli had originally wanted Grace Kelly for the role of Marilla Hagan, but Miss Kelly was getting ready for her impending marriage to Monaco's Prince Rainier and ruled it out. Lauren Bacall had

dedicated her time recently to taking care of her husband Humphrey Bogart, staying home and seeing him through one of the difficult phases of his bout with cancer, which had entailed both surgery and a long and excruciating series of post-operative X-ray treatments. Miss Bacall felt that a bout of work for her would boost her sagging spirits but she was still somewhat apprehensive about leaving her ailing husband.

Bogart himself sensed that his wife needed a break from the sickroom routine and, since he was feeling better, encouraged her to go for the part whey they heard about it.

Shooting was to begin in mid-September 1956, and with Bogart showing definite signs of improvement, Miss Bacall began preparing for the job in August. Apparently the return to a sort of normalcy was a tonic for both of

146

Once married, designer Bacall and sportswriter Peck begin to discover that the temperaments, lifestyles and coteries of their respective professions may not be as compatible as they would like.

them, because on the first day of shooting, with scenes around the swimming pool at the Beverly Hills Hotel, Bogie and their two children came to visit the proceedings. Later, when they were shooting scenes on a sailboat at a local marina, Bogart anchored his own boat *Santana* nearby and, during a break, Bacall and Peck came aboard and joined him for lunch.

According to Miss Bacall, the entire project was a delight: As she recalled later in her book, *By Myself, Designing Woman* offered "a lovely, funny script, a terrific part, and I was happy about working." In all, she thought "that movie was one of my happiest film experiences...."

The picture gave both of its co-stars excellent chances to play some broad comedy scenes, considerably broader for Peck, as Mike Hagen, than the lighter, more restrained romantic comedy of *Roman Holiday*.

Bacall and Peck get very able comic support throughout from Dolores Gray and a superb cast.

Designing Woman decorated Radio City Music Hall beginning May 16, 1957, and *Cue* magazine thought it "...a very fast and wildly funny newlyweds' comedy of errors...a tasty spicy, high comedy entertainment dish... whipped together into hilarious fun by... Wells and ... Minnelli, with willing assists from a first-rate cast...."

The New Yorker's John McCarten didn't agree and said, "...this doesn't add up to much, and I'm afraid that Mr. Peck and Miss Bacall are far too earnest a team to be successful at this kind of comedy...."

Bosley Crowther, in *The New York Times*, pointed out that "this pseudo-sophisticated romance...bears more than a passing resemblance to that old Spencer Tracy-Katharine Hepburn film *Woman of the Year* (MGM, 1942)...it obviously makes an endeavor to generate the same kind of verve and general sardonic humor. ... It does, too—at least in certain stretches...some of the verbal exchanges...have a nice little splash of wit about

them. Good dialogue has been written by George Wells. ... We wish Mr. Wells had not resorted to the ancient device of jealousy as the cause of the matrimonial trouble. ... There is also something a little chilly and forbidding about Miss Bacall. Miss Gray seems a whole lot more obliging. Frankly, we think Peck picked the wrong girl. ... Mr. Peck makes a better deadpanned comic than sports writer. ... Vincente Minnelli keeps things moving tolerably until the end, when it bursts in a splurge of ostentation that is silly and in somewhat dubious taste...."

Gregory Peck takes it on the nose from Chuck Connors, playing a threatening hoodlum who's not an admirer of Greg's investigative sports columns.

147

Arriving in Rio Arriba, Gregory Peck is stopped by suspicious townspeople, unidentified blacksmith, Kathleen Gallant, Herbert Rudley, Robert Griffin, Barry Coe and George Voskovec, who at first mistake him for the hangman they await to conduct the executions of a band of murderous bank robbers.

The Bravados

20th Century-Fox   **1958**

Cast

Gregory Peck (Jim Douglass), Joan Collins (Josefa Velarde), Stephen Boyd (Bill Zachary), Albert Salmi (Ed Taylor), Henry Silva (Lujan), Kathleen Gallant (Emma), Barry Coe (Tom), George Voskovec (Gus Steinmetz), Herbert Rudley (Sheriff Eloy Sanchez), Lee Van Cleef (Alfonso Parral), Andrew Duggan (Padre), Ken Scott (Primo), Gene Evans (Butler), Jack Mather (Quinn), Joe DeRita (Simms), Robert Adler (Tony Mirabel), Jason Wingreen (Nichols), Robert Griffin (Banker Loomis), Ada Carrasco (Mrs. Parral), Juan Garcia (Pepe Martinez), Jacqueline Evans (Mrs. Barnes), Alicia del Lago (Angela Lujan). With the Ninos Cantores De Morelia Choral Group.

Credits

Producer, Herbert B. Swope, Jr.; *director*, Henry King; *screenplay*, Philip Yordan, based on the novel by Frank O'Rourke; *music*, Lionel Newman; *cinematography*, Leon Shamroy; *editor*, William Mace; *sound*, Bernard Freericks, Warren B. Delaplain; *art directors*, Lyle R. Wheeler, Mark-Lee Kirk; *set decoration*, Walter M. Scott, Chester Bayhi; *wardrobe*, Charles LeMaire; *assistant director*, Stanley Hough; filmed in CinemaScope and Technicolor. (99 minutes)

"Henry, how the heck is it that you always know exactly where you're going to do something?" asked Darryl Zanuck when director Henry King informed him instantly that he knew exactly the location he was going to use for his next picture.

"Because," replied King, "I'm always looking."

This conversation took place circa early 1947; the picture involved was *Captain from Castile*, which King had told Mr. Zanuck he wanted to shoot in Morelia, Mexico. A decade later King would return to Morelia to shoot *The Bravados*, his fifth picture with Gregory Peck. Unlike their previous Western, *The Gunfighter*, a small black-and-white production, much of which took place on one set, *The Bravados*, shot in Technicolor and CinemaScope, is a chase picture spread across the scenically variegated terrain of Central Mexico, among the steep mountains, the canyons, grasslands and forest groves of the states of Michiocan and Jalisco.

Gregory Peck's first Western since *Only the Valiant*, in 1951, *The Bravados* was written by Philip Yordan, a veteran screenwriter. As it emerges on screen, the picture is fairly tightly written, undoubtedly a result of Henry King's revisions of Yordan's work. Although he never received or, apparently, asked for a screen credit for writing, King was in the habit of reworking, to various degrees, the screenplays for his projects before shooting began; he has estimated that about fifty percent of *The Bravados* script was his own contribution. What does emerge is essentially a "revenge" drama, dealing with the brutalizing effect on the revenge-seeker himself of the violence he commits and probing the conscience of a man who takes the law into his own hands.

Peck plays Jim Douglass, who joins a posse hunting down four escaped killers because he thinks they are the ones who raped and murdered his wife.

Romantic interest is provided in an otherwise unromantic tale by the presence of Josefa

Barry Coe, whose fiancée has been abducted by the fleeing criminals, is a member of the pursuing posse which Gregory Peck joins and subsequently leads.

Gregory Peck asks Sheriff Herbert Rudley and deputy Ken Scott to let him have a look at the prisoners, whose execution he has come to Rio Arriba to witness.

On execution-day's eve, Joan Collins, as a Spanish-American beauty who'd spurned Gregory Peck's attentions in the past, appears more attentive when he accompanies her to church after turning up in Rio Arriba a few years later.

At the Mexican border, the posse turns back, but a determined Gregory Peck bids goodbye before continuing to track the remaining outlaws into Mexico.

Velarde, an aristocratic beauty played by British actress Joan Collins.

The Bravados marked the twelfth collaboration between director King and photographer Leon Shamroy, who had, in fact, directed the photography of the four previous King-Peck projects as well.

For Gregory Peck himself, the character of Jim Douglass was something of a reverse from that of Jimmy Ringo in *The Gunfighter*. Unlike Ringo, Douglass is driven by hatred to track and kill; he seeks the deadly confrontation.

Deeply troubled to learn that he has killed three men for a crime they did not commit, Gregory Peck embraces his daughter, Maria Garcia Fletcher, in the church where a priest offers him hope of absolution.

The picture opened at New York's Paramount Theater on June 25, 1958. In a June 4 review, *Variety* praised the picture and noted that "Peck in one of his best performances…is taciturn but compelling; you know what he is thinking, and his climactic scene is a powerful one.…"

In *The New York Times*, A. H. Weiler reported that the film was "executed intelligently in fine, brooding style against eye-filling, authentic backgrounds.…" Weiler did feel that the tension was reduced somewhat when Douglass's reasons for pursuing the men are revealed, that the romantic angle was unnecessary and that the characters of the villains were not clearly defined, but he said that "Despite these flaws, which are fundamentally minor, the film emerges as a credit to its makers. … Peck performs in rough, moody, laconic fashion. He is a tough, calculating, somber gent who lends conviction to a role that could be a stereotype.…"

"The chase is the thing," said Paul V. Beckley in the *New York Herald Tribune*. "Henry King…has elaborated the cat-and-mouse… theme into wide proportions. … For all its beauty, the landscape is something of a distraction from a dramatic point of view. … Yet the picture has a sense of bigness like the land in which it was made, and King's understandable enthusiasm for the scenery is a part of it. As Peck tracks the men…gunning them one by one, the cruel realities are not dwelt on but neither are they avoided.…"

According to *Time* magazine, the picture "attempts to draw a useful moral, but it is just too goldurn slow on the draw. … The paradox of public innocence and private guilt is strongly framed in the ending, and the point of the story…is almost cruelly pressed home. … Cowboy Peck gives the impression that he felt more comfortable in that gray flannel suit.…"

Cue magazine, however, found that "Peck is excellent, as always.…" And Arthur Knight, in *Saturday Review*, wrote that the production "…marks a welcome return to the taut style and keen pictorial sense that distinguished… *The Gunfighter*. … Through superior direction and a thought-provoking theme, *The Bravados* emerges as one of the best Westerns in a long, long time."

Gregory Peck, as Eastern-dressed Baltimore gentleman and former sea captain James McKay, arrives in the Western ranching community of San Rafael. The three lads leaning on the hitching rail nearby are Peck's real-life sons, Carey Paul, Stephen and Jonathan.

The Big Country

United Artists   **1958**

Credits

Producers, William Wyler, Gregory Peck; *director*, William Wyler; *screenplay*, James R. Webb, Sy Bartlett, Robert Wilder, based on the novel by Donald Hamilton; *adaptation*, Jessamyn West, Robert Wyler; *music*, Jerome Moross; *cinematography*, Franz Planer; *editor*, Robert Swink; *art director*, Frank Hotaling; *set decoration*, Edward G. Boyle; *second-unit photography*, Wallace Chewning; filmed in Technicolor and Technirama. (166 minutes)

Cast

Gregory Peck (James McKay), Jean Simmons (Julie Maragon), Carroll Baker (Patricia Terrill), Charlton Heston (Steve Leech), Burl Ives (Rufus Hannassey), Charles Bickford (Major Henry Terrill), Alfonso Bedoya (Ramon), Chuck Connors (Buck Hannassey), Chuck Hayward (Rafe Hannassey), Buff Brady (Dude Hannassey), Jim Burk (Cracker Hannassey), Dorothy Adams (Hannassey Woman), Chuck Robertson, Bob Morgan, John McKee and Jay Slim Talbot (Terrill Cowboys), Ralph Sanford, Harry V. Cheshire, Dick Alexander (Guests), Jonathan Peck, Stephen Peck, Carey Paul Peck (Boys).

The Big Country was the first film on which Gregory Peck's name would appear as "producer" and, Peck told an interviewer during the picture's production, it was in Rome that he had caught the producing bug—from William Wyler.

Out of their mutually pleasant experience making *Roman Holiday* grew the Peck-Wyler co-production partnership responsible for *The Big Country*. After this, their second picture together, was completed, however, Wyler told

Charlton Heston plays ranch foreman Steve Leech, who's not only disdainful of Gregory Peck's apparent dudeness but, as it turns out, also very jealous that this Easterner is engaged to his boss's daughter.

a newspaper reporter in New York, "I'll never make another picture with Greg Peck...and you can quote me." Dissolve partnership.

As Peck has observed, *The Big Country* is "a sort of *Grand Hotel* Western," with "a whole gallery of characters. They all have big scenes and fit into the main theme."

Producers Peck and Wyler spared no expense to make the picture live up to its name. A part of Wyler's attraction to this project was his keen desire to use the setting, the vast landscape of "the big country," as a counterpoint to the small-minded creatures who inhabit it and fight against its stunning beauty.

For Peck, producing the picture brought him, he says, a new awareness of production details to which someone who was only acting would usually remain oblivious. A producer, he found, is "always aware of money going down the drain."

The disagreement between Peck and Wy-

Although firmly and happily betrothed to the luscious and impulsive Carroll Baker, heiress to the huge Terrill ranch, Gregory Peck is soon troubled by the discovery of some rather basic differences in opinion and attitude between them. Carroll's not too pleased, either.

ler arose, in fact, over costs, specifically, what Peck considered Wyler's extravagance: "He overshot by an hour's length, which had to be cut." They wound up with a picture just under three hours long and "went way over our budget." The original budget, projected for $3 million, was revised to $3.5 million. "We spent," says Peck, "4.1 million."

Neither Peck nor Wyler is the sort of man to carry a grudge very far, if at all, and the attrition of time has eroded whatever strain the picture made on their mutual regard.

The Big Country opened on October 1, 1958, at New York's Astor Theater, with a gala charity premiere benefitting the National Jewish Hospital at Denver, a non-sectarian tuberculosis and respiratory-disease treatment center. The screening was followed by a midnight supper at the Waldorf-Astoria hotel, where patrons of the hospital mingled with the filmmakers and other celebrities attending.

Some of the reviews were already in. *Variety* (August 13, 1958) praised the film as "massive in its pictorial splendor…one of the best photography jobs of the year. … Although the story…is dwarfed by the scenic outpourings, *The Big Country* is nonetheless armed with a serviceable, adult Western yarn…about the meaning of bravery and the value of a sane, peaceful approach to hot-headed issues. … Peck gives one of his better performances…."

In *Time* magazine (September 8, 1958), the picture was called "…a starkly beautiful, carefully written, classic Western that demands comparison with *Shane*. … In both *Shane* and *High Noon* the plot tautened on one spare, straight line—the hero awaiting an unwanted showdown with an implacable enemy. … In contrast…Wyler's…drama hinges not on a fateful decreed clash…but on a succession of real choices to be made by each of the characters, each choice affecting the lives of all the others, and creating in turn a new set of choices. … The story is acted out against a landscape in which the splash of blood

Rivalry over Jean Simmons's friendship ultimately erupts into violence between Chuck Connors and Gregory Peck in *The Big Country*.

Gregory Peck shares his ideas for resolving a longstanding local feud with head-turning schoolmarm Jean Simmons, whose inherited ranch he aims to buy and operate as a part of his peace plan.

Accompanied by Alfonso Bedoya, Gregory Peck confronts the stern and obstinate Rufus Hannassey, played by Burl Ives in an Oscar-winning role, with an idea for settling the Terrill-Hannassey dispute, while Jean Simmons looks apprehensive and Chuck Connors skeptical.

Chuck Connors appears to have the upper hand over Gregory Peck in a tense confrontation witnessed by Jean Simmons and Burl Ives.

provides the only bright color...."

In *Saturday Review* (August 23, 1958), Arthur Knight called *The Big Country* "a fairly complex and sophisticated affair. ... Wyler," he said, "has mastered the problems of composing and directing for the new screen shapes beyond any of his contemporaries. What he has failed to do is obtain performances of matching force and effectiveness. ... Peck underplays to the point of listlessness, Ives intones his lines flatly and heavily." Baker, Simmons and Heston were, he felt, "little more than adequate. ... For this, however, the writers must share responsibility. In their eagerness to prove a moral, they overlooked the necessity of exploring, explaining and making credible their characters."

Bosley Crowther, in *The New York Times*, October 2, 1958, felt that Wyler and his co-workers "have attempted to make...the most

bellicose hymn to peace ever seen. ... The verbal construction and pictorial development," he said, "are measured, meticulous, robust and ringing with organ tones. ... Those verbal encounters and violent battles are like something on the windy plains of Troy. ... This quality is best represented by Mr. Bickford and Mr. Ives who glare and roar at each other like a couple of fur-bearing gladiators. Mr. Peck...and Mr. Heston...stoke up the spirit of contention to a lesser degree. ... For all this film's mighty pretensions, it does not get far beneath the skin of its conventional Western situation and its stock Western characters...."

In the *New York Herald Tribune*, Paul V. Beckley sounded a more favorable note, calling the picture "...king-size and astutely and enthusiastically made...magnificently, overwhelmingly photographed. ... Foremost among its qualities is an acute sense of the West's bigness. ... Wyler, in giving full attention to the themes and incidents of his story, has shown such relish in the telling, such a richness, that the workmanship becomes economical, always to the point, never diffuse. ... The acting is good throughout...this is pre-eminently a director's picture and among Westerns a real beauty."

Someone else who shared that sentiment saw the picture in his private screening room in Washington, D.C., and *The Big Country*, a resounding commercial success, has been reported to have been President Dwight D. Eisenhower's favorite film. Eisenhower loved Westerns and musicals and when *The Big Country* was completed, a print was shipped to Washington, where it was screened in the White House theater four times in a row for an appreciative president.

With a group of his cowboys, Charles Bickford pays a riotous surprise call on the ranch of rival Rufus Hannassey while Hannassey's wife, Dorothy Adams, and one of his children cower in the background.

Pork Chop Hill

United Artists 1959
A Melville Production

Credits

Producer, Sy Bartlett; *director*, Lewis Milestone; *screenplay*, James R. Webb, based on a work by S.L.A. Marshall, U. S. Army (Ret.); *music*, Leonard Rosenman; *cinematography*, Sam Leavitt; *editor*, George Boemler; *sound recording*, Earl Crain, Sr., Roger Hermanic; *sound effects*, Del Harris; *production design*, Nicolai Remisoff; *set decoration*, Edward G. Boyler; *technical advisor*, Capt. Joseph G. Clemons, Jr., U.S. Army. (97 minutes)

Cast

Gregory Peck (Lt. Clemons), Harry Guardino (Forstman), Rip Torn (Lt. Russell), George Peppard (Fedderson), James Edwards (Cpl. Jurgens), Bob Steele (Kern), George Shibata (Lt. O'Hashi), Woody Strode (Franklin), Norman Fell (Sgt. Coleman), Robert Blake (Velie), Biff Elliott (Bowen), Barry Atwater (Davis), Michael Garth (S-2 Officer), Ken Lynch (Gen. Trudeau), Paul Comi (Sgt. Kreucheberg), Abel Fernandez (McKinley), Lou Gallo (P. I. Officer), Cliff Ketchum (Cpl. Payne), Martin Landau (Marshall), Bert Remsen (Lt. Cummings), Kevin Hagen (Cpl. Kissell), Dean Stanton (MacFarland), Leonard Graves (Lt. Cook), Syl Lamont (Sgt. Kuzmick), Gavin McCloud (Saxon), John Alderman (Lt. Waldorf), John McKee (Olds), Charles Aidman (Harrold), Chuck Hayward (Chalmers), Buzz Martin (Radio Operator), Robert Williams (Soldier Runner), Bill Wellman, Jr. (Iron Man), Viraj Amonsin (Chinese Broadcaster), Barry Maguire (Lt. Attridge).

"Remember this, you've got a hundred and thirty-five men, all of them thinking of the peace talks at Panmunjom. It's a cinch they won't want to die in what may be the last battle...."

Under this admonition, U.S. Army Lieutenant Joseph G. Clemons, Jr., must lead his men, King Company, in a difficult assault on a hilltop position occupied by North Korean and Chinese Communist troops. Within this framework, Gregory Peck's and Sy Bartlett's first Melville Production tells a story of wartime valor and sacrifice.

James R. Webb, another alumnus, with Peck and Bartlett, of *The Big Country*, wrote the screenplay, based on the very professional account of the battle by U.S. Army Brigadier General S.L.A. Marshall, one of the world's foremost military historians.

To direct their picture, Peck and Bartlett sought out Lewis Milestone, then concentrating on television work, whose credits included what are generally regarded as two of the finest pictures ever made about men in war and the subject of war itself: *All Quiet on the Western Front* (1930) and *A Walk In The Sun* (1945). With those two pictures, *Pork Chop Hill* marked, for Milestone, the completion of a trilogy of films dealing with the three major military conflicts in which Americans had fought in this century.

Lt. Clemons, as played by Gregory Peck, is steadfast, stalwart and methodical in his commitment to carrying out his assignment and

As commander of King Company, "Lt." Gregory Peck reviews with Rip Torn the limited options he has for successfully capturing a disputed hilltop.

Faced with imminent enemy counterattack, Harry Guardino and Gregory Peck survey the bomb-cratered and rubble-strewn terrain for which American soldiers have been asked to give their lives.

leading his men successfully up the hill and over the top. But his unflinching determination to complete the mission does not blind him to the terrible cost in terms of human lives. His concern for his men is second only to his devotion to duty. Clemons is a courageous man, but not recklessly so, nor does he seek glory for himself. He keeps both his wits and his wit about him.

Variety mildly criticized the filmmakers for casting a black man in the deserter's role: "It's amazing that Webb should have chosen a Negro…it could have been a white man, and the effect would have been the same. The producers…surely are aware that the tendency to generalize where a Negro is involved is far greater and more harmful…."

The dramatic rationale behind making this character a black man comes clear during the confrontation between Franklin and Clemons which enables the movie to make a minor statement about racial problems and deprivation in the United States.

"I don't want to die for Korea," Franklin tells Clemons. "What do I care about this stinkin' hill? You oughtta see where I live back home. I sure ain't sure I'd die for that…."

"Peck's performance…is completely believable," said *Variety* (May 6, 1959). "He comes through as a born leader, and yet…has his moments of doubt and uncertainty. This is no customary Hollywood hero and the picture gains immeasurably from the human factor with which Peck imbues the role…."

"Hollywood has come a long way to be able to make war films such as *Pork Chop Hill*," continued *Variety*'s critic, "a grim, utterly realistic story that drives home both the irony of war and the courage men can summon to die in a cause which they don't understand and for an objective which they know to be totally irrelevant…an important reminder of the futility of war. … As war pictures go, this one makes most of the rest look pale."

Pork Chop Hill opened at New York's Roxy

Pinned down by intense and unexpected enemy resistance, Gregory Peck takes stock of his company's tactical situation.

Preparing for enemy insurgence, Gregory Peck emerges from the hilltop bunker that serves as company headquarters and on which a G.I. with an ironic sense of humor has posted a sign dubbing it the "Korea Hilton Hotel."

Theatre on May 29, 1959. The next day, in *The New York Times*, Bosley Crowther reported that "Milestone knows how to stage these things and he has here the further advantage of a highly responsive cast. ... Gregory Peck is convincingly stalwart. ... Rip Torn is cheerfully professional. ... George Shibata ... is excellent. ... A good dozen other fellows—notably Woody Strode—are moving and amusing in G.I. roles. ... The readiness to incorporate [the troops'] resentments in the account and demonstrate this new brainwash technique are worthy of highest commendation. ... And the audacity of Sy Bartlett in producing such a grim and rugged film, which tacitly points out the obsoleteness of ground warfare, merits applause."

In the *New York Herald Tribune*, Paul V. Beckley called the picture "a realistic and sober film with touches of wry G.I. humor and an extraordinary honest view of officers both in the line and in the higher echelons. ... Among all war films it is unusual for an utter lack of bombast, mawkishness, or the customary misunderstanding of the circumstances of infantry action. ... It reflects in its quiet comprehension a fundamental change in the attitude toward war, certainly the attitude toward the fighting men. ... For Milestone this film marks a trilogy. ... In terms of pure military authenticity I should say this one tops them all...."

Time magazine (June 8, 1959) saw the picture as "heart-racking," but claimed that its "imagination of the battle is inevitably untrue to the events; the fighting scenes are almost too spectacularly realistic, and too often they transpire in the middle distance, surrounding the spectator but somehow never quite touching him. The moviegoer never really gets to know the fighting men...but then, on the other hand, the film does not sentimentalize or patronize its heroes. ... Milestone seems determined to proclaim the dignity of the individual at the moment, in the heat of battle, when it seems to matter least...."

In a tense confrontation with a mutinous Woody Strode, Gregory Peck explains to the black infantryman that, in this confrontation with a communist military power, the stakes are equal for all of the fighting Americans regardless of race.

Hollis Alpert, in *Saturday Review* (May 16, 1959), thought that, as a picture about war, *"Pork Chop Hill* is one of the very best...."

Above all, *Pork Chop Hill* is a battle hymn to the American foot soldier, the infantrymen drawn from the ranks of average citizens and forged into a citizens' army. We may argue whether any glory at all may be drawn from warfare, but we need not question the truth of the courage and strength and tenacity amply demonstrated in this unpretentious and very moving motion picture.

Gregory Peck himself is understandably proud of the film that he and his partners produced, and it is typical of the man that he has praise as well for his fellow actors:

"It's one of the outstanding war dramas, with a cast of men who really seem to belong. They are not 'names,' but each boy contributes a great performance. ... What more can one ask?"

A grim-faced and exhausted Gregory Peck leads the handful of survivors from King Company down the hillside after they have successfully—but at great cost in lives—resisted an enemy counterattack and finally been relieved by the arrival of replacements.

Gregory Peck comforts Deborah Kerr after his relentless questioning about her background brings her to the point of hysterical confession that she has in fact lied about her past life in order to gain acceptance in the world she thought would otherwise reject her.

Beloved Infidel

20th Century-Fox   **1959**

Credits

Producer, Jerry Wald; *director*, Henry King; *screenplay*, Sy Bartlett, based on the book by Sheilah Graham and Gerold Frank; *music*, Franz Waxman; *title song*, Paul Francis Webster, Franz Waxman; *cinematography*, Leon Shamroy; *editor*, William Reynolds; *sound*, E. Clayton Ward, Harry M. Leonard; *art directors*, Lyle R. Wheeler, Maurice Ransford; *set decoration*, Walter M. Scott, Eli Benneche; *costumes*, Bill Thomas; *assistant director*, Stanley Hough;

filmed in CinemaScope and De Luxe Color, with Stereophonic Sound. (123 minutes)

Cast

Gregory Peck (F. Scott Fitzgerald), Deborah Kerr (Sheilah Graham), Eddie Albert (Bob Carter), Philip Ober (John Wheeler), Herbert Rudley (Stan Harris), John Sutton (Lord Donegall), Karin Booth (Janet Pierce), Ken Scott (Robinson), Buck Class (Dion), A. Cameron Grant (Johnson), Cindy Ames (Miss Bull).

Deborah Kerr and Gregory Peck in happier beach-house moments in *Beloved Infidel*, Hollywood's version of columnist Sheila Graham's story of the love affair she had with F. Scott Fitzgerald.

Of all film genres, the one in which success is perhaps the most elusive is that of screen biography. If it does nothing else, *Beloved Infidel* stands as a testament to that verity.

According to Peck there seem to have been two schools of thought about the project at the studio—they divided along the lines of whether to make the picture with writer F. Scott Fitzgerald as an incidental character in the life of Hollywood gossip columnist Sheilah Graham, or whether to make the picture with Sheilah Graham as an incidental character in the final episodes of Scott Fitzgerald's life. The two schools of thought apparently were never reconciled.

During the production of the picture Peck saw it on a simpler level, as "a story of a man who is trying to recapture his talent and a rather silly girl who happened to meet and fall in love. Somehow they bring out the best in each other."

After Al Hayes finished his screenplay, producer Jerry Wald sent it to Sheilah Graham for her approval. He didn't get it. She read the screenplay and said she hated it.

"Which part of it?" Wald asked.

"All of it!" she replied.

Wald and Hayes and Graham met in Wald's office to try to resolve their differences. Hayes admitted to them that he really didn't like either of the characters and Graham told Wald that she thought he should find another writer. The next complaints about the screenplay, however, came from a source with far more weight than Sheilah Graham.

Beloved Infidel was to be Gregory Peck's last picture under his contractual commitment to 20th Century-Fox. He had serious reservations about accepting the role and it was only the presence of his old friend and mentor Henry King as director that led him to agree to it in the first place. When *he* read the Alfred Hayes script, he too found it completely unacceptable. The Fitzgerald character Hayes had drawn and whom Peck was expected to play was as completely unattractive to Peck as he had been to Sheilah Graham and Greg thought that neither the fictional Sheilah Graham nor any movie audience would have wanted to stay in his company for very long.

"I couldn't see what charm she could have found in such a character," Peck observed.

Peck told Wald he would not do the picture using the current screenplay. Robert Alan Arthur was hired to make extensive revisions and he too failed to come up with an acceptable version. Peck asked Wald to postpone the production while an entirely new script was written, but because of co-star Deborah Kerr's other commitments, it couldn't be long delayed. On an emergency basis, Peck's friend and sometime production partner Sy Bartlett, who was also an experienced writer, took on the job next, writing the screenplay while the picture was actually in production and eventually winding up with the script credit.

Above all, Gregory Peck knew that he could not portray the writer with any kind of physical veracity. Fitzgerald was a relatively short man in stature, with pale blond hair and gray-blue eyes and an open, enthusiastic manner.

"I'm no night-club imitator," he remarked during production. "I can only do what I can to capture the essence of the man and hope that his friends will feel that I haven't done him violence."

At one point in the production, the film-makers ran afoul of the movie industry's Production Code—in effect, its morality guide—and its administrator, Geoffrey M. Shurlock, who was, in effect, Hollywood's censor. In

Relaxing on a sunny California beach, recovering alcoholic writer Gregory Peck probes less-than-candid columnist Deborah Kerr about her cloudy past life.

contention was whether or not Gregory Peck could use the word "bitch," which was in the script and which he thought was important for one bit of dialogue and perfectly justifiable within the dramatic context of the picture. We may be sure that Peck would not treat such a matter lightly. In 1959, such language was still taboo in the movies and, although Greg made a strong case for keeping the word in the script, the request was turned down.

Of course, Gregory Peck's own innate dignity and our perception of him as reliable and agreeable both in person and in the character roles with which he is most popularly associated does tend to undermine the credibility of the drinking-bout scenes and the drunken loutishness he is called upon to display as sometime aspects of Fitzgerald's behavior.

Sheilah Graham herself found Greg's por-

trait unbelievable on a number of levels and has remarked that "even Bing Crosby" would have been better. She has also characterized the picture as, in a word, "dreadful." So much for pleasing everyone.

Beloved Infidel did make one bit of film history: it was the first commercial Hollywood production given for showing in competition at the San Francisco Film Festival, which was in its third year.

The New York premiere was held in November at the Paramount Theater, as a benefit for the Damon Runyon Fund; the picture opened its run on November 17, 1959, about a year after the publication of Sheilah Graham's book of the same title.

In *The New York Times*, Bosley Crowther called it "Generally flat and uninteresting. ... While there was a certain amount of frenzy in the memoirs of Sheilah Graham, there is only a routine sort of fumbling between a man and a woman in this film leading to nothing more engrossing than a sense of futility. ... [The moviemakers] went on the evident assumption that the simple dropping of names...the unrestrained calling of 'Scott' and the mention ...of the novels of Mr. Fitzgerald would be sufficient to impress an audience. ... It definitely is not. ... There is no more reality in these names than there is in the postured performance of Gregory Peck. His grim-faced monotony as a washout is relieved in a couple of critical scenes by some staggering and bawling as a drunkard, but that is hardly enough. ... Deborah Kerr...is likewise unconvincing and emotionally implausible...."

Paul V. Beckley, in the *New York Herald Tribune*, was more inclined to accept the film at face value: "If it is not likely to pry any cheers out of Fitzgerald devotees, it is nevertheless an intensely told love story with some tender moments and some fairly desperate ones. ... I have the feeling this picture is going to stir a good many hearts, if not minds. ... The film describes with frankness but more taste than one might have expected the tormented if intense passion of Miss Graham and Mr. Fitzgerald. ... While it minces no words nor evades the facts of the situation, it does not simper or gawk or make any effort to shock. ... Peck, although his manner and mannerisms won't persuade most writers that he is one of them, nevertheless manages to turn in one of his most pungent performances...."

Gregory Peck himself felt that what seemed to be most lacking in the picture was a sense of F. Scott Fitzgerald himself and of what really made him an interesting character; explanations of Fitzgerald as a person and as an artist were simply missing. Somewhere between the picture's inception and its release, says Peck, "Fitzgerald got lost...and the picture turned out to be a soap opera about a Cinderella from London who came to Hollywood and took care of a noisy drunk...."

What there was was a glossy Jerry Wald production, filmed in DeLuxe Color and CinemaScope largely in the Fox studios, but with some pretty backgrounds shot in England, New York and southern California. It was obviously made with the best of intentions all around and its overall effectiveness is, as clearly noted, debatable. Unsuccessful it may be in capturing accurately and compellingly the story of the doomed writer and the woman with whom he spent his last days, but boring it is not; the people involved in its manufacture knew a thing or two about screen entertainment that makes even their failures interesting.

"It is impossible," Henry King later observed, "to put one's finger on just what went wrong" with *Beloved Infidel*, but he still considered it "a passable" movie, noting that not every work can be a masterpiece of moviemaking.

A relapse into alcoholism brings a drunken Gregory Peck to follow Deborah Kerr onto a train and cause an embarrassing disturbance in a sleeping coach.

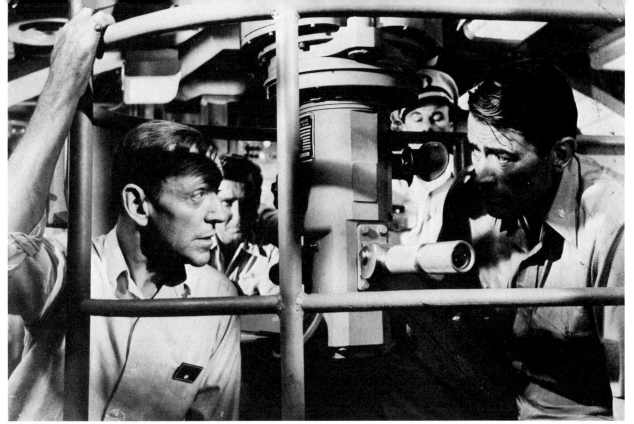

On a reconnaisance submarine mission to search for signs of life in the radiation-ridden northern hemisphere, physicist Fred Astaire and commander Peck consider the lifeless landscapes they have surveyed and face the grimness of the prognosis for mankind.

On the Beach

United Artists 1959

Credits

Producer and Director, Stanley Kramer; *screenplay*, John Paxton, based on the novel by Nevil Shute; *music*, Ernest Gold; *song*, "Waltzing Matilda," lyrics by A. B. Patterson, music by Marie Cowan; *cinematography*, Giuseppe Rotunno; *editor*, Frederic Knudtson; *auto race photography*, Daniel L. Fapp; *art director*, Fernando Carrere; *production design*, Rudolph Sternad; *costumes*, Joe King; *special effects*, Lee Zavits; *sound effects*, Walter Elliott; *assistant director*, Ivan Volkman; *technical advisor*, Vice-Admiral Charles A. Lockwood, U.S.N. (Ret.); *Royal Australian Navy Liaison*, Lt. Comm. A. A. Norris-Smith. (134 minutes)

Cast

Gregory Peck (Dwight Towers), Ava Gardner (Moira Davidson), Fred Astaire (Julian Osborn), Anthony Perkins (Peter Holmes), Donna Anderson (Mary Holmes), John Tate (Admiral Bridie), Lola Brooks (Lt. Hosgood), Guy Doleman (Farrel), John Meillon (Swain), Harp McGuire (Sundstrom), Lou Vernon (Davidson), Ken Wayne (Benson), Jim Barrett (Chrysler), Basil Buller Murphy (Sir Douglas Froude), Keith Eden (Dr. Fletcher), John Royle (Senior Officer), Frank Gatcliff (Radio Officer), Paddy Moran (Port Man), John Casson (Salvation Army Captain), Kevin Brennan (Dr. King), C. Harding Brown (Dykers), Grant

Taylor (Morgan), Peter Williams (Prof. Jorgenson), Harvey Adams (Sykes), Stuart Finch (Jones), Joe McCormick (Ackerman), Audine Leith (Betty), Jerry Ian Seals (Fogarty), Katherine Hill (Jennifer Holmes), Cary Paul Peck (Boy).

———————◆◆———————

"This is a would-be shocker which plays right up the alley of a) the Kremlin and b) the Western defeatists and/or traitors who yelp for the scrapping of the H-bomb. ... See this picture if you must (it seems bound to be much talked about), but keep in mind that the thinking it represents points the way toward eventual Communist enslavement of the entire human race."

Thus did the editors of the *New York Daily News* relieve the fullness of their minds in regard to *On The Beach*, in an editorial on December 18, 1959. They were not alone in their denunciation of the picture on these grounds.

In a press conference, Gregory Peck was asked about the controversial nature of the picture and its story. Peck responded that he thought the movie's theme "a subject which needs airing, which needs dramatizing." He dismissed suggestions that his career might be harmed by his starring in a controversial film, pointing out that some well-meaning friends had once warned him that his future would be jeopardized if he made *Gentleman's Agreement*. But the role had helped, rather than hurt, his career.

Welcoming American submarine commander Gregory Peck and his sub into port down under, Australian naval officer Anthony Perkins discusses the grim situation confronting the survivors of a catastrophic nuclear war.

Producer-director Stanley Kramer was no stranger to controversy or off-beat subject matter either. After working his way up through the Hollywood ranks from prop-boy to film cutter to writer to producer, Kramer established his reputation, in partnership with writer Carl Foreman, as a maker of socially significant low-budget pictures. Among them were *Home of the Brave* (1949), *Champion* (1949), *The Men* (1950), and *The Wild One* (1954). Kramer's most successful picture during this period was *High Noon* (1952), written by Foreman and directed by Fred Zinnemann.

Since Kramer wanted to make a picture which could play on an international basis and not offend anyone (by possibly assigning even theoretical guilt for unleashing the ultimate holocaust), the movie vaguely ascribes the blame for the conflict's outbreak to "some poor bloke somewhere who probably thought he saw something on a radar screen" and knew that if he hesitated to push a button his own country might be wiped out....

Above all, it was Stanley Kramer's intention that *On The Beach* would transcend politics, nationalism and political-economic ideology. His aim, he remarked at the time, was to make a picture that "reflects the primary hopes and fears on the minds of *all* people today."

In yet another military role (his ninth), Gregory Peck's reserved, stalwart and determined manner perfectly fit the character of U.S. Navy Captain Dwight Lionel Towers, commander of the nuclear submarine *Sawfish*. According to Peck, he modeled his character after U.S. Navy Commander W. R. Anderson, of the first American nuclear submarine, *Nautilus*.

Ava Gardner, playing opposite Greg for the third time, is Moira Davidson, the early-middle-aging daughter of an Australian rancher, whose life seems particularly unfulfilled and who seems to have found no purpose in it other than to drink her way through.

The renowned Fred Astaire made his dramatic acting "debut" as Julian Osborn, the boozy, all-too-wise-and-knowing scientist assigned to the *Sawfish*'s cruise to take readings of the residual radioactivity in the northern hemisphere and assess the possibility that it might be diminishing fast enough to allow for some survivors. *On the Beach* was Astaire's 31st movie since his screen debut in 1933 in *Dancing Lady*.

Most of *On the Beach* was shot in Australia, where most of the action takes place. Post-production work, editing and scoring were done in Hollywood, with composer Ernest Gold adapting the popular Australian song "Waltzing Matilda" as the picture's main theme and weaving it beautifully and poignantly into his effective score.

Kramer's original intention was to premiere the picture simultaneously in 25 cities around the world on December 17, 1959. The premiere site that attracted the most attention was Moscow, and not only because *On the Beach* would be the first full-length American feature to have a premiere in the Soviet Union. Everyone was also keenly interested in the Russians' reaction to the picture.

Negotiations for the Moscow premiere were handled privately with the Russians by Stanley Kramer and United Artists representatives rather than through regular U.S. government channels.

For the official occasion—the World Premiere—producer-director Kramer and Gregory Peck and his wife Veronique traveled to Moscow as guests of the Soviet government. The trip was a brief one; the Pecks arrived the night before the premiere and, as Greg has recalled, "were only in town two days and we wanted to see everything."

Before the screening, Peck had been a little bit apprehensive that the Russians might somehow take offense at the picture, but after-

In an attempt to locate the source of some mysterious radio signals emanating from a radioactive environment, Gregory Peck sends a crewman ashore near San Diego.

While Gregory Peck and Ava Gardner listen, disillusioned but thoroughly pragmatic scientist Fred Astaire discusses the calamity which mankind has brought upon itself.

With Gregory Peck, Anthony Perkins and crewmen in the sub's mess room, Fred Astaire sums up the dreadful prospect for humanity and how the world came to its grim predicament.

wards he found that they accepted it virtually without quarrel: "No one I talked to, including many high in the Soviet cultural program, found the film controversial. ... They called it a dramatic warning."

Some of the viewers also expressed doubts that the picture would be shown to the general public because, according to one Soviet official, it was "too pessimistic, too shocking, and our people would not like it." The doubts seem to have been well founded.

The following morning Peck had the Russian reviews translated and found that the critics were unanimous in their approval of the film. "There were," he said in an interview back in New York, "no political slants or angles. They took it as a good theme, didn't see anything political in it at all."

A special screening of the picture for Washington officials and others was no mobbed that it had to be shown twice the same day. Before the screening Senator Wallace F. Bennett of Utah made a speech slamming the picture, calling it "an imaginative piece of science fiction, a fantasy, and not a dramatization of what would probably happen in the event of nuclear war."

The "stung" responses of some of those who attacked the picture indicated perhaps that *On the Beach* had, in fact, struck sharply at a vulnerable and weak spot of certain vested interests.

New York Governor Nelson Rockefeller even suggested that the movie might be subversive: "Now," he pointed out, "a basic objective of any military operation is to break the people's will to resist. I don't know how many of you have seen the movie *On the Beach*. I know some of my kids saw it, and I want to tell you, that is a great way to destroy people's will

to resist, because they come out of that movie saying, 'There is nothing we can do!'"

The New York Times, in an unusual move, devoted an entire "Topics of the Times" editorial page column to the picture, with the comment that "Its message is vigorous and meaningful for all of us...seldom has a filmed message been conceived on so grand a scale."

In New York, the film's December 17 premiere was held at the Astor Theater, with a benefit celebrating the 75th Anniversary of the American Academy of Dramatic Arts. Critical response tended to break down along lines of intrinsic individual cynicism.

Esquire's Dwight MacDonald, for example, attacked the film as "slick, vulgar, sentimental, phony...equipped with a plot of special banality." The Peck-Gardner love affair also came under attack and one wag commented, somewhat incorrectly, that "the world doesn't end with a whimper; it ends with a bang." John McCarten, in *The New Yorker* magazine, briefly commented on the characters and their personal dramas and then dismissed it all with "...all this seems pretty irrelevant if we remember that we are supposed to be looking at the way the world might die...."

On the other hand, *The New York Times* critic Bosley Crowther found that *On the Beach* "has a graphic authority about it that makes it not at all hard to believe...." Crowther thought that the film's scientific premise might be somewhat shaky, but held that its importance "does not in the least depend on its being scientifically indisputable...the way in which this film drives home its precept is by convincing us that people are strong and good, that they have fortitude and tenacity, that they are capable of extending compassion and love...." He thought the picture "splendidly done—crisply written, with intelligence and economy, wisely directed...in a clear, terse style, and played by a cast that is uniformly fine in every role...."

When he finally can accept that his American wife and family have died in the nuclear holocaust, Gregory Peck is free to express his tender feelings for Ava Gardner.

With humanity's time running out, Gregory Peck and Ava Gardner take in the world's last auto race, a free-for-all affair in which their friend Fred Astaire drives to victory.

In a later article, Crowther responded to some of the more fatuous attacks on the movie, particularly those of the ilk of Senator Bennett and Governor Rockefeller: "The acerbity with which some authorities have lashed out ... is indeed uncommonly surprising and hard to understand. It is as if they have peevishly resented its awesome warning about the fright of nuclear war and have missed the obvious point that its drama is purposefully based on an extreme hypothesis. ... It appears," said Crowther, "that the impact of this picture...is profound. People leave it in sober, contemplative and evidently resolute moods."

John Beaufort wrote in the *Christian Science Monitor* that "*On the Beach* matches the somber warning of its theme with the jolting impact of its dramatic force...."

In *Saturday Review*, Arthur Knight reported that "...the earlier, land-locked passages...are heavy with the sense of actors acting. But once the *Sawfish* casts anchor... the screen begins to tingle with excitement...." Knight thought Kramer's direction of the auto-race sequences "masterful" and called it "the apotheosis of all auto races, with the self-destructive impulses of the drivers at last matching the death-wish of the spectators...."

Knight did have some quibbles: "For all the virtues of ideology and execution, however, there are still some curious lapses... one wonders at the complete absence of corpses. ... It is equally difficult to believe that people would remain as calm and self-possessed as the people here...it all seems a bit too perfect...but these are minor details in a film that aims at something big and emerges as something tremendous...."

Years later, the message of *On the Beach* is still, alas, just as topical and pertinent as it was when the picture was made. And perhaps, in light of the massive stockpiling and spread of nuclear weapons in the intervening years, it is more timely than ever; likely, given the apparent psychopathology of *Homo sapiens*, it will remain valid for a long time to come. In any event, no public officials in recent years have seemed so ever-ready to belittle the consequences of nuclear warfare on the ecosystem of the planet we live on, and the general consensus among informed opinion is that any survivors of a nuclear war would in all likelihood envy the dead.

And surely, there can be few people who have seen this picture who will ever lose their visual memory of its last scene:

Wind-blown paper and debris swirling among the waving trees of a deserted, refuse-strewn city square; a wind-tossed billowing banner stretched on poles set on either side of stone steps leading up to the Corinthian-columned facade of the Melbourne Public Library, where people were gathered earlier for a religious revival service. Now, there are no people, no movement save for the wind, no sign of life. As the last few bars of "Waltzing Matilda" are played out to a dirge-like beat on the soundtrack, we are in three quick cuts jolted closer, closer and closer to the banner and its block-lettered proclamation:

THERE IS STILL TIME...BROTHER.

169

The "international-look" cast of *The Guns of Navarone* included James Darren, Stanley Baker, David Niven, Gregory Peck, Anthony Quinn and Anthony Quayle.

The Guns of Navarone

Columbia Pictures   1961
A Highroad Presentation

Credits

Producer, Carl Foreman; *director*, J. Lee Thompson; *screenplay*, Carl Foreman, based on the novel by Alistair MacLean; *music*, Dimitri Tiomkin; *cinematography*, Oswald Morris; *additional photography*, John Wilcox; *editor*, Alan Osbiston, Raymond Poulton, John Smith, Oswald Hafenrichter; *special effects*, Bill Warrington, Wally Veevers; *art director*, Geoffrey Drake; *costumes*, Monty Berman, Olga Lehman; *sound*, John Cox, George Stephenson, Vivian C. Greenham; *assistant director*, Peter Yates; *songs* sung by Elga Anderson; *narrator*, James Robertson Justice; filmed on locations on the Island of Rhodes, in Cinema-Scope and Eastman Color. (157 minutes)

Cast

Gregory Peck (Captain Mallory), David Niven (Corporal Miller), Anthony Quinn (Andrea Stavros), Stanley Baker (C.P.O. Brown), James Darren (Spyros Pappadimos), Anthony Quayle (Major Franklin), Irene Papas (Maria Pappadimos), Gia Scala (Anna), James Robertson Justice (Jenson), Richard Harris (Barnsby), Bryan Forbes (Cohn), Allan Cuthbertson (Baker), Michael Trubshawe (Weaver), Percy Herbert (Grogan), George Mikell (Sessler), Walter Gotell (Muesel), Norman Wooland (Group Captain), Albert Lieven (Commandant), Tutte Lemkow (Nicholai), Cleo Scouloudi (Bride), Nicholas Papakonstantantinou (Patrol Boat Captain).

After completing his work with Stanley Kramer, Gregory Peck joined Kramer's former partner, Carl Foreman, for *The Guns of Navarone*, an adventure movie of epic scale that was not only Peck's most successful picture financially until *The Omen*, fifteen years later, but also had three directors and started a movie-making trend, on two levels, that has not yet run its course and seems likely to continue for a long time to come.

Here in one package are embodied both the specialized-team-adventure-caper film and what has come to be dubbed the "global production." The "global production" concept involves casting a film with actors of various nationalities (the creative team may also be pan-national) to give the resultant picture the widest possible international appeal.

The Guns of Navarone is based on the book by British adventure-novelist Alistair MacLean. According to Foreman, who purchased the screen rights to it in the summer of 1958, he was attracted to MacLean's story, he says, by the author's "gift for keeping his audience enthralled by the pace and drive of his tale. The novel had six colorful major characters, providing an opportunity for casting as many international stars."

As Captain Mallory, the mission's ultimate leader, American Gregory Peck headed the film's international cast. "Why me?" Mallory asks his gruff, lovable old commander (James Robertson Justice), who has just asked him to sign on for the possible suicide mission.

"Well," replies Commander Justice in his familiar sonorous basso-profundo voice, "you speak German like a German, Greek like a Greek and before the war you were the greatest mountain climber in the world."

Mexican-born ethnic-for-all-seasons Anthony Quinn plays a Greek resistance fighter, Colonel Andrea Stavros, who in addition to being a key member of the Navarone sabotage team also carries a murderous grudge against Mallory, whom he blames for the earlier deaths of members of his family.

Gregory Peck and Anthony Quinn pause on a cliffside ledge to catch their wind during an exhausting and, for the audience, breathtaking ascent straight up above a roaring Aegean Sea.

When mountain-climbing expert Gregory Peck reencounters Anthony Quinn, an old associate who blames him for his own family's death, their meeting is less than friendly.

Apparently betrayed by someone in their own group, Stanley Baker, David Niven, Gregory Peck and Anthony Quinn find themselves captured by the Nazi military.

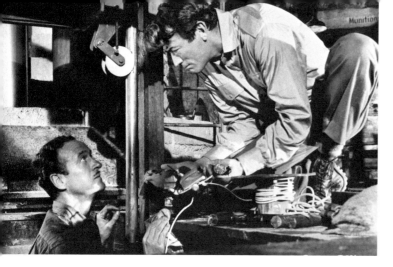

The cast's British contingent, which included Richard Harris and Bryan Forbes in lesser roles, was headed by David Niven.

The women Foreman wrote into MacLean's story are played by the outstanding Greek actress Irene Papas and Italy's attractive and talented Gia Scala.

Dimitri Tiomkin was Foreman's choice to write the film's music. The much-honored and prolific Russian-American composer had won his first Oscar for the memorable music for *High Noon*, another for *The High and the Mighty* (1954) and a third for *The Old Man and the Sea* (1958), as well as having scored *Duel in the Sun* (q.v.), *The Men* (1950), and *Giant* (1956), among many others.

When the picture opened in New York on June 12, 1961, at the Criterion and Murray Hill Theaters, *New York Herald Tribune* critic Paul V. Beckley called it "a good, bone-hard, manly military adventure....Script... direction, and the intense performances of a fine international cast make it one of the most exciting 'big' pictures around. ... Peck may seem at times a trifle wooden and his German

After Irene Papas has summarily executed their betrayer, Gregory Peck, in a stolen Nazi uniform, takes the pistol she has used away from her.

Aiming to blow up the guns with the maximum amount of damage to the Nazis and anxious that their sabotage not be detected beforehand, David Niven and Gregory Peck devise what they hope is a foolproof detonator.

accent too obviously American...but his not too introspective, somewhat baffled manner is manly and fitted to the role he plays. ... The picture progresses by nodules of shattering excitement...a textbook example of how to manipulate the elements of suspense...."

In *The New York Times*, Bosley Crowther reported that "Carl Foreman is beginning to blast himself a niche in the hall of fame of adventure-film producers that is surmounted by the bust of ... De Mille. ... This big, robust action drama...is one of those muscle-loaded pictures in the thundering tradition of De Mille. ... It moves swiftly and gets where it is going. ... Thompson has directed...with pace and seen to it that the actors give the impression of being stout and bold. ... One simply wonders why Mr. Foreman...didn't aim for more complex human drama, while setting his sights on those guns...."

According to *Cue* magazine, the picture was "...a rip-roaring spectacular movie entertainment...pure movie adventure, filled with cliches but presented so skillfully and so jampacked with action that you haven't time to sneer before you start to cheer...the cast could hardly have been bettered."

Variety reported that "...Peck is suitably laconic yet authoritative as the officer who takes over when Quayle becomes a casualty. ... From the start of the credits, patrons will be beguiled by an ambitious, splendidly produced piece of entertainment-plus...."

For *Time* magazine it was "the most enjoyable consignment of baloney in months..." and *Newsweek* commented that "...Foreman had attempted here to mix message with adventure, but his action speaks louder than his words...for physical adventure the makers of this film get the highest marks...."

The New Yorker critic felt, on the other hand, that it was "...one of those great big bow-wow, or maybe I should say bang-bang, movies that are no less thrilling because they are so preposterous. ... Let me confess that I was held more or less spellbound all the way through this many-colored rubbish...."

Disguised as Nazi soldiers, Gregory Peck and David Niven work feverishly to plant explosive charges on the big guns before their ruse is discovered.

New York Post critic Archer Winsten was unequivocal in his praise: "When students of movie form foregather to study ways of mingling suspense with maximum melodramatic excitement henceforth, they will have to analyze *The Guns of Navarone*. ... What makes the suspense all the more impressive is the calibre of the men, those sterling actors, who know how to toss a quip or a grenade with equal sangfroid. Coolest, of course, is Gregory Peck, but...Quinn ... Niven and...Baker are hardly less so. ... The women, too ... are bred to the manner of battle. ... There is no single letdown in this whole mighty build-up to cataclysm. ... The picture grips you ... with an astounding power...."

While critics quibbled about the message, audiences responded in droves and the picture rolled up net rentals of $13 million in the United States and Canada alone, making it the top domestic grosser of the year, with worldwide rentals more than doubling that figure.

It was voted the best picture of 1961 in the 39th annual *Film Daily* poll of critics, reviewers and commentators; beyond its special effects Oscars, was nominated for Academy Awards in the Best Picture, Best Direction and Best Screenplay categories; and the Hollywood Foreign Press Associaton voted it Best Picture and Best Score awards.

The success of *The Guns of Navarone* prompted Carl Foreman to plan a sequel, *Force Ten from Navarone*, also to be based on a MacLean story. It was first announced in 1967 but was not produced until 1977, with Foreman's only involvement apparently in writing the "screen story" about an Allied mission to blow up a bridge in Yugoslavia. Actors Robert Shaw and Edward Fox played the Peck and Niven roles respectively—and respectably—but the picture, released in the winter of 1978, failed to duplicate the amazing success of its predecessor.

A coldly calculating Robert Mitchum, bent on revenge, quietly tells a grim-faced Gregory Peck exactly why he is determined to get even with the man whose testimony had sent him to prison years before and that he can't be dissuaded.

Cape Fear

Universal-International   1962
A Melville-Talbot Production

Credits

Producer, Sy Bartlett; *director*, J. Lee Thompson; *screenplay*, James R. Webb, based on the novel, *The Executioners*, by John D. MacDonald; *music*, Bernard Herrmann; *cinematography*, Sam Leavitt; *editor*, George Tomasini; *art directors*, Alexander Golitzen, Robert Boyle; *set decoration*, Oliver Emert; *sound*, Waldon O. Watson, Corson Jowett; *assistant director*, Ray Gosnell, Jr.; *costumes*, Mary Wills. (105 minutes)

Cast

Gregory Peck (Sam Bowden), Robert Mitchum (Max Cady), Polly Bergen (Peggy Bowden), Lori Martin (Nancy Bowden), Martin Balsam (Mark Dutton), Jack Kruschen (Dave Grafton), Telly Savalas (Charles Sievers), Barrie Chase (Diane Taylor), Ward Ramsey (Officer Brown), Edward Platt (Judge), John McKee (Officer Marconi), Page Slattery (Deputy Kersek), Paul Comi (Garner), Will Wright (Dr. Pearsall), Joan Staley (Waitress), Norman Yost (Ticket Clerk), Mack Williams (Dr. Lowney), Thomas Newman (Lt. Gervasi), Alan Reynolds (Vernon), Herb Armstrong (Waiter), Bunny Rhea (Pianist), Carol Sydes (Betty), Paul Levitt (Police Operator), Alan Wells, Allan Ray (Young Blades).

"Amoral"… "an exercise in sadism"
… "close to pornography"…!!!
"What on earth is Gregory Peck
doing in a movie like this?"!!!

When Gregory Peck, Sy Bartlett, James R. Webb and J. Lee Thompson teamed to turn John D. MacDonald's 1958 novel *The Executioners* into the taut suspense-thriller that resulted, they likely never had a glimmer of suspicion that their project would provoke such condemnatory outcries and controversy.

Essentially, MacDonald's story is of an ex-con psychopath's revenge against the man whose testimony had sent him to jail eight years earlier for a brutal sexual assault on a woman. Peck would play Sam Bowden, the lawyer who had witnessed the crime while on a business trip and whom the law· apparently cannot now protect against the marauder who stays just within its limits while setting the stage to accomplish his evil plan. The seemingly helpless lawyer is ultimately forced to use the wife and daughter he is trying to protect to bait a trap for the predatory criminal, a trap that just might destroy them all.

The filmmakers approached actor Robert Mitchum to play Peck's antagonist, Max Cady. Mitchum's almost trademark air of heavy-lidded, sleepy-eyed menace, exemplified forever by his terrifying portrait of a psychopathic Bible-quoting murderous minister stalking a pair of small children in Charles Laughton's legendary *Night of the Hunter* (1955), would seem to have made him a logical choice for his *Cape Fear* role.

Polly Bergen, absent from the screen for eight years, was persuaded to return for the role of Peck's wife, Peggy Bowden.

In addition to the principals, noteworthy performances are given by Martin Balsam, as the police chief to whom Bowden turns at first for protection; Jack Kruschen, as the guileful attorney Max Cady hires to run interference with the police and end their harrassment of him; Barrie Chase, as a woman victimized by

Playing a sadist to the hilt, Robert Mitchum confronts Gregory Peck to remind him of the score he intends to settle.

When Gregory Peck tries to have Robert Mitchum run out of town, Mitchum's lawyer, played by Jack Krushen, skillfully uses the law to protect the perpetrator and hamper Peck's efforts to protect his family.

Mack Williams, veterinarian, explains to Gregory Peck that the family's pet watchdog has been poisoned.

The happy marriage between Gregory Peck and the lovely Polly Bergen is threatened by the unexpected appearance of a relentlessly vengeful stranger.

Cady; Telly Savalas, as a private eye; and Lori Martin as Bowden's young daughter.

For Peck, this marked his first return to work in the South since making *Twelve O'Clock High* in Florida and southern Alabama in 1949.

The two harshest critical reactions to the film came from *The New Yorker* magazine's Brendan Gill and *Esquire's* Dwight MacDonald. Said Gill, "In case you were thinking of dropping in on *Cape Fear*, don't. It purports to be a thriller but is really an exercise in sadism, and everyone concerned with this repellent attempt to make a great deal of money out of a clumsy plunge into sexual pathology should be thoroughly ashamed of himself. What on earth is Gregory Peck doing in such a movie?"

MacDonald was not entirely negative:

"Robert Mitchum," he said, "is really terrifying as the psychopath; it's the best performance of his I've seen since his tough and weary captain in Lester Cowan's *Story of G.I. Joe*...." But MacDonald thought the film's final tense moments "close to pornography. ... I don't enjoy seeing a cat play with a mouse, and I got no pleasure from seeing Mr. Mitchum—huge, brawny and sweatily bare-chested—toy first with the frantically terrified ten-year-old and then move on to conquer her shrinking, pleading mother...."

"A cold-blooded, calculated build-up of sadistic menace and shivering dread is accomplished with frightening adroitness," reported Bosley Crowther, reviewing *Cape Fear* in *The New York Times* after its April 18, 1962, opening.

The *New York Herald Tribune's* Paul V. Beckley called the picture "...a *tour de force*...

study in terror that verges on the horror genre. ... Mitchum's performance," said Mr. Beckley, "sets a new high (or low) in villains."

Before the picture was released in England, it encountered problems of an official nature: After viewing it, Lord Morrison, President of the British Board of Film Censors, called *Cape Fear* unequivocally "a nasty film." The board subsequently demanded, according to director J. Lee Thompson, 161 cuts, which Thompson felt would "mutilate and emasculate" the film.

Thompson was so disturbed over the demanded cuts that at first he urged Peck and Bartlett not to distribute the picture in England rather than knuckle under to the Censor Board's demands. But a compromise was finally reached; the film was cut by about six minutes and when it was released in January 1963, by Rank Film Distributors, the *Punch* critic commented, "I don't agree that the film is objectionable because Cady is a sexual sadist; the spring of the action is the existence of his threat, not the nature of it. And the much advertised cuts by the censor...were not obvious to me."

Above all, it was perhaps *Saturday Review*'s Arthur Knight, less frightened than some of his nervous colleagues, who remained the most level-headed about *Cape Fear*, which, he said, "comes off as old-fashioned, suspenseful melodrama that has no purpose beyond scaring the daylights out of you...sometimes the scares are patently manufactured...but just as often they are the legitimate terrors of a war of nerves. ... Mitchum proves again ... a resourceful and expressive performer.... Gregory Peck is equally commendable in a role that is, I suspect, far more difficult—that of the man who is acted upon...."

Gregory Peck, commenting on the film, proved again his own lack of egotism by joining in the praise for his co-star; "It's Bob's picture," he said to a reporter, "best performance he ever gave!"

When the regular institutions of law enforcement fail to adequately protect him, Gregory Peck finds that he must fall back on self-reliance in order to defend his wife and child from the marauding Mitchum.

178

To Kill a Mockingbird

Universal Pictures

Credits

Producer, Alan J. Pakula; *director*, Robert Mulligan; *screenplay*, Horton Foote, based on the novel by Harper Lee; *music*, Elmer Bernstein; *cinematography*, Russell Harlan; *editor*, Aaron Stell; *sound*, Waldon O. Watson, Corson Jowett; *art directors*, Alexander Golitzen, Henry Bumstead; *set decoration*, Oliver Emert; *costumes*, Rosemary Odell; *assistant director*, Joseph Kenny; *narrator*, Kim Stanley. (129 minutes)

Cast

Gregory Peck (Atticus Finch), Mary Badham (Scout Finch), Phillip Alford (Jem Finch), John Megna (Dill Harris), Frank Overton (Sheriff Heck Tate), Rosemary Murphy (Miss Maudie Atkinson), Ruth White (Mrs. Dubose), Brock Peters (Tom Robinson), Estelle Evans (Calpurnia), Paul Fix (Judge Taylor), Collin Wilcox (Mayella Ewell), James Anderson (Bob Ewell), Alice Ghostley (Stephanie Crawford), Robert Duvall (Boo Radley), William Windom (Gilmer), Crahan Denton (Walter Cunningham), Richard Hale (Mr. Radley), Steve Condit (Walter Cunningham, Jr.), Bill Walker (Rev. Sykes), Hugh Sanders (Dr. Reynolds), Pauline Myers (Jessie), Jester Hairston (Spence Robinson), Jamie Forster (Hiram Townsend), Nancy Marshall (School Teacher), Kim Hamilton (Helen Robinson), Kelly Thordsen (Burly Man), Kim Hector (Cecil Jacobs), David Crawford (Tom Robinson, Jr.), Guy Wilkerson (Jury Foreman), Charles Fredericks (Court Clerk), Jay Sullivan (Court Reporter), Barry Seltzer (School Boy), Dan White, Tex Armstrong (Men).

"Gregory Peck was the only actor we ever had in mind," says Alan J. Pakula, producer of *To Kill a Mockingbird*. "He was our first and only choice for the role of Atticus Finch."

Pakula and his director partner Robert Mulligan had only one previous picture to their mutual credit when they read novelist Harper Lee's glowing reminiscence of a childhood in Alabama in the depths of the Great Depression. They knew immediately that they wanted to make the movie and directed inquiries to Miss Lee's agent, who informed them that other filmmakers were also interested in the film rights. Pakula and Mulligan asked Miss Lee to withhold sale until they could enter a bid. She agreed and they immediately sent a copy to Peck, hoping he would agree to play the lead.

"I hadn't known these two young fellows," Peck recalled later, "but I had seen a picture that was well done, about a baseball player named Jim Piersall; the picture was called *Fear Strikes Out*, with Anthony Perkins and Karl Malden, very, very well done and sensitively directed. That's all I knew about them, but they sent me the book and called me and asked me to read it.

"I got started on it and of course I sat up all night and read straight through it. I understood that they wanted me to play Atticus and I called them at about eight o'clock in the morning and said, 'If you want me to play Atticus, when do I start? I'd love to play it.'

"I thought the novel was a fine piece of writing and of course I turned out to be right about that, because it won the Pulitzer Prize

and it's still being read in high-school literature classes and the paperback goes on selling. But more than that, I felt it was something I could identify with without any stress or strain, I felt I could climb into Atticus's shoes without any play-acting, that I could *be* him. And I felt that I knew those two children. My own childhood was very much like that. It was not in the true South, it was in Southern California, but it was nevertheless a small town where we ran around barefooted in the summertime and lived in trees half the time and rolled down the street curled up in an old rubber tire. So I fell into that very readily, both as the father and with an understanding of the children."

Miss Lee's touching book about the warm relationship between a widower father and his children and about racial injustice in the American South had been on the best-seller list for some six weeks by the time Pakula and Mulligan concluded their purchase agreement with the author. And her novel not only had been awarded the 1961 Pulitzer Prize for fiction, but was to eventually sell over six million copies as well, increasing, the filmmaking

partners felt, their responsibility to be faithful to the original text both in story and mood.

Pakula and Mulligan's first choice to write the screenplay was Miss Lee herself, but she was working on a new book in Monroeville, Alabama, where she lived with her father, and was reluctant to leave and come to work in Hollywood, which would have been necessary if she undertook the task. She was, of course, concerned about the adaptation of her book and was very much relieved when informed that the filmmakers had secured an agreement with fellow-Southerner Horton Foote to write the script.

An exhaustive search was undertaken to fill the pivotal roles of the three children in the film—nine-year-old Mary Badham was picked for Scout and 13-year-old Phillip Alford was chosen to play Jem. Mary, the daughter of a retired Army general, had never acted before and Phillip's experience was limited to school pageants in his native Birmingham.

Nine-year-old John Megna, a child actor who had already appeared on Broadway in *All The Way Home*, got the lesser role of Dil. Other Broadway actors, notably Frank Overton, Rosemary Murphy, Ruth White, Brock Peters and Estelle Evans, were used, rather than Hollywood-character types, in the film's supporting roles, as the filmmakers sought to achieve a certain freshness in the film that they thought would have been vitiated by faces already familiar to moviegoers.

A great deal of consideration was given to filming the picture in the South and Pakula and Mulligan scouted throughout the region for locations that would be suitable for a film set in the 1930s. Harper Lee's hometown, Monroeville, which had served as the model for the book's fictional Maycomb, was looked at first, but it had changed considerably during the intervening thirty years, with TV antennae, neon signs and updated storefronts rendering it impossible to use. The decision was finally made to film the picture entirely in Hollywood on the Universal backlot.

Art directors Alexander Golitzen and

As lawyer Atticus Finch, Gregory Peck visits the home of the black man he has been defending against an unjust assault charge brought by the father of a white girl.

Henry Bumstead supervised the construction of Maycomb on 15 acres of the Universal lot.

Production got underway in February 1962, and things worked beautifully from the start. Gregory Peck feels it was director Mulligan's sense of delicacy in working with the children, aided by the general "family" feeling that seemed to gather around the production and the crew, that made the children seem natural on screen. And, accordingly, says Peck, "It was altogether a marvelous experience to work with them."

In large part, the moving and subtle effect of *To Kill a Mockingbird* derives from the fact that although the picture is clearly concerned with civil rights issues, with intolerance and with the injustices suffered by black people in the South (for that matter, bigotry knows no regional boundaries), it does not propagandize. Peck, as Atticus, does not deliver orations on the subject and his courtroom speeches are confined to the business directly at hand; he does not take to a soap box with polemical assaults on the evils of segregation and racial intolerance and the picture makes its very meaningful points in a quiet, indirect and mightily more effective manner.

Gregory Peck was asked if, during the making of a film like *To Kill a Mockingbird*, one got the feeling that perhaps such a picture might have some sort of power to sensitize hard hearts in the cause of justice, might create some understanding in people that wasn't there before they saw the film.

"You can never be sure," the actor replied, "what effect a picture of this kind that does deal with a social issue will have. I never overrate the importance of a social philosophy or message, if you like, in a film. But I think one does perhaps get the idea that people will not only be moved and held and entertained but perhaps they'll carry a thought away with them. Perhaps they'll carry it with them for a while, perhaps they'll discuss it with their friends and it may have some effect eventually in a change of social attitude one way or another. I think that's as much as we can be

sure of, but that sort of thing does happen."

To Kill a Mockingbird opened at New York's Radio City Music Hall on February 14, 1963. *Variety*'s reviewer called it "a major film achievement...that ranks with the best in recent years. ... For Peck, it is an especially challenging role, requiring him to conceal his natural physical attractiveness yet project through a veneer of civilized restraint and resigned, rational compromise the fires of social indignation and humanitarian concern that burn within the character. He not only succeeds, but makes it appear effortless, etching a portrayal of strength, dignity and intelligence...."

The *New York Herald Tribune*'s Judith Crist thought "Gregory Peck...indeed impressive as the father with loving wisdom, the lawyer... dedicated to striving to give his motherless children a sense of decency amid the indecencies of bigotry in a small Southern town. ... But the scene stealers in this excellent film... are Mary Badham ... Phillip Alford...and John Megna. ... The story may seem slightly sentimental...but its stature and lasting substance stem from the beautifully observed

While friends and relatives of his client look on apprehensively, Gregory Peck confronts James Anderson, the father of the girl whose false testimony has led to the conviction of an innocent and well-meaning man.

relationship between father and children and from the youngsters' perceptions of the enduring human values in the world around them."

In *The New York Times*, Bosley Crowther called the picture a "fine film," but he did have a complaint: "There is so much feeling for children..." said Crowther, "so much delightful observation of their spirit, energy and charm...that it comes as a bit of a letdown at the end to realize that...it doesn't tell us very much of how they feel...as their father, superbly played by Gregory Peck, goes through a lengthy melodrama of defending a Negro...." Despite his disappointment, Crowther did think that Mulligan had achieved "a bewitching indication of the excitement and thrill of being a child..." and that the "charming enactments of a father and his children in that close relationship that can occur at only one brief period are worth all the footage of the film."

"In her famous novel," commented *Time* magazine, "Harper Lee...framed an Alabama melodrama that etched its issues in black and white...made a tomboy poem as full of hick fun as Huck Finn, a sensitive feminine testament to the Great American Childhood. ... Mulligan and scenarist Horton Foote have translated both testament and melodrama into one of the year's most fetching and affecting pictures. ... Peck, though he is generally excellent, lays it on a bit thick at times...the children are fine...."

Show magazine called the picture "one of the solidest Hollywood films in a decade," and Richard Mallet, critic for the British humor magazine *Punch*, reported that "the children in

particular are strikingly good, good enough to distract from the excellence of Mr. Peck's performance. Here is a solid, kindly, dignified, conscientious citizen; never before has he shown such authority."

But for producer Pakula, director Mulligan, writer Foote and star Peck, the dearest words of praise were undoubtedly those from Harper Lee herself, who was simply delighted with their work and remarked, "I can only say that I am a happy author. They have made my story into a beautiful and moving motion picture. I am very proud and very grateful."

Although *To Kill a Mockingbird* did not actually go into release until February 1963, it had qualified for 1962 Academy Award consideration by playing in Los Angeles before the end of that year. It received nominations in the categories for Best Picture, Best Direction, Best Supporting Actress (Mary Badham), Best Screenplay based on material from another medium, best black-and-white cinematography, best black-and-white art direction and set decoration, and Gregory Peck received his fifth Best Actor nomination.

When the awards were presented, Mary Badham lost out to Patty Duke, who was laureled for her portrayal of the child Helen Keller in *The Miracle Worker*; David Lean took the director's Oscar for the best picture, *Lawrence of Arabia*, and the photography prize went to *The Longest Day*'s team. But Horton Foote carried home an Oscar for his screenplay and Alexander Golitzen, Henry Bumstead and Oliver Emert were honored for their artwork.

Gregory Peck once again faced stiff competition in the Best-Actor nominations, which also cited the performances of Burt Lancaster, for *Birdman of Alcatraz*; Jack Lemmon, for *Days of Wine and Roses*; Marcello Mastroianni, for *Divorce—Italian Style*; and Peter O'Toole, for *Lawrence of Arabia*. The customary hush descended over the audience as the nominees were announced and everyone waited for the

While tense spectators look on in the courtroom, Gregory Peck tries to persuade the jury that his client had no ill intentions toward the girl he is accused of attacking and that the charges against him are false.

Gregory Peck, brother Phillip Alford, cook and a neighbor regard Mary Badham's objections to having to wear a dress to school with a mixture of amusement and unyielding sympathy.

Sheriff Frank Overton looks on as Gregory Peck prepares to demonstrate his keen ability as a sharpshooter when called upon to put a rabid dog out of his misery and eliminate the animal's threat.

Gregory Peck and Mary Badham have a serious discussion about tolerance and justice.

opening of the envelope containing the winner's name. In a moment it was opened and, bouyed upon and propelled by the tumultuous and loving applause of his peers, a beaming Gregory Peck was on his way to the stage to claim at last the prize that had always eluded him before. The Oscar was his!

To Kill a Mockingbird was also chosen to represent American filmmaking at the 1963 Cannes International Film Festival and was shown in Cannes on Saturday, May 18. It drew mixed reactions from the festival audience: Several times during the film there was applause as Atticus fought in the courtroom to save Tom Robinson; at the end, however, there were a few boos and catcalls scattered among the hearty applause and "bravos."

Following the screening, there was a press conference where more than a hundred international reporters and critics jammed into a room and Greg Peck faced a barrage of questions about both the film and American race relations.

More than a dozen years later, Peck reflected on both his personal triumph and on the role for which he received the ultimate Hollywood acclaim: "Atticus Finch was probably the most completely well-rounded character that I've every played. But I can't say that it's the most difficult thing I've had to do. On the contrary, it was one of the easiest. The part fitted me so well it was like climbing into a favorite suit of clothes. I knew all about that man, those children and that small-town background, because of my own early life. It was wonderful being given the Oscar, but I feel deep down that I've done better acting in more unsuccessful pictures that didn't come off as a whole." Still, says Peck, "*Mockingbird* is my favorite film, without any question."

Debbie Reynolds and Gregory Peck, archetypal American pioneer types, become lovers during a westward wagon-train journey in MGM's spectacular Cinerama epic of the winning of the American West.

How the West Was Won

Metro-Goldwyn-Mayer–Cinerama   **1963**

Credits

Producer, Bernard Smith; *directors*, Henry Hathaway (The Rivers, The Plains, The Outlaws), John Ford (The Civil War), and George Marshall (The Railroad); *screenplay*, James R. Webb, based on the *Life* magazine series, *How the West Was Won*; *cinematography*, William H. Daniels, Milton Krasner, Charles Lang, Jr., Joseph La Shelle; *second unit cinematography*, Harold E. Wellman; *editor*, Harold F. Kress; *color consultant*, Charles K. Hagedon; *special visual effects*, A. Arnold Gillespie, Robert R. Hoag; *art directors*, George W. Davis, William

When gambler Gregory Peck decides to join a westward-ho wagon train and team up with Thelma Ritter and Debbie Reynolds, wagonmaster Robert Preston, himself romantically interested in Reynolds, doesn't take kindly to the idea of the proposed arrangement.

(Marty), Charles Briggs (Barker), Jay C. Flippen (Huggins), Clinton Sundberg (Hylan Seabury), Joe Sawyer (Ship's Officer), John Larch (Grimes), Jack Pennick (Corporal Murphy), Craig Duncan (James Marshall), Claude Johnson (Jeremiah), Rodolfo Acosta (Henchman), James Griffith, Walter Burke (Gamblers). *Narrated by* Spencer Tracy.

Ferrari, Addison Hehr; *set decorations*, Henry Grace, Don Greenwood, Jr., Jack Mills, *makeup*, William Tuttle; *assistant directors*, George Marshall, Jr., William McGarry, Robert Saunders, William Shanks, Wingate Smith; *music*, Alfred Newman; *lyrics*, Ken Darby; "Home in the Meadow," lyrics by Sammy Cahn; "Raise a Ruckus," "Wait for the Hoedown," and "What Was Your Name in the States" lyrics by Johnny Mercer; *folk singing*, Dave Guard and the Whiskeyhill Singers; *recording supervisor*, Franklin Milton; filmed in Cinerama and Technicolor. (155 minutes)

Cast

Gregory Peck (Cleve Van Valen), Debbie Reynolds (Lilith Prescott), Carroll Baker (Eve Prescott), James Stewart (Linus Rawlings), Agnes Moorehead (Rebecca Prescott), Karl Malden (Zebulon Prescott), Robert Preston (Roger Morgan), Thelma Ritter (Agatha Clegg), George Peppard (Zeb Rawlings), Carolyn Jones (Julie Rawlings), Lee J. Cobb (Marshall), Henry Fonda (Jethro Stuart), Eli Wallach (Charlie Gant), John Wayne (General Sherman), Harry Morgan (General Grant), Raymond Massey (Abraham Lincoln), Russ Tamblyn (Reb Soldier), Walter Brennan (Colonel Hawkins), Richard Widmark (Mike King), Brigid Bazlen (Dora), Andy Devine (Peterson), Mickey Shaughnessy (Deputy), David Brian (Attorney), Kim Charney (Sam Prescott), Bryan Russell (Zeke Prescott), Tudor Owen (Harvey), Barry Harvey (Angus), Jamie Ross (Bruce), Mark Allen (Colin), Lee Van Cleef

Gregory Peck was one of the 13 stars and ten co-stars who all played second fiddle to the splendiferous scenery and rousing action in *How the West Was Won*, MGM's epic and exciting Cinerama production that cost only a little bit less than the $15 million President Thomas Jefferson paid France for the entire Louisiana Territory in 1803. And Peck's own participation was limited to only one of the film's five sections that traced the adventures and fortunes of an American pioneering family, the Prescotts, from 1839 to the late 180s. The picture's scope was so wide that three directors were employed to get it all on film.

Henry Hathaway directed sections one, two and five, John Ford was responsible for the Civil War sequence, and George Marshall worked on the railroad segment. Richard Thorpe, another director under contract to MGM, directed some of the picture's transitional sequences but did not receive screen credit. Actual filming began in May 1961, near Paducah, Kentucky; the picture was ready for release 18 months later.

Peck plays a smooth-talking, self-assured and dashing gambler, Cleve Van Valen, who winds up married to Lilith Prescott, the younger daughter, played by Debbie Reynolds, the only Prescott, in fact, whose life spans the entire picture.

For the actors, of course, appearing in a Cinerama production, with its 147-degree field-of-view camera system, posed some problems not ordinarily encountered in regular movie work. Frequently they could not look directly at the person to whom they were speaking their lines, since the Cinerama process bends the screen and when projected they would appear to be talking to the scenery instead of at the actor on the other side of the curved screen. It was also necessary for the actors to maintain a constant awareness of their movements, of how close they were to the triple-lens camera and to tailor their gestures and expressions accordingly.

In New York, *How the West Was Won* opened at Loew's Cinerama Theater on March 27, 1963. "Cinerama has always been big," said Paul V. Beckley in the *New York Herald Tribune*, "but now it is bigger. The movie...has given it dramatic dimensions that it never had. ... The visual excitements are plentiful. ... I think the word epic is fitting here. ... [The directors] have used Cinerama to make a return to the kind of film-making that hasn't been seen at such a magnificent level since the days of the silent pictures. There may be a tendency to corn, but corn here is growing the way it ought to. ... [It is] not only a tribute to the American past, but to American movie-making."

"Here is as thrilling a picture as we have ever seen," commented Kate Cameron, giving the picture the *Daily News*'s highest (four-star) rating. "It is the Western to end all Westerns. ... Debbie Reynolds handles her important assignment with superb confidence. James Stewart, Carroll Baker, George Peppard, Thelma Ritter and Gregory Peck are also outstanding...."

According to Hollis Alpert, *Saturday Review*, "As might be expected, [the picture] provides little of value on the winning of the American West, but it does provide a considerable amount of excitement and spectacle. ... The sheer work put into [it] amounts to a monumental statistic in itself and it is rather a shame that all the bigness does not make for a more lasting impression...."

The New York Times's Bosley Crowther was almost alone in finding absolutely nothing worthwhile in the picture, in viewing it through what seemed to be a singularly curmudgeonly eye: "What's been done," said Crowther in his initial review, "is to stitch together a mammoth patchwork of western fiction cliches. With little or no imagination

Vivacious Debbie Reynolds proved the ideal sort of woman for gamblin' man Gregory Peck, equally at home on the range, on a saloon stage or merely standin' by her man.

and, indeed, with no pictorial style...the three directors...have fashioned a lot of random episodes, horribly written by James Webb, into a mat of outdoor adventure vignettes that tell you nothing of history...."

Motion Picture Academy members found a few things to admire and voted Oscars to James Webb for the screenplay; to Harold Kress, for the film editing; and to the MGM sound department for its achievement in sound recording on the picture. The production itself was nominated as Best Picture and nominations also went to its quartet of cinematographers.

Moviegoers apparently agreed with those favorably inclined critics: *How the West Was Won* became one of the film industry's top money-making films of the year and went on to ultimate world-wide grosses in the vicinity of $50 million.

As an Army Air Force psychiatrist who's also up to his neck in administrative problems, Gregory Peck lays down the law of the ward to Tony Curtis, the upstart corporal who has his own way of dealing with mental patients and their problems.

Captain Newman, M.D.

Universal Pictures
A Brentwood-Reynard Production

1963

Cast

Gregory Peck (Captain Josiah Newman), Tony Curtis (Cpl. Jackson Laibowitz), Angie Dickinson (Lt. Francie Corum), Eddie Albert (Col. Norval Algate Bliss), Bobby Darin (Cpl. Jim Tompkins), James Gregory (Col. Edgar Pyser), Jane Withers (Lt. Grace Blodgett), Bethel Leslie (Helene Winston), Robert Duvall (Capt. Paul Cabot Winston), Dick Sargent (Lt. Alderson), Larry Storch (Cpl. Gavoni), Robert F. Simon (Lt. Col. Larrabee), Crahan Denton (Maj. Gen. Snowden), Gregory Walcott (Capt. Howard), Martin West (Patient), Syl Lamont (M. Sgt. Arkie Kopp), Vito Scott (Maj. Alfredo Fortuno).

Credits

Producer, Robert Arthur; *director*, David Miller; *screenplay*, Richard L. Breen, Phoebe and Henry Ephron, based on the novel by Leo Rosten; *music*, Frank Skinner; *music supervision*, Joseph Gershenson; *cinematography*, Russell Metty; *editor*, Alma Macrorie; *sound*, Waldon O. Watson, William Russell; *second unit director*, Robert D. Webb; *art directors*, Alexander Golitzen, Alfred Sweeney; *set decoration*, Howard Bristol; *assistant director*, Phil Bowles; *costumes*, Rosemary Odell; location shooting in Arizona; Eastman Color. (126 minutes)

Although Gregory Peck himself provided the original impetus that led to the production of *Captain Newman, M.D.*, it was actually his long-time friend, professional reader Syl Lamont, who brought Leo Rosten's 1961 novel to Peck's attention as a possible screen project. The actor was immediately attracted to the character of the Army psychiatrist presiding over a military hospital's neuropsychiatric ward.

As Peck recalled later, "Syl shoved me into a corner, pushed me into a chair and handed me the book. I could see that it would make a picture even though I knew it had been kicking around Hollywood with no takers since its publication." Universal's chiefs agreed it would make a good picture and paid Leo Rosten $250,000 for his book. Producer Robert Arthur, long associated with Universal, was put in charge of the project and Richard L. Breen was signed as screenwriter.

Additional work on the script was done by Henry and Phoebe Ephron, the husband-and-wife writing team whose screenplays included *The Jackpot* (1950), *There's No Business Like Show Business* (1954), *Desk Set* (1957) and *Take Her She's Mine* (1963). David Miller was taken on as director.

In preparation for his role as Captain Joseiah Newman, Peck conferred with several Beverly Hills psychiatrists, spending hours on end talking with them and observing them in his determination to give the character the verisimilitude he felt Capt. Newman must have. He also spent several days observing the behavior of both staff and patients in a real mental hospital and in addition read dozens of medical articles and journals on the subject of mental health and illness.

Although the movie unabashedly juxtaposes comedy and pathos, the filmmakers worked with a clear awareness that too much laughter in a basically serious story would have been harmful to the overall piece.

Much of *Captain Newman, M.D.* was filmed at Universal Studios in Hollywood, but to simulate exteriors and other aspects of the

Gregory Peck is mystified by the cool manner in which Tony Curtis, without any medical or psychiatric training, is able to defuse tense situations in the mental ward and by the easy rapport that seems to exist between Curtis and the patients.

Trying to discover the source of the emotional trauma that is obviously causing the violent outbursts that plague Airman Bobby Darin, Gregory Peck proposes using a "truth serum" type drug to bring forth whatever memories Darin is repressing.

Angie Dickinson and Syl Lamont look on as Gregory Peck tries to calm hysterical Bethel Leslie, who is upset on hearing from her husband that his mental illness may have its roots in his civilian and marital life rather than in his military experiences.

book's Camp Colfax, location of the fictional hospital, a former U.S. Cavalry outpost, Fort Huachuca, 74,000 acres in the Arizona desert east of Nogales and near the Mexican border, was borrowed from the Army.

Captain Newman, M.D. opened at New York's Radio City Music Hall on February 20, 1964. In the *New York Post*, critic Archer Winsten said the picture "could not miss if it contained half of its attractions, and in the lead is Dr. Gregory Peck...so amiable that he can charm crude commanding officers and madmen alike out of their violent worlds. ... In a long series of wonderfully entertaining and pleasing confrontations and episodes ... Peck is wonderful as a person, and he's wonderful as a doctor. ... The picture is completely absorbing...."

The *New York Herald Tribune*'s Judith Crist called it "that rare Hollywood film about mental illness that does not reduce it to the level of low comedy and/or Grand Guignol. ... This, with the more positive virtues of good humor and some excellent characterizations, is almost enough to make us overlook the fact that the film is, au fond, a sort of 'Ben Casey' cum 'Dr. Kildare' in khaki, with a comparatively judicious admixture of schmaltz and corn. ... On the plus side, we have Gregory Peck's stability to lend authority to Newman. ... But Laibowitz ... ends up on the minus side, an anachronism as portrayed by Tony Curtis ... Darin's...contortions are at best embarrassing. ... Miller's direction misses no opportunity to underline the obvious...."

In *The New York Times*, Bosley Crowther was more lenient: "Hats off to Capt. Newman, M. D. He's the latest of the fine heroic breed of medical practitioners and healers turned loose on the...screen with the motto 'Mens sana in corpore sano' all but emblazoned on his chest. ... Certainly the precept of that motto is implicit in everything done by the noble and kind physician Gregory Peck adroitly plays. ... Bobby Darin plays the kid touchingly. ... Tony Curtis makes a thoroughly irrepressible card. ... As for the structure of the picture, it does tend to jump about between solemn and comic situations to the point of monotony. This [however] is its gravest shortcoming...."

Nurse Angie Dickinson provided the welcome touch of femininity and the romantic interest (not to mention capable support) for Gregory Peck in *Captain Newman, M.D.*

Omar Sharif, as a priest torn between allegiance to his vows and duty to secular authority, tries to dissuade former terrorist Gregory Peck from a pointless journey and ultimate confrontation that can end only in tragedy.

Behold a Pale Horse

Columbia Pictures
A Brentwood-Highland Production
Credits

1964

Cast

Producer and director, Fred Zinnemann; *screenplay*, J. P. Miller, based on the novel, *Killing a Mouse on Sunday*, by Emeric Pressburger; *music*, Maurice Jarre; *cinematography*, Jean Badal; *editor*, Walter Thompson; *sound*, Jean Monchablon; *art director*, Auguste Capelier; *set decoration*, Maurice Barnathan; *production designer and associate producer*, Alexander Trauner; *costumes*, Elizabeth Haffenden, Joan Bridge; *opening montage*, courtesy of Nicole Stephane and Frederic Rossif; *assistant director*, Paul Feyder. (112 minutes)

•

Gregory Peck (Manuel Artiguez), Anthony Quinn (Captain Vinolas), Omar Sharif (Father Francisco), Mildred Dunnock (Pilar), Raymond Pellegrin (Carlos), Paolo Stoppa (Pedro), Daniela Rocca (Rosanna), Christian Marquand (Lieutenant Zaganar), Marietto Angeletti (Paco Dages), Perette Pradier (Maria), Zia Mohyeddin (Luis), Rosalie Crutchley (Teresa); with Mollie Urquhart, Jean-Paul Molinot, Laurence Badie, Martin Benson, Jean-Claude Berck, Claude Berri, Claude Confortes, Michael Lonsdale, Alain Saury, Jose-Luis Vilallonga, Elizabeth Weiner.

Knowing that a trap is being set for him, Gregory Peck seeks information.

"And I looked and behold a pale horse, and his name that sat on him was Death. And Hell followed with him."

From that Biblical verse (*Revelation*, 6:8) came the title for the Gregory Peck-Fred Zinnemann production based on Emeric Pressburger's novel *Killing a Mouse on Sunday*. Actor Peck and director Zinnemann teamed their respective companies to make the Brentwood-Highland Production for Columbia Pictures, with Zinnemann as its producer. While the working relationship seems to have been a cordial and successful one, critics and moviegoers found the picture itself something of a disappointment.

Producer-director Zinnemann was particularly well-suited to handle a picture with a European background and sensibility.

In essence, *Behold a Pale Horse* is a revenge drama with Peck playing a Spanish Loyalist called Manuel Artiguez, a former terrorist and bandit and now largely forgotten resistance leader who seems to want only to be left alone. But across the Spanish border waits Captain Vinolas of the Spanish Civil Guard, a Republican who has sworn to capture Artiguez, whom he almost nabbed during the war and has pursued with the zeal of a fanatic ever since. Vinolas is played with oily effectiveness by Anthony Quinn, in his third picture with Peck.

Interior scenes for *Behold a Pale Horse* were shot in studios in Paris. Exteriors were shot during the summer of 1963 in the actual French locations where the story's events unfold—in the province of Bearn, within 50 kilometers of the Spanish border, in the Basque-Pyrenees region, and at Lourdes. Location shooting had been planned for Spain but the Spanish censor read the script and objected to one line of dialogue. He wanted the line cut.

When Zinnemann refused to change the script, Spanish officials retaliated; not only was the production itself banned from Spain but all Columbia pictures were also withdrawn from circulation there and Spanish revenues due Columbia were frozen in the country's banks.

"When we were forbidden to shoot the picture in Spain," says Peck, "we moved across the border into France and shot around Pau and Lourdes in the Basque country, which looks like the terrain on the other side of the Pyrenees."

About a year after the company ended its location work, *Behold a Pale Horse* opened in New York at the Victoria and Sutton Theaters, on August 13, 1964. Gregory Peck attended the gala premiere at the Victoria, where audience response to the picture was noticeably subdued, in part, Peck felt, because of what seemed to be problems with the sound and acoustics.

"Let's say I sweated through every frame," he remarked of the experience.

The morning following the premiere did not ease Peck's discomfort; even though all of them found some aspects of the picture commendable, three of the four newspaper reviewers wrote unfavorable reports.

"A beautifully photographed, well-directed film and a disappointing one," said Judith Crist in the *New York Herald Tribune*. "Not all the dramatic clips of the Spanish Civil War [with which the picture begins]...nor the veritable babel of accents can lend refreshment, significance or depth to the story. ... Nor do the protagonists...Peck, looking appropriately baggy-eyed, paunchy and unkempt. ... Quinn, looking appropriately Neanderthal and well-groomed...Sharif looking appropriately liquid-eyed and dedicated. ... Never once does the conflict...suggest personal principle or political philosophy or social comment. ... The failure ... is Zinnemann's.

Omar Sharif is subjected to questioning by Anthony Quinn to reveal the whereabouts of Gregory Peck.

Having captured the interest and the imagination...he backs away from the issue. Without courage to comment in retrospect or in contemporary terms, he might just as well have kept us at home. ... [From] Zinnemann we deserve much more than this—handsomely presented, seriously undertaken though the film is."

"Consistent Fred Zinnemann, the man who has never made a bad picture, again applies his infinite care to a subject which benefits therefrom, but remains earthbound," remarked the *New York Post*'s Archer Winsten.

Bosley Crowther, in *The New York Times*, commented that "It is a shame that a film made as beautifully...and that has as much atmosphere in it as this one unquestionably has should be short on dramatic substance and emotional urgency. But that is what is missing...."

In the *New York Daily News*, Kate Cameron disagreed. Awarding the film a four-star (highest) rating, she said it "compels attention from its opening scene to its fadeout, as it unfolds an absorbing drama. ... Peck and Quinn, and the other members of the cast, play their roles with complete conviction. Peck's characterization...tops his prize-winning performance in...*Mockingbird*. ..."

Peck, though naturally disappointed, was not altogether surprised by the lack of positive response to the picture: "Zinnemann and I did realize that the background and the Spanish character would be a bit obscure for Americans. And since the film is so understated, I was always a little doubtful about how it would go over here."

Behold a Pale Horse was not a success in the United States. In retrospect, Peck has indicated that he thinks a part of the fault lay in the film's failure to commit itself to a viewpoint, to take a moral stand instead of merely posing questions. Moviegoers—particularly the young—without a previous emotional involvement in the Spanish Civil War, who hadn't lived through the period, remained unaffected and unmoved by the picture, which dealt indirectly with a very large event

(the war itself and its lingering effect on the people who fought it), but without bringing the many ramifications across clearly or with any passion. It didn't, Peck now feels, rise to the kind of noble and tragic climax inherently demanded by the material. Still, he says, "it had lovely things in it." All of Fred Zinnemann's works, Peck points out, are "beautifully...meticulously done."

In any event, the world is still plagued with terrorism and banditry spawned by passions that boil over in the Basque area of France and Spain. And today, *Behold a Pale Horse* reminds the viewer of the sad tenacity with which human beings unfortunately hang on to their hatreds and endlessly squander their energy in pursuing dreary vendettas to their bitter and almost inevitably self-destructive ends.

Having knowingly walked into a trap set for him by Spanish police, Gregory Peck is unwilling to surrender without a fight.

Trying to elude agents who are out to capture him for the secret formula which only he knows, Gregory Peck flees into New York City's Central Park.

Mirage

Universal Pictures

Cast

Gregory Peck (David Stillwell), Diane Baker (Shela), Walter Matthau (Ted Caselle), Leif Erickson (Crawford Gilcuddy), Kevin McCarthy (Josephson), Jack Weston (Lester), Walter Abel (Calvin), George Kennedy (Willard), Robert H. Harris (Dr. Broden), Anne Seymour (Frances Calvin), House B. Jameson (Bo), Hari Rhodes (Lieutenant Franken), Syl Lamont (Benny), Eileen Baral (Irene), Neil Fitzgerald (Joe Turtle), Franklin E. Cover (Group Leader).

Credits

Producer, Harry Keller; *director*, Edward Dmytryk; *screenplay*, Peter Stone, based on a story by Walter Ericson; *music*, Quincy Jones; *cinematography*, Joseph MacDonald; *editor*, Ted J. Kent; *art directors*, Alexander Golitzen, Frank Arrigo; *set decoration*, John McCarthy, John Austin; *sound*, Waldon O. Watson, Corson Jowett; *production manager*, Wallace Worsley; *assistant director*, Terence Nelson. (108 minutes)

•

Dictionaries define the noun "mirage" as the name given to "an optical phenomenon that creates an illusion"—usually of water in a desert—or as "something that is illusory or insubstantial." In other words, a mirage is something that appears to be where or what it isn't; i.e., an optical illusion. All in all, a rather fitting title, whether tongue-in-cheek or not, for a movie whose success is largely dependent on its keeping the viewer dazzled with visual tricks and enigmas to distract attention from the loose ends of plot threads lying all about.

For the basic plot of *Mirage*—well, amnesia's back and it's got Gregory Peck again, 20 years after Ingrid Bergman and Michael Chekov cured him in *Spellbound*. And the picture itself aspires somewhat to Hitchcock-thriller status, but unlike most of the Master's works, it doesn't hold up too well on close examination, a little bit like a scarecrow dressed in the emperor's new clothes. For most of the way, however, the ride is swift enough.

All the elements of the stylish contemporary thriller are present, including oblique references to work involving atomic radiation, mysterious California research laboratories, megacorporations run by militaristic megalomaniacs ("The Major"), impersonal killings by cold-blooded hoodlums for hire, bright young executive types who always "follow instructions" without question because they're

Research-foundation-head Walter Abel, who employs scientist Gregory Peck in high-level work, listens as Peck tells him of his discovery which may have profound and positive impact on the search for world peace.

paid three times what they're worth, peace-foundation heads who harbor dark secrets, attractive and well-attired and slightly vague young women who seem neither to spin nor to sew, a psychiatrist who "doesn't want to know …" and apparently dotty and daft senior citizens who turn out to be homicidal maniacs—not to mention the suggestion that murder can occur in executive suites without drawing public attention.

Mirage's director Edward Dmytryk had

A number of New York streets and locations provided backdrops for the dramatic action and chases in *Mirage*.

In a flashback, Gregory Peck recalls his last meeting with Walter Abel before the latter plunged to his death from the window in the background and thereby triggered the amnesia which haunts Peck throughout *Mirage*.

been in films since 1923, directing many "B" pictures and gaining a reputation as a stylist with some tough adult thrillers in the 1940s, *Murder My Sweet* (1944) among them. Dmytryk, whose wartime works included *Hitler's Children* (1943) and *Back to Bataan* (1945), later became a victim of the anti-Communist witchhunts and left the United States after directing *Crossfire* (1947), which, like *Gentleman's Agreement*, dealt with anti-Semitism. He worked in Europe several years before returning to America and scoring a solid hit with *The Caine Mutiny* (1954), followed by such

In a final confrontation with the forces of evil who want to steal his formula for their own personal power interests, Gregory Peck finds himself in the clutches of Leif Erickson, Diane Baker and Kevin McCarthy.

films as *Raintree County* (1957), *The Young Lions* (1958) and *A Walk on the Wild Side* (1962).

Walter Matthau is superb in his all-too-brief role as Caselle, the private eye who turns out to be a neophyte (Peck's his first case), somewhat skeptical ("trying" to believe Peck's strange story) and a bit insecure ("Tell ya one thing. It's kinda scary," he tells David when they're faced with some undeniable and seemingly inexplicable incongruity).

Mirage opened in New York on May 26, 1965, at the DeMille, the Coronet and at neighborhood theaters. "This exercise in mayhem, murder, mental instability and moralizing…evolves as an interesting, fairly taut, if not especially credible, chase-mystery," said A. H. Weiler in *The New York Times*. "Mr. Peck's performance is serious, properly confused and natural. Walter Matthau turns in a fine, easy-going stint. … Characters played by Diane Baker…Leif Erickson … and Mr. Abel … remain partial enigmas. If, like the film's good doctor, a viewer doesn't take too much stock in this amnesia, *Mirage* comes off as a diverting thriller…."

The New Yorker magazine's critic praised the picture: "It's the genuine article, dating back in spirit to the Upper Middle Hitchcock, or Intricate Puzzlement, period of movie thrillers, and I salute it with respect and relief. Peter Stone…Dmytryk…and Gregory Peck have hurled themselves with commendable sober relish into their assorted tasks, and the results kept me close to the edge of my seat up to the moment of denouement…."

"*Mirage* pieces together a compelling puzzle that exists in a man's mind," said Kathleen Carroll in the *Daily News*. "The mystery… remains elusive to the very end. One's curiosity is not totally satisfied. … Peck is everybody's affable, straightforward guy and the character he plays, at his understated best, immediately arouses sympathy…."

Peck himself has said in interviews that he feels that the film didn't fully come off, that it didn't realize its full potential and suffered from a pedestrian cinematic approach while it desperately needed a modern one. According to Peck, the story was basically "a shell game, and it should have been treated more as a ballet of cinematic suspense."

A lull in the fast-paced, high-style action in *Arabesque* gives Gregory Peck and mystery woman Sophia Loren an opportunity to find themselves and get down to more basic and more enjoyable business.

Arabesque

Universal Pictures

1966

Cast

Gregory Peck (David Pollock), Sophia Loren (Yasmin Azir), Alan Badel (Nejim Beshraavi), Kieron Moore (Yussef), John Merivale (Sloane), Duncan Lamont (Webster), Carl Duering (Jena), George Coulouris (Ragheeb), Ernest Clark (Beauchamp), Harold Kasket (Lufti), Gordon Griffin (Fanshaw).

Credits

Producer and director, Stanley Donen; *screenplay*, Julian Mitchell, Stanley Price, Pierre Marton, based on the novel, *The Cipher*, by Gordon Cotler; *music*, Henry Mancini; *cinematography*, Christopher Challis; *editor*, Frederick Wilson; *art director*, Reece Pemberton; *sound*, John W. Mitchell, C. Le Messurier; *assistant director*, Eric Rattray; filmed in Panavision and Technicolor. (105 minutes)

Gregory Peck and Sophia Loren, who may or may not be on his side, on the run through one of several London landmarks that provide backgrounds in *Arabesque*.

Gregory Peck is an ordinary type chap who unexpectedly gets caught up in a mysterious intrigue with all sorts of people suddenly out to capture or kill him because they think he has this piece of paper that contains information they want and there's this attractive woman whose identity is something of a mystery and who may or may not be on Peck's side. ... Wait a minute. Isn't this where we just came out—*Mirage*? No, this is *Arabesque*.

On a simplistic level it might appear that producer-director Stanley Donen simply got the idea to remake *Mirage* in high-style and Technicolor and set it in London, but this time the elusive slip of paper contains not a magic formula but supposedly a 4000-year-old Hittite hieroglyphic; instead of executive-suite greed, perfidy and power-mongering, the swirl around Peck involves spies, assassination plots and Middle Eastern oil politics, and, best of all, the mystery lady is played by the incomparably beautiful Sophia Loren. And *Arabesque* is a charming, witty, romantic entertainment without a heavy thought in its

head; there may not be a laugh a minute, but the pace of this colorful comedy-thriller never lags long enough for one to notice—or care.

Arabesque opened in New York on May 5, 1966, at Radio City Music Hall, a perfectly glamourous setting for a cinematic jewel. Critic Wanda Hale gave it the *New York Daily News*'s highest (four-star) rating, calling it "the spoofingest spoof yet on espionage adventure, with a handsome pair you'd least expect to take part in the wild, wonderful nonsense. ... The dignified Peck and the elegant Loren let themselves go on a mad, mirthful spree. ... Donen...aimed only at entertainment. He hit the bull's eye.... Dialogue...is smart, crisp and suggestive, the best delivered by Peck. ... Donen...has outdone all the recent spy pictures in thrills, suspense and delicious humor...."

"About 10 minutes after *Arabesque* gets underway," said Grace Glueck in *The New York Times*, "you'll lose track of its plot completely, and that's as it should be. ... [It] provides ... Op photography, lush decor, gimmicky locations and hair-raising pursuits. ... Loren...is not called upon to act but to Dior. ... A Yank exchange professor...is played with Good-Guy affability by Gregory Peck. ... A climax scene ... should make chase buffs swoon. ... That, and the striking photographic effects... make the picture worth sitting all the way through...."

The *New York Post*'s Archer Winsten found the picture less engaging: "After a while you not only don't know who's who, you don't care either. ... This is the more remarkable because Gregory Peck...is an appealing figure, and Sophia Loren is breathtakingly whatever it is you have thought she is. ... It may not be much of a picture when you add it all up... but it does ring the bell as a superior travelogue, equipped with splendid stars, electric with motion, and chockablock with fast-moving engines of excitement...."

Variety's critic thought the picture packed "certain saleable ingredients, such as the names of Gregory Peck and Sophia Loren... but doesn't always progress on a true entertainment course. Fault lies in a shadowy plotline and confusing characters, particularly in the miscasting of Peck in a cute role. ... There are chases, murders and attempted assassinations to whet the appetite, as well as misuses of comedy. Peck tries valiantly with a role unsuited to him...."

Finally, *Life*'s Richard Schickel lauded the entire light-hearted, light-headed production: "For all of us who have suffered at least a twinge of nostalgia for the opulent fantasy life we enjoyed while curled up at the knees of our vulgar cinematic grandmothers—there is good news: *Arabesque* is here. ... The England in which these two gloriously handsome people chase and are chased...is that green and pleasant land where even the rains serve a romantic purpose. ... Mr. Peck and Miss Loren are admirably suited to this landscape. ...This is only commercial film-making at its mindless, marvelous best...."

As the events of *Arabesque* draw to a close, Gregory Peck realizes that Sophia Loren is in as much danger as he is, even though she herself displays uncanny instincts.

Kieron Moore, and John Merivale prepare to administer a powerful psychotropic drug to Gregory Peck in hopes that he will reveal the information they seek.

Arabesque's action even takes its participants to the Royal enclosure at Ascot racetrack, where Gregory Peck was called upon for some acrobatic stunt work.

After retired Army scout Gregory Peck takes in Eva Marie Saint, a white woman formerly held prisoner by Apaches, and Nolan Clay, the half-breed son she bore during her captivity, he finds his ranch under attack by a renegade Apache killer who wants the boy back.

The Stalking Moon

National General Pictures   **1969**

Credits

Producer, Alan J. Pakula; *director*, Robert Mulligan; *screenplay*, Alvin Sargent, based on the novel by Theodore V. Olsen; *adaptation*, Wendell Mayes; *music*, Fred Karlin; *cinematography*, Charles Lang; *editor*, Aaron Stell; *sound*, Jack Solomon; *art directors*, Roland Anderson, Jack Poplin; *set decoration*, Frank Tuttle; *costumes*, Dorothy Jeakins, Seth Banks; *assistant director*, Don Kranze; location scenes filmed in Nevada, in Panavision and Technicolor. (111 minutes)

Cast

Gregory Peck (Sam Varner), Eva Marie Saint (Sarah Carver), Robert Forster (Nick Tana), Noland Clay (Boy), Russell Thorson (Ned), Frank Silvera (Major), Lonny Chapman (Purdue), Lou Frizell (Stationmaster), Henry Beckman (Sgt. Rudabaugh), Charles Tyner (Dace), Richard Bull (Doctor), Sandy Wyeth (Rachel), Joaquin Martinez (Julio), Red Morgan (Stage Driver Shelby), Nathaniel Narcisco (Salvaje).

•

Given the artistic, critical and commercial success of *To Kill a Mockingbird*, their previous venture together, one can imagine that Gregory Peck found the prospect of making another picture with Alan J. Pakula and Robert Mulligan an attractive one indeed. It would be the first Western for the producer-director team, whose subsequent films had included *Baby the Rain Must Fall* and *Inside Daisy Clover* (1965) and *Up the Down Staircase* (1967). Adding to the attraction would be that superficially, at least, the story of *The Stalking Moon*, like that of *The Gunfighter*, is about just one thing: a man's fight to survive.

The filmmakers' objective was to make a simple, scary story of suspense and endurance in a Western setting, a de-romanticizing the genre and stripping it of its myths even while dealing with a mythic theme in, according to one critic, archetypal terms. The intentions were obviously good ones; the result is mixed—and even set off a small critical controversy when it was released.

Gregory Peck plays scout Sam Varner, a veteran of 20 years' service with the U.S. Army in Arizona, who is retiring to the little New Mexico ranch he's bought by mail order and paid for over the last eight years.

Eva Marie Saint, who won a Best Supporting Actress Oscar for her role opposite Marlon Brando in *On the Waterfront* in 1954, is Sarah Carver.

As a director, Robert Mulligan has said that he has always been attracted to "good yarns and rich characters" and more concerned with putting them clearly across on screen than with the hardware of cinema and bravura technique. Bearing him out, *The Stalking Moon* unfolds in a simple and straightforward cinematic style. There is an austerity to its execution that matches the austerity of the story and the landscapes within which it takes place.

Understatement can sometimes be its own undoing, over-emphasis on detail can sometimes lead to neglect of the overall view, and

The climax of *The Stalking Moon* involves a one-on-one hand-to-hand struggle to the death between Gregory Peck and Nathaniel Narcisco, as the Apache.

While trying to salve a leg wound, Gregory Peck has to keep a constant lookout for the Apache killer with whom he duels in *The Stalking Moon*.

Wounded Gregory Peck, unable to track his Apache quarry, waits for the quarry to come to him in the Pakula-Mulligan production *The Stalking Moon*.

less can sometimes add up to too much and not enough at the same time. At its core, *The Stalking Moon* is a simple chase story, but the chase goes on much too long.

When *The Stalking Moon* opened in New York at Loew's Tower East on January 29, 1969, critical reaction ranged from good to negative:

Life's Richard Schickel, in a laudatory review, praised the film for its mythic content, saying, "it is an examination in archetype of good and evil linked in a death grapple. It has the simplicity and fascination of a myth dredged up from the unconscious of the race." Forthwith, both he and the picture were taken to task by Pauline Kael in *The New Yorker* for what she felt was a near-racist approach to the Indian: "For many years, big budget Westerns have generally tried to be respectful and sympathetic toward Indians, and now ... *The Stalking Moon* goes back to the most primitive movie image of the vicious savage...." For Ms. Kael, the movie was a clear example of "dehumanizing the enemy as a way of justifying our own inhumanity....Since some people don't care about people," she pointed out, "if you want to show that a killer is *really* evil, you have him kill a dog" and then—as Salvaje does—murder the dog's distraught old master. "*The Stalking Moon* doesn't have a sense of shame—only a sense of what 'grabs' you...."

Ms. Kael did comment that "The role of the decent superman requires an actor like Peck—an actor of proved authority—and Peck is very good in it," but in sum, her feeling was that "movies can open us up to complexities and I don't think we should applaud [as Mr. Schickel did, she noted] this kind of infantile, primitive regression...."

Knowing what we do of Pakula, Mulligan and Peck, it is clear that they would never make a "racist" film by design. Their intention was to create a good drama, not a sociological tract. According to some of the publicity material they distributed, the filmmakers saw the film on one level as a symbolic representation of the struggle between the white settlers and the Apaches, for the land of the American Southwest. In whatever terms *they* saw it, however, moviegoers found it less than gripping entertainment and the picture was less than a hit.

The New York Times's Vincent Canby reported *The Stalking Moon* "classically pure and simple in outline. ... A beautiful movie—and one that may be too tasteful for its own good...."

Eva Marie Saint, Noland Clay and Gregory Peck in a relaxed publicity shot for *The Stalking Moon*.

Camilla Sparv and Gregory Peck find themselves captives of arch villain Omar Sharif in Carl Foreman's treasure hunt, *MacKenna's Gold*.

MacKenna's Gold

Columbia Pictures 1969

Credits

Producers, Carl Foreman, Dimitri Tiomkin; *director*, J. Lee Thompson; *screenplay*, Carl Foreman, based on the novel by Will Henry; music, Quincy Jones; *song*, "Old Turkey Buzzard," lyrics by Freddie Douglass, sung by Jose Feliciano; *cinematography*, Joseph MacDonald; *second unit photography*, Harold Wellman; *additional photography*, John Mackey, Don Glouner, Farciot Edouart, Richard Moore; *editor*, Bill Lenny; *second unit director*, Tom Shaw; *special effects*, Geoffrey Drake, Abacus Produc-tions (John Mackey and Bob Cuff), Willis Cook, Larry Butler; *stunt co-ordinator*, Buzz Henry; *sound*, Derek Frye, William Randall, Jr.; *art directors*, Geoffrey Drake, Cary Odell; *set decoration*, Alfred E. Spencer; *production designer*, Geoffrey Drake; *costumes*, Norma Koch; *assistant director*, David Salven; *production manager*, Ralph Black; location scenes filmed in Arizona, California, Oregon, and Utah, in Super Panavision and Technicolor. (128 minutes)

Only while captive Gregory Peck's tied to a post would Omar Sharif dare to attempt the sort of physical abuse he's dishing out here in trying to get Peck to reveal the whereabouts of a fortune in gold.

Gregory Peck disarms a dishonest Apache, played by Ted Cassidy, in one of several struggles in *MacKenna's Gold*.

Cast

Gregory Peck (Mackenna), Omar Sharif (Colorado), Camilla Sparv (Inga), Telly Savalas (Sgt. Tibbs), Keenan Wynn (Sanchez), Julie Newmar (Hesh-ke), Ted Cassidy (Hachita), Eduardo Ciannelli (Prairie Dog), Dick Peabody (Avila), Rudy Diaz (Besh), Robert Phillips (Monkey), Shelley Morrison (Pima Squaw), J. Robert Porter (Young Englishman), Anthony Quayle (Older Englishman), John Garfield, Jr. (Adams' Boy), Pepe Callahan (Laguna), Madeleine Taylor Holmes (Apache Woman), Duke Hobbie (Lieutenant), Trevor Bardette (Old Man), Lee J. Cobb (The Editor), Raymond Massey (The Preacher), Burgess Meredith (The Storekeeper), Edward G. Robinson (Old Adams), Eli Wallach (Ben Barker); *Narrator*: Victor Jory.

When producer-writer Carl Foreman left the United States during the days of the blacklist for self-exile in England, he had a reputation as a successful producer of serious low-budget, socially-conscious films; his *Home of the Brave* (1949) had cost only $235,000. Sixteen years later, after the enormous success of *The Guns of Navarone*, he returned to America as a producer of epics and with a $14.5-million budget for *Mackenna's Gold*, planned as a blockbuster Western to be filmed in 70mm Panavision and released by Columbia Pictures as a Cinerama roadshow presentation. The movie was in production for more than two years and although it was filmed more than a year earlier than *The Stalking Moon*, it was released later, delayed, probably, by post-production problems and perhaps by a reluctance in some quarters to release it at all.

It is a rare Gregory Peck film that fails on practically every level; clearly, *Mackenna's Gold*

Gregory Peck, Ted Cassidy, Omar Sharif and Eli Wallach, as one of The Gentlemen from Hadleyburg, are ready for any action as they watch more treasure-hunters arrive at their canyon encampment.

is one of those rarities. Carl Foreman himself wrote the screenplay for *Mackenna's Gold*, based on Will Henry's novel; and Oscar-winning composer Dimitri Tiomkin, who'd scored *The Guns of Navarone*, joined him as co-producer on the project. J. Lee Thompson, of *Navarone* and *Cape Fear*, was hired to direct, with photography supervised by veteran Joseph MacDonald. A large staff of technicians assisted them in the film's production. The end result of their efforts is an unmitigated disaster, proving that even the most successful can have their lapses.

With the unequivocal benefits of hindsight, we can speculate that perhaps too much money was lavished on a low-budget story that simply couldn't carry the burden of a big-budget treatment.

Interviewed during the production, Peck compared the picture stylistically to an earlier work: "I guess it's more like *Duel in the Sun* than any other Western I've done. It's almost a Western fantasy—a quest for a storied mother lode."

Mackenna's Gold opened in New York on June 18, 1969, but it had been released in March in Philadelphia, where *Variety*'s critic reviewed and praised it: "Although Carl Foreman has packed the cast…with some top names…and…has a good story…it is his producer's touch that saves the film from being a program western…."

When the film finally arrived in New York, *The New York Times*'s Vincent Canby reported it "a Western of truly stunning absurdity…a thriving example of that old Hollywood maxim about how to succeed by failing big…."

Neither Carl Foreman nor Gregory Peck has allowed himself any illusions about the picture's lack of either commercial or artistic success. Foreman could see that something had gone wrong and he was disappointed, he said later, in the results. He had sought to make a commentary on men and motives as a reaction to latter-day ignoble behavior patterns (maybe the whole thing was actually intended as a "parable" about the Nixon Administration). And The Gentlemen from Hadleyburg were related, for Foreman, to the

Camilla Sparv and Gregory Peck plot their getaway from Omar Sharif and his band of outlaws and other undesirables in *MacKenna's Gold*.

cowardly townspeople in *High Noon* (which he had also written) who would not help their marshal (Gary Cooper) when he faced a moment of crisis and needed them; less than heroic, they put self-interest ahead of social duty.

Peck lumps *Mackenna's Gold* with several of his concurrent pictures that came at a time when his own career problems paralleled those of the movie industry as a whole. Says Peck, "I have done several pictures that I probably shouldn't have done…things like *Mackenna's Gold*, like *Marooned*. They weren't very good. The public didn't go to see them and the notices weren't all that great. So I'd call them bad pictures. But they were the best that were offered.

"I didn't do them only for the money—it just took a while for me to rid myself of the habit of getting up early in the morning and going to the studio. I knew they weren't worth much when I read the scripts. But as soon as I started work on them, damned if I didn't start believing in them.

"It just goes to prove," says Peck, "you can't be an actor and Pauline Kael at the same time."

Gregory Peck's distinguished good looks and bearing have often led him to be called upon to play military heroes, diplomats, lawyers, lawmen and a variety of professional men. Here he is a Nobel Prize-winning scientist.

The Chairman

20th Century-Fox
British Title *The Most Dangerous Man in the World*
An Apjac Production (Arthur P. Jacobs)

1969

Credits

Producer, Mort Abrahams; *director*, J. Lee Thompson; *screenplay*, Ben Maddow, based on the novel, *The Chairman*, by Jay Richard Kennedy; *music*, Jerry Goldsmith; *cinematography*, John Wilcox, Ted Moore; *editor*, Richard Best; *sound*, Dudley Messenger; *art director*, Peter Mullins; *set decoration*, Arthur Taksen; *costumes*, Anna Duse; *makeup*, Trevor Crole-Rees; *production manager*, David Korda; *location manager*, Tim Hampton; *assistant director*, Ferdi-nand Fairfax; filmed on locations in London, Wales, and Taiwan and at Pinewood Studios, London, in Panavision, Color by DeLuxe. (104 minutes)

Cast

Gregory Peck (Dr. John Hathaway), Anne Heywood (Kay Hanna), Arthur Hill (Lt. General Shelby), Alan Dobie (Air Commodore Benson), Conrad Yama (The Chairman),

Zienia Merton (Ting Ling), Ori Levy (Alexander Shertov), Eric Young (Yin), Burt Kwouk (Chang Shou), Alan White (Colonel Gardner), Keye Luke (Professor Soong Li), Francisca Tu (Soong Chu), Mai Ling (Stewardess), Janet Key (First Girl Student), Gordon Sterne (U.S. Air Force Sergeant), Robert Lee (Hotel Night Manager), Helen Horton (Susan Wright), Keith Bonnard (Chinese Officer), Cecil Cheng (Soldier), Lawrence Herder (Russian Guard), Simon Cain (U.S. Signal Corps Captain), Anthony Chinn (Chinese Officer), Edward Cast (Audio Room Technician).

<hr />

The Chairman, Gregory Peck's next project with director J. Lee Thompson, following *Mackenna's Gold*, was a generally effective thriller. Set against the background of the enigmatic People's Republic of China and its Red Guard revolution, it dealt with such timely topics as the possible alleviation of world hunger, the East-West struggle for world political influence, and with the question of whether a scientist's actions should be determined by narrow nationalistic loyalties or by world-wide humanistic considerations.

Peck plays John Hathaway, a Nobel-prize-winning American scientist who is recruited by American and British intelligence authorities in London to steal the formula for a unique agricultural enzyme that's apparently been discovered in Red China and carries profound implications for the future of mankind.

The Chairman went into production in the late fall of 1968, after Peck had finished work on *The Stalking Moon*. Few pictures up to that time had dealt with life behind the so-called Bamboo Curtain and the filmmakers went to considerable lengths in pursuit of authenticity for the project. Producer Mort Abrahams, director Thompson, actor Peck and other members of the production staff spent many hours in meticulous research. Among other things, they looked at all the available newsreel footage they could find that depicted the Chinese people and their contemporary Communist culture.

The Chairman opened in New York in multiple theaters on June 25, 1969, only a

A romantic evening with Anne Heywood stands in stark contrast to the dangerous espionage assignment that Gregory Peck is about to undertake inside Communist China.

week after *Mackenna's Gold* appeared. Critical reaction was mixed—and interesting—but not enthusiastic. In the *New York Post*, Archer Winsten commented that "some of the first shots of Peck's plane arriving in Hong Kong are so spectacularly good that it seems a shame they got booted out...and had to make the rest of the picture in England's Pinewood Studios and on a mountainous hillside in Scotland [sic]. ... The rest of the picture looks like studio, sounds like studio and is made like studio stuff. ... Peck doesn't know how to be bad...but this time he gets mighty little assistance. ... It's an idea picture in which the idea, though noble, is old, tired and presented without flair...a picture that flaps its wings the same old melodramatic way but barely gets off the ground despite Peck himself leading the way."

Howard Thompson of *The New York Times*, thought the picture "...an ambitious new thriller...[that] begins so brilliantly...that makes provocative entertainment for the first half, hits a snag, begins to fall apart and come in for a tame, wobbly ending...."

Kevin Thomas, in *The Los Angeles Times*, said: "...the kind of Hollywood hokum that can yield lots of fun and excitement if you're willing to go along with it...and because of the convincing charm of its star Gregory Peck it's

Although ostensibly in Red China on a mission of science, Gregory Peck is in reality involved by unscrupulous Western intelligence agents in an attempt to obtain a secret agricultural formula from a Chinese scientist.

not hard to do…for no one is more skilled or experienced in making getting out of tight spots believable. … If Peck's adventures are pure hokum, *The Chairman* nonetheless possesses plenty of underlying levels of seriousness for those who care to consider them.…"

In England, where the film was released as *The Most Dangerous Man in the World*, Richard Mallet reported in *Punch* that it was "…as different as could be from the James Bond stuff and all the imitations. The hero… is a teacher…and Mr. Peck is able to make him suitably conscientious.…It could be regarded as no more than a handsome… thriller, but that touch of conscience gives it a certain distinction."

Conrad Yama is a believable Chairman Mao Tsetung, facing Gregory Peck over a ping-pong table for one of the most important games in scientist Peck's life.

Avid students wave Mao's *Little Red Book* at Gregory Peck when he's caught up in a Cultural Revolution demonstration while guided by Zienia Merton.

Playing a capable NASA chief, Gregory Peck, addresses the problems of a crew stranded in orbit in *Marooned*.

Marooned

Columbia Pictures   **1969**

Credits

Producer, M. J. Frankovich; *director*, John Sturges; *screenplay*, Mayo Simon, based on the novel by Martin Caidin; *cinematography*, Daniel Fapp; *editor*, Walter Thompson; *aerial photography*, Nelson Tyler; *special visual effects*, Lawrence W. Butler, Donald C. Glouner, Robie Robinson; *sound*, Les Fresholtz, Arthur Piantadosi; *production designer*, Lyle R. Wheeler; *set decoration*, Frank Tuttle; *costumes*, Seth Banks; *associate producer*, Frank Capra, Jr., filmed in Panavision and Technicolor. (131 minutes)

Cast

Gregory Peck (Charles Keith), Richard Crenna (Jim Pruett), David Janssen (Ted Dougherty), James Franciscus (Clayton Stone), Gene Hackman (Buzz Lloyd), Lee Grant (Celia Pruett), Nancy Kovack (Teresa Stone), Mariette Hartley (Betty Lloyd). *At Mission Control*: Scott Brady (Public Affairs Officer), Craig Huebing (Flight Director), John Carter (Flight Surgeon), George Gaynes (Mission Director), Tom Stewart (Houston Cap-Com). *Air Force Officers*: Frank Marth (Space Systems Director), Duke Hobbie (Titan Systems Specialist), Dennis Robertson (Launch Director), George Smith (Cape Weather Officer). *News Commentators*: Vincent Van Lynn (Cannon), Walter Brooke (Radin), Mauritz Hugo (Hardy), Bill Couch (Russian Cosmonaut), Mary-Linda Rapelye (Priscilla Keith).

209

Tension mounts as options diminish for NASA administrator Gregory Peck and mission control technicians at the space flight center in Houston.

Gregory Peck starred in *Marooned* because he did not appear in *Ice Station Zebra* (1968). When that Cinerama adventure-epic about a U.S.-U.S.S.R. confrontation in the Arctic was originally planned, Peck was to have starred as an American submarine commander. The film was at that stage of planning sponsored by Columbia Pictures, but because of producer Martin Ransohoff's dissatisfaction with the script, the production was mothballed. When it was eventually reactivated, Peck was unavailable, Rock Hudson took the role, and the movie was made under the aegis of MGM. To settle their joint commitment, Columbia offered Peck the role of the National Aeronautics and Space Administration's Chief of Manned Space Flight in *Marooned*.

As Charles Keith, Peck plays the American space program administrator with the awesome responsibility of deciding the fate of three astronauts who are perilously trapped in earth orbit because of an equipment malfunction. The life-or-death burden is a heavy one, but one for which the shoulders of Gregory Peck are typically well suited in a drama about the durability of human courage and the frailty of machines.

While *Marooned* was in production, the entire company stopped work to watch the December 21, 1968, launch of an actual space flight, Apollo 8, which made the first manned voyage around the moon. They studied the mission carefully to heighten the authenticity of their own work, and U.S. astronauts Frank Borman, James Lovell and William Anders provided perfect role models for *Marooned* astronauts Richard Crenna, James Franciscus and Gene Hackman.

The movie story itself anticipated the American Skylab program of the 1970s, when astronauts went aloft to work for prolonged periods in an orbiting space station.

Marooned also ironically anticipated some future events in the real-life American space program.

Despite the care with which it was obviously crafted, despite the intense attention to detail and to rendering all facets of the space program it dealt with as much fidelity as possible, and despite the urgency of its story, audiences did not turn out for it, and *Marooned* was not a hit.

The picture was given a premiere sendoff in Washington on November 10, 1969, at the Warner Theater, with NASA and other government officials and members of the National Association of Theater Owners' convention in attendance. In New York, *Marooned* was the premiere attraction at Walter Reade's plush new Ziegfeld Theater, where it opened on December 17, on a reserved-seat basis and with an intermission. Critics praised some aspects of the production and damned others.

For *Variety*, it was "gripping drama...part documentary, part science fiction. Superbly crafted, taut, a technological cliffhanger... [with] convincing and often touching performances." But, said *Variety*'s reviewer, the "major flaw is a hokey old-fashioned Hollywood Renfrew-to-the-rescue climax that is dramatically, logically and technologically unconvincing.... Peck...is a pillar of quietly concerned strength under unbelievable stress...."

In *The New York Times*, Howard Thompson called it "a handsome, professional and future-minded drama...admirably intelligent all the way, with a good cast headed by Gregory Peck."

Frances Herridge of the *New York Post* reported, "If you are enthralled...by all the maneuvers of space shots, *Marooned* is for you. ... Moviegoers who like action will have to be patient in the first half, where the script stays with strict realism. But the second half drains every bit of drama out of the situation, with contrivances, unfortunately, that get more and more corny. ... Even when the script rings false, the actors don't. ... Lee Grant is particularly good. ... Peck is coolly himself as the unemotional Chief...."

Regardless of the critical reaction, NASA thought the filmmakers had done a good job and awarded the picture an official commendation for its accuracy at portraying the behind-the-scenes story of the U.S. space program and its many diligent workers. And legend has it that *Marooned* actually inspired the idea for the American-Russian Apollo-Soyuz spacecraft rendezvous and link-up staged successfully in the summer of 1975.

Despite a top-flight cast, audiences were turned off by some of the obviously faked special effects in *Marooned,* a factor which, in part at least, contributed to the picture's failure.

Professional disagreements take an argumentative personal turn as Gregory Peck and David Janssen heatedly debate the question of rescue for the marooned astronauts.

The faces of astronaut David Janssen and administrator Gregory Peck register their deep concern as the struggle to save an imperilled crew goes on.

An illicit romance between a sheriff and a criminal's daughter is not always a bed of roses, as Gregory Peck discovers when he tries to persuade a reluctant Tuesday Weld to leave her family.

I Walk the Line

Columbia Pictures   **1970**

Credits

Executive producer, Edward Lewis; *producer*, Harold D. Cohen; *director*, John Frankenheimer; *screenplay*, Alvin Sargent, based on the novel, *An Exile*, by Madison Jones; *music*, Johnny Cash; *musical supervisor*, Robert Johnson; *cinematography*, David M. Walsh; *editor*, Henry Berman; *supervising editor*, Harold F. Kress; *art director*, Albert Brenner; *set decoration*, Marvin March; *costumes*, Lewis Brown; *sound*, Tom Overton, Arthur Piantadosi; *assistant director*, Philip L. Parslow; filmed in Panavision and Eastman Color. (95 minutes)

Cast

Gregory Peck (Sheriff Tawes), Tuesday Weld (Alma McCain), Estelle Parsons (Ellen-Haney), Ralph Meeker (Carl McCain), Lonny Chapman (Bascomb), Charles Durning (Hunnicutt), Jeff Dalton (Clay McCain), Freddie McCloud (Buddy McCain), Jane Rose (Elsie), J. C. Evans (Grandpa Tawes), Margaret A. Morris (Sybil), Bill Littleton (Pollard), Leo Yates (Vogel), Dodo Denney (Darlene Hunnicutt).

•

"Sheriff…sheriff. Your wife says bring home the corn," crackles a woman's somewhat strident Southern-accented voice on the radio of a sheriff's patrol car.

The electronic intrusion interrupts what seems to be a reverie as Gregory Peck, whom we've found standing with his back to us and looking across the water at the huge concrete dam that holds back a large shimmering lake, turns, gets into the car and drives off without answering, heading across the dam itself.

As he drives through the rural Tennessee hill country, we ride with him, passing by weather-beaten, broken-down farm houses, paint-faded storefronts and rust-saturated automobile graveyards, all of them attended by people who seem to be as broken-down and weather-beaten and faded as their surroundings. We scan their faces, the old and the old-before-their-time, hard-bitten and tight-lined faces, the human wreckage that seems a counterpart to the used-up, crushed-up and thrown-away vehicles littering the landscape. These sad and haunting eyes all seem to search for something they seem to know they'll never find. They look as if someone forgot to tell them that the Great Depression had ended long ago. The sheriff also seems to feel them looking constantly at him, paying attention to his progress every bit of the way. Being sheriff is a high-visibility job.

These are the scenes that open *I Walk the Line*, to Johnny Cash's vocalizing of the song which gives the movie its title and tells us that a man's got to walk the straight and narrow and keep careful check on himself, on his emotions and on what's going on around him. These are the scenes that establish a social, geographical and thematic context for the story that follows. This is "September country"—in more ways than one.

"September Country" was the working title of this movie directed by John Frankenheimer from a screenplay by Alvin Sargent, based on the Madison Jones novel, *An Exile*. Sargent had also written the script for Peck's recent *The Stalking Moon*. When the Johnny Cash song was added, the film's title was changed to match.

According to the director, he saw *I Walk the Line* as "basically about what can happen to a sensitive man when he's really in the wrong environment, how society can destroy an individual. [It's] a film about an older man who for

Gregory Peck, the Southern sheriff who is led astray by a moonshiner's daughter, and wife Estelle Parsons consider the sad state of their deteriorating relationship in John Frankenheimer's *I Walk the Line*.

His romance with Tuesday Weld having led to his involvement in concealing a murder, Gregory Peck races after her when he discovers that she and her family have taken off.

all the wrong reasons falls in love with a young girl and decides to throw his whole life away to have her go off with him...a very personal small film about freedom of choice." Unfortunately, most of the characters in the movie appear to make only bad choices.

This role was a major change of pace for actor Peck from his recent and usual involvement in epic-style heroics. He is not altogether successful in it, but he does create a generally sympathetic character through whose surface

When Gregory Peck tries to rescue Tuesday Weld from her own family, she interferes, wounding him with a meat hook before departing to leave him behind to face the ruins of his life.

simplicity we can occasionally glimpse some complexity within.

I Walk the Line opened in multiple theaters in New York, on November 18, 1970. Howard Thompson, in *The New York Times*, called it "a minor drama that ends up chasing its own tail and falling to pieces quite literally in the middle of the road. There, at the fadeout, stands an anguished Gregory Peck. ... Before it flattens into tedium and starts churning around in clanky melodrama, this picture, which begins nicely, promises more. ... It was admirable of Peck to try such a role in a hillbilly context after his usual expensive showcases. He performs with laconic restraint ...even looks like a Cumberland...sheriff.... But he emerges a dull knucklehead who rates little sympathy. ... Sargent's adaptation ... sends the picture careening over a bumpy road. And even an intelligent director like John Frankenheimer, with his unobtrusive evocation of the locale, the regional faces and some authentic sideline dialogue, can't hold it together."

The *New York Post*'s Archer Winsten found it "...a tragedy of such simple components that the power and beauty of the performances come through unimpeded by any complexity or oddity. ... This situation...enables ...Frankenheimer to utilize fully his very considerable artistry. He has attempted much more difficult assignments in the past but perhaps has never succceeded with such ease and mastery of his material. Gregory Peck also benefits by the change of role...gives a performance of unexpected depth...."

I Walk the Line died at the box-office, perhaps in part because Gregory Peck's fans wouldn't buy him in this downbeat role, however sensitive his portrait of Henry Tawes; or perhaps the Johnny Cash songs gave the picture too much of a "country" cachet that kept the vital urban audiences away. Everyone is likely to have his own ideas.

Peck's own personal feeling is that the picture suffered from both insensitive cutting and the post-production addition of the Cash songs. "The picture I made," he says, "was a much better picture than the one that showed up on the screen." Others would likely feel that they did the best they could with what they had.

Gregory Peck is neither grinning nor bearing it very well as gunmen Robert F. Lyons, John Chandler and Pepe Serna taunt barfly Susan Tyrrell.

Shoot Out

Universal Pictures   **1971**

Cast

Gregory Peck (Clay Lomax), Pat Quinn (Juliana Farrell), Robert F. Lyons (Bobby Jay), Susan Tyrrell (Alma), Jeff Corey (Trooper), James Gregory (Sam Foley), Rita Gam (Emma), Dawn Lyn (Decky), Pepe Serna (Pepe), Joan Chandler (Skeeter), Paul Fix (Brakeman), Arthur Hunnicutt (Page), Nicolas Beauvy (Dutch Farrell).

Credits

Producer, Hal B. Wallis; *director*, Henry Hathaway; *screenplay*, Marguerite Roberts, based on the novel, *The Lone Cowboy*, by Will James; *music*, Dave Grusin; *cinematography*, Earl Rath; *editor*, Archie Marshek; *art directors*, Alexander Golitzen, Walter Tyler; *set decoration*, John McCarthy; *sound*, Waldon O. Watson; James Alexander, Ronald Pierce; color by Technicolor; filmed on locations in New Mexico. (95 minutes)

Occasionally one gets the impression that in Hollywood movies are not made so much as they are re-made. *Shoot Out* appears to have been turned out by producer Hal Wallis, director Henry Hathaway and scriptwriter Marguerite Roberts with the hope of recapturing the *True Grit* mystique with which they had made so successful a film—and gained John Wayne a well-deserved Oscar—two years earlier. This time around they trotted out Gregory Peck as the gun-totin' cowboy saddled with an unwanted female companion, but instead of *True Grit*'s spunky and engaging 14-year-old

Dawn Lyn is the almost too-cute little girl whose welfare becomes Gregory Peck's unwanted concern in *Shoot Out*.

Unflinching and fearless, Gregory Peck tells a trio of gunmen who've been dogging his trail that they should let their employer know that he's determined to settle an old score.

Mattie Ross, Peck winds up with little Decky, who is six-years-old and cute. *Oh*, so cute.

Henry Hathaway had previously directed Gregory Peck in his segment of *How the West Was Won* and had directed Wallis's *Sons of Katie Elder* (1965) as well as *True Grit*. Unfortunately, *Shoot Out* has none of the excitement, style and charm that makes *True Grit*, a star vehicle for John Wayne, the rewarding and entertaining movie *it* is.

The picture opened in New York in a multiple theater engagement on October 13, 1971. "It seems a lot," said Roger Greenspun, reviewing *Shoot Out* for *The New York Times*, "to expect a little seven-year-old-girl…to hold together a whole feature film full of inept adults, but that is what somebody must have expected of Dawn Lyn…given the story, the director and the rest of the cast. … *Shoot Out* is no more than another variation of the eternal tale of the Westerner…who seeks revenge on the pal who betrayed him but is himself pursued by…killers until a showdown in which everybody gets his except Mr. Peck, who unaccountably gets marriage and a family.…"

Wanda Hale, of the *Daily News*, was more receptive and gave the film a three-star rating. Said Miss Hale: "Hathaway, an old hand at Westerns, works up his suspense by degrees, keeping the star on the edge of danger but only once in difficulty when the leader of Foley's punks gets over-zealous and at that moment we know he is doomed. … *Shoot Out* is a well turned story."

A wounded Gregory Peck is hauled along on a litter as he and his Indian companion in crime attempt their getaway over arid terrain.

Billy Two Hats

United Artists 1974

Cast

Gregory Peck (Deans), Desi Arnaz, Jr. (Billy), Jack Warden (Gifford), David Huddleston (Copeland), Sian Barbara Allen (Esther), John Pearce (Spencer), Dawn Little Sky (Squaw), W. Vincent St. Cyr (Indian Leader), Henry Medicine Hat (Indian), Zev Berlinsky (Indian), Antony Scott (Indian).

Credits

Producers, Norman Jewison, Patrick Palmer; *director,* Ted Kotcheff; *screenplay,* Alan Sharp; *music,* John Scott; *cinematography,* Brian West; *editor,* Thom Noble; *sound,* Brian Simmons; *special effects,* Les Hillman; *production designer,* Anthony Pratt; *wardrobe,* G. W. Nicholls; *property master,* Sam Gordon; *assistant directors,* Paul Ibbetson, Howard Grigsby. (80 minutes)

An American Western, written by a Scotsman, produced and directed by Canadians and photographed entirely on location in Israel capped a string of failures for Gregory Peck and brought the actor to an important point of resolve regarding his acting career and his future.

It is easy to understand the initial attraction Peck must have felt toward this story about the relationship that grows between an older Scottish outlaw and the young Indian half-breed with whom he becomes associated, because within the context of what is essentially a character study, *Billy Two Hats* also has something to say about the stupidity of racial bigotry.

For Gregory Peck there was some irony in shooting scenes of the American West around the Israeli city of Ashkelon. In *David and Bathsheba*, filmed more than twenty years earlier, as King David he had had a line of dialogue that read, "Publish it not in the streets of Ashkelon"; that Biblical epic had been filmed in Arizona—and now Peck had come to the Holy Land itself to film a Western.

As Deans, Peck plays a failed outlaw, a salty, bearded, Bible-quoting Scotsman consigned to wandering the dry and dusty West while dreaming of the green hills of his native Scotland.

Striving to perfect an authentic-sounding Scottish accent for Deans, Peck devoted a considerable amount of preparatory time to working very carefully with a Scots dialect expert, but the result is not entirely successful. Of course, a totally authentic Scots dialect might have rendered Deans's dialogue largely unintelligible to non-Scottish audiences and obviously some middle road had to be taken.

Basically, the film deals with the camaraderie and warmth that develops between Billy and Deans, whose bungled bank robbery makes both of them fugitives, pursued unrelentingly by Sheriff Gifford.

Desi Arnaz, Jr., is more than adequate as Billy, the credibility of his performance undoubtedly enhanced by his rank then as a relative newcomer to film. Jack Warden skillfully creates an obnoxious Sheriff Gifford.

Billy Two Hats was completed in 1973 and released in England in April 1974. It garnered a favorable comment from the *London Observer*'s Russell Davies, who noted that although his enthusiasm for the genre wasn't the greatest, "I begin to see the virtues of the Western. ... As genres go it seems to be providing the most consistent level of entertainment these days. *Billy Two Hats*...is quite a nice little Western. Considering what an extraordinary melange of experience and rawness, bogusness and authenticity the picture is...it comes off surprisingly well...."

New York magazine's Judith Crist panned the movie as "an international mishmash of a Western that is as gloomy and pretentious as it is imperfectly awful..." and James Murray, in New York's *Amsterdam News*, commented that it "is a perfect example of why many seasoned observers feel that the [Western] genre should be abandoned for a while...."

Gregory Peck himself holds no illusions about *Billy Two Hats*, though he finds it not without some virtue: "It was a little picture that didn't amount to much...the story was weak, the plot was diffuse, but there were moments...there were scenes that were fluid, that were well done and life-like and genuine. It has some lovely scenery...but basically the screenplay was flawed and not completely thought out, not well constructed. But I liked the character and I liked doing it. We thought it was an interesting little Western anecdote to tell but we must have been wrong. But you write those things off when that happens and you think, 'Well we did out best.'"

"But," said Peck reflectively, in an interview in November 1974, "I've decided now not to do any more of those. ... I get offered quite a few scripts, but to be quite honest about it, I haven't had an outstanding script offered to me for a couple of years. And to go on doing a succession of *Billy Two Hats* would be embarrassing. I don't like it when pictures go out and get lost and no one goes to see them, because you put just as much effort into it. You spend all those days and nights...get up early and learn your lines and study your character. And you work just as hard or harder on a bad script as you do on a good one. And at this point in my life, it's embarrassing to have a picture go out and get lost like that. So I'm just not going to do any more of those. I'll retire first. I'll go to the south of France or take up charity work rather than do a series of mediocre pictures."

After Gregory Peck is wounded in their getaway, he and Desi Arnaz, Jr., make camp for the night during their flight from justice.

Sian Barbara Allen, the lovely young wife of a grizzled and much older rancher, befriends Gregory Peck and Desi Arnaz, Jr., with whom she also has an affair.

219

Escaping a pack of killer dogs which have attacked him in a deserted Italian cemetery, Gregory Peck impales his arm on the iron fence that surrounds the graveyard.

The Omen

20th Century-Fox   **1976**

Credits

Executive producer, Mace Neufeld; *producer*, Harvey Bernhard; *director*, Richard Donner; *screenplay*, David Seltzer; *music*, Jerry Goldsmith; *cinematography*, Gil Taylor; *editor*, Stuart Baird; *art director*, Carmen Dillon; *special effects*, John Richardson; *associate producer*, Charles Orme; *assistant director*, David Tomblin; filmed in England, Italy and Israel in Panavision and DeLuxe Color. (111 minutes)

Cast

Gregory Peck (Robert Thorn), Lee Remick (Katherine Thorn), David Warner (Jennings), Billie Whitelaw (Mrs. Baylock), Leo McKern (Bugenhagen), Harvey Stephens (Damien), Patrick Troughton (Father Brennan), Anthony Nicholls (Dr. Becker), Martin Benson (Father Spiletto), Sheila Raynor (Mrs. Horton), Holly Palance (Nanny), Robert McLeod (Horton), John Stride (The Psychiatrist).

Following the disappointing failure of *Billy Two Hats*, the latest in a string of unsuccessful pictures, Gregory Peck went into a period of self-imposed retirement from acting and directed his attention for a time to film production. He was lured back in front of the cameras in 1975 by a script which read, he says, "like a good pulp thriller." It was a fortuitous return, for *The Omen* became the biggest hit of his entire career and changed Peck's mind about retiring to a life behind the camera.

The idea for this quasi-religious supernatural thriller about the birth of the anti-Christ (which allegedly would signal the beginning of the end of the world) originated with a Los Angeles advertising executive and Biblical-prophecy buff, Robert L. Munger, who took it to producer Harvey Bernhard. Bernhard raised some development money and hired David Seltzer to write a script based on Munger's suggestions. Seltzer, who has emphatically denied *any* religious pretensions for the story he subsequently developed, took a bit of prophetic doggerel verse as his screenplay's motif:

"When the Jews return to Zion
And a comet rips the sky
And the Holy Roman Empire rises
Then you and I must die.

"From the eternal sea he rises
Creating armies on either shore,
Turning man against his brother
'Til man exists no more."

The verse is alleged, by Seltzer, to have come from the "Book of Revelations," an apparently fictional tome so-called to lead the unwary to mistake the source for the Biblical book of "Revelation," which prophesies the second coming of Jesus Christ and the end of the physical world. In any event, no such rhyme can be located in the Judeo-Christian Holy Bible.

Bernhard and Seltzer took their screenplay, entitled *The Anti-Christ*, to Warner Brothers, whose devil-possession picture *The Exorcist* (1973) had been a smash. Warners took a seven-month option on the property but let it languish. When the Warners' option

Gregory Peck comforts his wife, Lee Remick, and son, Harvey Stephens, after they have witnessed the child's nanny commit suicide by hanging herself during a birthday party.

was about to expire, an agent brought the script to the attention of Richard Donner, a successful director of commercials, television series (including *Twelve O'Clock High*, based on the 1949 Peck movie), documentaries and TV-movies. When he started reading it, Donner found the script impossible to put down and as soon as he finished he went to see Alan Ladd, Jr., chief of production at 20th Century-Fox, and asked him to read the script over a weekend, since the option would be up for grabs again on the following Monday morning. Ladd protested that his weekend agenda was already overloaded but Donner persisted until he agreed to take a look at it. Around midnight on Sunday, Ladd called Donner and told him that if he could put the production together, Fox would provide the financial backing for it. On Monday, Fox added *The Anti-Christ* to its production schedule.

Peck did feel that the screenplay had "some loopholes." He thought, for instance, that as an ambassador, Robert Thorn had to be too intelligent a character to unquestioningly accept a substitute child, as he does, without first asking to see his own dead son and without researching the adoptee's background. He also felt it unlikely that a man of Thorn's social position would have deceived his wife about the child, whom they name Damien, even though the script makes it clear that he does so out of love and concern for her

One of the factors that kept the budget down was that Donner and his creative team did extensive pre-production planning and devised back-up plans to be put into effect whenever an originally scheduled shot gave them a potentially production-delaying problem.

Before production got underway, it was discovered that there was a European picture with the title *AntiChristo*, so the working title on the Bernhard-Donner-Seltzer project was changed to *The Birthmark*, a reference to the three numerical sixes which allegedly appear somewhere on the body of every minion of the devil. Donner also had some reservations about certain aspects of Seltzer's script, which originally contained more in the way of literal appearances of demons and cloven-hoofed Luciferians than shows up on screen. His own preference was for a more restrained and ambiguous approach, for a picture that might leave some doubt about what was really going on. Seltzer agreed with Donner's viewpoint after they discussed it and within a week presented the director with a revised screenplay that reflected the new ideas.

A crucial part of *The Omen*'s success lies in its crafty and carefully planned manipulation of its audience's expectations. Donner and Seltzer sat down before shooting started and plotted the script out meticulously minute by minute to create the sort of titillating sensations one associates with the sudden ups and downs of a roller-coaster ride. They worked out a pattern of shocks and lulls which would condition the viewers to one sort of rhythm which they could suddenly reverse to create maximum surprise. They structured the film to shock then lull, shock then lull, shock and then—when the audience was expecting a lull—shock again, maximizing the effectiveness of the thrill. When, for example, Katherine Thorn survives a hair-raising fall from a high stair-landing onto the floor of a hallway, the audience is relieved to see that she is still alive and apparently saved from danger. But moments later the horror is amplified when

and from a heartfelt desire to spare her the painful knowledge of her own baby's death. But Peck saw that the movie was essentially "a sort of roller coaster thrill ride for the audience" and besides, as the filmmakers pointed out, even Hitchcock movies have plot holes.

Lee Remick, an accomplished actress who combines both talent and beauty in equally large measures, was cast as Katherine Thorn, the unsuspecting and loving wife and mother who awakens too late to the full import of the seemingly inexplicable tragedies which befall her household and family and who may be unknowingly nurturing the child of the devil.

Plans were made to begin shooting the picture in London in October 1975, with Shepperton Studios as production base. It was budgeted at $2.5 million, a modest amount for an 11-week shooting schedule, particularly considering the fact that much of it was done on location, which usually entails considerable expense. The movie did, in fact, run over budget; Donner brought it in for $2.8 million, an amazingly low figure which makes its subsequent blockbuster success all the more impressive.

During their drive through a safari park, Lee Remick and Harvey Stephens are violently attacked by a troop of normally benign baboons who become agitated at the sight of the boy.

she plunges to her death from the window of a hospital where she's recovering.

Despite the fact that there are a number of violent deaths in *The Omen*, Donner took care to keep the gory aspects to a minimum and there is probably a good deal more blood in the minds of the audience as it watches than actually appears on screen. When Lee Remick falls to her death, for example, the only blood we see is a little trickle from the corner of her mouth.

Overall, Donner's approach to the picture was to attempt to give it two levels of possible interpretation. Beyond the obvious literal one—that Damien *is* the son of the devil and that the plague of tragedies that befalls everyone around him results from Satanic influences—Donner tried to leave open the possibility that in actuality Robert Thorn might be having a nervous breakdown and, descending into madness, has become obsessed with the idea, accentuated by a series of bizarre coincidences and encounters with several eccentric persons, that his adopted child is the anti-Christ.

Peck's performance is carefully orchestrated to allow this sort of interpretation: He has moments of lucid certainty that others around him are insane—the priest who insists that Damien is dangerous, for instance.

As much care and careful plotting went into the advertising and release plans for *The Omen* as had been devoted to its structure and production. Since the picture had been made from an original screenplay, it lacked the sort of pre-sell impetus attending the release of a picture like *The Exorcist*, which had the publicity benefit of having been based on a best-selling novel, so the public appetite for *The Omen* had to be whetted from scratch. Twentieth Century-Fox's advertising executives set an initial publicity campaign budget at $2.8 million, equal to the entire cost of the picture itself.

The Omen was scheduled to open on June 25, 1976, and during the six- to ten-week period preceding the date, Fox began running some 1300 trailers in theaters across the United States. The trailer campaign was augmented in early June by a two-round break of an unprecedented 547 sneak previews. The sneak previews were an astounding success, selling out 95 percent of their possible seats, with standing-room-only and turnaway crowds in many situations. Over 700,000 people saw the picture in these previews and they immediately constituted a powerfully large word-of-mouth advertising corps—the very best kind of publicity a movie can get.

Indicative of the interest stirred up by the sneak previews was the effect they had on the sale of the paperback novelization of David Seltzer's screenplay, which was published a few days before the picture opened simultaneously in 516 theaters in some 321 cities: The book sold out its entire first shipment within hours after it appeared in bookstores in New York, Los Angeles and several other major cities. It quickly established itself as the nation's No. 1 best-selling paperback and by the end of the year had sold more than 3.5 million copies and was still going strong.

When *The Omen* opened on a Friday, it immediately proceeded to break every existing record for an opening weekend in Fox's 41-year history, amassing a total gross of nearly $4.3 million in its first three days. Extra performances were scheduled in many theaters to handle the crowds. As the picture took off into the stratosphere, Fox unveiled a revised ad campaign based on the successful word-of-mouth premise: Millions of people have seen *The Omen*, the ads said, and "For those of you who haven't seen it yet, we urge you to do just

223

one thing. Ask anyone who's seen it. Anyone."

Apparently a lot of people took the ad's advise and liked what they heard. *The Omen* went on to grosses far in excess of $100 million. *The Guns of Navarone* had been Gregory Peck's most successful picture up to this time, but *The Omen* quickly eclipsed that movie's own strong boxoffice showing. Eventually, the total advertising expenditures for the picture reached the neighborhood of $6 million, and in terms of generating dollars in return for dollars spent, it may well have been one of the most successful ad and publicity campaigns since David O. Selznick launched *Duel in the Sun* thirty years before.

The Omen's reviews were generally good. *Variety*'s critic saw the picture at one of its sneaks: "The Satanic-suspense melodrama, fallen into artistic disrepute after *Rosemary's Baby* and *The Exorcist*, resumes its class status again with *The Omen*. ... Peck [is] well cast as a career American ambassador. ... Production credits are all tops...."

New York Daily News's Kathleen Carroll gave the picture a three-and-a-half star rating and reported it "truly a rare find: the horror movie that displays real thought and intelligence. ... Peck gives one of the peak performances of his career...."

For the *New York Post*'s Frank Rich, *The Omen* was "a very cagey, though far from airtight horror movie. ... If that Biblical stuff really turns you on ... you'll probably be able to forgive *The Omen* its narrative trespasses and be carried away by its surefire scare tactics and classy production values. But...you may find yourself constantly distracted by the holes that permeate the...plot. ... Given the script's drawbacks, there's no denying that director Richard Donner has gotten everything out of the material that he possibly can. ... The cast is equally reassuring. ... Peck is a more pre-

possessing diplomat than any appointed by recent Washington administrations and Miss Remick continues to be about the loveliest woman on earth."

In *The New York Times*, second-string movie critic Richard Eder called the picture "...a dreadfully silly film, which is not to say that it is totally bad. Its horrors are not horrible, its terrors are not terrifying, its violence is ludicrous—which may be an advantage—but it does move along. ... The movie takes its details with no seriousness at all. It is not a put-on—it is terribly solemn, in fact—but it often seems like one...."

When *The Times*'s chief critic Vincent Canby got around to writing about the movie, he commented that "William Friedkin's *The Exorcist*...seemed pretty dreadful at the time but...alongside *The Omen* now looks like a work of cinematic art...."

The film's release was not without some controversy. A number of theologians, many of whom had been horrified at the public's unquestioning embrace of and delight in the lurid and fraudulent religiosity of *The Exorcist*, took an equally dim view of *The Omen*'s subject matter and its treatment of it. The U. S. Catholic Conference assailed it as "one of the most distasteful [movies] ever put out by a major studio." A religious publication, *Christianity Today*, called the picture "a muddle of prophecy—pre-Sunday school stuff," and *Cinema Sound*, a Lutheran magazine, described it as "mystery and truth reduced to simplistic entertainment."

The movie's ending, with Gregory Peck attempting to stab the anti-Christ child to death, was seen by some as condoning "using the weapons of evil to fight evil...the antithesis of Christ's message." There were also ministers who denounced the film as "worse than sheer hokum."

David Seltzer countered that as far as he was concerned, the movie had no religious pretensions whatsoever. It was, he maintained,

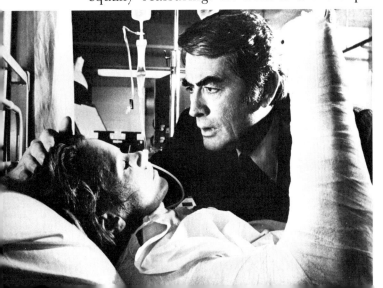

After his wife, Lee Remick, is seriously injured in a fall caused, unbeknownst to them, by their son, Gregory Peck visits her in the hospital before setting off on a trip to Italy to seek some answers about the bizarre and violent events which are enveloping his family.

Resting after dressing his wounds, Gregory Peck contemplates the awesome and mind-boggling discovery he and photographer David Warner, who has accompanied him, have made in the old cemetery from which they have barely escaped.

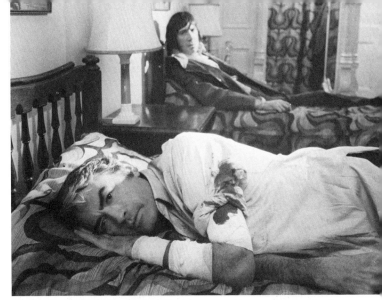

"pure escapism. I wanted to see if I could write something really outlandish and really commercial."

Noting that *The Omen* and other films like it were made for purely economic reasons and usually attended by people looking for cheap thrills, the Vatican Radio issued a proclamation decrying its popularity: "The religious institutions are anything but enthusiastic about this type of interest in the devil." After citing alleged possible negative social side effects that might be attributed to such movies, the Vatican commentary further observed that "Nothing and nobody prevents movies from dealing with Satan. But in front of such a serious theme tackled for reasons and towards ends absolutely consumeristic and economical, the proverbial tail of the devil comes to one's mind."

Richard Donner replied to the Vatican attack, saying that he was surprised at the Church's negative reaction in light of the fact that the film served, he thought, to inform people about the devil's work. "They must admit," he said, "that the devil can be alive and well on planet Earth, and if so, isn't it important to gather our religious strength to ward off this evil? The best way to do that is to have an informed public. *The Omen* is certainly not a film about the devil winning, but a warning of his presence."

Donner cited a review of the film in an American National Council of Churches publication which commented that "This is a must film. If nothing else it will provoke parishioners into reading the Bible."

In Hollywood, of course, nothing impresses like success—and movie-making is by and large an imitative business, not an innovative one. The success of *The Omen* confirmed what a good many producers and studio executives suspected, based on the earlier success of *The Exorcist*, and everybody ran to jump aboard the devil-movie bandwagon. By the end of October, 1976, Alan Ladd, Jr., told a

reporter that he thought that "almost every movie company has five or six devil movies in the works."

He knew whereof he spoke, since Fox and Harvey Bernhard had also announced that they were planning not one but *three* sequels to *The Omen*. One would deal with Damien's later childhood (the Devil goes to prep school—or vice-versa, as it turned out), the second with Damien in his teen years, and the last would deal with the anti-Christ from his middle age, when he would apparently come fully into his powers, to Armageddon, the end of the world—and, promised producer Bernhard, "It won't be with atomic bombs. It'll be far more frightening!"

Attempting to find out the truth about his son, Gregory Peck is attacked with supernatural strength in a climactic struggle with the boy's new nanny, Billie Whitelaw, who tries to kill him to protect the child.

MacArthur

Universal Pictures   **1977**
A Richard D. Zanuck—David Brown Production
Credits

Producer, Frank McCarthy; *director*, Joseph Sargent; *screenplay*, Hal Barwood, Matthew Robbins; *music*, Jerry Goldsmith; *cinematography*, Mario Tosi; *editor*, George Jay Nicholson; *production designer*, John J. Lloyd; *set decoration*, Hal Gausman; *special effects*, Albert Whitlock; *sound*, Don Sharpless, Robert L. Hoyt, Jim Troutman; *makeup*, Jim McCoy, Frank McCoy; *stunt coordinator*, Joe Canutt; *assistant directors*, Scott Maitland, Donald E. Zepfel; *chief technical advisor*, D. Clayton James, Ph. D.; filmed in Technicolor and Panavision. (128 minutes)

Cast

Gregory Peck (Gen. Douglas MacArthur), Ed Flanders (President Harry S Truman), Dan O'Herlihy (President Franklin D. Roosevelt), Ivan Bonar (Gen. Sutherland), Ward Costello (Gen. Marshall), Marj Dusay (Mrs. MacArthur), Art Fleming (The Secretary), Russell D. Johnson (Adm. King), Sandy Kenyon (Gen. Wainwright), Robert Mandan (Rep. Martin), Allan Miller (Col. Diller), Dick O'Neill (Col. Whitney), Addison Powell (Adm. Nimitz), Tom Rosqui (Gen. Sampson), G. D. Spradlin (Gen. Eichelberger), Kenneth Tobey (Adm. Halsey), Garry Walberg (Gen. Walker), Lane Allan (Gen. Marquat), Barry Coe (TV Reporter), Everett Cooper (Gen. Krueger), Charles Cyphers (Gen. Harding), Manuel De Pina (Prettyman), Jesse Dizon (Castro), Warde Donovan (Gen. Shepherd), John Fujioka (The Emperor Hirohito), Jerry Holland (Aide), Philip Kenneally (Adm. Doyle), John McKee (Adm. Leahy), Walter O. Miles (Gen. Kenney), Gerald S. Peters (Gen. Blamey), Eugene Peterson (Gen. Collins), Beulah Quo (Ah Cheu), Alex Rodine (Gen. Derevyanko), Yuki Shimoda (Prime Minister Shidehara), Fred Stuthman (Gen. Bradley), Harvey Vernon (Adm. Sherman), William Wellman, Jr. (Lt. Bulkeley).

"Duty...honor...country...."

The balding, gray-haired old man, in a dark business suit, speaks the words slowly, meticulously and in carefully measured tones, his voice slightly tremulous, as he looks out over a sea of gray-uniformed Army cadets seated attentively in the main mess hall of the United States Military Academy at West Point. It is 1962. Diffused sunlight filters through stained-glass windows, softly filling the vast, cathedral-like vaulted-ceilinged room, touching the banners of the states that hang in progression along its side and brushing the heroic mural at the end of the room with its faint glow.

Although his frame is slightly stooped and sagging, there is an unmistakable aura of grandeur about this figure and the eyes with which he fixes his youthful audience are still those of an eagle. He pauses, then continues: "Duty...honor...country. Those three hallowed words reverently dictate what you ought to be, what you can be, what you will be...."

Those three hallowed words are the motto of the corps of cadets, the wellspring from whence the U.S. Army officers of the future will come; the words are emblazoned on its crest as surely as they must be emblazoned on the soul and spirit of General Douglas MacArthur, who, at age 82, is delivering his

227

Gregory Peck, as the 82-year-old Douglas MacArthur, returns to West Point, where his own military career had begun, for a final address to the cadet corps, his theme one of "Duty ... Honor ... Country," in a poignant scene at the beginning of *MacArthur*.

farewell address to the young soldiers who are in training at the Academy from which he himself graduated 59 years before, first in his class and senior officer in the corps. Across the intervening years is emblazoned a remarkable, magnificent and not infrequently controversial career which made the man truly a legend in his time and an American hero for all time.

Thus begins—and ends—*MacArthur*, the picture that traces the crucial events of the last two decades of the general's life, from his 1942 evacuation of Corregidor in the Philippines, with the famous pledge, "I shall return," to his touching goodbye at West Point, to which we return in the film's concluding moments. As the general, Gregory Peck gives one of the finest performances of his career in a role for which there was some stiff competition.

When Richard D. Zanuck, David Brown and Frank McCarthy announced their inten-

tion to produce *MacArthur*, on September 6, 1972, they touched off a casting game of worldwide proportions, with scores of star-grade actors suggested for the title role.

As an independent production team, Richard Zanuck, son of Darryl, and David Brown were responsible for several eminently successful films, including *The Sting* (1973) and *Jaws* (1975). Both had been executives at 20th Century-Fox when the studio backed Frank McCarthy's production of *Patton* (1970). After that success, McCarthy, himself a retired brigadier general, became interested in a film about MacArthur and set about meticulously researching the life of the general. The core of McCarthy's research was conducted in the military archives at the Marshall Library in Lexington, Virginia; his work there and elsewhere provided much of the material from which scenarists Hal Barwood and Matthew

228

Robbins, winners of the Best Screenplay award at the Cannes Film Festival for *The Sugarland Express* (1973), derived their script.

Peck himself spent months in preparation for his portrayal of MacArthur, devoting more time and care to researching it than he had for any of his previous movie roles. He read everything he could find about the man and consulted with MacArthur experts and many people who had known the general personally.

Before shooting the scenes of MacArthur's farewell to the cadets, someone asked Greg if he had gone so far as to dream that he *was* MacArthur. "No," he replied, "but I did have the typical actor's dream that I got up in front of four thousand people and couldn't remember a word."

During production, at least, actor Peck and producer McCarthy had no disagreements themselves over the course their picture should take or over Peck's portrayal. The vital thing, they felt, was to get into the general's skin, to present him as a complex human being and avoid the pitfalls of the nightclub impersonation approach which, Peck averred, "would become boring after five minutes." Thus, rather than relying on extensive makeup devices to give the actor a cosmetic resemblance to the general, a simple "MacArthur look" was decided upon, with Peck rejecting the "tour-de-force makeup" the studio experts at first prepared for his transformation.

Whether *MacArthur*'s best moments lie on some cutting-room floor is a question that really cannot be taken beyond conjecture. At some point, Universal and the producers decided that releasing a three-hour version of the film would be out of the question and several versions appear to have been tried out on preview audiences. The print which *Variety*'s critic saw (and liked) on June 9, 1977, in Hollywood ran 128 minutes, reduced apparently from an earlier one that ran 144 minutes. Gregory Peck objected to some of the cuts that had been made and made known his feeling that the picture was weakened by them, but he would not be critical of his colleagues: "I always hoped," said Peck, "the picture would be a historical drama that would illuminate the era. I hoped that because of the drama of the confrontation between Mac-

From the bridge of the *U.S.S. Nashville*, Gregory Peck observes the bombardment and assault on Red Beach at Leyte, as the Americans begin their campaign to retake the Philippine Islands from the Japanese.

As General MacArthur, Gregory Peck meets with his Commander-in-Chief, President Franklin D. Roosevelt, played by Dan O'Herlihy, on board the *U.S.S. Baltimore* at Pearl Harbor, to discuss the progress of the war against Japan in the Pacific.

Arthur and President Truman, young people might become interested and reappraise their thinking."

"I'm not going to say that I'm unhappy with the outcome," the actor told an interviewer. "It was important to have both MacArthur and Truman represented fairly. But these events are 26 years in the past. I thought we could let MacArthur have his full due. Some of his strongest diatribes were removed from the picture. Diatribes against the Joint Chiefs of Staff, China, the British, against anyone opposing his retaking all of Korea."

Critical reaction to the picture was divided. Because of the subject matter and because Frank McCarthy had produced both films, comparisons with *Patton* were inevitably raised, even though there is an obvious disparity between the two generals on any number of levels.

According to *Variety*'s review, "It's not a back-handed compliment to say that *MacArthur* is as good a film as could be made, considering the trully appalling egomania of its subject.... Gregory Peck [stars] in an excellent and remarkable characterization.... Unlike *Patton*, which was loaded with emotional and physical action highlights, *MacArthur* is a far more introspective and introverted story...."

The New York Times's Vincent Canby thought that while "its subject is not as colorful as *Patton*...*MacArthur* comes in a close second." While Canby felt the movie "covers too much ground too quickly (and thus superficially)," he considered it "extremely effective in delineating the extraordinary contradictions in the man," and said that "Gregory Peck is remarkably good. He not only looks and sounds like the general, he also makes the character disgracefully appealing, even when he is being his most outrageous.... In addition, the actor displays a wit that gives an edge to the performance and humanity to a character who it might well have been impossible to be around. ...[MacArthur's] speeches are so cannily handled by the film and Mr. Peck that one is constantly finding oneself at equal distances between the sneer and the tear.... Though the movie gets a number of laughs at the expense of the general's vanity and rightist political sympathies and aspirations, the final tone is one of respect and awe. This, I suspect, is something that will be difficult for people who like easy judgments to accept. One of the reasons *MacArthur* is so disturbing is because,

Fulfilling his solemn vow, "I shall return," Gregory Peck wades triumphantly ashore on Leyte after an American beachhead has been secured and the counterattack against the Japanese forces has been successfully launched.

The war against Japan having been brought successfully to an end, Gregory Peck adds his signature to history as General MacArthur presides over the Japanese surrender aboard the battleship *U.S.S. Missouri* in Tokyo Bay while General Wainwright (behind him, played by Sandy Kenjon), other Allied commanders and U.S. sailors look on.

at unexpected moments, it's so moving."

In *Newsweek*, Jack Kroll commented that the film "doesn't have the flair and panache of *Patton* but in many ways it cuts deeper and churns up more food for thought.... This prosaic, limited, naggingly honest film finally achieves a strangely touching quality, thanks mainly to Gregory Peck, whose voice and bearing evoke exactly the 'transcendent sincerity and essential rectitude' that historian Trumbull Higgins found in one of the most enigmatic heroes in American history.... *MacArthur* is hardly a brilliant film, but it has a certain dogged integrity, and the figure of MacArthur as hero and bogeyman remains a crucial one...."

"Peck plays the Red-baiting, noisy, obtuse man perfectly; actors' instinct makes them seem uncannily two of a kind," wrote Penelope Gilliat for *The New Yorker* magazine. "This blockbuster film is an act of homage to egocentricity and love of war."

Time's Richard Schickel disagreed: "One must regretfully conclude that Gregory Peck is not the ideal choice to play MacArthur. He is a pleasant man, good at playing troubled, conscientious, reasonable characters. But he is perhaps the least self-centered of actors, and while he tries hard to adopt the grand MacArthur manner he just cannot manage it. The fire, the touch of lunacy, is not there, though Peck does nicely...when he portrays the aged general, flames banked, the mood autumnal.... The Great Commander never operated

in a climate of caution, and there is no good reason why this movie should...."

Kathleen Carroll, *New York Daily News*, said that the movie "misfires almost completely. Unlike the snappy, smartly executed *Patton*, *MacArthur* is so stiff-necked and gener-

ally undistinguished that it leaves one wishing that Hollywood had allowed this old soldier to fade away quietly...As played by the ramrod-straight, ever-dignified Gregory Peck, he is a regal, imposing figure, but Peck's unbending performance gives no hint of MacArthur's inner complexity or his deeper convictions.... Given the strong anti-war sentiment of the country, it's hard to imagine that there are many people who are really interested right now in the life of an imperious soldier who was America's answer to Julius Caesar."

For *Saturday Review*'s Judith Crist, "A lack of feeling—more specifically a lack of viewpoint—appears to be the hallmark of *MacArthur*.... There is something surprisingly old-fashioned about this production, not only in its multimillion-dollar recreation of recorded history on a Hollywood backlot but also in its noncommittal but reverential approach to...the admittedly controversial figure.... So surface plain and familiar is the character created by the...screenplay and embodied by Gregory Peck that a textbook tone dominates the screen...."

After he has been fired by President Truman for insubordination in Korea, Gregory Peck receives a tumultuous hero's welcome and a New York ticker-tape parade when he returns to the United States.

Having been relieved of duty by his President, Gregory Peck appears before the U.S. Congress to deliver Gen. MacArthur's famous and moving "Old soldiers never die..." speech

During a top-secret conference with his Nazi co-conspirators, Gregory Peck discovers that their meeting has been bugged and the details of their master plan for the resurgence of the Reich may have been overheard.

The Boys from Brazil

20th Century-Fox   **1978**

Credits

Executive producer, Robert Fryer; *producers*, Martin Richards, Stanley O'Toole; *director*, Franklin J. Shaffner; *screenplay*, Heywood Gould, based on the novel by Ira Levin; *music*, Jerry Goldsmith; *cinematography*, Henri Decae; *editor*, Robert E. Swink; *production designer*, Gil Parrondo; *set decoration*, Vernon Dixon; *costumes*, Anthony Mendleson; *art director*, Peter Lamont; *makeup*, Bill Lodge, Christopher Tucker; *special effects*, Roy Whybrow; *sound recording*, Derek Ball; *assistant directors*, Jose Lopez Rodero, Terry Churcher; *technical advisor*, Dr. Derek Bromhall; filmed in Panavision and De Luxe Color, on locations in Portugal, Austria and the United States. (182 minutes)

Cast

Gregory Peck (Dr. Josef Mengele), Laurence Olivier (Ezra Lieberman), James Mason (Eduard Seibert), Lilli Palmer (Esther Lieberman), Uta Hagen (Frieda Maloney), Steven Guttenberg (Barry Kohler), Denholm Elliott (Sidney Beynon), Rosemary Harris (Mrs. Doring), John Dehner (Henry Wheelock), John Rubinstein (David Bennett), Anne Meara (Mrs. Curry), Jeremy Black (Jack Curry, Simon Harrington, Erich Doring, Bobby Wheelock), David Hurst (Strasser), Bruno Ganz (Professor Bruckner), Walter Gotell (Mundt), Michael Gough (Mr. Harrington), Wolfgang Preiss (Lofquist), Joachim Hansen (Fassler), Guy Dumong (Hessen), Carl Duering (Trausteiner), Linda Hayedn (Nancy), Richard Mar-

233

As Dr. Josef Mengele, the infamous Nazi geneticist and war criminal, Gregory Peck presides over a Nazi function in a South American country where surviving remnants of Adolph Hitler's Third Reich are surreptitiously hatching an insidious plot to restore their late Führer to power.

ner (Doring), Georg Marischka (Gunther), Gunter Meisner (Farnbach), Prunella Scales (Mrs. Harrington), Raul Faustino Saldanha (Ismael), Jurgen Anderson (Kleist), David Brandon (Schmidt), Monica Gearson (Gertrud), Wold Kahler (Schwimmer), Mervyn Nelson (Stroop), Gerti Gordon (Berthe).

Fresh from his portrayal of an almost archetypal American military hero, Gregory Peck went on next to play perhaps the quintessential Nazi villain, Dr. Josef Mengele, the dreaded embodiment of evil known, feared and loathed as "the Angel of Death" to the thousands of inmates at the Auschwitz concentration camp, where he conducted horrible tortures in the perverted name of medical and genetic research. The role also gave Peck an opportunity to play opposite another of the world's most renowned actors.

Based on Ira Levin's best-selling novel, *The Boys from Brazil* is an intended thriller centering around the unfolding and unmasking of a monstrous plot hatched by Mengele from the depths of his postwar South American hideout. Through his diabolical scheme, he hopes to set the stage for the world-wide resurgence of the defeated Third Reich which had plunged the world into the abyss of war on an unparalleled scale and whose hideous and twisted philosphy brought terror, suffering and death to millions of human beings.

Peck was at first reluctant to take a role which stood in total opposition to his longtime "good-guy" and humanistic screen persona; he hadn't played a thoroughly villainous type since *Duel in the Sun*, 30 years earlier. But after much urging by the film's director, Franklin J. Schaffner, he was finally persuaded because, in part, of the acting challenge it represented in demanding a total reversal of character type. In that light, it was, Peck thought, "a plum role," offering him an opportunity to indulge his craft, to create the consummate evil personality and, he hoped, to bring a truly rabid mentality to screen life.

In addition, Peck was also motivated to take the part because it offered an opportunity as well to further remind people of the horrors perpetrated by Naziism and its dedicated ministers and servants like Mengele. He also thought it would impress upon them the fact that Mengele, unlike most of the Nazi heirarchy who either perished in the Third Reich's own version of *Gotterdammerung* or were later brought to trial for their crimes against humanity, is thought to still be alive and hiding somewhere in South America, probably in Paraguay. As the actor put it, he would be playing "a human rattlesnake," and the decision to do so was obviously not made lightly by someone who has always taken into consideration the moral underpinnings of the characters he has chosen to portray. Even though he personally loathes everything Mengele represents, Peck thought it important to bring the evil creature to the screen, "so people will never forget that horror."

For the role, Peck's appearance was altered more extensively than for any previous screen undertaking, even more than for the elderly MacArthur, a role which involved considerably more in the way of actor's nuance than makeup.

Beyond the chance to revel in abject villainy, Peck found another cause to take pleasure from his involvement in *The Boys from Brazil*; working with Laurence Olivier, who stars as Ezra Lieberman, a fictional counterpart of famed Nazi-hunter Simon Wiesenthal who, like the character modeled after him, has devoted his life to tracking down the remain-

At his deep-jungle South American hideaway, where he has operated a secret genetics laboratory and conducted horrible experiments on some of the local Indians, Gregory Peck confers with fellow-Nazi James Mason about putting their master plan into operation.

ing Nazi criminals who escaped punishment and melted back into society, concealing their ignoble pasts from their neighbors and contemporary associates.

As Lieberman's sister, Esther, Berlin-born beauty Lili Palmer lends her lovely and warm presence—and smile—to the picture, always worrying about her dedicated and driven brother and cognizant of the toll his life's cause has taken on him, both physically and spiritually.

James Mason also stars as Colonel Seibert, the security chief for the Nazi underground which has managed to keep itself alive over the years since the Reich's fall.

Financial backing for the production was provided by British mega-producer Sir Lew Grade. The film rights for Ira Levin's novel were purchased for $250,000 and the picture was originally budgeted at $6 million, a figure which was nearly doubled by the time the project was completed.

The Boys From Brazil opened at New York's Ziegfeld Theater on October 5, 1978. Its critical reception was in general not a good one. Whereas many people had evidently found the Ira Levin novel gripping, the film's critics tended to feel that the large-scale production it had been accorded made the movie considerably less so, that what was essentially melodrama in the vein of all those World War II "nasty-Nazi" pictures had been overblown into something the filmmakers thought should be taken more seriously. Granted, the plot is a bit farfetched and the treatment is a bit heavier than the material perhaps could stand, but it does not deserve to be lightly dismissed.

"It is all pretty silly stuff," said Richard Schickel in *Time* magazine, "but the peculiarity of this film…is the expensive sobriety with which it has been mounted…. Schaffner seems determined to overwhelm our disbelief with production values—a strategy that frequently threatens to succeed. To begin with,

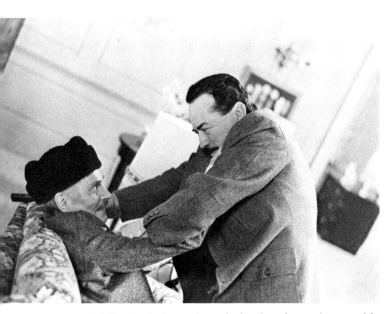

While Peck has plotted, he has been inexorably tracked by Laurence Olivier, as a Jewish Nazi-hunter who has become aware of the menace Mengele has unleashed, and the paths of these bitterest of enemies ultimately cross in a Pennsylvania farmhouse where a life-and-death struggle ensues.

While a pack of fierce Dobermans finally holds Gregory Peck at bay, Nazi-hunter Laurence Olivier tries to convince young schoolboy (and unaware Hitler clone) Jeremy Black to summon the police in the suspenseful final moments of *The Boys from Brazil*.

there is the fascination of watching Gregory Peck, Mr. Integrity himself, playing Mengele. He…seems to be enjoying his change of face and pace. But no more than…Olivier, no less, relishes playing the old Jew…. Yet in the end the self-conscious importance of the film produces a rather queasy feeling, for really this story is no more than a crude exploitation …of what amounts to a penny dreadful fantasy…."

In *Newsweek*, Jack Kroll commented that "…the movie's meat is the bravura acting of Laurence Olivier, Gregory Peck and James Mason…. Fresh from a thoughtful, under-rated portrayal of Douglas MacArthur, Peck throws his characteristic decorum to the dogs and plays Mengele as a monstrous, ranting genius of moral idiocy. Olivier's ironic, subtle acting as usual has a thousand nuances."

In *The New Yorker*, Pauline Kael noted that "when veteran American actors are cast too strongly against type, they look ridiculous. Who could accept John Wayne or James Stewart—or Gregory Peck—as a Nazi sadist?…

Although *The Boys From Brazil* failed to live up to expectations, either artistically or commercially, it did give Gregory Peck an opportunity to realize a long-time dream. "One of my lifetime ambitions," he remarked afterwards, "was to work with Laurence Olivier—and I was thrilled as well to play scenes with James Mason, whom I've always admired…."

British intelligence officers Gregory Peck and Roger Moore are led to exotic locales in their search for a German agent who is responsible for Allied shipping losses in the Indian Ocean.

The Sea Wolves

United Artists 1980

Credits

Executive producer, Chris Chrisafis; *producer*, Euan Lloyd; *director*, Andrew V. McLaglen; *screenplay*, Reginald Rose, based on a novel, *The Boarding Party*, by James Leasor; *cinematography*, Tony Imi; *editor*, John Glen; *production designer*, Syd Cain; *art director*, Maurice Cain; *costumes*, Elsa Fennell; *makeup*, Neville Smallwood; *sound*, David Hildyard; *special effects*, Kit West, Nick Allder; *assistant director*, Bert Batt; *associate producer*, Harold Buck; *technical advisor*, Major-General Lewis Pugh, C.B., C.B.E., D.S.O.; Colin Mackenzie; Major W. E.

Catto; Vice Adm. R.K.S. Gandhi, I.N.; Capt. Hans Joachim Krug; Karl Breitkopf; Fritz Dimsak; Erich Sautter; Karl Tiegel. (120 minutes)

Cast

Gregory Peck (Lt. Colonel Lewis Pugh), Roger Moore (Capt. Gavin Stewart), David Niven (Lt. Col. Bill Grice), Trevor Howard (Jack Cartwright), Barbara Kellerman (Mrs. Cromwell), Patrick Macnee (Maj. Yogi Crossley), Patrick

237

A mustachioed Gregory Peck brings an air of imposing authority and rugged British reserve to his role as Col. Lewis Pugh.

Allen (Colin Mackenzie, S.O.E.), Bernard Archard (Underhill), Martin Benson (Mr. Pinhas), Faith Brook (Mrs. Doris Grice), Allan Cuthbertson (Melborne), Kenneth Griffith (Wilton), Donald Houston (Hilliard), Glyn Houston (Peters), Percy Herbert (Dennison), Patrick Hoit (Barker), Wolf Kahler (Trompeta), Terence Longdon (Malverne), Michael Medwin (Radcliffe), John Standing (Finley), Graham Stark (Manners), Moray Watson (MacLean), Brook Williams (Butterworth), George Mikell (Capt. Rofer), Jurgen Anderson (German First Officer), Morgan Sheppard (Lovecroft), Edward Denith (Lumsdaine), Clifford Earl (Sloane), Victor Langley (Williamson), Mark Zuber (Ram das Gupta), Robert Hoffman (U-boat Captain), Dan Van Husen (First Officer), Rusi Gandhi (The Governor), Keith Stevenson (Manuel), Scot Finch (Croupier), Farid Currin (Room service waiter), Mohan Agashe (Brothel Keeper), kruger (Martin Grace).

Gregory Peck's 49th film as an actor marks a welcome return to heroic high adventure in the *Guns of Navarone* mold and, in fact, reunites him with his *Navarone* co-star David Niven.

The Sea Wolves is based on a true incident, a super-secret clandestine operation conducted in 1943, during World War II, and not made public until the publication of James Leasor's book *The Boarding Party* in 1978.

In one of the most carefully guarded and daring operations of the war, a brave group of aging civilians, members of the Calcutta Light Horse, a volunteer cavalry unit that had last seen action during the Boer War in 1900, undertook a dangerous mission to silence a German spy ship, the *Ehrenfels*, which had been transmitting information on Allied shipping to Nazi U-boats from the safety of the neutral port of Marmagoa in the Portugese colony of Goa, on the Indian Ocean. *The Sea Wolves* recounts the thrilling story of that extraordinarily heroic undertaking.

Gregory Peck plays Lt. Col. Lewis Pugh, a real-life character who, as Director of the Special Operations Executive in India during the war, handled and supervised various clandestine operations vital to the Allied war effort. He is the leader of the C.L.H.'s valiant mission to put the German spy vessel out of commission.

David Niven plays Lt. Col. W. H. (Bill) Grice, who as Chief of the Calcutta Light Horse leads his courageous volunteers under Pugh's command, bringing his usual gallantry to the dangerous assignment. As Capt. Gavin Stewart, the dashing Roger Moore plays an S.O.E. operative who not only revels in the risky business his work entails but also finds time for romantic adventures as well.

The Sea Wolves is directed by Andrew V. McLaglen, son of the late Oscar-winning actor Victor McLaglen and a prolific and successful director of high-adventure action dramas. Involved in motion-picture making since 1944, Andrew McLaglen began his directorial career in 1952, with such films to his subsequent credit as *McLintock* (1963), *Shenandoah* (1965), *The Devil's Brigade* (1968), *Hellfighters* (1969), *Fools Parade* (1971), *The Last Hard Men* (1977) and *The Wild Geese* (1978).

The screenplay is by Reginald Rose, a writer for stage, screen and television, whose scripts include the highly praised *Twelve Angry Men* (1957), based on his own play, *Man of the West* (1958) and *The Wild Geese*. Because of England's Official Secrets Act, the story of the C.L.H.'s remarkable exploit was withheld from the public for 35 years and could only be told when the information became de-classified. The movie was filmed on locations in New Delhi and in Goa, now a part of India, where the actual events took place.

According to a story in the March 4, 1980, *Hollywood Reporter*, Peck "was a little apprehensive about making his British accent sound authentic when surrounded by genuine Britishers such as Moore, David Niven and Trevor Howard." But, the *Reporter* went on, "Moore told him 'if Olivier can play MacArthur at *Inchon!*, you can certainly get away with playing a British lieutenant.'"

Whether *The Sea Wolves* lived up to its makers' hopes is problematic. In its July 9, 1980, issue, *Variety's* critic reported that the picture "teems with romantic heroism routinely told... Gregory Peck, Roger Moore and David Niven in performances that don't stretch any of them but suffice for popular appeal under...McLagen's competent direction...[it's] unabashed flag-waving, a salute to the Calcutta Light Horse.... Rose's scenario delays most of the suspense and action to the final bloody minutes ... [but] the pace could be quicker....For those who complain they don't make them like that no more, this one's a reasonably entertaining answer."

When the picture opened in multiple theaters in New York City on June 5, 1981, The *New York Post's* Archer Winsten remarked that its "most notable distinction ... is the roster of famous old movie stars assembled from both England and America" and that "this casting seems appropriate...." The *Daily News's* Ernest Leogrande reported, "...fact or no, this movie of an improbable World War II adventure has been made as half action yarn, half imitation James Bond thriller," but noted that near its end, in "an interestingly unexpected turn of attitude," the movie registered the fact "that far from being a lark, war is indeed hell, with no concessions for nationality."

The New York Times's critic, Vincent Canby, had mixed feelings, commenting that "if the film sounds like a geriatric *Guns of Navarone*, that's more or less the way it plays, even though it has a good cast....The movie... looks authentic and, for the most part, it is played by the kind of seasoned professionals who bring to any movie the weight and conviction they have acquired in other, much better circumstances...."

Finally, *New York's* David Denby dubbed *The Sea Wolves* "...a dear, silly old action movie... a sweet epitaph for a movie genre that has been put out to pasture."

Whatever the picture's ultimate merits or shortcomings, the filmmakers' intentions were undoubtedly noble ones, witnessed by their dedicating it to the memory of the late Earl Mountbatten, himself an honorary Commander of the Calcutta Light Horse and a real-life hero, many times over, very much in the heroic tradition of the most familiar Gregory Peck on-screen personae.

Roger Moore and Gregory Peck let an uncooperative Marc Zuber know they mean deadly business in their determination to put a stop to costly Nazi spy activities in Southern India.